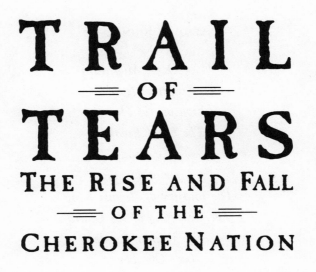

TRAIL
OF
TEARS
THE RISE AND FALL
OF THE
CHEROKEE NATION

TRAIL

— OF —

TEARS

THE RISE AND FALL

— OF THE —

CHEROKEE NATION

JOHN EHLE

ANCHOR BOOKS
DOUBLEDAY
NEW YORK LONDON TORONTO SYDNEY AUCKLAND

An Anchor Book
PUBLISHED BY DOUBLEDAY
a division of Bantam Doubleday Dell Publishing Group, Inc.
1540 Broadway, New York, New York 10036

Anchor Books, Doubleday, and the portrayal of an anchor
are trademarks of Doubleday, a division of Bantam Doubleday
Dell Publishing Group, Inc.

BOOK DESIGN AND PHOTO INSERT BY WILMA ROBIN

Library of Congress Cataloging-in-Publication Data
Ehle, John, 1925–
Trail of tears / John Ehle.
    p. cm.
    Bibliography: p.
    ISBN 0-385-23953-X
    1. Cherokee Indians—History. 2. Cherokee
Indians—Removal. 3. Indians of North America—
Southern States—History. 4. Indians of North
America—Southern States—Removal. I. Title.
E99.C5E55 1988   88-1386
975′.00497—dc19   CIP

to Marshall De Bruhl

ACKNOWLEDGMENTS

The writings of William McLoughlin, Thurman Wilkins, and Dwayne H. King introduced me to the world of Cherokee history, and I am particularly in debt to them. Dr. King, among other duties, is editor of the *Journal of Cherokee Studies*, the only journal published by an Indian tribe to consider its own history.

Also, I gratefully acknowledge the help of Professor William Anderson of the History Department of Western Carolina University, George Frizzell, archivist in the library there at Cullowhee, Tom Underwood of the Sequoyah Museum, and Gary Carden and Joan Greene of the Cherokee Museum in Cherokee, North Carolina.

My editor, Marshall DeBruhl, and I grew up in Asheville, not far from Cherokee, and as children we absorbed many impressions of the Cherokees and stories of their past. Early in life we became aware, as they taught us, that the earth is flat and is suspended from its four corners by great ropes, and in the center of the Earth live the Principal People, the Cherokee.

—John Ehle
Penland, North Carolina

NOTE

In 1770 Thomas Jefferson's income as a lawyer is figured to have been three thousand dollars, and his income as a planter using his 5,000-acre estate about two thousand. These figures help to establish a comparison of monetary value between today and 1770: perhaps a ratio of thirty to one.

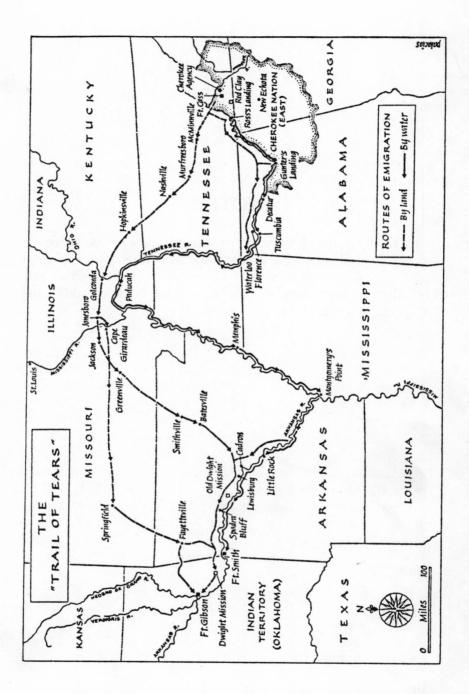

THE "TRAIL OF TEARS"

ROUTES OF EMIGRATION
------ By land
——— By water

1

Investigations were made in the seventeenth and eighteenth centuries to determine whether the American Indians were the lost tribes of Judah; and it was pretty well proved both yes and no, and unprovable either way, which made it an excellent topic for study and exploitation, one populated by warm bodies and tear-stained faces and beautiful, waiting children. James Adair, an Irish trader who lived among the Cherokees for forty years, decided the Indians were indeed one of the lost tribes and wrote seventy thousand words on the subject at a time when printed words were dear. He used as evidence such topics as their division into tribes; their language and dialects; their festivals, feasts, and religious rites; their absolutions and anointings; their laws of uncleanness, their avoidance of unclean things; their practices of marriage, divorce, and punishment for adultery; their ornaments. . . . Adair was one of a series of writers who held similar views, among them Gregorio García in his *Origen de las Indios de el Nuevo Mundo* (1607), Bartolomé de las Casas, Thomas Thorowgood in his *Iewes in America* (1650 and 1660), John Eliot in his *Conjectures*, Manasseh ben Israel, Cotton Mather, Roger Williams, William Penn, Charles Beatty in *The Journal of Two-Months Tour* (1768).

The Cherokees were often selected for distinction because they were inheritors of a dignity beyond their rather simple means and even referred to themselves as the "principal people." Their lands were the center of the Earth. All else radiated outward from there.

Naturalist and social historian William Bartram reported on them:

> The Cherokees in their disposition and manner are grave and steady; dignified and circumspect in their deportment; rather slow and reserved in conversation; yet frank, cheerful and humane; tenacious of their liberties and natural rights of men; secret, deliberate and determined in their councils;

> honest, just and liberal, and are ready always to defend their territory and
> maintain their rights.

Male and female, they were hospitable but uneffusive. The men
appeared to be respectful but remained aloof, were secure within
themselves. They would shake a stranger's hand silently while
looking off toward the horizon, securing their own independence.
They never bowed to any other creature; they were not even
willing to nod. They spoke one at a time, deliberately and with
many motions, then fell silent, listened without looking at their
companion.

They were of a copper color and proud of it, referred to
Europeans as "ugly whites," were lighter than their Indian neighbors, the Creeks and Choctaws and Iroquois. They were lithe,
tall, erect, without noticeable deformities. Their spoken language
was musical, punctuated by guttural, breathy breaks. The men
enjoyed ball games, hunting, and warfare. Indeed, warfare was
their favorite activity and occupied much of each winter.

They were a clean people, when compared to the white English, German, and Scots-Irish settlers drifting in, infiltrating
their territory, most of whom were satisfied to bathe in autumn
and not again till spring. The Indians "went to water" often,
considering water, the sun, and fire to be three holy gifts of the
Great Spirit.

The Cherokees were polite, except that the men, particularly
the young, were easily offended and quick to react, often violently; and whiskey made many of the men argumentative and
testy. Women were not supposed to drink.

The maidens were particularly appealing for whites, as well
as for Indians. Louis-Philippe, while duke of Orléans (later he
was King of the French), traveled to the Cherokee country in
1797. He remarked that "There are several of these Indian women
who are very pretty and I was very struck by the coquettishness
of their manners. It is an entirely different kind than their neighbors, and they could hardly have been taught better by French
women." He noticed that a guide, when the fathers or husbands
had their heads turned, "barely concealed his games with the
wives or daughters and they were so little bashful that one of

them who was lying down put her hand, in my presence, on his trousers and said to him, with a disdainful air, 'Ah, sick.' " He described a group of women picking berries as disclosing their beauties to the fluttering breeze, and bathing their limbs in the cool, flitting stream.

A Cherokee woman had more rights and power than European women. She decided whom she would marry, and the man built a house for her, which was considered her property, or else he came to her or her mother's house to live. The house and children were hers. She and her brothers reared them. If she bore too many children, or if a child were deformed, she had the right to kill the unwanted infant. Should the father kill one, he would be guilty of murder. To obtain a divorce, she packed her husband's clothes in a bag and set it outside her door. She was free to marry someone else, and so was he. Many divorces occurred, many remarriages. A system of serial monogamy developed, and adultery was common, even though frowned upon. The Cherokees, unlike most tribes, did not generally enforce laws against it. One exception in the 1700s was an incident in which the men of a village arranged to make an example of an annoyingly promiscuous woman: in the woods near the town thirty males persuaded her to consent in series.

The year was 1771. When the Cherokee woman lay down to bear a baby, she did not know that the child she was about to deliver was to be a leader, a chief among his people. It was for her a fond hope, a dear hint of a promise. Mothers were allowed to suspect as much. The house in which this particular mother lived, in which she lay down on a reed bed to deliver, was made of saplings tied to corner posts, with plaster inside and outside. The house had an earthen floor. In the middle of the roof was a smoke hole for the fire. The place was the town of Hiwassee, on the Hiwassee River at Savannah Ford, located in territory then claimed by the state of North Carolina, sooner or later to be formed into the state of Tennessee. The river was a bawling, brawling torrent off the west slope of one of the highest mountain ranges in eastern America, which white traders called the Great

Smokies, a range so varied in temperament and aspects that it was thought to be imbued with a life of its own.

Four midwives attended Ridge's mother at this birth. She had borne before—three sons, all now dead by reasons of the cold hand of sickness, perhaps laid on them by an enemy nearby: a neighbor jealous of her and her happiness, or one who despised her husband because of an old argument or fancied wrong; or perhaps the curses had first been made in another Cherokee village against a resident there, and a local shaman, the priest or medicine man of the Cherokees, had thrown the curse away, had deflected it toward the Hiwassee, where it had fallen on her sons.

As labor pains began, she asked to be carried outdoors. The smoke annoyed her; she said she could be carried on the deer hide on which she lay. It was natural for a Cherokee mother to want to be a close part of the earth and forest and open sky, to smell the odor of mold and blooms, to lie, body writhing, on the same plot as held the dead of the past, the same pad used by the swift panthers, the wolf, the fox, the grunting, solemn sow bears.

The shaman told the midwives to leave her where she was for the moment. He was reciting chants from his place near the fire, invoking the aid of the flames, a vital element, as much a living being as the midwives or the sweaty, naked mother who wanted the cooler air. He was concentrating to sense the presence of a witch. While the mother and a midwife watched, he slowly, deliberately, respectfully raked some of the fire's coals into the ridge walls of a small rectangle. From a pouch he took a pinch of tobacco and dropped it into the center of the enclosure. The tobacco burned evenly. He grunted, satisfied. It is well enough, safe enough, he said.

The mother was carried in the deerskin to the yard outside, where her husband and his closest friends waited. She was laid on a grassy mound, her eyes toward heaven, her lips moving in a silent appeal of her own, the shaman trailing along, now hovering, now returning to the fire to make other tests.

A cry from him. This time the tobacco had flared up. He demanded silence, attention as he crept to the other side of the rectangle of coals. His voice was urgent, crackly. The father and two of the midwives crowded inside the house and looked on as another pinch of tobacco blazes. The two women cried out. This time the smoke was drawn to the north, was bent in that direction, revealing that a witch was coming and was from the north. Swiftly the shaman worked, his deliberate chants rising, filling the room. The mother was brought inside once more; one of the midwives stood in the narrow doorway. The shaman called out the warning words, fending off, protecting, while stirring the red embers of the living, breathing fire. The labor pains heightened as the woman pushed the baby into being, the midwives assisting.

This fourth child was also a boy. Gratefully she put him to her full breast to suck. The shaman cried out in anger. He reminded her that she knew better. He snatched the babe from her, even while she tearfully protested, gave it to a midwife: the baby will have tea for seven days, a tea the shaman will brew, and nothing else, and the result will be that even witches will be unable to harm him; also, the brew will bestow magical powers, so that the boy will in time be able to see what to others is invisible, and he can leave his body whenever he chooses, can leave his body during illness, for instance; he will be able to change his form, too, to become a raven, and to fly.

The infant eagerly accepted the tea the midwife fed him, sucked the leather nipple greedily. He will be a hungry hunter; they are the best. He will be a brave warrior with many Creek scalps.

The mother waited for all of them to be done with her baby. Experience had taught her there was no argument persuasive enough to move the shaman, one chosen by her because of his high reputation. Her private view was that he was better with witches than with babies; and as for new mothers, he had no curiosity about her condition, had left her without a sip of the tea he had brewed.

To fly like a raven. To leave one's sick body in a coma. To see many forms invisible to other people: all that she wanted for him, for her new baby. She wanted him to be a chief among his people, a hunter as expert and respected as his father, a warrior to save his people from enemy Indians and whites. But she believed a mother would not have milk in her tits if it were not intended to be used.

The shaman doctor dozed off. She accepted her baby from a midwife and cradled him in her arms. As the midwives sat around her so that the doctor would not see should he snort awake, she put his little mouth to her breast and let him suck.

Fly like the raven if he wants to, she thought, but he must live a full, happy life on this earth, too.

The mother's own father was a Highland Scot. A few dozen of that nationality—another people nominated to be the lost tribe of Judah—had over the years moved into Cherokee country, most of them traders arriving from Charleston, buying furs with guns, powder, lead, cloth. They married pretty Indians and became fathers of their children. Sometimes they came to long for their other home, their parents and kin, or even a lover left there, and as often as not they left on a trip, making assurances of return. Be back in one year, by the next green corn dance. . . .

One year became two, became three and longer. Illness had delayed him, or lack of money for the long journey, or the appeal of other loving women. Who can say? No criticism intended by his Cherokee wife and children.

My father is here tonight beside my baby, the mother thought; my father is proudly watching his grandson suck his breakfast from his daughter, the baby three-quarters Cherokee, more than enough. A few drops of Cherokee blood were required, that was all, to give him a place in the family, full citizenship in the nation, this blood kin of Attacullaculla, the high chief. Even though the chief was of the Wolf clan and Ridge of the Deer, Attacullaculla would perhaps come here to see his kinsmen and would, if asked, talk for half a day about his experiences, even the journey to England he had made as a child to marvel at a thousand sights and mysteries—one of them the King.

The shaman awoke. He looked toward her, slowly got to his feet, yawning, stretching, and stepped outdoors. A major moon tonight, a sky fire just over there beyond the first hill, and it helped to light his way.

The two struggles of the Cherokees during Ridge's long lifetime were their effort to protect their territory from the intrusion of white settlers and their attempt to adapt their culture in order to meet the appeals and pressures of the cultures of the white man.

As to the first, as of 1771—the probable date of Ridge's birth —they claimed territory in what in time became the states of Virginia, Kentucky, North Carolina, Tennessee, South Carolina, Georgia, Alabama, and Mississippi, their lands including the southern Appalachians, the fertile piedmont of northwestern Georgia, and the Tennessee Valley, with all the waters flowing off the western and eastern escarpments of the Smokies and the Unakas. In 1770 this land was occupied by about twelve thousand Cherokees. Three thousand males were of suitable age to take up arms, and about two thousand females were of bearing age. Much of this land was also claimed by other tribes and by the British and French, and it was desired by the Spanish.

The borders were not marked, but the land was patrolled by the Cherokee men throughout the colder half of each year. In course of time they had in bloody skirmishes fought back advances of the Creeks, the Iroquois, especially the Senecas, the Shawnees to the south—who later drove them north—the Chickasaws, the Catawbas; and they had in turn conquered land claimed by them.

Late autumn, winter, early spring were the times for patrolling, with groups of twenty to forty warriors policing a territory. These excursions were masculine adventures, with risk of torture and death for each participant, and the risk for each family of losing members. The profession of warrior was a favored, most honored one. The stark, ever-present alternative to war was death or enslavement of men, women, and children. Cherokees were reminded to consider the Catawbas of a generation ago, warn their sons about that powerful people, once feared, who neglected their guard: the Cherokees themselves moved east, conquered them, captured five hundred of their warriors, and sold them at the slave market in Charleston. The five hundred were sent to work on Caribbean islands: a double gain for the tribe, in that an enemy was defeated and their own people were able to pay all their bills.

The whites were now an even greater threat than Indian tribes, whites settling on land sold by the Cherokees, then moving onto unsold land, a tide uncontrolled by their own governments, even uncontrollable, a people with land their single thought, knowing nothing as dear as land to own. If one killed them, as Cherokees sometimes did, at once their place was taken, and white neighbors replied with deadly revenge.

The military struggle was ages old and was a way of life. As long as the Cherokees won, they were satisfied.

The other, the cultural struggle, was also one of survival. The Cherokee must come to terms with the white man's attainments. What do we have or can we get that will obtain for us guns and powder, cloth, lead and iron and silver, knowledge of their language, ability to count, to write messages? How do they make music in a wooden box? Can wood sing? How do they awaken it with a bow? When I first heard it speak, Attacullaculla admitted, I leaped back, afraid. How much do you want, Unaka, for a box full of music? How long will the music last—a season, two seasons? How do you measure the value of music? Here is a piece of cloth you offer, and I know its length and cost, but music is unknown in price. It has always been the wind sounds, the drum, the river, the cry of a mountain lion, the voice of a woman. How much would I owe you for five boxes of music?

We can defeat the enemy in battle, Attacullaculla explained to friends, if they are Choctaws or Creeks or whites. One can kill a white easily enough, but what then will we do for what we want of theirs? Where do their secrets hide?

Sell furs. We can't always do that. The beaver and deer grow scarce. Sell slaves. The Catawbas to the east—disease-ridden, drunkards—sell them. A band of Creeks coming over our border, sell them.

Sell land. There is plenty of land.

Sad are the lullabyes an Indian mother sings to her baby as she measures the time from day to day, danger to danger.

A boy growing up would usually eat at home and would be limited to two meals a day in order to strengthen his willpower and appetite. At mealtime his mother and father, brothers and sisters would be present, as might visitors who had arrived without notice. These strangers would present themselves simply by saying "I am here."

"So you are," the mother would say.

They would be members of the mother's clan visiting from another town, or local clan members who had sniffed out the best meal.

Food would include warm boiled beans, bread—a corn and bean batter baked in corn husks in the house fire—and fish or meat: deer, rabbit, squirrel, or pork, either baked or stewed.

A Cherokee boy living in a town was not taught by his father. He was taught by the other men of his town, particularly his mother's brothers. It was through the mother that he gained clan identity, which afforded him citizenship. There were seven of these clans. One did not marry within one's own clan, for the members were family. In each of the forty-three Cherokee towns, the seven were represented. The members of the Bird clan (to name one) were responsible for feeding and protecting and serving the needs of members of the Bird family. The women were in charge of their own houses and owned the children. Communal areas were set aside for each woman and her daughters to raise vegetables, and the women cooked meals and cared for the babies. The men were in charge of a boy's training. In a town the boys of all seven clans or families were sometimes trained together, sometimes singly. The boy Ridge came to know several fathers, most of them his uncles. He also had a word for mother, but it designated more than one person, often including his blood mother's sisters and other women of the Deer clan.

If two uncles disagreed about an element of discipline, additional votes would be sought until a consensus was reached. The father might give his opinion, but he was never asked to do so. All boys of a village received the same instruction. Deviations were not acceptable.

A man's duties included trading goods, providing game, deciding with his wife where he would live, including the decision to move the family to another town; he had the power to represent himself in the council house, where daily the men gathered to smoke tobacco and deliberate. He could trade such items as he made; some men fashioned silver decorations. He could give gifts, could chide and praise his children and those of his sisters. He never struck a son. Nobody was allowed to strike a Cherokee boy of any family. It was thought to be demeaning to show lack of respect for his dignity. Discipline was achieved through ostracism and mockery. The father might acquire wealth, in terms of horses or jewelry or guns, but if he continued to live in a town, he must reckon with the relative poverty of others all around; he must help other clan members as the need arose or draw their scorn and maybe suffer from their shamans serving as sorcerers.

The Cherokee boy learned Cherokee words in the accent of his mother—one of three distinct accents, to some extent distinct languages of the tribe. He had furry toys, and he had pets. He was coaxed and encouraged, tolerated and amused. He was not reprimanded, more often was chided. Even as a baby and as a naked young boy playing in the town streets he was honored, highly regarded, a husband-to-be, a lord someday of a village, a powerful person just now little who would have authority over his own being and the life and death of others.

He also had the company of the little people and other rarely seen creatures, the Nunnehi, present all around. The little people ranged in height from one to three feet; they lived in patches of broom sage, the cavity in the rocks behind the waterfall, the laurel slicks on the dry, steep mountainsides where a boy was cautioned not to go. The little-people men had beards to their little-people toes and long gray hair, and often they wore multicolored caps. The females were beautiful, exquisitely delicate. The little people were Cherokees, of course; that is, they spoke the language. For instance, their name as a group was Yvnwi Tsunsdi, and the individual names of the females were like the music of the river, while those of the men more closely resembled thunder. They ate corn and beans and venison and rabbit, just like the Cherokees. They had dances. They would sit for hours at a time in the little-people council house, unwinding stories, laying out matters of justice and government.

Where are they, a child might ask?

Why, just here, I suppose. No, they are over there. They are always with you. You can't see them, though they allow little children now and then to see them. And even I saw them once in a while when I was your age, whenever they wanted to be seen for foolishness' sake, or affection's. More often, I heard them. They sing pretty as birds, and you can hear them dancing in among the rocks.

They could also be heard in the claps of thunder.

As Ridge grew older, he could play with them by going near the bushes at the edge of the woods, could talk to them, displaying his storehouse of words. He could take them food, leaving it for them on a wooden shingle, and when he returned, the food was gone. That was proof.

These rituals were not devised by his mother to entertain him, or to entice him into a world of fairy stories. Not at all. She had known the little people well, all her life had depended on them, had accepted their companionship in times of sickness and loneliness. Whenever she was lost, they helped her find her way. Whenever her cow strayed—the cow she shared with her sister— they helped her find it, even though it was in the third meadow, in a canebrake beside the river.

Not that little people were always helpful. Whenever a stone falls nearby, one of them threw it. Whenever rocks begin to tumble across a mountain path, the little people are up there, high above, snickering. Say an old woman cannot dress herself because of them. If she has a deerskin with which to hire a shaman, he will chase them away, make them leave her alone, and for added pay will even make them carry the water for her, and clean her house, shell her ears of corn, which, dear old thing, she can no longer do herself.

The boy must learn to hold secret his sightings of them. Do not report what you hear them say, Ridge, not for seven days— which is a long time for a boy to wait—or you will suffer illness or accident. And as you get older and go into the woods and onto the mountain, should you come upon a beautiful maiden, do not risk going off with her, for she might be a Nunnehi, a band of people from the highlands. Although they will protect you if you are lost, even feed you if you are hungry, the beautiful women are dangerous and they are possessive—not like a Cherokee woman. In the hidden places in the earth where they live, night is day, and day is night. Think of that. And what is right to do becomes wrong, and what is wrong becomes right. But they do know the paths, all of them.

When your grandmother died, it was the little people who came from far off and took her by the hand and led her to the place where Kanati lives, the Great Spirit of all.

The boy would be a hunter. This decision was a tribal matter, not one of choice for the family. A mother could not decide that her son would not hunt, that he would be a shaman instead. All boys hunted. If when older he wanted to be a shaman, very well, he could apprentice himself.

He was taught that all animals had been friends before the death of the deer had made them antagonistic. The animals had sufficient reason for their present embitterment, and were not enemies. Their manners, habits, wants, habitats must be learned. Also, it was necessary to learn to surrender oneself to the whole of animal life, of which the Cherokee were the lordly part, and for which they were in a sense responsible.

When Ridge was but five years of age, the routine skirmishes between Indians and Indians and between Indians and whites erupted in a war. At the council house were war dances; the young men painted their faces and bloodied their bodies. Ridge heard fierce threats against white people.

As the war progressed, the boy listened to the young warriors who came through Hiwassee, often nursing wounds, their horses often wounded as well; and their stories were of a white storm so fierce that there was no stopping it. They spoke of six thousand white riflemen killing and plundering, burning all the towns, every house and storehouse, destroying all animals and crops. Into the woods, flee to the woods, the local head shaman said, claiming to have warned the people of this approaching anger. Ridge heard that a band of young Cherokees had massacred thirty or forty white people living on the Catawba River in North Carolina, and this was the response, the whites not seeking thirty or forty lives, which would be proper and expected, but the life of every Indian.

Ridge's mother and father decided to flee Hiwassee. He could remember the canoe his family used and the two days of water journey, much of it spent paddling up a rushing stream. His parents chose a cove, one jutting into the flank of high mountains, where water flowed from the earth and game was abundant. The family hid their canoe near the proposed house site and for several nights slept on the deerskin and bearskin blankets on the ground, under the moon and stars, before deciding to stay here. His uncles—where were they? His other mothers, the aunts and neighbors, were no longer around. Mates for games and learning about darts and arrows, where were they? Where were the haunts hereabouts of the little people? Where was the orderly village to which he was heir, and where his mother was the pivot of the world?

Why did his father tremble with anger, even now, whenever he mentioned the whites?

His father and mother measured a place for their house and drove four poles into the ground at the corners, then two others to serve as the doorway. They placed saplings between the poles, tying them. Ridge helped to daub the cracks between them, then plaster the walls inside and out. The roof was also of saplings, these covered first with clay, then with thatch. A hole in the center let the hearth smoke out. A shield was built so that wind could not sweep unobstructed into the house through the narrow, low doorway. Once finished, the house lent a sense of safety; but even so, Ridge's family were fugitives in their own country: the Cherokee had been defeated in war.

Another Cherokee family moved into the next big cove and was welcome. Other visitors sometimes stopped by, families and warriors. One man had to have a bullet dug from his thigh, another from his chest. He said a price had been offered by one of the white men's governments for an Indian's scalp taken by a white soldier: thirty-five English pounds, a fortune. And the scalps being taken were women's, children's, as well as men's. Who knew the difference? The bounty was lordly, and there were white men on every trail, at every fording place, waiting. They fought each other to have the chance to kill an Indian. They stole scalps from each other. The leather most precious now was not otter or mink or red fox or beaver, but Indian.

That was a marvel to a boy, and made him rather proud.

This warrior died, and Ridge's father was able to recall one of the traditional prayers.

There was no particular moment when peace arrived. Perhaps somewhere far off a treaty ended the war, but in the mountain cove only rumblings of arguments were heard. Life here involved the senses, and them only.

This was a place for deer and trout and teaching the boy how to track, how to use his bow, his reed arrows. It was the place for two good meals each day and deep sleep at night.

Shallow was the draft of the place, however. There was no medicine, no instruction by uncles, no sense of community, and both parents were prisoners to the needs of their own children, an exceptional situation for both, particularly for the father. Even so, the family persevered month by month, safe here. The reports were that the towns were completely ravaged, all stock and crops destroyed. Hundreds had been killed, scalped by the whites. The Cherokees had fled, evaded, escaped unto the deep woods; hundreds of them were fugitives in the higher mountains, hiding out.

A Charleston merchant who traded with the Cherokees observed that "War is their principal study and their greatest ambition is to distinguish themselves by military actions." He also wrote, "Their young men are not regarded till they kill an enemy or take a prisoner."

All of that was a bygone time. Perhaps their days of war were not completely over, but the days of glory were gone. Victory was no longer assured. A wounded giant, the Cherokee warriors nursed their wounds and occupied themselves with incidental raids, with picking up stray laggard enemy soldiers.

Attacullaculla came by, mounted on a beautiful pony, an entourage of twenty warriors with him. He embraced the lad and sought out a private place to talk with him and his father. As always, he had news of big plans, of sweeping change, of accommodation, adjustments. The whites called him the Little Carpenter, because of his short stature and craftsmanship with treaties and trades; over the years he had maneuvered the Cherokees into positions of power with both French and English. At times he had even negotiated with the Spanish, as European nations ma-

neuvered for position in the heart of the continent, particularly
the Mississippi Valley and sought the help of the Indians. He told
Ridge and his father that the American colonists had been recently fighting the British. The British were winning and they
were asking for Cherokee help. They had offered a prize of great
value to their friends, the Cherokees. They offered to force all of
the American settlers to leave, offered to throw them off Cherokee
land and forbid them to return. So Attacullaculla and the Cherokee council a few months ago had consented; and the warriors
had put on war paint and attacked the white settlers along the
Holston River, only to find the men away, fighting the English.
Then the whites returned as victors. They were victors over a
whole English army. They had killed the general and his red-
headed woman. And now they were home and had sent word that
they would revenge themselves on the Cherokees.

He spoke using long pauses, as the awful weight fell: the
distant victory, the far-off killing, the usurping whites, the new
war threatening at this minute once more, even again, to slaughter and burn. Had he been wise in siding with the English? he
asked.

Soon after this visit, Cherokees met white soldiers on the
banks of the Holston and fought to the death. The river ran red.
White Colonel John Sevier, a leader of the Holston settlers, lost a
son; the son fell between two Starnes youths, all three just back
from the Battle of Kings Mountain. The Indians retreated; so did
the whites.

Raids continued, white and red, cruel skirmishes, Indians
now, then whites attacking, families fleeing, falling, until finally a
treaty, peace for a while, provided the youthful hotheads on each
side would accept it.

Go from here, that was the idea of many of the young people,
move on west, cross the Mississippi.

The land there is claimed by other tribes, but we can defeat
them, take it away. Or let the white men take it, then trade for
ours. We must escape this country. So went many arguments. It
was an old controversy, given new urgency. The arguments were

heard by Ridge and his family, who went on hunting, living to themselves.

Ridge was now ten.

Colonel John Sevier sent the Cherokees a letter. A growing number of Cherokees could speak English, but only a few could read it. James Vann could read English, had books at his house, among them volumes of English poets, and he was sent for.

> Chiefs and Warriors——
> We came into your Country to fight your young men, we have killed not a few of them, and destroyed your Towns. You know you began the war, by listening to the bad Councils of the King of England, and the falsehoods told you by his Agents. We are now satisfied with what is done, and may convince your nation that we can distress them much at any time they are so foolish to engage in a war against us.
> If you desire peace, as we have understood you do, we, out of pity, to your women and children, are disposed to treat with you on that subject, and take you into friendship once more. We therefore send this by one of your young men, who is our prisoner, to tell you, if you are also disposed to make peace, six of your Head Men must come to our agent, Maj. Martin, at the Great Island within two Moons. They will have a safe passport, if they will notify their approach by a Runner with a Flag, so as to give him time to meet them with a Guard, on Holstein's River, at the Boundary line. The wives and children of those men of your nation that protested against the war, if they are willing to take refuge at the Great Island until peace is restored, we will give them a supply of provisions to keep them alive. Warriors listen attentively—
> If we receive no answer to this message until the time already mentioned expires, we shall then conclude you intend to continue to be our enemies, which will compel us to send another Strong force into your Country, who will come prepared to stay a long time, and take possession though as conquered by us, without making any distribution to you for lands.
> Signed at Kai-a-tee, the 4th day of January, 1781, by
> > Arthur Campbell, Col.
> > John Sevier, Lieut. Col.
> > Joseph Martin, Agent and
> > Major of Militia

Full of promises, peace would arrive from time to time. It would settle over the countryside like a blanket. Then abruptly a few white men would kill or capture several Indians, or a small band of Indians would take a family prisoner and torture and kill the men. There were many Indians and whites who did not care for peace just now. Treaties didn't bind such men. No colony or state could tell John Sevier what to do. His followers lived in a world far from white courts and government. They were a tough breed of settlers, staking their claims on their own deeds and desires. Some of them were of French stock, many German, most English, others Scots-Irish and Highland Scot. Each group had reason to be suspicious of the others. They were second- and third-generation Americans, halfway around the world; they were tenacious, tough fighters who had moved westward from Virginia and North Carolina. They were farmers of the highest ability and were making progress, were taming the wild. Not many had owned land before. For generations they had worked the land of royalty or of some landlord living far away. They had been told growing up that they would never have land of their own. Even here in America most people could not afford land, except for the fact that in certain places of risk and danger, a family could own, actually own, a whole valley, provided they had nerve enough to fight off its wild beasts and its savages. This chosen country had land that had never felt a plow; it had been enriched over centuries. Give it up? The settlers would not leave their new fields, the friends they had made, the roads laid out and mountainsides burned free of forests, the breeding stock they had brought over the mountains, each man's cabin, barn, crib, smokehouse, stone-walled springhouse, the cellar dug, the pens, fences, because of Indians or because of white government officials who worked from a drawing room and had never soiled their linen cuffs, who preferred that they not stir up trouble. Nor did these settlers care to hear pleas for Indians, who had slaughtered white neighbors and broken their bones, who worshiped false gods, who had land beyond measure and yet begrudged others this one valley.

Make the land bloom, make it rich with good crops. Keep it for our children. Keep it ours.

There were in several cabins along the Holston River copies of a message from one of the Cherokee chiefs—Onitositaii, com-

monly known as Old Tassel—a few years back, translated rather
elaborately, its meaning nonetheless starkly clear:

> It is a little surprising that when we entered into treaties with our brothers,
> the whites, their whole cry is *more land!* Indeed, formerly it seemed to be a
> matter of formality with them to demand what they knew we durst not
> refuse. But on the principles of fairness, of which we have received assur-
> ances during the conducting of the present treaty, and in the name of free
> will and equality, I must reject your demand.
>
> Suppose, in considering the nature of your claim (and in justice to my
> nation I shall and will do it freely), I were to ask one of you, my brother
> warriors, under what kind of authority, by what law, or on what pretense
> he makes this exorbitant demand of nearly all the lands we hold between
> your settlements and our towns, as the cement and consideration of our
> peace.
>
> Would he tell me that it is by right of conquest? No! If he did, I should
> retort on him that *we* had last marched over his territory; even up to this
> very place which he has *fortified* so far within his former limits; nay, that
> some of our young warriors (whom we have not yet had an opportunity to
> recall or give notice to, of the general treaty) are still in the woods, and
> continue to keep his people in fear, and that it was but till lately that these
> identical walls were your strongholds, out of which you durst scarcely ad-
> vance.
>
> If, therefore, a bare march, or reconnoitering a country is sufficient
> reason to ground a claim to it, we shall insist upon transposing the demand,
> and your relinquishing your settlements on the western waters and remov-
> ing one hundred miles back towards the east, whither some of our warriors
> advanced against you in the course of last year's campaign.
>
> Let us examine the facts of your present eruption into our country, and
> we shall discover your pretentions on that ground. What did you do? You
> marched into our territories with a superior force; our vigilance gave us no
> timely notice of your manouvres [sic]; your numbers far exceeded us, and
> we fled to the stronghold of our extensive woods, there to secure our
> women and children.
>
> Thus, you marched into our towns; they were left to your mercy; you
> killed a few scattered and defenseless individuals, spread fire and desolation
> wherever you pleased, and returned again to your own habitations. If you
> meant this, indeed, as a conquest you omitted the most essential point; you
> should have fortified the junction of the Holstein and Tennessee rivers, and
> have thereby conquered all the waters above you. But, as all are fair advan-
> tages during the existence of a state of war, it is now too late for us to suffer
> for your mishap of generalship!
>
> Again, were we to inquire by what law or authority you set up a claim,
> I answer, *none!* Your laws extend not into our country, nor ever did. You

talk of the law of nature and the law of nations, and they are both against you.

Indeed, much has been advanced on the want of what you term civilization among the Indians; and many proposals have been made to us to adopt your laws, your religion, your manners and your customs. But, we confess that we do not yet see the propriety, or practicability of such a reformation, and should be better pleased with beholding the good effect of these doctrines in your own practices than with hearing you talk about them, or reading your papers to us upon such subjects.

You say: Why do not the Indians till the ground and live as we do? May we not, with equal propriety, ask, Why the white people do not hunt and live as we do? You profess to think it no injustice to warn us not to kill our deer and other game from the mere love of waste; but it is very criminal in our young men if they chance to kill a cow or a hog for their sustenance when they happen to be in your lands. We wish, however, to be at peace with you, and to do as we would be done by. We do not quarrel with you for killing an occasional buffalo, bear or deer on our lands when you need one to eat; but you go much farther; your people hunt to gain a livelihood by it; they kill all our game; our young men resent the injury, and it is followed by bloodshed and war.

This is not a mere affected injury; it is a grievance which we equitably complain of and it demands a permanent redress.

The great God of Nature has placed us in different situations. It is true that he has endowed you with many superior advantages; but he has not created us to be your slaves. *We are a separate people!* He has given each their lands, under distinct considerations and circumstances: he has stocked yours with cows, ours with buffaloe; yours with hog, ours with bear; yours with sheep, ours with deer. He has, indeed, given you an advantage in this, that your cattle are tame and domestic while ours are wild and demand not only a larger space for range, but art to hunt and kill them; they are, nevertheless, as much our property as other animals are yours, and ought not to be taken away without our consent, or for something equivalent.

Those were the words of the Indians. But they were not binding on these whites, who were living beyond words, claims, even dangers; men and women desperate, devoted to the land.

Of an evening Ridge could hear the war drums of a distant village, and as he grew older, approaching warrior age, he longed to respond to them. He and his father visited the war dancers who had painted vermilion on their faces, a red circle around one eye, a black circle around the other. Their dance was slow, insis-

tent. Most of the warriors who danced wielded black and red
clubs, the colors of fearlessness and blood. The warriors clubbed
the invisible enemy. As they slowly moved around a circle,
around the outdoor fire, their monotonous, pounding music
sounded against the nearby hills and the high mountains. The
boy Ridge, aged ten, was emotionally moved, his pride as a Cherokee was fanned, until one night he joined in the dance, moving in
the circling procession. A warrior pulled him out of the dance
and his father, laughing with the others, led him away.

Rumor had told the family that the English had lost the great
war, the settlers had won; therefore, the Cherokees had lost, too.
In any case, war dangers were temporarily absent, and the family
decided to leave their cove. Once they decided to do so, they chose
a few possessions to put into the canoe and traveled by river,
making their way to their old town of Hiwassee, on the Hiwassee
River, which had been badly damaged.

They went on to the nearby village of Chestowee, one built
long ago by the Yuchi and used by them before the Cherokees
drove them off, conquest providing ownership in the historic pattern.

Here Ridge helped with the building of his mother's third
house, and his father, Dutsi, was accepted in the local council.
The boy and his younger sisters were taken into the clan's affection. His home was with his parents. His uncles, his mother's
brothers, were living close enough to share their influence. There
were in the town scores of other members of the Deer family.

The boy's training began once again and had a more ritualis-
tic tone. He must learn together with many boys how to use his
weapons: the spear, the blowgun, the bow and arrow, and the
tomahawk. Often he was left near the river to study the animals
that came to the water. Other days he was taken into the hills, left
deep in steep, laurel-clad places, entangled hells that were made
of branches so tightly interwoven that a grown man could be held
captive. He was taught to fast during the day, to go all day without saying a word or making a sound, to move long distances
without complaint, to track all animals—the easiest being the
bear—and to study their nocturnal habits, their ways of resting,

their sleep. He was taught patience, and reverence for silence and for the friendly voices of the forests. He was taught to accept for himself a single separate place in the family of creatures. He learned to determine whether a hunt will be successful; to do so the hunter sweeps ashes from the home fire into a heap and sprinkles tobacco on them. If the tobacco does not catch fire, the hunter's effort will be futile. If it does catch fire, success is promised, and if the flame is big, then big game will be encountered; and the direction of the tobacco smoke, the length of time it lingers will direct the best day for the hunt, today, tomorrow, just now.

By killing animals wantonly, forebears had caused the remaining animals to curse man with disease. The plants had come to his rescue and offered such cures as possible, which the shamans knew. Even so, the curse remained.

A Cherokee would not kill a wolf, which was a messenger to the spirit world. Elders admitted to learning much from them, by listening to their lonely sounds. Killing a wolf caused game to disappear and rendered useless the hunter's weapon until it underwent a cleansing ceremony performed by the *ada'wehi*, the shaman-magician. If such a one were not available, the hunter could do much toward saving the weapon by placing it in a swift stream overnight. Then he must clean it thoroughly, or he could give it to a child to play with, make it into a toy for a time. He must be aware, however, that retribution from the wolves could be expected, revenge: death for death.

The hunter could cleanse himself in the river each morning while reciting the sacred prayer, and again at evening he must go to water and cleanse himself and pray. The water was a guardian element, holy, as was fire, that red-tongued guardian resting near his breast. Hunting was an occupation, a profession, and it was like all Cherokee professions, those for women and those for men, embedded in religious rites. They were not wedded to a personal God, and did not seek special favors, either—except a request that the wind might be favorable the next day. The Cherokee did not seek changes in nature's order, but did ask to be accepted as part of that order, given a place in it, safe in the forests and fields from his detractors and enemies, as well as from evil spirits, which abounded.

At puberty, all Cherokee boys were required to move on to advanced instruction, that of the warrior. An initiation ceremony, welcoming Ridge to manhood, was held. He was dedicated by his family to the warrior's ways, which were different from those of the hunter. While the hunter sought kinship with other creatures and offered salutation even to those he must kill, the warrior was a brutal instrument of vengeance, the deliverer of death to others. He must put in the eyes of his enemy the same fear a rabbit has on seeing the panther close by. No escape, only most painful death, is left to the enemy. Unerringly, unhesitatingly the warrior must slay him or capture him.

The hunter was friend of the beast he killed, but the warrior was *a-sgasi-ti*—dreadful to the man. The beast was friend; the enemy was abhorrent and must be slain.

After the indoctrination, after Ridge's dedication as a student warrior, the young man was told not to associate for one week with females of any age, not even to sit near them, and not to touch or be touched by them. Once the week was over, a chief, Old Tassel, prayed to the Great Spirit for the boy, asking that he be given courage and ruthlessness. The chief then fed him corn and pieces of a partridge.

The mother was overjoyed that Ridge, who was big and muscular and handsome, took readily to the warrior's life; however, she did hope he would not unduly hate anybody, even the white people. The white men had killed their own God, as she told Ridge; they were strange, very strange, she admitted to her children. She told them her own grandfather often talked to God as if he knew him, as if God were his father. That made the children laugh. To them God was a spirit, not a personality or judge or advocate. The children sat in awe, dumbfounded by the stories about their marvelous grandfather, proud to be one of his, even though they knew the whites to be their enemy.

Ridge had his grandfather's soft hair, instead of an Indian's more coarse, straight hair, and his features were a mixture of Indian and white, his complexion light. He was a handsome, powerful person, even as a youth.

The men and boys lived for three sports: hunting, warfare, and ball games. These were the mighty three. All boys longed to do well in them, and praise and glory fell on success.

Even though there were three distinct Cherokee dialects and seven clans, there was but one ball game, and it was played town against town. Occasionally the Cherokees played against Creeks or Chickasaws, or other Indian tribes, with horses or slaves or immense tracts of land wagered. A young man, such as Ridge, could not expect to play on a national team; he was an amateur, a student, who practiced the use of the stick.

In his first game, his town was playing a neighboring town. Betting was heavy. Blankets, horses, three Negro slaves, a Chickasaw boy, a white boy captured in a raid a month earlier, a gun—all of these were staked by the citizens. The head shaman of Ridge's town was chanting and performing incessant ceremonies, as were the two shamans from the opponents' town. The elders were making speeches at the council houses. There were songs and dances in the street.

Ridge and the other player had been in training for four times seven days. Ridge had been put under a *gaktunta*, a taboo. He must not eat rabbit—a favorite food; it was because the rabbit loses its wits when under stress, and the tendency might carry over to the ball player. The meat of the frog was forbidden because its bones are brittle. Young birds or animals were forbidden. The player must not during training touch an infant. Certain fish could not be eaten, and certain herbs—lamb's quarter (orache), used as greens, was one—because its stalk was easily broken. All hot foods were forbidden, along with salt. He must not touch a woman.

The penalty for breaking any rule was public humiliation and punishment so harsh it could result in a trainee's death—at least the threat was always present.

The trainees developed abilities to tackle, to throw the ball, to use the hickory stick—a wooden spoon with a loose webbing of Indian hemp or thongs made of twisted squirrel skin. A young man, having purchased a stick, made one, or inveigled his uncles to provide one, was allowed to burn or cut designs into it, to paint it if he chose, and to decorate it with feathers. In any event he guarded it, kept it at hand, kept it away from the others' touch, particularly an enemy's or a woman's; her touch would surely weaken it and—for a day or so at least—make it unusable. All this the boy, Ridge, had learned.

The night before the game, a dance began in a field. It started soon after dark, and people walked in from several miles around, drawn by the monotonous, hypnotic beat of the music. The women softly sang the chorus of the ball songs, punctuated by shouts from the men, and the night resounded, the mountain walls catching and echoing the appeal for victory.

Both sexes took part. The male dancers were the ball players scheduled for tomorrow. They revolved around the fire, chanting responses to the sounds of a rattle, a gourd filled with pebbles, carried by another man, who circled around on the outside. Seven women, each representing one of the clans, danced toward the men, then wheeled and danced away, keeping time to a drum, chanting the refrain of the songs, replying to the voice of the drummer, who was seated on the ground on the far side of the fire. The drum, made like a keg with a head of stretched ground-hog skin, was partly filled with water, and the skin was moistened. The drummer used a single stick.

The women dancers were replaced by others, but the ball game's players danced the night through in the same small circle, except when a shaman called them to follow him to the river, where he chanted his secret prayers to his mystic acquaintances, sometimes bleeding the men.

The women during the dances did not smile. Their songs were plaintive, in the minor key, as are all Cherokee songs, but often the stanzas were amusing. Even so, they did not break their solemnity, the monotony, the shuffling back and forth all night long without as much as a coquettish glance. The drummer pieced out the words of his songs, promising a festive game tomorrow, a high score to be made by his team, acknowledging rewards that awaited them, demeaning the prowess of the rivals. The women replied with their plaintive refrains and shuffling.

At dawn, the close of the dance, green pine boughs were thrown upon the fire and the smoke enveloped the dancers in yet another form of exorcism. The players dressed in ordinary clothes and took time to entwine bits of bat wing into their stick and its net, to help instill swiftness.

The game was played on a field located between the rival towns, all the people for miles around attending. On the way to the field, Ridge and the other players made four stops in order to go to the river with a shaman. During each stop the players were allowed a rest time to sit down, but only on the ground, not leaning against anything or anyone. They were able to adjust the netting on their sticks and appeal one to another for confidence. After the fourth stop, at the close of the ceremony, the main shaman exhorted the players to do their best, assured them the omens were favorable, reminded them of the stakes and glories to be won, and promised to use his powers to drive their opponents into the Darkening Land. This fiery peptalk was delivered by the best speaker among the holy men, exciting shouts in reply, choruses of yells resembling the yelps of dogs. On reaching the playing field, a meadow alongside the river, the shaman again led with four yells, the last a long quaver, the players responding with another yell.

Weary from the long night of dancing and the many ceremonies, Ridge was ill prepared for yet another river ceremony, followed this time by the painful scratching rite, administered by a sharp comb with seven teeth. Seven and four were the Cherokee's sacred numbers. The teeth were made from sharpened splinters from turkey quills, mounted so that they could be pushed out to the length of a small tack. Ridge stripped, along with the other players, and the shaman seized their arms and plunged the teeth into the flesh of their shoulders, raking the teeth down to the elbow, leaving seven white lines that began to redden as blood responded. The shaman repeated again, again, again, to make in all twenty-eight lines; four times seven.

Their arm below the elbow received twenty-eight red lines. The other arm. The left leg, above and below the knee. The other leg.

An *X* was made across the breast, connecting the gashes on each shoulder. Then another *X* on the back, so that, finally done, the shaman had made almost three hundred gashes on each player's body, all of which by now were bleeding. Ridge accepted the torture willingly, not revealing pain. He even tried to joke about it. Men did not flinch, did not cringe, even while the teeth scratched through their flesh, making a rasping sound. Actually, some of the men, to make their blood flow more freely, scraped their wounds with wood or stone chips.

The shaman gave each player a root, or piece of one, which he had blessed; it was sassafras or some other, as he chose, and he absorbed its magic and spat the juice onto their wounds, rubbing it into their blood.

After this was done, the men plunged into the water.

Ridge's dress for the game was a breechcloth tied at the waist by a cord that would break if tugged. He wore an ornament made of eagle's feathers to give clear signs, a deer's tail to give swiftness, and a snake rattle to make himself feared. The rattle sounded as he moved his head. Along with the other players, he marked his body with paint and charcoal. The charcoal was made from wood taken from a tree that had been struck by lightning, but not killed. The players rubbed their bodies with grease or the chewed bark of the slippery elm or sassafras. Beyond these standard practices there were individual idiosyncracies, charms found through experience to work: rubbing each limb with the hind leg of a turtle to acquire stoutness; bathing with a decoction of wild crabapple wood, because even when thrown down a crabapple tree supports its trunk with its spreading tap; lathering on a lotion made of wild rushes, because their stalks, no matter what is done to them, will not lie flat upon the ground. Some of the players whipped themselves with hickory switches, to make their muscles more supple.

One of the shamans now, once again, conjured the more dangerous opponents, seeking to blind them or cause their bones to break. The oldest shaman drew in the dirt an armless figure and put a hole into its heart, into which he dropped two black beads. He covered them with earth and stomped them. That was almost certain to weaken the other team.

Yet again, the players were taken to the water, this time to a bend where the shaman could look eastward while facing upstream. The players stood side by side on the riverbank, the shaman behind them. A helper at his side spread out two cloths, red and black, on which were placed the sacred beads, red and black, the number equal to the number of players, the red representing Ridge's team. With a red bead in his right hand and a black in the other, the shaman prayed to the Long Man, the river:

> O Long Man, I come to the edge of your body. You are mighty and most powerful. You bear up great logs and toss them about where the foam is white. Nothing can resist you. Grant me such strength in the contest that my enemy may be of no weight in my hands—that I may be able to toss him into the air or dash him to the earth.

In a similar strain he prayed to the Red Bat in the Sun Land to make him expert in dodging; to the Red Deer to make him fleet of foot; to the great Red Hawk to render him keen of sight; and to the Red Rattlesnake to render him terrible to all who oppose him.

The shaman now called each of his players in turn by name and clan, and prayed for him until he was satisfied that the player was standing on the seventh heaven, the highest state of spiritual compliance. Then he called down curses on the opponents, calling their names and the clans of the most feared ones. Finally he stabbed the soft earth and buried each black bead and stomped it; then, as he instructed them one by one, each player dipped his stick into water, touched it to his lips, then took water in his hand and bathed his head and breast.

The whoops and shouts of the players preceded them to the playing field, where several hundred spectators waited, men, women, children, babies slung on mothers' backs.

> The ball ground is a level field by the river side, surrounded by the high timber-covered mountains. At either end are the goals, each consisting of a pair of upright poles, between which the ball must be driven to make a run, the side which first makes twelve home runs being declared the winner of the game and the stakes. The ball is furnished by the challengers, who sometimes try to select one so small that it will fall through the netting of the ball sticks of their adversaries; but as the others are on the lookout for this, the trick usually fails of its purpose. After the ball is once set in motion it must be picked only with the ball sticks, although after having picked up the ball with the sticks the player frequently takes it in his hand and, throwing away the sticks, runs with it until intercepted by one of the other party, when he throws it, if he can, to one of his friends farther on.

The opponents were escorted onto the field by their shamans, these players also scratched, decorated, equipped with ball
sticks. The yells of their supporters were meant to elate them and
to terrify the opposition. Betting continued all along the side-
lines. It was agreed that each team would field twelve players.

The shamans moved reverently to the bushes alongside the
river, to secrete themselves, to continue prayers and chants; runners would take them news of the game as it proceeded.

Ridge took his place, his family watching. Everybody he had
ever known in his life was watching. An elder advanced with the
ball. He reminded the players to keep their tempers, and with a
loud *"Ha! Taldu-gwu!"* he threw the ball into the air and the
twenty-some pairs of ball sticks clattered together. One of the
players caught the ball in his stick and, throwing off an opponent,
ran with it toward the goal; but two men caught him, took him to
the ground. Out from the heap of bodies rolled the ball. With a
throw a player sent the ball high over the heads of the spectators,
and the players followed it, charging through the crowd, spectators fleeing right and left. One player was seized around the
waist, raised in the air, and hurled to the ground with force
enough to break his collarbone. Spectators pulled him by his feet
out of the way and the game continued.

Twelve runs constituted victory. The game, begun at noon,
lasted until sundown. By then Ridge and the other players who
remained were weary to death, hungry, virtually dead on their
feet. The opposing team collapsed, as close to despair as life can
tolerate, leaving their entire town in a fit of gloom. Ridge's team
members, revived by victory, returned to the water with their
shaman to perform a ceremony meant to protect them from the
revengeful chants of their opponents. Then they dressed. At last
they were allowed to rest and eat.

Ridge was given his father's horse for the ride home. Of the
twelve goals he had scored only one, but that was a feat for a new
player, and he had been in the thick of tackles and struggle for six
hours; he had run the length of the field—about two hundreds—
countless times. Bloody and sore, he was a proud young man,
mounted on his father's pony, accepting the adoring looks of the

pretty ladies, recognizing the pride and fear in his mother's eyes, grateful for her concern for him.

She could not touch him, nor could his sisters, nor any other woman, for one week.

Ridge's parents became ill. Both were quite sick, and his mother's brothers came at once and hired a shaman they respected. For the next weeks the house was a place of retching and groaning, of brews concocted, of herbal scents, of words uttered in fever. The medicine man ordered the sick couple taken out of doors into the cold and laid naked on a bearskin; when that failed to work a cure, he had them brought to the river, where he immersed them in cold water. Ridge listened to his dear mother scream in her delirium.

The couple did not die. The curse, which Ridge decided must be one deflected from afar, was in turn deflected from them by the shaman, whom Ridge and his uncles paid the bearskin the parents had lain on.

Chief Old Tassel, while standing under a flag of truce, was shot by a renegade white man named Kirk, and the news excited the young Indians. Ridge was seventeen when the war dance began in his village. At first only a few older men joined in. They sat in council, reasoning, considering, sharing worry, reciting yet again the grim litany of wrongs done by whites, yet warning of their own recent failures while fighting them. Ridge's sister and younger brother drew him away from the center of town, took him to their house, where the two parents sat near a fire, even now in summer. It was while there that Ridge told his sister to shave his head; he would accept no delay. He wanted the traditional warlock left, he told her. Later, as he requested, she tied to the lock a few red feathers with white tips. She painted his face. She reminded him that he must support the family, should their parents die; even so, he told her, the whites must be punished.

Ridge was one of twenty men from his village to join two hundred or more from other villages, each dressed in loincloth, each armed with the best weapons he could provide for himself: gun, bow, spear. Each carried a hatchet for scalping. Each had a mount. Ridge's was his father's horse, which was old and obstinate. Reports came in of other warriors assembling and of parties of whites forming, alarmed by reports of an Indian uprising. A party of whites was said to be nearby, mounted and armed with guns.

An old Indian orchard stood nearby, the bent trees heavy with ripe fruit, and the local chiefs decided to ambush the whites there. The warriors hid themselves around the orchard. Once thirty to forty whites had crossed the river—the Little Tennessee, near the deserted town of Settico—and came upon the fruit, they began to pick, enough to take a supply along, the men moving from tree to tree. They were laden with apples when the terrifying war whoops of the Cherokee sounded. The first volley of shots and arrows felled ten of them. The other twenty or so rode toward the fording place, only to find Indians there, too. About fifteen of the whites succeeded in crossing through the deeper waters of the river, but of these, many were wounded. A Cherokee overtook a soldier, pulled him from his horse. The two fought, the white man throwing the Indian into the river, even as another Indian joined in. Ridge came forward and killed the white man with his spear. He seized his victim's hair with his left hand and with his right drew his father's scalping knife around the top of the man's skull, pulling the scalp free.

Around him, other Indians mutilated the bodies of the dying and dead whites, decapitating one and opening the body to rip out the heart and guts.

News of this skirmish, and of others, alarmed the frontier settlements. The whites sent an army to punish the Cherokees; the retaliation of the whites was fierce, their soldiers burning villages, destroying crops. It was the bloodiest white–Indian fighting for years; and Ridge was a hero in it.

Dragging Canoe gathered together an army and faced the whites with two thousand Cherokees and a thousand Creeks, Ridge among them. At the first skirmish, the army of whites under General Martin became demoralized, quickly buried their dead to discourage Indian mutilation of corpses, and retreated. Dragging Canoe, with young Ridge, sought out Colonel John Sevier, or who had been raiding, burning towns and crops, but

Dragging Canoe repulsed his troops. The Cherokee army was then divided into smaller units, some pursuing General Martin, others set to raid the white settlements, and more ordered to harass Colonel Sevier's men.

Ridge was one of the warriors to attack John Gillespie's station on the Holston. Before the engagement the Cherokees captured several men working in the nearby fields, then attacked the stockades. The Cherokees overcame the defenses, killed all the men, and took twenty-eight women and children prisoners. They burned the station to the ground.

Some of the braves wanted to kill the twenty-eight prisoners. The whites would do as much, they argued. These avengers were young hotheads eager to have a frolic, a festival to celebrate their victory. Their leader, John Watts, a half-breed, demanded restraint, then led them against two other Holston stations.

They were always successful. But that winter when their army was camped under the western shoulder of the Great Smokes, the white forces of Colonel Sevier surrounded their camp and surprised them with a mounted charge, ending in hand-to-hand encounters, a fierce struggle in which 145 died. Ridge, though wounded, survived. The defeat was cruel and bitter to the Cherokees.

After seven months of war, he turned toward home. His father in his lifetime had taken only one scalp; the son already had several. He returned home victorious, at eighteen an experienced warrior, to be greeted by one of his sisters with the news that both of their parents were dead. Before their death the shaman had performed all the rites, including several water rites, but the spell sent against them had overcome his power and their resistance.

Two generations earlier the shamans as a group had failed when the tribe had suffered smallpox. The shamans decided that the disease had been sent to punish the adulterers, and the cure was to have them lie, breast bare, in the open, for that must have been their position when their acts were performed. The disease spread, overcoming the simple diagnosis and treatment, and the shamans turned to their water cure: they sweated a patient, then shocked the body by submersing it in the cold river. Many died. Twenty-five in one day in one river, Ridge had heard. Half of the Cherokee died. More than ten thousand Cherokees were lost in the epidemic. The shamans as a group humbled themselves, admitted their failure, even as now the sole shaman of Ridge's parents admitted his.

2

Because history was passed down by the shamans by word of mouth, details were never dependable and were often confusing. Every shaman frequently, routinely, recited chants that made no sense; but they were what he remembered and indeed, had often been transmitted by his teacher in piecemeal, garbled form.

In any event, the Cherokee had, by reports of history, once traveled for a long while, stopping for a period in a cold climate. They had once been closely related, were perhaps neighbors and kin to the Iroquois, whom they called "uncle." They referred to the Creeks and Chickasaws as elder brothers and saw themselves as uncles to the Choctaws.

The Cherokees in build resembled the Iroquois, with whom they shared a similar language; the Creeks, Choctaws, and Chickasaws were Muskogean speakers. Farther off, the Shawnees were of the altogether different group that spoke Algonquian.

These were the principal tribes vying for control of the Mississippi Valley, all of which were at war with the whites. Some of them wanted peace, but with whom were they to treat? As for the whites, their newly won independence from England had resulted in thirteen colonial state governments. Georgia claimed the territory of Alabama and Mississippi, as did the Cherokees, Choctaws, and Creeks. The state of North Carolina claimed land to the crest of the Appalachian Mountains and beyond that to the Pacific Ocean, the same land claimed by Cherokees and many other tribes. Furthermore, the thirteen states had formed a central government that declared its right to jurisdiction over foreign affairs, including Indian affairs. This government was now seeking to redeem from the new states their claims over the western lands. The patchwork was complex.

Meanwhile the English, defeated in the East by the colonies, were still powerful in the Mississippi Valley. The French were

present, as were the Spanish, in the southern portions of the
Cherokees' range. All three claimed certain jurisdiction, as did
the Indian tribes, this new American central government, the
thirteen states, and the quasi-legal colonies of white settlers on
the frontier in eastern Ohio, Kentucky, western Virginia, and
Tennessee, the frontiersmen.

Assuming that the Cherokee council wanted to negotiate
with the white man, with what group was it to negotiate? There
were several claiming rights to part or all of the land claimed by
Cherokees, Creeks, Chickasaws, and others. Some of the white
man's claims were older on certain portions of the land than were
those of the Cherokees. Men still alive could recall when the tribe,
pushed westward by the whites, had conquered some of the Tennessee property, chasing off other Indians.

The jurisdictions of the states, the new American government, the English, the French, the Spanish governments, the
Cherokees, the Creeks, and other tribes were overlapping, contra-
dictory. Force of arms was the conventional way to establish ownership; that was the type of claim the Indians respected most. But
whom did one fight? There were so many, and they were growing
and splintering.

As for Cherokee government, it rested on the councils of
many towns, with an annual central council of independent
chiefs, all seeking consensus. Without officials, without courts,
without titles or wills, without contracts, without banks or accounts, without written records, and with some of the chiefs willing to accept bribes, in the central council consensus was often
impossible, disagreements common. The local chiefs might refuse
to comply or cooperate. From time to time there had been more
than one Cherokee government, or none at all. The Chickamau-
gas, for instance, were Cherokees who had recently resented the
council's unwillingness to go to war to the death with the whites;
they had their own chiefs, but did meet at council. Many of the
Chickamaugan Cherokees were moving westward, however, seeking land there.

Government actions under these conditions were not dependable.

A treaty had been signed at Hopewell, South Carolina, in

1785, when Ridge was fourteen. This one, signed with the new United States government's congressional delegation, guaranteed Cherokee territory against further intrusions of whites. The government next ordered the white intruders to vacate Cherokee lands or forfeit protection, but the Holston River settlers and those whites spreading their farms between the Holston and French Broad rivers would not leave. This dispute had led to more battles and the death of Chief Old Tassel under a flag of truce. Now a new peace treaty would doubtless lead to the forfeiture of still more land. On and on, the Cherokee and white governments seemed to sway and totter like old men. It was a time of despondency. When Attacullaculla had led the Cherokees into war beside the English—why, the English had lost, and in the treaty with the new United States government much Cherokee land was taken away. Error could so easily be made even by the wisest chiefs, especially now with so many governments. The costs could be high.

The shamans had always objected to whites marrying Cherokee women, unless the husbands came to live in the Cherokee towns and became one with the tribe and its customs. There were many of these whites, among them soldiers who had fought for the English, or men who had refused to fight in the war, or men who had suffered disappointment in love or life. They did become Cherokee, and their children belonged to the mother's clan, but these whites were never pleasing to the shamans. They would not allow the wife's brothers to instruct the children; as often as not they moved out of town onto land of their choice and established an independent home; they often brought black slaves to work for them; they did not share their food and wealth with other Cherokees, but hoarded it; they imported whiskey.

Their children did not speak Cherokee; they spoke English. They were not members of any religion, even the white man's, and sometimes they cursed God in casual conversation. They bred and reared many children, while the Cherokees arranged for small families. They claimed that more and more land was needed for their use and for the use of their slaves.

The shamans were ever fretful, seeing a breach in the cultural armor of the people that would, if not mended, reduce the Cherokee to the state of the black bear. According to one of the tribal accounts, once long ago a few Cherokees had forgotten their responsibilities to their clansmen, and as a consequence hair grew longer on their bodies and they began to move about on all fours. They ignored the warning of their priests and even failed to revenge the death of fellow clansmen. Eventually they forgot the Cherokee language. In this way the bear was formed, and the bears were ever after made to serve the needs of the Cherokee, their distant kinsman, and to provide meat and fur.

The white men's children were Cherokee because of the mother's blood. The white men were Cherokee through their wives. But the men did not come to the council houses.

And the men wrote wills, papers that apparently lived on even after their death. Their children inherited all of the accumulation. Nothing was buried with them or burned or shared with the neighbors. And the farm—look at that whole valley, one farm. They cannot use all they grow and must ship it to other parts.

Pots, pans. Cherokee women became fretful, jealous of the wives of these white men who had so many pots—often more pots than people at their table. And cloth enough for clothing, even diapers for their babies, even rags for cleaning.

The Cherokee women would go to the homes of clan sisters married to whites in order to marvel at their riches and watch spellbound the work of the spinning wheel, the copper and iron pots full of dye, the looms manufacturing. From dawn to night the wives of the whites worked, and their daughters did, too— even when there were slaves about, everybody worked. And if you slackened, you were whipped, whether black or white.

The shamans said: Women, teach your daughters not to want colored dresses, not to want cooking pots, not to want a wheel to spin yarn, or a loom, a candlemold, a wagon, a buggy, a carriage, a book. . . .

Do not, either, listen to the whites talk about roads. Cherokees do not need roads. These white Cherokees want them, but only to get crops to market, to import more slaves and smelly cattle and to send their children to schools. They and their half-breed sons will build taverns on these roads and put ferries at the river crossings, and thereby make more wealth. They will charge the poor Indian to cross his own river. Do not listen to them.

At this time of transition, of unrest and change, a sixteen-year-old boy named Joseph Brown was traveling with his family through Indian country in order to reach land issued to his father by the new United States government in recognition of his having fought the British at the Battle of Guilford Courthouse. There were several holdings that the father owned, land recently ceded by the Indians on the Duck River, the Cumberland, and the Tennessee, land taken from them because they fought with the British.

The family was moving past the lower Cherokee towns in two big boats. Traveling together were the boy, his father and mother, two brothers, three sisters, and five other white men. Creek and Cherokee Indians in four canoes met them, displaying flags of truce and announcing friendship. The Indians showed no guns or hatchets and were represented by an English-speaking man, part white, part Indian, who said he was James Vann and who assured them the Indians meant no harm. By this ruse Indians came aboard the two boats even as others appeared in canoes and showed weapons, declaring the family to be prisoners.

Carrying a sword, one Indian approached the boy and his father, who were in the stern of the boat. The Indian caught the boy's arm, perhaps to jest with him, and the nervous father angrily laid hands on him and ordered the Indian to leave the boy alone, which he did. As soon as the father turned his back, however, the Indian cut his head off. The boy fled to the bow of the boat, arriving as his mother and two little sisters, aged five and seven, and a brother, eight, were being taken away in Indian canoes.

The boy and the five white men were set ashore where an elderly stranger, also white, was waiting, watching. He and James Vann decided that the boy would be safe, being of value as a slave, but that these Creeks, now that they had scented blood, might want to kill the white men. The Cherokee's chief was away and could not help control them. The boy, Joseph, was invited by the white man to come home with him, but Joseph hesitated to accept; he was in a state of shock and was terrified for his life. His eldest brother told him by all means to escape this place, if he could.

The old white man led him down the road, all the time explaining that the Indians might launch a frolic, now that blood was smelled. They will not kill you, a boy, he said, unless they become so excited that they lose all their senses. As for your brothers, I dare not say.

Guns began firing, and the old white man paused, turned to listen; after the sound had stopped, he moved on.

His wife, also white, had a French accent. The old man said she had been captured near Mobile and had lived as a Cherokee since. She welcomed Joseph, but directly a fat old woman, an Indian, came into the cabin and began scolding her. The white man and his wife spoke English to each other, and Joseph learned that his brothers and the others of his party were dead and that this old Indian squaw did not want a boy to be left alive to go tell the white men about the massacre.

The old man, whose name was Tunbridge, told the boy not to fear for his own life, that he would be spared. Tunbridge had the boy sit on the edge of the bed, and he took position in the doorway to wait for the Indians. The warriors arrived drunk and spoke at length. Tunbridge calmly replied to their threats, speaking Cherokee to them. The boy judged that his age was important; if he was old enough to tell others of the deaths and lead white soldiers here, then the town might be destroyed.

The boy scrunched up his body as small as he could. Tunbridge calmly told the Indians that this boy, Joseph, was his son's prisoner, that they could not harm him. Infuriated, the Indians finally pushed past him and, knives and hatchets in hand, took hold of the boy. Tunbridge's wife began crying out, no doubt anxious about her cabin being the scene of an execution; so the Indians' leader, a large, strong man, jerked the boy to the door. Joseph turned to old Tunbridge and begged to be allowed to live for half an hour.

It's not worth it, Tunbridge told him.

The Indians stripped off Joseph's clothes and cast lots for them. Meanwhile the French woman hovered and circled, pleading for his life, or for the sanctity of her cabin site: Joseph could not tell. In English she asked Tunbridge to make them take Joseph up on the mountains where the wolves could eat his corpse, not to kill him here in her yard.

Old Tunbridge did try to argue with the Indians. He told her they agreed to take the boy to Running Water, about four miles off. As no white people were there, they could have a frolic knocking the boy over.

Joseph fell on his knees and prayed to be saved, but nobody paid him the slightest attention.

Once the Indians made ready to leave the old people's yard, they gave Joseph his pants, which he pulled on. Along the road the Indians began arguing over some matter or other, and Joseph fell on his knees and prayed, preparing himself to accept death here and now. After five minutes he opened his eyes and saw an Indian smile at him, then some others smiled, and he judged to his immense relief that he was to be spared.

At nightfall the local Cherokee chief returned and was mightily displeased by this frolic, one endangering his town. He told them, Joseph learned, that he himself had never stained his weapons with white man's blood, only with that of the Shawnee, and it was unwise to kill white people in his town's vicinity. He was furious, and so was Tom Tunbridge, who also arrived, a warrior son of Tunbridge's wife by a previous marriage, who did not like the theft of the boy from his parents' house. Tunbridge was a big man, at least six feet tall, a warrior with many white and Indian scalps.

The chief talked to Tunbridge and his French mother. He said the boy would be accepted as an Indian, and he himself would look after him. He was to call the chief uncle and Tom Tunbridge brother; the boy's long hair must be cut off in Indian fashion, and he must dress like an Indian.

The boy consented to all of this gladly, and the old French lady herself shaved his head. She took away his pants and gave him a piece of coarse cloth about four feet long and a foot wide, to pull tight between his legs. He also wore a short old shirt. He was sent into the acres of gardens to work with others Indians, about fifty of them. The sun burned him that first morning, so that he became ill, but he kept working. There was no time for rest, not even for mourning the death of father and brothers. Where his mother and sisters were nobody seemed to know.

Several months later his presence became known to white settlers, who purchased his freedom, and his mother and sisters were also located, purchased, and freed.

Whites helped to decide which chiefs were paramount: they were the ones the whites preferred to deal with. Always they were the warrior chiefs, never the shamans, as in previous days. Specifically, they were the warrior chiefs most willing to negotiate, who could be bribed. One of them was a brutal chief of the lower towns, his name Doublehead, a complex man thirsty for power, one in need of the best horses and slaves, in need every so often of bloody revenge and violence.

One of the young warriors Doublehead singled out for praise and special treatment was Ridge, brave, loyal, patriotic. Nonetheless, the boy had faults. At least, he had one: he was not cruel enough to be feared.

Doublehead had noticed this problem on a trip to Kentucky. The men were out of tobacco, so they raided a white family on the trail, took the tobacco, and killed them. When they returned to camp, Ridge wept. Now, as Doublehead saw it, there was nothing to weep about, except being left out of the raiding party; that showed a willingness to kill, but even so, weeping was weakness.

Doublehead took the young man along on several raids. Sometimes they were accompanied by a nephew, Bob Benge (sometimes called Bench), who was an even more famous raider than Doublehead, having successfully attacked settlements in western Virginia and northeastern Tennessee, so many a bounty had been placed on his head by Virginia. In the spring of 1793, Benge and Doublehead, with a group of warriors, attacked the Ratcliff settlement, where they killed four whites and withdrew without losses. They made other raids, Doublehead's brother, Pumpkin Boy, along with Ridge and a few others, teaming up to capture horses and slaves. They rode fast horses and struck by surprise, doing much mischief.

Later, when the band was in the uninhabited barrens of

southwestern Kentucky, raiding whites passing through; they were hidden near a watering hole on the Nashville-Kentucky road when a Captain Overall, who was known to be an Indian fighter, and a friend of his named Burnett came along. The band killed them and secured their nine packhorses, then scalped the two and drank their whiskey. Doublehead when drunk was always dangerous, and he decided to eat Overall and Burnett. This ritual was, he reminded the men, an Iroquois custom, not a Cherokee one. In any event it would terrify the settlers, who would judge that their bodies, too, might soon be in Doublehead's bowels.

He cut strips of flesh off the two men and broiled them. He broiled their hearts and brains, too, then served them to his nephew Benge and his brother, Pumpkin Boy, and to the others, some of whom would eat only a bite or two. Ridge ate none of either man, not even of the heart, which surely was a sign of weakness.

One March, Benge was in western Virginia. He set up an ambush on a high mountain road, where he and his men saw three white men and their supply train approaching. Benge recognized one of the men, a Moses Cockrell, famous as an Indian fighter on the Holston, who had often claimed publicly that he would like to meet Benge in personal combat. Benge told his men to kill the two companions, and with only a tomahawk he leaped onto the road, facing Cockrell. The frontiersman forgot his boastful ambition and hurled his big body down the mountainside, crashing through bushes, Benge following, barking Cherokee whoops. Cockrell, bellowing in terror, ran two miles to a cabin on Waller's Creek. As he leaped the cabin fence, Benge threw his tomahawk, missed, and Cockrell reached the cabin safely. Benge returned to the pack train, which now belonged to him.

This was the type of action that attracted the younger Cherokee warriors, Ridge among them. Ridge made many raids with Doublehead and Benge. There was challenge and danger, and amusement, too, sorting through the possessions in the house of a Scots-Irish or German family, or going through the stock of a pack train, taking home whatever loot was given to him. His share he would sell, or share, or give to the young lady he was starting to court.

George Washington and other national leaders fully intended to honor the claims of the Cherokee for their land, as stipulated in the treaty of Hopewell. They had scores of reports of anarchy and killings all along the Cherokee boundaries, and late in 1792, both Washington and Thomas Jefferson signed this proclamation:

Proclamation

By the President of the United States

Whereas I have received authentic information, that certain lawless and wicked persons of the western frontier, in the State of Georgia, did lately invade, burn and destroy a town belonging to the Cherokee Nation, although in amity with the United States, and put to death several Indians of that Nation; and whereas such outrageous conduct, not only violates the rights of humanity, but also endangers the public peace; and it highly becomes the honour and good faith of the United States to pursue all legal means for the punishment of those atrocious offenders; I have therefore thought fit to issue this my proclamation, hereby exhorting all the citizens of the United States, and requiring all the officers thereof, according to their respective stations, to use their utmost endeavors to apprehend and bring those offenders to justice. And, I do moreover offer a reward of Five Hundred Dollars, for each and every one of the above-named persons, who shall be so apprehended and brought to justice, and shall be provided to have assumed or exercised any command or authority among the perpetrators of the crime aforesaid, at the time of committing the same.

In testimony whereof, I have caused the seal of the United States to be affixed to these presents, and signed the same with my hand. Done at the city of Philadelphia, the twelfth day of December, in the year of our Lord, one thousand, seven hundred and ninety two, and of the Independence of the United States in the seventeenth.

By the President
GEORGE WASHINGTON
THOMAS JEFFERSON

No one claimed the reward.

Washington requested the Cherokees to send their leaders to a peace conference at the town of Coyatee, or "Sacred Old Place," to meet with federal commissioners. The older chiefs accepted and in June 1793 they arrived at the town, among them Hanging

Maw, Otter Lifter, and Scantee. A few younger chiefs arrived, as well, several of them present for the opening sessions. Doublehead and John Watts were due to arrive. Bob Benge had refused to attend.

The territorial governor, William Blount, was heartened by this show of cooperation. He was so optimistic that he at once departed for Philadelphia, the temporary federal capital, to arrange a meeting there for the Cherokee leaders with President Washington himself. He left the other representatives of the new American government to deal with the Indians and white settlers. Not present were the more bitter enemies of the Cherokees, among them the men from the Holston settlements.

On June 12, in the dead of night, a volley of shots awoke the white and Cherokee delegates, and a company of mounted militia raced through the town, shooting into the houses, cutting down Indians and whites alike. The chief federal commissioner Major Thomas King, was sleeping with Chief Hanging Maw's daughter and was decidedly unprepared for the assault; he admitted to recovering as best he could and leaping out a back window. Other government agents were fired upon as they sought to make their escape. Chief Hanging Maw and his wife were wounded. As the shooting ended, dying were chiefs Scantee and Fool Charlie, a white woman named Betty Katagista, a white man named Rosebury, and seven other Indians.

The invading militia occupied the town, and only through the pleading of the whites did they spare the other Indians and the town from burning.

The reason for the attack was that a group of Indians, among them Ridge, had killed a white man and his son near Knoxville and had taken twenty horses. The raiders had come through this very town, Coyatee, sold a horse to one of Hanging Maw's sons, and moved on. The militia was trailing them and in their excitement had exceeded their orders.

Ridge was present during this series of murders.

The older Cherokee chiefs hurriedly dispatched a delegation to President Washington, urging that peace be negotiated in spite of the attack. Among the delegates sent was Doublehead himself, who proudly took the President by the hand.

Made furious by the Watauga settlers' attack, President Washington, Virginia's Governor Blount, and the federal commissioners ordered that arrests be made. The fiery captain of the errant
militia was, indeed, arrested and tried; however, he was a friend
of Colonel Sevier, and in his trial, which was marked by irregu-
larities, he was found not guilty of any crime.

The young Cherokee chiefs responded by calling out their
warriors. Bob Benge, John Watts, and Doublehead invited a number of Creeks and Shawnees to join in. A large array of young
warriors assembled, Ridge among them. The war drums, the
dancing, the shaman's chants were heard through every night.

John Watts decided that the wise action was to destroy Knoxville, the largest village on the Cherokee border, and he persuaded Bob Benge, Doublehead, and Chief James Vann, the half-
breed, to join him. They brought together a force of a thousand
warriors. On the way to Knoxville Doublehead insisted that the
army pause to loot all the settlers' cabins, to steal blankets,
clothes, hams, corn, to kill and scare whites, and to burn the
barns. As a result, the movements of the army were announced to
the world. Knoxville, Watts decided, was alert and prepared. Left
available for easy plunder nearby was one small fort, Cavett's
Station, which he decided to attack. He ordered his army to sur-
round it. Only one family of thirteen people was there. The Watts
army outnumbered the whites many times over, but the whites
defended themselves killing five of the braves before John Watts,
to save further deaths, offered to assure the white family of safety
if they would surrender. Bob Benge, who spoke English himself,
approached them and worked out the arrangements for their
safety.

Doublehead was not consulted. The gates of the fort were
scarcely open before he fell on the white family, wielding an ax.
John Watts tried to stop him; but Doublehead's Creek friends
soon joined him. Benge and Watts rushed about trying to save the
women and children, but even they were attacked by Doublehead
and the Creeks. Finally James Vann rode his horse into the mob
and pulled a white child up behind his saddle. Doublehead saw
him and with a leap broke the child's head open with his ax.

Baby killer, Vann shouted at him. Doublehead swung the ax at Vann.

John Watts took personal possession of a white boy, Alexander Cavett, Jr., and entrusted him to three Creeks, ordering them to take him to a safe place. They did so, and killed him there.

In a few minutes the splurge ended; sanity returned. Resentment was everywhere. Among the chiefs, John Watts as war chief of the Cherokees was embarrassed.

Bob Benge was dismayed by the revolt of his uncle Doublehead and openly criticized John Watts for his inability to control the situation. He withdrew his men.

Ridge, one of the young warriors present, admitted his abhorrence of Doublehead's murders; he later said he looked another way, unwilling to witness what he could not prevent.

John Watts, still with the main body of his army, moved northward across the Clinch River, then on to the Tennessee and the Etowah, where the army entrenched itself. When the Indians discovered a group of white soldiers half a mile downriver, they left their fortifications and ran to kill them, exposing themselves to the main white army of about six hundred men under Colonel Sevier, who had set the trap. The Indians lost many men, guns, supplies, blankets, horses. They fell back in disorder from Sevier's attack, crossing the Coosa River.

They confronted Sevier at Hightower, also known as Etowah, but lost there, too, a major, final defeat.

Ridge returned home, his confidence shaken in the capability of Cherokee arms; he began to rearrange his thoughts about the war-worthiness of his tribe and the reliability of any shaman to ward off the white enemies. He had by now moved with his younger brothers and sisters to the village of Pine Log and had built a house alongside the river near several other houses occupied by members of the Bird clan.

On returning he did his absolution in the river near where a shaman chanted his bleak intonations, then in misery he walked through the parceled field to his fiancée's house, stood for a while in the doorway looking at her, Susanna, his dejected manner announcing the defeat the Cherokees had suffered.

He was not to touch her, or she him, for a week's time, by shamans' rules.

She cooked his supper. All he had been allowed while warring was a bowl of meal each day, and he was hungry. He was lean and spent, waves of weakness gripping him, as at the close of a ball game. The depression of defeat was lodged in his big body.

He told her the blood and bones specifics of the losses, described the chiefs' excesses. He ate the bowl of beans—all she had. I will go hunting now that I'm home, he promised. I will hunt deer, not men, he told her.

He confessed his disappointment in Doublehead, who was, he felt, at least half mad, and in John Watts, who could not, dared not, control him.

He said there was talk of getting three thousand rifles from the Spanish in New Orleans, with three thousand more for the Creeks, and other rifles for other tribes. The Indians might make a stand, all together, and stop the whites' advance; but short of unified action, war was useless.

One of the better shamans came by and sat with him for a long while; he burned a dust of tobacco to test for spirits, to tell if any were near. He expected no reward or pay and got none.

More raids. Horses, slaves were taken. What better work was there for a warrior? Just now he was no more successful than were the shamans; everything Cherokee was sour and rancid.

Bob Benge rested for a season before taking a small group of warriors to the Holston River in Virginia, where he was feared, and resuming his raids there. He boasted he would capture every black slave living along the Holston, which terrified planters and slaves alike.

Dreams told him to stop the raids and return home, but he rejected the warning. One night he captured a white family; he killed the man and kept the woman, a Mrs. Livingston. He was walking beside her, explaining that he meant to sell her into slavery or to exchange her for Cherokee prisoners, when several whites' rifles marked and shot him. Even as he bled his life away, a white man, Lieutenant Hobbs, scalped him.

Now and then a writer would be present for such occurrences and would submit a report to an eastern newspaper:

Knoxville, Nov. 29——

On the 24th of October last, a party of Indians fired upon John Leper and another man, near the house of the former on the east fork of Red River, Tennessee county. On the same day, another party of Indians killed and scalped Evan Watkins, within one hundred yards of Col. Winchester's Mill in Sumner county.

These two places are 70 miles distant from one another. On the 25th of the same month, a party of twelve fellows were discovered crossing the road between Bledsoe's Lick and Shaver's Cabins. On the following day, Cornet Evans was fired upon between Bledsoe's Lick and Colonel Winchester's by four fellows; and on the 26th the spies discovered a party of thirteen Indians crossing the Cumberland River, towards the settlements, within five miles of Colonel Winchester's.

These several parties, appearing in and about the settlements nearly at the same time, spread an unusual degree of alarm among the inhabitants. Families in general throughout the neighborhood shut themselves up in their stations, and all intercourse ceased for several days, except by patrolling parties. The people exclaimed, Congress could not know their sufferings, and have the feeling of men, or they would take measures to give them effectual protection.

On the fifth instant, a party of fifty Indians, on the waters of Red River, Tennessee county, fell upon the families of Col. Issac Titsworth, and his brother, John Titsworth, and killed and scalped seven white persons, wounded a negro wench, and took a white man, three children, and a negro fellow prisoners. Pursuit was given by the neighboring militia, and the Indians discovering their approach, tomahawked the three children and scalped them, taking off the whole skin of their heads. The white man and negro fellow were either killed, or carried off. Our informant from Mero district, supposes these murders to have been committed by Creeks.

On the 12th instant, the Indians killed John Covington on his way from Red Bank, on the Ohio, to Muddy River in Kentucky.

On Thursday afternoon, a company of travellers arrived in town from Mero district. For the news from that quarter, we refer our readers to the following copy of a letter:

Dear Brothers,

Yesterday, I was a spectator to the most tragic scene I ever saw in my life. The Indians made an attack on Col. Sevier's station, killed Snyder, his wife, one child, King's wife and child, one of Col. Sevier's children, and another wounded and scalped which must die. On hearing the guns, four or five of us ran over. We found the poor old Colonel supporting his house with his wife. It is impossible to describe the scene to you. Mr. James, who goes and was an eye witness, can give you the particulars. The crying of women and children in town—the bussle and consternation of the people, being all women and children, but the few who went over to Sevier's, was a scene which cannot be described. This is a stroke we have long expected and by every intelligence we hourly expect this place to be assailed by the enemy—Colonel Sevier is now moving, and the town will not stay longer than Mr. James's return. My wife lies on her bed, so bad that it would be death to move her. Thus we are situated. This place, without any doubt, will be evaluated in a day or two unless succour is given by the people from the interial parts. Pray ask the influence of Major Tatum Douglass and all our friends with General Robertson to guard us, or at least help us safe away.

    Adieu, ANTHONY CRUTCHER

Autumn, 1794, Chief John Watts led a group of the more dependable, predictable chiefs in negotiations for peace on the frontier, at Tellico Blockhouse, a peace now sought desperately by the white settlers and by most Cherokee chiefs.

The Creeks were even yet opposed to peace. A Creek party would raid an area, and cruel mischief would result. One January a white soldier, Elijah Walker, was killed by Indians twelve miles south of the new town of Nashville. Also that day, on the frontiers of Hawkins County, a white man was killed and four were wounded by Indians. On January 27 a party of ten marauding Creeks was killed. This type of action cried out for an arrangement, an agreement, peace.

3

James Vann and Charles Hicks discovered alternatives to traditional Cherokee ways; both half-breeds lived near the town of Pine Log, where Ridge had moved. Hicks was a planter, using black slaves to work his choice land. A mild person, generally agreeable, given to good humor, he nursed a crippled hip. He accepted the pain, uncomplaining. Much of his time he spent officially assisting an influential white man, Colonel Return J. Meigs, known to Cherokees as White Eagle because of his hair. Hicks was the translator and adviser to Meigs, and in the course of events he frequently met Ridge and came to recognize in him great strength.

Ridge was interested in Hicks, who was a reader of books, particularly English literature. A book was expensive. To take one's wealth and spend it on what had no value to touch, smell, taste, an object that made no sound, intrigued Ridge. Apparently the books exuded magic. A book housed people, he discovered; they lived in its pages. A book told stories to those having its secrets. It issued the thoughts of others. Ridge was baffled by the magic. The Cherokee had developed their five senses to a high degree, and almost all thoughts had to do with experiences a person could see, hear, feel, smell or taste. A book went beyond, as Hicks had told him. The Cherokees did not even have words for what was not known to the senses. Even courage, affection, forgiveness, honor were not communicable in Cherokee, but apparently in English books such concepts were often presented.

Hicks himself was peculiar. Cherokee men did not farm. Hicks did. By custom an Indian man might choose to help his wife girdle and later burn a forest, and might help her clear away heavy brush; these acts were not offensive to the Great Spirit, but most surely offensive were Charles Hicks's daily occupations on his farm. Lightning did not strike him, however, illness did not attack him, or strike him down. The shamans did not claim to understand.

The other intellectual chief was James Vann, who had opposed Doublehead at Cavett's Station, the interpreter who had captured the two boats of Joseph Brown's family. He was a planter, owner of many slaves, a Cherokee, the son of a trader. Any Cherokee could assign to himself for his own use land not being used by other Cherokee; he was allowed to develop it. In years past this practice had meant that a family might take a plot for a family garden and, within walking distance, space for a house and a few hog pens. Not so modest were Vann's allotments, which included an entire valley worked by scores of slaves he had brought from Charleston or bought from raiders and others who had been bred and reared in his slave houses. He had more than a hundred horses and four hundred head of cattle. He owned a store and a tavern.

Ridge would trade with Vann, bring him items to buy that he had taken in raids. Whenever sober, Vann was a friendly, reliable, even-tempered human being, eminently fair. Drunk, which was his one daily adventure, he was wild and vengeful. His two wives loved him but had reason to fear him. His slaves feared him. He favored the use of the whip to settle his disappointments. A stranger who seduced his sister was bound to Vann's whipping post and given seventy lashes. Vann carried out the punishment himself. A white woman who stole from him—he lived in fear of thieves—was strung up by her thumbs until she confessed; she repeatedly cried out her guilt before he cut her down.

Even as a minor chief, Vann had considerable political influence because of his wealth. He had often opposed Doublehead, a higher chief, and had even dared to speak against him publicly. Vann accused him of taking bribes from the federal government for land and road rights.

Ridge, who also distrusted Doublehead, was attracted to Vann's political stands and to his wealth. Vann was having a big house built at the time, the finest home any Cherokee owned or had ever owned, and Ridge along with others was impressed.

Ridge went courting in the traditional way. First he had prepared himself for a hunt; he found a deer and silently asked it for permission to kill it, then he shot it with his rifle, which he had taken in a raid. He dressed the deer and selected the parts he wanted: two for his hungry brothers and sisters; one roast for the neighbors, who helped take care of the family while he was warring; and the saddle of the deer for her, Sehoya, also called Susanna Wickett.

He left the remainder of the carcass for the wolves.

He packed the meat in the deerhide and carried it to the village. At dusk he carried the saddle to Susanna's home, arriving unannounced, and offered his gift to her mother, who knew at once its significance.

Susanna came from the darkness inside the house, moving shyly, without daring even to let him see her eyes, and invited him indoors, where she, as coaxed and coached by her proud mother, cooked a bit of the best part of the tenderloin for Ridge to eat, her brothers and sisters waiting, watching, whispering, giggling with delight and surprise.

Never more than a glance at him would Susanna allow herself, and a nervous smile. Flushed, pleased, embarrassed by cooking meat for him, she accepted him as her suitor.

One requirement of their courtship was to seek the opinion of a shaman. The oldest of the village shamans sat them down and performed a simple tobacco ceremony, making a test for witches and other afflictions, and after chants he pronounced them acceptable as partners.

Ridge was feted by his male friends, a ceremonial meal in a house near the town's council house, featuring jokes and instruction and much hilarity, with hints and promises of the pleasures awaiting him and warning of his awkwardness. Susanna was a high-spirited young lady, and pretty, and had been properly chaperoned and protected, so there would be an immediate release at the moment of opening her body, which experienced men told him might be more joyous than he could cope with.

Nearby in another house, Susanna was being prepared in less rowdy manner, she also feted with her favorite foods and waited on by other young ladies not yet married. After the feasts the male guests took places inside the council house; the women guests entered and stood across from them. Attendants led Ridge into the council house, where he stood with his attendants. Susanna entered and was escorted to the other side of the room. One of Ridge's aunts, taking the part his mother would have played, brought him a venison roast and a blanket, gifts for sustenance and comfort. Susanna's mother slowly approached the girl; she gave her an ear of corn and a blanket. The relatives returned to their places, and slowly, a step at a time, Ridge and Susanna approached each other, she daringly looking into his eyes now. She took the blanket from him and folded it with her own, then gave him the corn, and he handed to her the roast. The town's main chief came forward and joyously announced "the blankets joined."

Ridge, when only twenty-five years of age, was designated by his fellow citizens of Pine Log to attend the Cherokee central council, which met this time at Oostanaula. The council had little authority over any town or person, but did serve as a place for discussion of differences as yet unreconciled. There were only a few ancient laws to be enforced. Sometimes a treaty with another government would require ratification. It was an honor to be chosen, an added mark of respect, one not generally given young people. Watts and Vann had been involved in bringing the vote about; in their political maneuvers they were usually effective.

On reaching the council grounds, Ridge was shunned. He wore old clothes, as was his habit, and only two silver bits of jewelry. He had not decorated his horse, not even with such trophies of war as he had, and his horse, an old favorite, was mangy. Other young chiefs urged the elders not to seat him, but among the powerful chiefs were those who knew his courage as a warrior. They took Ridge by the hand and seated him in the area reserved for his clan, within the portion of the area usually reserved for the elders.

The council house, an open-walled, seven-sided building

with a peaked roof, was large enough for a hundred chiefs to take seats. Visitors stood around outside. The elders had first call for making addresses; but any chief could rise and speak his mind about the issues facing his town, or facing the Cherokees, and everybody would be quiet, grunting assent as they felt the need. He might speak of the evils of whiskey, or about the whites, or about an intertown spat. Once he was through, whether he took a minute or half an hour, there would be a pause to allow others the opportunity to gather their thoughts. Somebody would eventually rise. Always there was sobriety, order. Because it was considered rude to stare at a Cherokee man, the audience appeared to be inattentive; however, through frequent grunts they made known their agreement or disagreement.

These sober meetings went on all day long for several days, dances and games taking place at night. Large pots of food were prepared, and pigs and wild game and bird were roasted by the wives and daughters of the chiefs and the visitors. Visitors could attend, Cherokee or other tribesmen, government agents, traders, settlers. Certain agents were present as representatives of various American governments, federal and state, and of the British, French, Creeks, Shawnees, Iroquois, and more.

Not a word did Ridge say at that first council. Late in his second, after a long pause occurred in the chambers, he dared to rise, a young man in the presence of elders. He spoke timidly at first, then forcefully, the grunts of the chiefs encouraging him. His voice was deep, resonant, his manner dramatic. Visitors began to press forward against the railing as his golden words traveled out across the council grounds.

Ridge felt deeply about the subject he addressed. Cherokee law required revenge for the death of one's kin. Often in a hunt or in battle a man would be accidentally injured or killed by a companion, and in such cases members of that victim's clan were obligated to inflict similar punishment on the companion. This was known as the Blood Law, and until this moment it had never been challenged in council.

Ridge's proposals passed, and the ancient law was abridged. Admittedly, it would be difficult to administer a humane adjustment to an ancient ritual. As an older chief said, the ways of a people would live into the future. Several elders remarked on this subject.

The young man rose once more. His voice filled the council house and carried into the woods around. He told the council that the law must be enforced as the council had today decreed. He would enforce the new law himself. Should any man kill another without just cause as now defined, he, Ridge, would kill him.

The old chiefs did not laugh. They had to take this young orator seriously.

4

The new federal government wanted to educate the Indians and prepare them for full citizenship, which President Washington believed to be possible. The acculturation of the Indians would be brought about, according to Henry Knox, George Washington's Secretary of War, through the white man's "knowledge of cultivation and the arts."

In 1792 Congress appropriated funds for the agricultural portion of the thrust, and for teaching Indian women the domestic arts. Even at this date, the Cherokees were regarded as model Indians, singled out as a tribe likely to respond to enlightenment, and the federal agents who were sent to the Cherokees were under orders to succeed. They were to persuade the Cherokee men to take up farming instead of hunting and to abandon war; the women must plant cotton wherever practicable and learn to use spinning wheels and looms. Federal agents were ordered to provide tools, seed, instruction.

One year, as soon as the men had gone off on winter hunts, the agents visited the piedmont towns, bringing cotton seed and spinning wheels. The first crop was small, but it served to create a use for the wheels. The women helped to decide where the new looms should be placed, for the large equipment took up much of the space in a Cherokee house. Each village got one.

Susanna that first season harvested little enough cotton. Even so, when Ridge, after several months of raiding and hunting, came home, she had a yard of cloth to show him.

The Pine Log men were amused and delighted with their women's new sport. Next year, however, some of them were embarrassed to reckon the value of their wives' and daughters' cloth, made from a larger cotton crop; it was worth more than the hides they had gathered in the hunt.

Ridge's brothers and sisters looked to him for much of their support. He did the best he could, but remained poor. From time to time he and Susanna Wickett discussed moving to an untenanted valley, a place large enough for sizable crops, one not far from Pine Log where they could grow as much cotton as they pleased, along with grain and grass for cattle and horses and other livestock. Such was the advice of Meigs, the chief federal agent, and of Hicks and Vann. Ridge promised her they could have house servants, slaves—two or three anyway—to help with the work. He would steal the slaves from the whites. He would steal stock and a wagon, too.

Susanna was in favor of moving. She was always in favor of progress. The shamans opposed the new federal efforts, but she told Ridge he had proved he had no fear of white armies or Creek raiders, so why fear his own priests?

The two of them chose a piedmont area through which flowed Oothcaloga Creek. There were scores of beaver dams in the valley, and the beavers had cleared many of the trees. Hundreds of other trees Ridge and Susanna burned, with the help of slaves borrowed from Watts. Watts liked the valley so well he moved into it himself, as did Ridge's brother Oo-watie, who made his own improvements. So later did one of Ridge's sisters and her husband, each family clearing more land by means of fire and building pens and cribs, using slaves Ridge stole from white settlers' fields. Stealing slaves he compared to picking up gold nuggets from the land. Breeding stock was garnered that way, too, and, of course, he traded horses and slaves with Watts and Vann. He stole excellent horses for Vann, who loved fine horses as much as he loved his wives.

Ridge and Susanna themselves dug holes and spread the roots of seven apple trees, the first ever planted in Oothcaloga Valley, and filtered in the dirt, covering, closing over the roots, the two of them joyfully feeling the rich earth in their hands. The dirt, the two-room cabin, the valley, the animals here, even the beaver and deer and wolf and dog were kin.

Every day a white woman spent on the frontier was dangerous for her, her children, her husband, and their possessions. Constantly she was conscious of the danger of Indians.

Most of the settlers came from well-established families down East. Back home there was simply too little land for all of the children to farm, so these outcasts had accepted the invitation to buy land in what had been Indian country.

They worked hard, took their babies to the fields while they hoed, made hot bread at every meal, and prospered as farmers and as fathers, mothers, families. Now and again drifters would arrive and be sent along their way. Now and then scouts heralding new and even better land would come through and be given food and a bed for a few nights; however, the main citizenry was soon part of the land, wedded to it, improving it.

As they saw the situation, this land had never been owned before by anybody. The Indians had owned it in common but had never owned it in the sense of knowing it or having boundaries or possessing it personally. Land was now personally possessed by a white man, a white woman, a white family. Its boundaries were from the middle of this creek here at the sycamore, going north half a mile to the top of Arthur's Ridge, east along the spine of the ridge to the biggest damn hickory you ever saw, which I put three gashes in—my boys and me could not reach around it, fingertip to fingertip; then south direct as an arrow to the creek, the sycamore. Now, mister, that's about three hundred acres and it's mine, bought from Mr. Robertson and surveyed off of his holding, and anybody knows, who knows my woman and me, that no damned Indian or government will ever put us off of it. So help me, whatever God there is.

Now you take my wife's brother, is working land that's been wore out, has to be fertilized to make it move a weed. She wrote him to come up here, bring his family. We can get him fifty acres of bottomland and any amount of hills he wants—I've already talked to Mr. Robertson. Her brother is the sort of man we want here. He's a worker, let me tell you. This land will be a Garden of Eden here directly. We got a church built—did you see it? Steeple goes on soon as it's ready and we figure out how to lift it. Two stores are open. Have a pastor here one of these days. Have a sort of teacher now in Mrs. Morgan. Law, what a singing voice on that woman, can sing like a bird in a cage, and she teaches right smart of knowledge, my daughters tell me. You know what we're doing away out here at the end of the world, mister? I'll tell you: we're building our own new country.

In 1798, that year alone, the federal government gave Cherokees three hundred plows, thirty pairs of cotton cards, and any number of spinning wheels. The government also sent more looms and weavers to teach the Indian women who cared to learn. Growing sheep was their right, too.

The women most eager for cotton and wool were mixed-bloods or full-bloods married to mixed-bloods. They were also the ones most tolerant of white people and their ways. In general the full-blooded families insisted on being hunters and warriors. In the absence of regular, annual warfare, they staged a certain number of raids. These were challenging and dangerous and fed the young men's appetite for adventure. If caught stealing horses, the men were shot by white settlers or tried by federal agents. Either way, they would be judged by the enemy. In a sense they gambled with their lives and their family's welfare, and many of them learned to lie and deceive, two new characteristics for Cherokees. Ridge was philosophical about it. Now that he had a plantation and several slaves, he could afford to be critical of those making new thefts. He was hoping the Cherokees would convert themselves to new ways. He welcomed the overtures of the Moravian church, suggesting that they send teachers to the Cherokees; he favored the mission in council.

The Moravians were makers of work-and-worship brotherhood communities. They were Germans and in America had established three towns so far, in which only people of like mind were allowed to live. In the autumn of 1798, at the Cherokee council, two Moravian missionaries—Steiner and de Schweinitz —were supposed to offer to send teachers, who would also be ministers; but the devil had delayed their arrival at council, and by the time of their arrival the chiefs had all gone hunting.

They did meet with two federal agents and the commander of the United States Army garrison at Tellico, and they were able to see an old chief, Arcowee, who had helped negotiate the peace treaty with President Washington six years earlier. The old chief put on his best clothes and hung around his neck a ribbon bearing his silver medal from President Washington. He told the Moravians that he believed the book, the one called God's Word, was the source of the white man's wisdom and power. Through the secrets it contained, the Bible had given whites an advantage, making them able to conquer even the Cherokee. He said he would like to have these two white men share the secrets of this book with the Cherokees, so that they might become once again well and strong.

The Moravians told Arcowee that they were willing to send teachers of English, but their purpose would be to acquaint the Indians with their God and Creator and what he had done and suffered to save them.

Arcowee began a monologue about God, his own views, to give a better setting for their discussion. One need only look upon the water, without which we could not live, he told the delegates. God made it. The fire on the hearth, what a little thing, yet God has created it for our benefit; and what especially would the poor red man do if there were not fire, for they had not as many clothes as the whites. Everywhere there is fire hidden, he said. It can be drawn from small stones. The white man has an advantage in his ability to make use of nature. He mentioned the hugeness of the whites' ships and the smallness of the Indians' canoes. The whites have the Great Book from which they can learn all matters, and these secrets the Cherokee want.

The Moravians told him that all that was very well, but their own concern was the eternal souls of the Cherokees, which would live on this Earth for a short time only.

Arcowee continued. He told them that when the Great Father in the beginning created men, he had a great book. He offered it to the red men and bade them read it, but they could not. He offered it to the whites and as soon as they saw it they were able to speak aloud to one another from the book, and thus it has come about that the whites know so much that is not known to the red men.

The Moravians had a vision of saving souls, they told him.

The time appears to have come, he told them, when the red people should learn the book. He was not convinced about religion, but he wanted the book. He chided the two by reminding them that the Great Father had placed the red men here toward the going down of the sun and the white men toward the rising of the sun, but then the white men arrived in their great boats and received permission to build a town. The town did not suffice them. They took more and more land. When the white people first came to this country, they had the great book wherein is the Word of God, but they did not instruct the red man concerning it. He had heard of it since and wanted to know the secrets, and that only.

The Moravians understood his remarks, delivered in the measured, moderate, reasonable tones of Cherokee conversation. He was saying that the Indian was caught in an inferior status not due to his own fault, but because his white brother had not shared his book as he should have. In other words, the Moravians had failed thus far to do their duty toward their hosts in America, their equals.

The old chief concluded, his words translated into English: "I believe, therefore, that you have been inspired by the Great Spirit to be willing to come to us and to teach us. For my part I will bid you welcome. I believe that it will be agreeable to my people, as it is to me."

Other elders talked with the Moravians. Chief Kulsatahee of Hiwassee thought that the Cherokees would be glad to hear and know the words of God, but that "we are clumsy about such matters." Still, it might prove effective. When first it became necessary for us to cultivate the land and cotton seed, I thought we would not understand this. We are not intended for farming, it is not for the Indian, I thought. Yet we have now begun to learn about it. I think we will learn to know the great words in the Great Book, but it will go slowly. Many people think that we Indians are too evil, he told them, and have to become good people and that we are too unclean and brown, that we are savages like the Africans, that we are incapable of improvement. Did the Moravians believe this?

No, they did not.

George Washington said the Indian can be equal citizens.

Yes, and Jefferson said, "I believe the Indian, then, in body and mind equal to the whiteman." We love all people, the Moravians assured him. All are descended from Adam and Eve and are brothers. We love all people regardless of color, as does God. He is the creator and Father of all men, be they white, brown, or black.

This is not the view of the white settlers who have moved into our lands, the chief told them. A wonder they can have the same God and same Book as you. I like your attitude better, but it will take time for everybody to agree.

President Washington had said fifty years would be needed before Indians would be citizens, the Moravians said. This he had spoken several years ago; therefore, he had given as the goal the year 1839.

Kulsatahee asked what the Moravians would need from the Cherokee council.

Land for a Moravian community, the Moravians told them, with fields, orchards, mill, and shops for the work we will do.

Land, the prime need of the white man. It always starts with land. Kulsatahee said he would help as best he could in the council when it met next autumn. Land. The white man always wanted land.

Arcowee and Kulsatahee were chiefs in the "upper towns," where the effort for years had been to have peace with the white man. The "lower towns" had been built by those Indians forced to give up historic Cherokee sites to the east. They harbored more bitterness toward whites. The lower towns region, chiefly in middle Tennessee, had Chickasaws living to the west and Creeks to the south, and the chiefs had those two tribes to worry about, along with the whites. The lower towns' most powerful chief was Doublehead, who was year by year becoming wealthy, with many horses and slaves, and even a white secretary to deal with merchants as far away as New Orleans, French country. Doublehead saw no advantage to having these Moravians come here, and he influenced many other chiefs, among them The Glass, Dick Justice, and Taluntuskee to oppose it.

Sensing difficulty, the Moravians met with Doublehead, The Glass, Bloody Fellow, and some others of the lower towns.

Doublehead asked if they were to teach, or were meaning to preach their gospel.

The Moravians replied that they would do both.

No, they were told, no preaching of your gospel.

The Moravians insisted that they must go into all the world and preach the gospel to every creature.

Doublehead asked if children would be charged for room, board, clothing?

Yes, the Moravians replied, they would and must learn the value of money.

Then go home, Doublehead told them.

At the 1800 council meeting, in the autumn, the matter of the Moravian missionaries came up for a vote. Doublehead, the elected speaker of the council, used his power to delay the vote. Some of the elder chiefs favored a contract, and some of the younger ones spoke or lobbied for it, among them three who had formed an alliance in other matters as well: Charles Hicks, James Vann, and the young fellow who had done so well at the earlier councils, Ridge.

The two Moravians watched from the side as the central council debated. Even upper-town chiefs rose to speak against it, to disagree with their elder comrades, Arcowee and Kulsatahee. Most of those who spoke against the advent were full-bloods; those in favor were of mixed blood. Charles Hicks and James Vann had white fathers, as did Will Shorey and Richard Fields, all of whom addressed the council in favor. Standing to the side were white traders who had made homes among the Indians, who had much at stake in the tribe admitting teachers for their children. John McDonald, Samuel Riley, John Rogers, Daniel Ross, William Woodward, and others were among them, but none of them could speak publicly.

Hicks and Vann took Doublehead aside. The two of them were prepared to offer the Moravians a place regardless of the vote. The upper towns would not be denied. This might even lead to the upper towns withdrawing from the council, resulting once more in two national councils. Doublehead must reconsider, because Vann and Hicks were wealthy enough to start a school for their own children, and would do so if necessary.

Doublehead relented; he would allow a vote. The voting was slow and tense. After the tally, Doublehead rose to announce the decision. The measure had passed, permission had been given: for the first time in Cherokee history white missionaries would be welcome. Land would be provided; just where it was to be must yet be agreed on. It was, he continued, to be an experiment. Experiments do sometimes fail. The Cherokees will be the judges of these Moravians' conduct. We will judge whether they give proper attention to us and our children. The government agents are here today and understand this. If the missionaries do not keep their part of the bargain, they will have to leave, and you agents will help drive them out. It will be the Cherokees who decide.

After the council meeting, in the whirl of celebrating and relaxing, Doublehead claimed to be pleased to have done this favor for the Vann party. Now Vann could find ways to help him, he said, and ought to stop criticizing him. As for the two Moravians, he suggested that they pay him for having allowed the vote to proceed. He asked that they buy him a bottle of whiskey.

James Vann, who was not a Christian and never would be, as he confessed to one and all, took the two Moravians to his home and gave them food, and later showed them a house and farm nearby for sale. Such improvements as had been made could be purchased from a white man, Robert Brown; the land itself was Cherokee land and could not, need not be bought. The farm was on the federal road that Vann was trying to get authorized, and it was a mile or so from Vann's own quarters and tavern. There was a bold spring there, which travelers had learned to trust, near which they sometimes camped.

The Moravians liked the spot, liked being near Vann and Hicks, and they agreed to put the matter before the Lord. In all, the two missionaries visited four places they liked, and they chose to decide among them by lot. After prayer for God's guidance, a slip was drawn. On the slip drawn was written "James Vann's place."

Stillbirths occurred often among the Cherokees, and the shamans claimed that this condition grew worse because of the presence of whites among the people and the acceptance by many of white civilization. There were no statistics kept indicating whether mixed blood or full-blood Indians had more dead babies issuing from the wombs, or more babies to die in infancy; but everybody knew the whites bred more babies than the Indians, also had more of them grow to size, so there were secret meanings to be learned.

In the old days, in a live birth, the placenta was taken by runner to a mountaintop and buried. There were reasons for this practice, but not everybody could recall them, and shamans argued about most of them anyway. Rarely was the placenta carried off today. It was buried nearby to feed the roots of a fruit tree, and the bodies of dead infants were buried, too. Susanna was always one to weep at these burials.

Her first child to touch her, to suck and cry, was a girl, and Ridge, swelled in pride, named her Nancy. The second, born soon thereafter, in 1803, was a spankingly healthy, loud-voiced boy baby. This birth took place in their new house, on their plantation. She and Ridge named him John, the four midwives listening. He was perfect in body; he was not as large as a Ridge might be expected to be, did not promise to fulfill his father as to girth, Ridge admitted, but he would carry the same passions.

Susanna took the boy to suck at her body and with a smile promised to do as well again and again, now that she had begun to get the gist of giving birth.

The Moravian school was to be located near enough to serve Nancy and John, once they were old enough, and Susanna often frequented the compound, watched the solid, substantial buildings rise. The Moravians did not use Indian construction methods. Their German-type houses required months, years to complete, which thwarted those Indian parents who had children already old enough to learn. Susanna could afford to be more tolerant, but even she had cause to become apprehensive as years passed, the Moravians working on the joints of windows and doors while Cherokee parents waited.

When she heard that the Moravians would enroll only four students, only four, Susanna was upset, as were many Cherokee parents. After years of constructing buildings and of clearing pastures and fields, the facility was to teach only four.

The Moravians admitted their own disappointment but explained that their facilities were for boarding students and must also serve the staff. They pointed out that church services had been held over a period of many months, without so much as a single convert, which was distressing to them. The school was to be for the children of Christians, as they said they had always claimed, and there were no Cherokee Christian parents.

The chiefs were openly critical of them. James Vann urged conciliation, but he was compromised just now. He had for years sought to have a new federal road built through the nation. Doublehead opposed it; in fact, most lower-town chiefs opposed it, as they did other contacts with the whites. Along the road the federal government wanted to authorize inns, with stables for the travelers' horses, wanted to build ferries for river crossings, all such franchises for services to go to white men, because whites would be using the road. Vann was fighting for the road, but he also wanted inn and ferry franchises; furthermore, he was seeking a mail franchise. His greed made Doublehead jealous and furious. As for the federal agents, they felt pressure on them from Indians on the one side, and President Jefferson in Washington on the other, who told the agents at all cost to gain the land for the road to the west, even if it meant bribing some of the more important chiefs.

The lower-town chiefs claimed the Moravians were agents of this new President Jefferson, were merely disguised as missionaries. They were James Vann's spies here to gain a federal road.

The upper-town chiefs met to consider this deplorable state of affairs, and in June 1803, they noted in a letter to the Moravians that a long time had elapsed since a school was to be begun for the instruction of Indian youth. "We now consider that the Society have fallen through their good intentions toward us, as we discover no prospect of such business going on." The council gave them six moons to open their school or, as they chose, to get out.

The Moravians admitted their disappointment. The whole nation seemed to be against them and would, as one wrote, "fain see us gone. We now hear that Mr. Vann was of the same opinion."

The missionaries next approached the peripatetic, difficult Vann, and gave him yet again their view that missionaries were not here to keep school but to bear witness to the word of God.

Vann told them bluntly, as was his nature, that the Cherokees had no interest in the word of God and that, in any case, this purpose was not sufficient cause for the Moravians to stay in the country.

Their reception elsewhere was equally chilly. They had spent four years doing their buildings, which were even yet incomplete. Also they had made the farm, which was so productive it gave Cherokees cause for distress. They wondered if the Germans were more interested in wealth than in teaching their children. At the Moravian place one could trade a saddle of venison for corn or leather or cloth; the Germans were keen traders, wanted to trade with Cherokees, but they never had taught a Cherokee anything. As for their religious services, the Cherokees did not understand complicated ideas, particularly when expressed in foreign tongues, whether English or German, and they noted that not a single Moravian had learned a word of Cherokee. The Sunday services were simply gibberish, though the music was attractive.

When told that admitting more than four students ought to be possible for so rich a farm, because Cherokee children ate corn and wanted nothing else, the Moravians replied that the corn grew prolifically, that was true, but it must be "pounded and baked and this would be for us a great trouble and waste of time. It would be best if we limited the number to four."

They did agree that the four need not have Christian parents, for not one child qualified under that rule.

A small dormitory for students was now begun. Vann allowed his slaves to work on it, but only on Sunday, which upset the Christians. Even so, they accepted the help and paid each of the adult blacks fifty cents a day.

In October the national council met and had this lingering matter of these blessed Moravians on their docket, along with a few other bothers. The dormitory was not complete. No students had been admitted. These foreigners are farmers, not teachers, the chiefs concluded. Doublehead, Glass, Bark, and others spoke against their remaining. Vann and Watts were in a pout, stymied to silence by the wiles and ways of the obstinate Germans. The Moravians must admit more than four, by God, or be damned, Vann stated privately. There was only room for four, the Moravians insisted.

Ten students or be gone—you and your Jesus Christ God, Vann told them.

No, four, they insisted.

As the question swelled toward a vote in the council, the chief federal agent Meigs actually prepared to evict the Moravians. He was issuing orders when, miracle by miracle, a diversion, a Presbyterian minister, the Reverend Gideon Blackburn of Maryville, Tennessee, arrived at the council and asked to speak. He promised to send three or four schoolmasters at once, each one to teach twenty-five to thirty students. The students could live at home but would be provided their food and clothing without charge. The teachers would not be preachers. They would not start a model farm or a trading community. The effort would be to teach the young people to speak and read English and to do arithmetic. There would be hymns for singing, but no effort to convert them. Once they were able to open the secrets of the Good Book, if they chose Christianity, they would be received into the church, but it would be each individual's decision and would not require the commitment of the entire family.

The lower-town chiefs forgot their animosity toward whites and reveled in their dislike of Moravians only; all of the chiefs enthusiastically welcomed Reverend Blackburn. They knew little about him but accepted his assurances, and told the Moravians that the Cherokees had no more need of them. Meigs went ahead and negotiated with them, telling them that they must accept students and teach them, or must return their farm to the nation.

The Moravians consented. They would have the dormitory finished in another year, they promised. They expected to have room for seven students at that time.

The Moravian community in Salem sent them a black female slave to help with the milling, baking, laundry, and farm chores, but she proved to be shiftless. They asked Vann what should be done. He agreed to help them. With a bullwhip, he beat her.

5

Born to Ridge's brother Oo-watie (or, as he was more commonly called, Watie) and his wife, living near Ridge in the same beautiful Oothcaloga Valley, a son to be named Gallegina, the English name being Buck. Born soon after Susanna gave birth to John, Buck was dedicated to him as companion and friend. Darker of skin than John and with straight, black hair, Buck was distinctly Indian in appearance even as an infant, while John was European, a result of his white genes from his father's father's father. Each boy was one-sixteenth white.

The two boys began their lives together, living in their own favored world near James Vann's plantation, near the mission and school of the Moravians.

In recent autumns, once the crops were in, John Sevier and his brother Val, leaders among the white Tennesseans, would lead raiding parties against Indians in order to keep them respectful. Recently the campaigns had aborted. It was impossible to find an enemy. The Sevier men would hire an English-speaking Indian guide, and they would follow his direction, and it did not occur to Sevier that his party was being led astray. In September 1782, James Sevier, one of John's sons, served on one such expedition. In two letters he gives quite different accounts of what happened:

> We set out for the Indian country in the month of September, 1782. On the Highwassee river and Chiccamauga creek we destroyed all their towns, stock, corn & everything they had to support on. We then crossed a small range of mountains to the Coosa river, where we found and destroyed several towns, with all their stock, corn & provisions of every kind. The Indians eluded our march and kept out of our way in the general, although a few men, women and children were surprised and taken. We left the Coosa river for home about the last of October. . . . We all set out for our homes without the loss of a single man.

Marched first through the Upper Cherokee towns, who were at peace; got John Watts and a half breed of the name of Butler to pilot the army. At Tellico met old Hanging Maw who was friendly; the Hiwassee towns professed to be at peace and were not molested.

. . . [A]s the first incident of the campaign . . . they neared Chestue Creek, the advance guard met two Indians coming towards them in the path; the Indians broke and run. Major Val. Sevier took the lead in their pursuit but the Indians had so far the start that they would have got off but for James Sevier and 3 others forming a flanking party on horseback and had rode upon a very large mound; and while viewing it heard the disturbance ahead and in a few moments saw an Indian running at full speed and making for a canebreak near by; Sevier and his party dashed down the mound, cut off his retreat, seeing which the Indian suddenly stopped, raised both hands and uttered a most pitiful and imploring cry. He was taken captive. Col. and Major Sevier and Watts and Butler now coming up, the captive was questioned as to where the other Indian went and replied he had secreted himself under the creek bank. Col. Sevier desired Watts to call for him to come in and surrender and he should not be hurt. Watts raised a yell, and the Indian, sure enough, emerged from under the creek bank and gave himself up.

Went to several hostile towns on the Chickamauga creek. The Indians kept out of the way; destroyed their crops, towns, corn mostly in the fields, in which they would turn their horses. Camped several days at Bull Town on that creek. Watts sent and had Miss Jane Ireland brought in, who had been captured a year or so before on Roan's Creek, in Johnson County now. . . . (John) Rogers soon after came in. Jack Civil, a free negro, also came in.

Followed up Chickamauga creek and over to the head waters of Coosa, and on this route came upon the cabin of Patrick Clements, an Irishman, a British refugee who was living with Nancy Coody; both were captured, and Clements soon after broke and attempted to make his escape. Isaac Thomas shot and killed him. Nancy was kept prisoner.

Then passed to Spring Frog Town, on Coosa; and when at a distance from the town, a canoe of Indians was observed crossing the river; a party of men made chase but the Indians got over, abandoned their canoe, and dashed into a canebrake and were seen no more. An aged squaw had hid herself under the river bank; some of the Beans discovered her, but did not disturb her. One Ralston, an Irishman, came upon and shot her and took her scalp. The Beans and others tormented Ralston unmercifully, calling out at the top of their voices, "Who scalped granny?" Several voices in different directions would reply "Ralston." Ralston found no peace the rest of the campaign, but kept at a distance of a hundred yards from the army.

Above Spring Frog Town on Coosa was Estamarla, here between the two, Robert Bean at the head of a small scouting party, captured an Indian, a squaw, and several children. The Indian had a very pretty shot gun; Bean took it from him and gave it to Col. Sevier's servant Toby. This Indian was a small fellow but full of impudence: he would on every occasion utter the bittersweet denunciations against Toby; and the war of words between him and Toby was carried on greatly to the amusement of the soldiers.

On another occasion, James Sevier and a scout of three or four others, came upon a camp of two squaws and several children, captured them and took them to camp.

From Estamarla, went to old Nunack town, Vann's town, back to Hiwassee, destroying all in their way. Message was sent to the Lower Towns that a treaty would be held at Chota, and the Indians, glad of an opportunity to secure peace, attended, and aided by the friendly chiefs Hanging Maw, Old Connestota, and the Tassel, made peace, gave up the prisoners to the number of about twenty in all, and returned home early in November. Not a man of Sevier's army was killed or wounded.

The guide, John Watts, was apparently able to lead Sevier and his men only to towns that had been abandoned after the whites' attacks three years earlier, missing the new towns entirely.

In one of the later campaigns, Sevier was thought to have been killed, and the Indians celebrated his death. In fact, the corpse was that of a Mr. Bullard, one of Sevier's men, who resembled him. Bullard and a few other corpses were buried by Sevier's men in the floor of one of the houses of an Indian town, and the house was burned to save the bodies from mutilation. The body was found, mutilated, and commemorated as if it were Sevier's.

Ridge, Hicks, and Vann had come to be the three leaders of a political movement. Doublehead led the opposition. The two sides disagreed about nearly everything, including the desirability of adapting to white civilization and the disposal of Cherokee land. One would expect a partisan, such as Doublehead, to be fiercely protective of everything Cherokee, and so he was, except on occasions when he was willing to "treaty away" land. Each time he negotiated a treaty, his own wealth increased, until by 1803 he was rich beyond his white secretary's ability to measure. Watts, Vann, and now even Ridge, were exploring livestock and grain to the whites, but no more than was Doublehead. All four had plantations, and Vann, Ridge and Doublehead had other business interests as well, in stores and river crossings, where ferry

services charged for the transport of people, wagons, horses, cattle, hogs. Ferries required only the attendance of one or two
slaves and made rich profits.

To trade with whites, Doublehead even ordered built a large
boat equipped with two cannons to haul his goods and loot to
market down the rivers to New Orleans, it being easier to reach
that rich port than Charleston or those of the Chesapeake. At any
of these centers one could sell goods and buy whatever one
pleased; the world was for sale, including the strongest and most
handsome slaves, some of them newly purchased from African
tribes. An Indian did need a white to assist him, however, for his
word was not weighted fairly against a white man's.

As Hicks analyzed the situation, Doublehead was gaining annually in influence, largely because the traders and white agents
knew he would take bribes. He was one of the chiefs the whites
preferred to deal with, the government agents as well as the representatives of the land companies. White settlers were prohib-
ited by various state and federal laws from making land purchases
from Indians, but several of them were deeply involved in making such purchases anyway. Because Hicks sometimes worked for
Meigs and often translated for him and other federal agents, he
learned many secrets and told Vann and Ridge much about
Doublehead's maneuvers. Within the past five years, Doublehead
had arranged one cession in North Carolina and two in Tennessee, the last one involving loss to the Cherokees of their claims to
the hunting grounds between the Clinch River and the Cumberland Mountains. In 1804, the Cherokees had ceded part of Georgia, the so-called "Wafford Settlement." In October 1805, a larger
cession was suggested by the federal government, and the chiefs
dutifully came together at Tellico, Tennessee, where word was
passed among them that Doublehead was the chief the federal
agents wanted to negotiate with. They bought the Cherokee
claims on lands north of the Tennessee River from Hiwassee to
Muscle Shoals, the best hunting grounds still claimed by the
Cherokees, including the Cumberland Plateau and parts of Kentucky. Doublehead received many favors and considerations, including private ownership of various tracts of land; two such
tracts were at the mouths of the Clinch and Hiwassee rivers,

while his brother became the owner of a major holding at the mouth of Duck River.

Judge Richard Henderson was the North Carolinian land merchant who dared to purchase most of Kentucky and the better part of central Tennessee from the Cherokees, ignoring the British proclamation of 1763 forbidding such purchases. First he conferred with Virginian land merchant Patrick Henry, who considered coming in with him on such a deal; however, Henry withdrew, perhaps fearful of the legal complications. Deciding to proceed alone, Henderson sent fellow North Carolinian Daniel Boone, who had earlier recommended the purchase to him, to select the best Cherokee chiefs for negotiating, the ones more susceptible to bribes; and he traveled west to negotiate with them and Boone. He met with them again in 1775 at Sycamore Shoals, and this time he exchanged a cabin full of goods for the Cherokee claim to the land.

Having thus reduced the fears of white families, Boone found it easier to induce others to settle. Possession was nine-tenths of the law under British rule, in spite of British proclamations.

The Holston settlers and other Wataugans, many of whom had accompanied Henderson, at once purchased title to their land, already settled but never deeded. Previously they had held only a short-term lease from the Cherokees, which had expired. The title from Henderson's Transylvania Company, suspect though it might be in English courts, was better than anything they had.

In 1806 Doublehead began leasing his private holdings to white men, adding richly to his cash income, and by the next year, he was again negotiating on behalf of the Cherokees with Colonel Meigs, now the United States agent. Criticism of him and his habits increased but failed to dissuade him. Occasionally his critics were put to death. Doublehead was the most powerful chief, second to the principal chief in title but more favored by the whites and more adroit. There was no legal way to control him; the best, last hope had been the federal government, but Meigs obviously was working hand in glove with him, and according to Hicks he was under orders from Washington to do so.

President Jefferson was willing to treat with him and recently had gone so far as to recommend the migration of all eastern Indians to lands west of the Mississippi.

Ridge admitted to hating him, telling stories of his excesses in battle and his vengeful, barbarous conduct. Ridge, Hicks, and Vann often talked about how to stop him. Death—assassination—was the only solution, Vann contended. The blood law would require that male relatives of Doublehead, those of his clan, must revenge his death, but Cherokee blood law also directed that any Cherokee who sold Cherokee land could be killed without consequence.

Very well, they agreed. The assassins would be Vann, Ridge, and a third mixed-blood, Alexander Saunders, a close personal friend of Vann's. Vann had years ago drawn knives with Doublehead after calling him a traitor to his face, but the two had been restrained, held apart. Now another meeting would be arranged.

Vann was urged on in this plot by his favorite wife, the sister of Doublehead's wife. Doublehead had recently killed his wife's baby in her womb, and had gone on beating her until she died.

Ridge, Vann, and Saunders decided to slay him before the next council assembly; one was due in August to accept the annual federal annuity, which after the treaty of 1791 was payment for land purchased by the United States.

Vann was drinking heavily, preparing for the encounter. He was to strike the blow; he had asked for that right, to be first, because of his sister-in-law's murder. He drank so much and worried so much that on the road to the meeting he became sick and had to lie down. Finally Ridge and Saunders left him and went on.

At Hiwassee the two waited in McIntosh's Tavern. Reports said that Doublehead was at a ball game an hour's distance away. A rumor circulated that today at the game he had killed a man who had called him a traitor. All afternoon Ridge and Saunders waited. After dark Doublehead arrived, drunk. At once an old man accosted him, berated him for selling Cherokee land. Doublehead rebuked him and pushed him away. He sat down at a table alone. Ridge approached him. A candle was burning near his face. The two men knew each other, and Doublehead watched unafraid as Ridge approached. Ridge blew out the candle and shot him in the head.

Ridge and Hicks fled the tavern. Later they learned that even yet the powerful man lived; the bullet had entered under his ear and escaped through his jaw. At once Ridge and Saunders went to find him, and by dawn had trailed him to a loft in the house of a teacher at one of the Presbyterian schools. As Ridge and Saunders entered, Doublehead, enraged with pain, drew a dirk and charged. He tripped over a sheet. Ridge and Saunders fired, missed. Doublehead grabbed hold of Ridge, and the two strong men strained to kill each other. Saunders fired again, hit Doublehead in the hip. Saunders then struck Doublehead with his hatchet. The blade entered the forehead, breaking open his skull.

To pull the hatchet out, one man had to brace his foot against the fallen giant's head; both men grasped the handle.

Susanna knew what act her husband had left home to perform; bathed in fright she waited with her babies for his footsteps on the porch. That night she heard the arrival of his mount. Briskly he entered; stared at her somberly, nodded. He moved heavily to the lamp and blew out the light, then stood near the window, listening.

All his life, from here on, she realized, he would be listening.

Return J. Meigs accepted the death of Doublehead as a serious setback to his plans to acquire further lands in Tennessee, and he predicted that the Cherokee government would be left even less centralized than before, with the lower towns now free to squabble among themselves and to seek greater control over monies intended for both upper and lower towns. This would give the federal agents more responsibility to decide matters; otherwise, chaos would result.

There was no effort—none he could detect—to avenge Doublehead's assassination. The chief's excesses in life had alienated even his relatives. His death was universally welcomed. His two assassins were greeted warmly everywhere they went, and this man Ridge had been placed in charge of one of the two new light horse guards, which were to police and judge Cherokee crimes, with power to hold court and inflict punishment. Ridge had been elevated in power, so that now he was a force Meigs must reckon with. He was gaining in wealth, too—and not through bribes, about which Meigs knew almost everything. Ridge might one day become principal chief, Meigs decided.

Ridge's main handicap was James Vann, who was half crazy. Vann, another member of the new light horse guard, had taken it upon himself the other day to beat several Indians with a whip and with the butt of his gun, women as well as men, almost killing a few of them. It was not Cherokee custom to beat people. It was true that the laws held that men and even women were to be beaten for certain crimes, such as adultery; but Meigs knew of no such punishments applied in years past in spite of flagrant violations of those laws. Actually, the light horse had been created to protect whites and Cherokees from thieves, who were sometimes white, sometimes Cherokee. Vann—rich as a king, terrified that he would be robbed—was too quick to punish and far too severe. Ridge also was subject to theft, as he had crops, slaves, blooded horses, even wagons and a buggy, as well as ornate saddles; his wife had fine clothes, quilts, and blankets, dishes from abroad. They had a smokehouse stocked with bacon and hams, an apple house, a cellar for cider and cabbages and turnips and potatoes. She had herbs in abundance in a garden fenced so that not even a chicken could peck or scratch about her plants. Most thieves were, Meigs noticed, poor full-blood Indians who were hungry, driven to desperation by the virtual disappearance of wild game. Meigs could recall when there had been no thievery in the Cherokee nation itself, except against strangers; but now neighbors stole from neighbors.

He could not set the Indian world straight, he realized, though here or there he could make a move and now and then even please the officials in Washington, who apparently had decided to take the land Indians were not using and make it available to white settlers. They would not do it by force of arms; the Cherokees could even yet make that painful. President Jefferson preferred another way, to allow Indians to buy what they so much wanted and could not afford, then have the whites take their land claim in payment. That was the Jefferson way. Conquest, bribes, or trade, the three choices of government: he seemed to prefer trade, with bribes a second best. Meigs believed it to be inevitable that the Cherokees, as time went on, would lose everything.

Civilize the Indians: that also was a government goal, set by President Washington. Let them farm and weave. Some would, but most would rather starve and go about naked and sleep in each other's arms for warmth. Meigs admired the full-bloods and wished them well, but he had no confidence in their becoming civilized. He chose mixed-bloods for his own assistants; Hicks was the best he knew. Hicks was an example of a civilized Indian male. He was good humored, sober. Many Indian men could not control their actions when drunk—and who, by God, was the new importer of whiskey for Indians? Why the Presbyterian Reverend Blackburn, caught with an entire boatload of it. Now, that will choke off his support, close his schools, leave for the Cherokee children only that piddling effort of the Moravians. Civilization, indeed! Please notice that full-bloods prefer their own civilization, are not one damn bit willing to be painted white.

Black Fox—since Little Turkey's death in 1804 he had been principal chief—was a full-blood, proud to be unable to read or write or count, the chief of chiefs of a nation with problems so immense and diverse, as Meigs knew them to be, that a genius trained by a king's counselors could not govern. The principal chief had no power to govern, anyway, but only to try to influence. Consensus supposedly must be reached. Black Fox had no experience. How much can I give you, Chief Black Fox, for Muscle Shoals? Meigs actually asked him this question in private. The new chief knew of the deals Meigs had made with Doublehead and appeared to be willing to become rich; however, Meigs knew that he did not have the ability to deliver. One must do what one could, however, use the clay at hand. Meigs offered him five hundred dollars. That was not enough, Black Fox said. Meigs offered a thousand. That was not enough, either. So Meigs offered a thousand dollars and a brand new rifle. Now that touched the quick, but it was still not enough.

The next offer was a thousand dollars, a new rifle, and a hundred dollars annually for life.

That was enough. That was the bribe for Muscle Shoals. The principal chief's vote was arranged. But there would need to be the salving of other chiefs, of two, three, four, or more. Now that Doublehead was gone, leadership was splintered and expensive.

Meigs was able to buy several votes in his effort to obtain Muscle Shoals. The sale was agreed to at a meeting of chiefs on September 7, 1807. By the next day everybody within many miles knew that the chiefs had been bought, knew what they had received, and were jealous of them for having new guns.

Meigs wrote the Secretary of War, telling him he had carried out instructions and that the chiefs well deserved the "silent considerations" they had taken, now that criticism of their sale of land was hot and widespread.

Then, too, there was the matter of the ironworks. A white in South Carolina was willing to make an ironworks in the Cherokee nation—which was needed in Meig's view—but the white man required the Cherokees to cede him land at the mouth of Chickamauga Creek, where he had discovered the necessary supplies of iron ore, limestone, and waterpower. Meigs called a meeting at his agency, and the chiefs agreed that six square miles of this land would be ceded to the federal government so that it could then be leased to the South Carolinian, a man named Elias Earle.

Meigs told Earle to come along, enough chiefs had agreed. Earle bought equipment and hired men. He got as far as the federal pike near Vann's tavern; but there Ridge, with a force of thirty men, stopped the wagon train, which was being driven by eight South Carolina blacks and a wagonmaster named Bill Brown.

Ridge took Brown's rifle. He fired it to unload it—fired it close enough to Brown's head that the roar convinced him to listen closely. A brave, Callescawee, grazed Brown's cheek with a hatchet—not enough to draw blood, but close enough to silence his protests. Ridge had a written message, in English, which he read.

This is to inform you that the majority of the Cherokee Nation does not approve of the sale & purchase made to & by Colonel Earle of part of our lands on Chicamauga [sic] & that we have resolved not to permit any one to settle on the said land or to cut a road thither untill the said sale & purchase is ratified by Congress as well as by Chiefs of our nation in full council, on which subject we wrote to the agent. We therefore warn you not to cut a road, nor to do any work on the said land untill such ratification be had & obtained; for if you persist in going on you will be stopped by force, for which the bearer and others have our orders, so you had better take our advice and return back in peace.

Brown sold what tools and equipment he could on the spot. He sold some of the food and the feed, too, and turned south.

The state of Tennessee later proved less than wise, in Meigs's opinion, by turning down the transfer of the land to the federal government, so Earle sued the federal government, listing exaggerated costs (which Meigs tailored down to just under one thousand dollars), and the government was deliberating whether to pay him that or nothing. If the War Department paid him, they would doubtless take it out of the Cherokee annuity, as they did every white man's claim for damages, whether fair or not, or approved by the tribe or not. Certainly, this expense was not tribal: it had never gone to the council. A band of Cherokees and Creeks stealing four blacks from a field was not tribal, either; but the value of those four, if paid by the War Department, would come out of the annual annuity that was owed the Cherokees as a people, as provided for them by terms of past treaties.

Why did Vann send Ridge to stop the ironworks? Meigs wondered. Perhaps he wanted a bribe himself. He was irrational when drunk, and recently he stayed drunk. Ridge would not take a bribe. Meigs was sure of that. He stopped the ironworks because it was not legally granted. That must be his thinking. He was an idealist, an Indian with an idealistic bent. He opposed anything the least bit underhanded or devious. More and more trails led to Ridge; but they were, Meigs admitted, all straight trails.

An order more difficult to execute that came to Meigs from Washington, D.C., had to do with Indian removal to some place in the West. Meigs worked on this matter, too, which was well—if secretly—funded. The lower towns had always had many chiefs who wanted to move away from the whites, but they could not find a welcome from any of the western Indian tribes. Now the federal government was offering land in the Arkansas territory, beyond the Mississippi, fertile land with more wild game than existed here. Meigs bought the votes of four chiefs, mentioning the possibility that the lower-towns' people might sell out and move, even if the residents of the upper towns wanted to stay.

A deputation of upper-town chiefs traveled to Washington to complain that the lower-town chiefs kept for their part all of the plows and looms and the annuity, now that they had a majority vote in the national council, and the "Great Father Jefferson" had grieved with them about this matter of their internal government over which he had no control. On this trip the Secretary of War suggested a division of the Cherokee nation, or so he reported by letter to Meigs, between upper and lower; each of those Indians who remained in the East would have a farm for his ownership, "to be under the jurisdiction and laws of the U.S. & to become actual Citizens."

Meigs thought it would be best to send all of the Cherokees west, and to this end he bought the votes of four powerful chiefs, Black Fox and John Jolly, The Glass, and Taluntuskee, in support of emigration. At the autumn council Black Fox introduced the proposal. It was a resolution to send a delegation, entrusted with the mission, to see the President:

> Tell our Great Father, the President, that our game has disappeared, and we wish to follow it to the West. We are his friends, and we hope he will grant our petition, which is to remove our people towards the setting sun. But we shall give up a fine country, fertile in soil, abounding in watercourses, and well adapted for the residence of white people. For all this we must have a good price.

Meigs, on hearing the proposal, was in as great suspense as his girth and aged heart would allow. All that now was needed was the council's favorable vote to place the initiative before the tribe. The council sat in silence. Apparently nobody would choose to be the one to speak first in argument.

Ridge rose from his seat among the younger chiefs. His deep, melodious voice filled the council house:

> My friends, you have heard the talk of the principal chief. He points to the region of the setting sun as the future habitation of this people. As a man he has a right to give his opinion; but the opinion he has given as the chief of this nation is not binding; it was not formed in council in the light of day, but was made up in a corner—to drag this people, without their consent, from their own country, to the dark land of the setting sun. I resist it here in my place as a man, as a chief, as a Cherokee, having the right to be consulted in a matter of such importance. What are your heads placed on your bodies for, but to think, and if to think, why should you not be consulted? I scorn this movement of a few men to unsettle the nation and trifle with our attachment to the land of our forefathers! Look abroad over the face of this country—along the rivers, the creeks, and their branches, and you will behold the dwellings of the people who repose in content and security. Why is this grand scheme projected to lead away to another country the people who are happy here? I, for one, abandon my respect for the will of a chief, and regard only the will of thousands of our people. Do I speak without the response of any heart in this assembly, or do I speak as a free man to men who are free and know their rights? I pause to hear.

He heard well enough the ovation. Meigs watched, astonished. In the next little while, his own proposal was defeated, and Black Fox, The Glass, and Taluntuskee were broken, expelled from the council, disgraced. He watched—nobody even consulting him—as the council appointed a new delegation to visit Washington, D.C., to represent the interests of the Cherokees in forming a more effective self-government. One member of the six-man delegation, even though he was only in his thirties, was this man Meigs could not purchase, Ridge.

And it was Ridge who sought out Meigs afterward and invited him to accompany the group to Washington City.

The delegation consisted of two parts: three chiefs from the upper towns and three from the lower. The six did not agree on the goals for their mission, Meigs noticed, except that they and he would all travel together. They rode their finest horses and had pack horses, as well. The route chosen lay through Greenville, South Carolina, where they turned northeast through the piedmont of North Carolina, arriving at the Moravian town of Salem. While there the Indians began to grasp the goals of the Moravian mission back home at Spring Place, where Ridge and Susanna planned to enroll Nancy and John in a year or so. They discovered here a community of craftspeople, all busy, all of the same spiritual belief and consecration, all the adults rearing towheaded children in sturdy, half-timber, half-brick houses, every man and woman busy doing basic crafts, pottery, furniture making, weaving, tobacco curing, gunmaking. Also, each person was a musician, and magnificent sounds were created, these musicians reading notes on paper as arranged in Germany years ago. This magnificent music was yet another miracle to Ridge. Hundreds of revelations were here. The chiefs had never seen as productive a people as these, living off to themselves, isolated by choice from the rest of society. It was apparent to the chiefs that the seed planted at Spring Place had a world to grow into. Here was example of the tree to be grown.

Ridge peered into the bakery, sniffing the rich aromas; he bought a loaf to nibble on. At the apothecary he studied the row on row of dried herbs, offering their Cherokee names to the apothecarist. He studied the potter's kilns, watched the gunsmith turn a barrel, his brain compressing, sorting information. Not all could be remembered. Better first to learn to write words and figures. No chief in this delegation could remember everything.

They rode on through Virginia, passing east of President Jefferson's homeplace in the mountains there, and proceeded up the Shenandoah Valley, with its thousands of independent farms and small, busy towns, to the largest city Ridge had ever seen. This was 1808. At thirty-seven years of age, he came to Washington, Meigs and the others with him.

As they approached they smelled the aroma of wood burning from hundreds of fireplaces; the smoke carried westward across the bay, welcoming them with promises of warmth and food. Washington city spread out its beautiful wings, was a massive bird resting, stretching, sunning. They proudly rode into the capital, the home site of the president they had been advised to call father. Meigs recommended one of the boarding houses, and once the six delegates were housed, he wrote a note to the Secretary of War, telling him that the delegation had arrived, had brought no papers describing its mission, but awaited an audience.

The nation's capital building was unfinished, but many marble walls reflected sunlight. The chiefs walked into the building's cold heart, then into its two bellies, gaping at the hordes of black slaves and white overseers hauling and pulling slabs of heavy rock into their places, all the rock already cut to fit. The mind was compelled to tremble at such achievement. Above them a dome of stone and glass was being set in place, the weight greater than any ten men could lift.

A swamp lay along one side of Pennsylvania Avenue, muddy, rutted, with holes that appeared to have been made by pigs lathering mud on themselves. The president's house had several lights in its windows, flickering assurances of health, safety, of Mr. Jefferson's comfort inside, the largest home the chiefs had ever seen.

As they gaped, people gaped at them. Both whites and blacks made way for the Indians. Stories must fill their heads, Ridge decided, of wigwams and blanket-wrapped babies, of Hiawatha bathing before a waterfall, of braves cleaning the scalp of a giant brutish bear with a tomahawk, of bows sending arrows into the heart of a buck deer, of leisurely nights lounging near a fire, resting one's head in the lap of a willing maiden, daughter of the principal chief, and chewing on a whole pheasant.

The chiefs knew well the romantic notions of these citizens as they deferred to them, made more than sufficient room for them to pass. Of all the chiefs, Ridge was the one most stared at, his broad handsome face and noble bearing distinctly fitting the romantic images.

On December 21 the chiefs, with Meigs, prepared a written paper to leave with President Jefferson; the six delegates agreed on its content and signed it with their marks, and, dressed in clothes provided for them, took it to the White House, where they were received by Jefferson.

Father—The underwritten, chiefs of the Cherokee Nation instructed by their national council to come to the city of Washington & there to take by the hand their father the President, & express to him in behalf of their nation their sincere sentiments of gratitude and to say to him—that, for nearly eight years they have experienced his protecting and fostering hand, under which they progressed in agriculture & domestic manufactures much beyond their own expectations or the expectations of their white Brethren of the United States & that by the schools many of their children have made great advancement in the useful facts of english education, such as reading, writing, and arithmetic—that by means of these acquisitions the desireable work of civilization advances & will in future be accelerated & knowledge diffused more easily and widely amongst their people provided the same measures shall be [pursued] by your successor in office, which they please themselves will be the case, & that he will also hold them fast by the hand & that the magnanimity of the U. States will not suffer ten thousand human beings [to] be lost between whom & the white people the great Spirit has made no difference, except in the tint of their skins, for they believe that the great Spirit loves his red children as well as his white children & looks with equal eye on the works of his hands, & that their final destination is the same.

Father——

When you retire from the Administration of the great business which has been committed to your hand by our white Brethren, a consciousness of upright intentions will be your reward: a reward beyond the lash of contingencies—that the great Spirit will add yet many years to your useful life & that it may be happy is the affectionate wish of the red people whom we represent.

The man who welcomed them, the resident of the executive mansion, was gaunt—might indeed be ill—was tall and slender and gray. The chiefs had expected his hair to be red. Chiefs who had seen him years ago had said it was red, and had marveled at it. Ridge was impressed with his civility, his courtesy, the compassion in his eyes toward them, his Indians, his country's threat, friends, one-day-to-be citizens. As an Appalachian mountaineer he would have heard a hundred horror tales about massacres, kidnapping, house and barn burnings, barbarism, thefts. No sign of criticism in his face. No guards were with him, either. No fear of the chiefs was evident as he took each man's hand.

He told them that soon he was leaving office at the close of eight years as president. Before that term, he had served President Washington, so he had for many, many moons been away from home, from his family and farm, which he acknowledged was on land once owned by the Cherokees. He had always re-spected Indians, he said, as much as white men. He believed them to be equal. He had sought to stop the flow of whiskey and other forms of liquor into Indian territories, believing it to be danger-ous. He reminded them that no government is always kind, In-dian or white. The United States must adjust to forces at home, and to others in Europe: in France, where he had seen years of service as a younger man; in England, which he knew several Cherokee chiefs, perhaps fathers of his visitors, had visited; and in Spain.

He would write them answers to their message to him and to the particulars they had addressed to the secretary. At this mo-ment he would discuss his answers with them. He proceeded to review his written reply, assuring them all the while of his re-spect. To the upper-town chiefs he said,

> You inform me of your anxious desires to engage in the industrious pursuits of agriculture and civilized life; that finding it impracticable to induce the nation at large to join in this you wish a line of separation to be established between the upper and lower towns so as to include all the waters of Hiwas-see in your part; and that having thus contracted your society within nar-rower limits, you propose, within these, to begin the establishment of fixed laws and regular government.

The president told the upper-town chiefs that he approved of these goals, saying that they must agree on the boundary they meant to separate them, and offered to send government survey-ors to run the line.

In reply to their questions about government solidarity and the administration of law, the Cherokees must decide; no one has the right to say what shall be law for others, he told them. He suggested that they might follow the United States model, which he personally admired. In that case, each Cherokee town, and its surrounding countryside, would elect delegates to a central coun-cil by means of a vote of the majority of all voters. He understood that the present method was to find the consensus of men living in or near a town, but it was unclear who was empowered to vote. A vote should allow the younger and weaker members to partici-pate equally. At the council meetings, Colonel Meigs could advise

the members on parliamentary procedures, even as debates un-
folded, the members to decide on punishments for crimes, ownership of property, and other matters. Their father in Washington
favored assigning to every head of a family a piece of land to own,
to improve, and to pass along to descendants. These suggestions
might be of use to the upper towns.

The suggestion of the lower-town chiefs that they leave their
land and migrate westward to the Arkansas River interested him
intensely. He had four or five years earlier recommended that
Indian tribes consider a move to land where they would never be
bothered by white people again. He would welcome working out
ways for the lower towns to do so.

Meigs accompanied the chiefs as they returned to the boarding house. They were elated, impressed by the reasonableness and
charity of this gray Father. Although he had separated them further, using the division they had suggested to Meigs, he had
brought them into comradeship, made them members with him
of the country in a way not done as successfully before. All issues
had been discussed in his soft Virginia-mountaineer accent, all in
orderly series, all considerately.

Ridge did not favor a division of the Cherokee nation. He
decided that he and Hicks and Vann must lead the Cherokees into
unity and improvement. He longed to do so. But on his return
home, Hicks announced that he had resigned as Meigs's assistant,
giving as reason Meigs's penchant for bribing chiefs on large matters and small. The resignation or firing was a loss of influence
for the Vann–Hicks–Ridge group, and closed off access to secrets.
Hicks claimed that there was no cause too small for Meigs to lay
on a bribe, and the money—where did it come from, if not Washington?

Even beyond this, there was trouble brewing within the
ranks of this triumvirate. The chiefs affiliated with them were
drawing away from Vann. Even Alexander Saunders had been
ousted as Vann's closest friend. Apparently Saunders had sought
to limit Vann's excesses and had been dismissed. Now Vann ruled
his tavern, where he was his own favored customer, without allowing criticism from anybody. As a consequence he was becom-

ing crazier every day. The wealthiest Cherokee of all, he had developed his obsession that thieves were about; he believed he was to be robbed, was being even now robbed, had often been robbed. He knew he would not go penniless to his grave, there was too much accumulated for him or his wives and children ever to go hungry; but he wanted to be fat, to have the world, to own and possess, to dominate, to luxuriate, to command. In his drunken stupors, while slandering Saunders, he would admit that he was possessed by devils; he had lost his soul. To hell with it.

His favorite wife went to the Moravian services, sat alone, and prayed in broken English for him.

He beat her. Later he wept, said he loved her, asked for her help. She consoled him and he beat her again.

Her brothers called on him, told him not to beat her anymore. Do you understand how serious our warning is? they asked him.

The level of cruelty to which he would stoop when drunk became a subject of speculation, people at first denying what later could be proved. There was the time Vann had ordered a black girl to be tied to a stake, and she, having survived his beatings before, remained insolent. He had firewood stacked around her and called his cronies out of the inn to watch as her defiance crumbled. She had not stolen from him, had not plotted with thieves, she told him, please let her go.

Those were not the words he wanted to hear, so he left her there to reconsider. Poor child that she was, she could not decide whether she must confess or deny. She confessed, then begged for release, swore never again to steal. She was his entertainment for the night. He left her tied there, until he was weary of her, no longer entertained by her. Then he burned her alive at the stake.

When Ridge and Hicks came to him, anxious to confer with him about efforts reunite the nation, they found that he had just killed a white man and wounded another.

A day soon after that, while Vann sat alone drinking, a rifle barrel nudged open the door nearby. He turned to see who was entering, and did see, but was never able to tell the name of his executioner. No one else at the tavern saw who killed him. They speculated that perhaps it was his wife's brothers, or one of his

wives, or Alexander Saunders, or a relative of the white man he
had slain, or another Indian, or a slave, or even the commander of
the light horse—Ridge.

At the meeting of the nation's council that autumn, Ridge
and Hicks were appointed to a new national committee, thirteen
men who were to manage Cherokee affairs. One of their duties
was to prepare a constitution modeled on that of the United
States. In addition to this Committee, Ridge remained commander of one of the two light horse guards. As for the division
line between upper and lower towns, Hicks and Ridge were
among those arguing against establishing one at all. They persuaded the lower chiefs, won them over so completely that
Meigs's westward migration died, with only one chief, Taluntuskee, taking a small number of Cherokees with him "into the setting sun."

The Moravians had taken no pleasure in the Presbyterians'
whiskey debacle. Reverend Blackburn had been with the boat, or
was nearby, so the voyage must have been personally directed by
him; and the Creeks, who had captured it, were now wealthy
individuals, with 2,226 gallons of as powerful a whiskey as had
ever been obtained from the white devils. The Creeks, who were
less than friendly to whites and for that matter to everybody else,
allowed Blackburn and crew to go home safely and soberly.

Disgraced, Reverend Blackburn closed his schools. He ex-
cused the whiskey-laden boat by saying that he was seeking a
water route to the West.

John Ridge entered the Moravian school before his sister and
before Buck. He was a bit older than Buck, and even though
younger than his sister, the Moravians had not yet completed the
girls' dormitory. John entered November 12, 1810, and thick loneliness covered him at once. A scrofulous condition of the legs and
hips, which had afflicted him from birth, became painful. Susanna
was beside herself. The boy was only seven and it was his father
who had engineered his leaving home, who was sending him to
live with foreigners, all in order to get a white education. She
resented this deeply, and would not hear of Nancy ever leaving.

Sequoyah, also known as George Gist, depicted in lithograph by Charles Bird King holding the Cherokee syllabary which he invented. (COURTESY: Archives and Manuscript Division of the Oklahoma Historical Society)

Left, David Vann, painted in 1825
by Charles Bird King
for inclusion in McKenney's
National Indian Portrait Gallery.
Vann was several times treasurer
of the Cherokee Nation.
(COURTESY: The Thomas Gilcrease
Institute of American History
and Art, Tulsa, Oklahoma)

Below, Joseph Vann, son of Chief
Vann and owner
of the sumptuous Vann
House in Spring Place, Georgia.
(COURTESY: Archives and Manuscript
Division of the Oklahoma
Historical Society)

Ridge had designs in her case, too, was going to have her live near Spring Place with Margaret Vann, John's widow, until such time as the Moravian quadrangle provided a room for her.

The leaders of the school were man and wife, elderly Brother John and Sister Anna Gambold, she the teacher of academics, he of religion. They were kind and industrious, ambitious for their eight male students, and they had agreed to teach three girls from Mrs. Vann's, once their mothers agreed to give them up. John, the son of Chief Ridge, was delicate in health, had a limp because of an afflicted hip—apparently the same malady as Chief Hicks, Ridge's neighbor. He was light-skinned and his hair tended to have a wave in it. The child could easily pass for white. He spoke not a word of English, and although his mother had supplied him with several shirts and breeches, he wore clothes with discomfort, no doubt preferring Indian nakedness, or near nakedness—which was, of course, sinful.

The Moravians had been at Spring Place since the spring of 1801, and although Colonel Meigs had advised them occasionally, they had made progress without government funding. Their buildings were of the blockhouse style, set so as to enclose a square yard. They had planted an orchard of cherry, peach, and apple trees, as well as catalpas and chinaberry trees in the yard, and Sister Gambold had begun a herb garden.

Nancy and two other girls did arrive finally, so eleven children were enrolled. Each day soon after first light the boys had prayer, a heartwarming sight to Brother Gambold; eight little Indian boys kneeling, seeking God's kindness. And sometimes the three girls were present in time to join them. Classes took the morning hours, then recess consisted of two or three hours for eating and chores. These included work in the fields, gardens, or barn, Mr. Gambold and his brother overseeing, instructing the children. Occasionally there was no work, and the boys could go hunting, using their blowguns or bows. All of them, even sick John Ridge, were quick, sure shots and often would find squirrels enough for a stew. At about three o'clock the boys and girls took up their books again—or sometimes the girls went to their looms or practiced mending or cooking. The books were elementary, teaching English words. Songs in English were one of the better ways, the Gambolds discovered, to teach the children this foreign language, foreign to everyone present, as the Moravians spoke German as their native tongue. Sister Gambold found herself amused by the sound of the German accent being layered onto English sentences by the Cherokee children.

John learned swiftly. She found him to be bright indeed. In one year's time he had mastered English. After his cousin Buck arrived, the two led the school. And what a dear child Buck was, she discovered, generous with his affection, which admittedly the reserved John was not, and full of good humor, of which John had little. John was always the determined, dedicated Indian; Buck, who looked Indian, was delighted to learn that he might be like the whites.

Ridge and Susanna came often to see the children at Sunday services. On other days Ridge would drop by whenever he was in the vicinity. He might be expected at mealtime, and the custom of singing before and after eating particularly pleased him. Occasionally, he would attend the afternoon chores, though he was not a worker himself. He offered to send a slave to do the chores for his children and Buck, so that they might use their time more profitably; but the Gambolds declined. They had one slave and wished they had none, and boys and girls needed to learn to work.

On one occasion Susanna received notice that John had an infection in his eyes, and she gave the alarm to Ridge and the servants and rode in haste to Spring Place. She was relieved and happy to find the report exaggerated. "They seemed pleased with what we had done for him," Sister Gambold wrote, "and after they had eaten, they went away much soothed."

A visitor to Spring Place, a Catholic abbé, wrote to a friend in England,

> Judge of my surprise in the midst of the wilderness, to find a botanic garden, not indeed like that at Paris, or yours at Kew; but a botanic garden, containing many exotic and medicinal plants, the professor, Mrs. Gambold, describing them by their Linnean names. Your missionaries have taught me more of the nature of the manner of promulgating civilization and religion in the early ages by the missionaries from Rome, than all the ponderous volumes which I have read on the subject. I there saw the sons of a Chero-

kee Regulus learning their lessons, and reading their New Testament in the morning, and drawing and painting in the afternoon, though to be sure, in a very Cherokee style; and assisting Mrs. Gambold in her household work or Mr. Gambold in planting corn. Precisely so in the forests of Germany or France, a Clovis or a Bertha laid aside their crowns, and studied in the hut of a St. Martin or another missionary.

The Gambolds often talked to Susanna and Ridge about salvation, but neither professed acceptance, though they were considerate listeners, and they did enjoy the Moravians' music. It was infinitely more varied than the drumbeat of the Indians. Cherokee music—whether for a celebration, a wedding, or a burial—was much the same, and it was monotonous. Chief Ridge, on an occasion when they told him the story of God's sacrifice of Jesus, replied that he knew of it already: Charles Hicks had told him. Chief Hicks had offered to convert, to instruct the Indians, he said, but often received only contempt in reply. He implied that any tendency toward Christianity on his part would interfere with his leadership as a chief, but he did want to know about good and evil. He had killed people and had come to regret it. He would kill again only if the council directed it.

He listened, profoundly moved, as the missionaries told him that God forgave all sins if one prayed to him from the heart. Mrs. Gambold later wrote, "He seemed to understand our meaning perfectly."

He did accept the existence of God, but it was his own, not the one revealed by Scripture. Once he said to them, "Anyone can see the stars did not create themselves."

No Cherokee had become a Christian, here or elsewhere, in this decade. Chief Hicks could read English fluently and was studying the Scriptures, but he was not actually converted. The other chiefs had been to Spring Place only to inquire about earthquakes. A tremor had alerted three chiefs, and they came to learn the truth about God's anger. Then, too, a fierce storm had arrived from the southeast, had felled trees and flooded the river. Several Cherokees were curious to know if the Germans' God had sent it to frighten them.

Vann's estate was entangled in dispute, and the Moravians accepted the request of the family that they recommend a settlement. His sisters claimed that he had wrongfully kept slaves who were theirs, and the ones who survived, and their issue, were requested. The Moravians found their claim just and turned eighteen slaves over to them, eighteen of the eighty.

Then there were disputes about Vann's tavern, his ferry, his debts, his methods of making loans. All was a jungle, which perhaps only Vann himself had ever understood. One wife had left him, and to her and her children he willed nothing. His other wife, Margaret, got the right to live in the house comfortably, and her son inherited everything, his half-brothers and half-sisters nothing. A will was a novelty to Cherokees, and the full inheritance by one son was a departure from Cherokee patterns of the past. Everybody was unhappy—except the son and his mother.

The Moravians were more democratic than Vann had been. They divided his fortune so that debtors were satisfied, loans were renegotiated with contracts, money was distributed to Vann's children and wives. The great farm and house and most of the slaves went to the sole son. Afterward the Moravians wrote in English a series of recommendations for Hicks and Ridge, concerning new Cherokee laws that might improve the channeling of inheritance.

Margaret Vann petitioned the Moravians to accept her as a convert, and her decision fired excitement in the Gambolds. It promised a God-sent change. After all these years, at last the Christian message had borne fruit. The Moravians examined her according to doctrine and found her acceptable for baptism. They were required to use the lot system to obtain God's approbation, which they did at once; but the slip was, to their shock, a rejection.

Margaret must pray about this, and study more, the Gambolds told her.

Months later, a second lot was taken, and it also proved negative.

The Moravians began to talk about leaving this particular people, this place of God-mandated disappointments. After further prayer and study, a third lot was taken. It was negative.

It was terribly distressing. The Gambolds' work was rejected by God, thwarted by God. This was not a Cherokee vote, it was God's. They had instructed the woman patiently in every aspect of the faith. Surely God realized Margaret's mother-in-law and sisters, along with most of her children, decried her decision and mocked her and had cursed the missionaries. Surely God realized Margaret was sole proof that the vineyard could bear. Admittedly she was not perfect. She had had a hard life. She had been married to a difficult husband. She had, however, suffered and studied, and she had a pleasant appearance and had influence.

O my God in Heaven, the Gambolds prayed, deliver us from this blight.

Again the lot was taken. And God said yes.

Joy. Joy, even though pious. Celebrations. The little brass ensemble played several of the more boisterous Protestant hymns, and the dear Margaret Vann, veteran of marriage to the devil himself, the mother of one brood of his children, was baptized into the Christian church, breaking asunder the walls of Cherokee times past.

Nevertheless, more work and blessing remained. Now baptized, Margaret longed for acceptance into church membership, and they wanted this for her. Preparations were made for her consecration.

Once more God was to be asked. There was no question about this matter, the Gambolds assured each other, because she had been accepted for baptism. She was pious, she had applied herself to mastering the doctrines and could even teach them to the Cherokee children. She was approaching sainthood.

The lot was taken, and God said no.

Lord in heaven, what message is this? Are we to despair? Are we to understand the lady is not even yet come of Christian age? Come, Margaret, sit with us. Here, take me by the hand. We must seek to understand. You know, God works in mysterious ways his marvels to proclaim, Margaret, his marvels to make known. They can be humiliating, God's ways. We must not blame God, however; we blame ourselves and pray together. You do understand the doctrine, now don't you, Margaret, that in olden days in Israel a lamb or bullock was slain as atonement for sin, and later

God sent his son to be sacrificed, he the perfect, unblemished lamb of God, and his sacrificial death was arranged to take away the sins of the world. His sacrifice serves all who accept him as their savior. Repeat all that, Margaret.

Yes, again.

She did so want to leave her house, where memories of James haunted corners, hallways, his raucous laugh filling the rooms, his smile dazzling her, his hand touching, caressing. James could be tender. He was as tender on occasions as ever he was vicious on others. Her life with him had been uproarious, disordered, emotionally draining, and now that he was gone she did so want the order and generosity of the Moravian community. She wanted the little room they had set aside for her use, and the bed for her nights of dreams and memories. She rather liked the Germans, and she loved the children.

God can be exasperating at times, she heard Brother Gambold admit to his wife.

The lot. Again. Once more. Humbly, reverently. Yes or no, God? Please be kind. Do pay attention. Even the Cherokees are watching. They have come to understand the lot; they understand what they want to. Draw out the answer from above.

Yes, it read, yes.

Thank you, Jesus.

Margaret, dear sister, you are ours, we are yours.

The brass instruments played on the grounds and the tables were loaded down with pork and bread. Margaret Vann, the storm-tossed woman, became the first Cherokee to make the complete passage. She was a Moravian at last. This Christian vineyard could bear, she the first fruit of it.

Meigs recorded three social movements taking place among the Cherokees just at this time. One was Christianity, still a small one. He had news that the Congregationalists might add impetus to the movement soon, sending their own and Presbyterian missionaries from New England.

Then there was the white culture every day challenging Cherokee ways—their medicine, their ways of weddings and child rearing and inheritance, their ways of warfare.

Third was the intense countervailing efforts of the Cherokee shamans, who were now calling for Indians to take off and burn their white man's clothing, abandon his ways, and go to water. One woman told Meigs: after dancing all night, some have thrown off their clothes into the fire and burned them up. He wrote, "Some of the females are mutilating fine muslin dresses and are told they must discontinue reels and country dances which have become very common amongst the young people. . . . A young Cherokee woman told me that she was told that the Cherokees ought to throw away the habits of the white people and return to the ancient manners, and that she told them that was nothing, that they ought to become good people and leave off stealing horses and drinking whiskey instead of destroying their clothes."

Meigs was having trouble in all aspects of his work, but most of all with the western movement. The government under Jefferson had favored fostering it, but once Madison became President the policy received less support. Fifteen hundred Cherokees had gone over the years, but these were fanatics, and their leaving left in charge the patriot party, Ridge and Hicks and their kind.

Madison was afraid that the Indians moving west would fall under British influence—or so Meigs decided—and would turn to fight the Americans. Meigs recognized that danger, himself. The men among the fifteen hundred who had gone west might well appear once more, with their war feathers on.

6

By 1811 rumors of an impending second war between the young United States and powerful old England were rife, and they stirred up fever among the Indian tribes. The war was shaping up in the Mississippi Valley, the belly of the continent, the lands between the Appalachians and the Rockies where a thousand streams flowed to the father of rivers.

The southern Indians who were faced with the need to choose sides were the Cherokees, the Creeks, the Choctaws, the Chickasaws, the Seminoles, and to the north the Sioux and the Shawnees. These last two had recently had shaman-led revivals, reasserting the traditional ways, accompanied by repudiation of the new United States. One of the warrior leaders of the North was Shawnee Chief Tecumseh, who had a cold heart for white settlers, considering them a race made of lake scum. He announced a southern tour in order to seek support for a confederation of all tribes living in the belly region of North America. Brother of the famous shaman Tenskwatawa, who claimed to be in constant contact with the spirit world, Tecumseh gave new hope to the shamans and young males. These young men were now limited even in horse stealing, and many of the old ones had come to watch in alarm as their people changed the long-established ways. The four annual ceremonial dances were shunted aside—only the green corn dance was likely to be held in some towns. And this was merely one example of the erosion of tradition. Tecumseh, storied chief of the Shawnee, was a traditionalist who feared no one, no ghost or spirit, no shaman, whether sorcerer or witch doctor or medicine man or priest, no warrior, no God, no other Indian, and certainly no white man.

He did favor the British over the Americans.

He was to meet first with the Chickasaws and Choctaws, then move on south to the Creeks, to attend their council meeting in October 1811. Ridge was appointed ambassador to represent the Cherokees at the Creek meeting.

As the announcement of Tecumseh's message flew from town to town, Cherokee elders reported mysterious happenings. Some saw ancestors long since dead who admonished them to erase among Cherokees all evidence of white culture. The people must return to ceremonies and reclaim their sacred towns. Three Cherokees, late in January 1811, reported a particularly elaborate vision. They had been on the crest of Rocky Mountain in northern Georgia. As reported to the Moravians and to the Cherokee council meeting at Oostanaula in February, the three of them, one man and two women, were on their way to visit friends when they came to a deserted house. Because the days in winter are short, nighttime falling early and suddenly, the three decided to remain there until morning. They entered the house and at once heard a violent noise in the air outside. They went out to see if a storm was brewing and saw a crowd of Indians descending from the sky, riding on black ponies, their leader beating a drum. The three Cherokees were frightened, but the ghost rider with the drum called to them:

> Don't be afraid; we are your brothers and have been sent by the Great Spirit to speak with you. God is dissatisfied that you are receiving the white people in your land without distinction. You yourselves see that your hunting is gone—you are planting the corn of the white people—go and sell that back to them and plant Indian corn and pound it in the manner of your forefathers; do away with mills. The Mother of the Nation has forsaken you because all her bones are being broken through the grinding.

A further pronouncement called on the Cherokees to admit only good whites to the nation, refusing places to the others. Some whites are corrupt, take Indian lands, obliterate established customs; some are criminals and drunkards, outcasts from the white world, and arrive to cheat and steal. Why would a skilled mechanic come to the Cherokee, leaving his own people who need his labor, except he be dishonest?

The drummer told the three listeners that the Mother of the Nation would "return to you, however, if you put the white people out of the land and return to your former manner of life."

The Cherokees were to return to harmony with nature. They were to move into towns and desert the plantations and farms. They need not, however, return to hunting as a way of life, or to outmoded weapons, or to warfare as an annual occupation, those being impossible now.

Another message had to do with moderation in their attitudes toward the whites. "You yourselves can see that the white people are entirely different beings from us; we are made from red clay; they out of white sand." The drummer said, "You may keep good neighborly relations with them, just see to it that you get back from them your Beloved Towns."

The drummer chastised them because of the light horse patrols, which for three years had been judge, jury, and punisher, all three, sometimes almost killing the accused by whipping. This, too, was excessive. "Your Mother is not pleased that you punish each other so hard; you even whip until blood."

He told the three scared visitors to tell what they had seen and heard to the Cherokees and the whites. They mentioned Meigs specifically as one to hear it. "If there is someone who does not believe it, then know that it will not be well with him." The drummer closed: "If you do not believe my words, then look up at the sky."

The three looked up: the heavens opened and a beautiful light appeared, and in the light were four white houses, and these, the drummer explained, were to be built for four white men who could be helpful to the nation with writing, who could teach Cherokees to read, write, and cipher.

Now, reports of this vision seemed to Ridge to come from Tecumseh and his brother, not from the heavens. Take one detail: the Cherokees had no sacred towns in the religious sense, as the Shawnees did. That was one detail only, but it might reveal the origin of the vision. In May 1811, the council met and once more this story was told, the instructions and warnings given to the chiefs and guests. The man among the three who had seen the vision closed by saying that if one would deny his message, the Mother of the Cherokees would strike him dead.

Ridge sat stone still as excited commentators roamed about the council house, most of them chiefs who were known opponents of acculturation with the whites; they were celebrating this revelation. Finally Ridge got to his feet and asked for audience, and when the noise subsided, he made his speech. "My friends, the talk you have heard is not good. It would lead us to war with the United States, and we should suffer. It is false; it is not a talk from the Great Spirit. I stand here and defy the threat that he who disbelieves shall die. Let the death come upon me. I offer to test this scheme of impostors."

Even as he finished speaking, angry delegates assaulted him. He struck back at them and several fell; like a great bear he batted off his assailants. Eventually they overcame him, toppled him, buried his big body under their own, pummeling him, trying to knife him. John Harris rushed to help and was stabbed. Jesse Vann joined in, as did others. Ridge, once on his feet again, continued to defy the nay-sayers and their shamans. Again furious chiefs assaulted him, but this time elder chiefs demanded order and enforced it.

Ridge, his clothing torn, bleeding from cuts, stood before them all. You see, he told them, I continue to live, so these prophets are deceivers.

Ridge was leader among the forty-six Cherokees commissioned to journey to the Creek council and hear Tecumseh. The meeting was to be at the Creek capital, Tuckabatchee, where the Tallapoosa River has its confluence with the Alabama. In all, five thousand Indians came to the council ground, representing Choctaws and Chickasaws as well as the Creek; also among them were white traders and land dealers, federal officials and state officers, and spies, many spies hired by England, the United States, Spain, by Tennessee, Georgia, Virginia, North Carolina, by many governments.

Now and again runners would arrive to announce Tecumseh's approach, just where he was, where he drank and ate, what he murmured. At last his company of men filed into the town square, riding beautiful horses. The entourage included six Shawnees, two Creeks who had lived with the Shawnees and knew both languages, six Kickapoos, and six from the Northwest, from the Sioux. These twenty were dressed in open buckskin hunting shirts, loincloths, leather leggings, and moccasins. Their clothes glittered with beads and beaded fringes, their hair was plaited in strands. Each wore a few feathers. Tecumseh wore two: one a white crane feather, the other a crane feather stained vermilion. He wore silver bands around his arms. A stripe of vermilion was painted under each eye. A single dot of red was on his shaved temple at the home of his soul, a circle of red was on his chest.

He dismounted, followed by his entourage. Young Creeks came forward to hold the mounts. He moved a few steps toward the welcoming chiefs and a gasp went up from the people, from those who had not known that the warrior was lame.

Even so, he danced that night, the Dance of the Lakes. He danced the part of the warrior, hurling himself about, a vigorous, distorted, terrifying, sometimes comical pantomime, his bowed leg striking its own beat. Naked, except for a breechclout and moccasins, he danced the night through.

Many present wished his brother had left his studies and come, too. Did Tecumseh believe the teachings of his brother; would a man of vengeance, a warrior, devote himself to the visions of a reclusive person, spirit-possessed? Of course, the Christian missionaries believed in similar revelations: they taught that God's spirit came to talk to Mary and Joseph, and to others, they believed in God appearing in a bush-fire on a mountain; and these Christian stories were no less extraordinary than the ones Tecumseh's brother was said to have told. Even dead people return to life in the Bible and bodily ascend into the sky; so they do for the Sioux and the Shawnee, and they apparently do so often since Tecumseh's brother began revealing his visions. The white man was created from the scum of the lakes, the Great Spirit hates the white man and longs for his death; those were his teachings.

Tecumseh would wait to speak until the spirit moved him, and the spirit did not move him the first and second days of the Creek council. Often the Creek chiefs would sit in silence, affording him the opportunity.

The third day he did not speak. Nor the fourth. Nor the fifth. A week passed and longer. On September 30 the Sioux chiefs accompanying Tecumseh rose to speak and told the Creeks they should fight the Americans. This seemed to be the heart of their proposal. A dozen Creek chiefs got to their feet, eager to comment, but Tecumseh stood. The council house became silent instantly.

Speaking in Shawnee, his words translated into many Indian languages, the warrior spoke to all. Aware of the white officials and spies attending, he must speak guardedly. He said his hatred of the Americans was as great as any Indian's, but his priestly brother had not as yet announced the time for war. Weapons were needed for a war, and those must be obtained. Also, there was need for unified action. The whites were powerful. They had taken most Indian land to the east and were hungry still. Once the entire country had belonged to the Indians, but the East was now white, and the number of Indians was small compared to the whites. He foresaw the extinction of the Indian in the East. What is needed is not a Creek war, or a Sioux war, or a Cherokee war, or a Chickasaw war, but for all tribes to form a confederation.

He spoke with power. His was the voice of a brilliant mind. His countenance lighted up, his erect body swelled with emotion, his personality dominated the multitude. I do not want to be at war with the Americans, he told them; be now in friendship, and prepare. Do not steal even a bell from Indian or white. For now let the white people alone to manage their own affairs.

He told them he was pro-British, if he must take the hand of any white man.

He told them of his own dealings with the Great Spirit and of his brother, Tenskwatawa, who was, he said, the great prophet. From the Great Spirit he had come to tell the Indians they must reaffirm their ancient ways, return to their own ceremonies, honor their shamans, cast out what was foreign. Only when the Indians were at one with the Great Spirit and each other, tribe by tribe; only when their lives were traditional; only when all tribes were as one in a confederation would he and his brother know the time had come for the Indians to go forth to meet the whites and to win success.

He fell silent. The council house was quiet. Big Warrior, a big man in body and the head chief of the Creek tribes, rose to his feet, assuming his right to speak first. Respectfully he asked Te-

cumseh questions. Did he mean war with whites was inevitable?
Did he mean to do away with schools, with cloth, with ploughs,
with agriculture as the Indians were now learning it? Would he
do away with cattle? Would he destroy all wheels?

Tecumseh's answers were indirect; the questions were obviously as annoying as beestings.

Big Warrior persisted in his questions a while longer, then
concluded by saying that Tecumseh's talk was meaningless, except that it had recommended peace. Tecumseh had said it was
not necessary for the Creeks to go to war. That was so, the Creek
chief said. That part was correct. Only that. As for the rest of it,
Creeks didn't need advice from Shawnees or Sioux.

Enraged, Tecumseh, looking directly into the eyes of Big
Warrior, told him his blood was white.

Big Warrior said that in his opinion the Great Spirit had not
sent Tecumseh to the Creeks.

Tecumseh said he would leave this place now, and on his
return home he would stamp his foot and the resulting tremor
would carry throughout the Mississippi Valley and affirm his
truth.

That evening the Cherokee leaders met with him. Ridge told
him he should not visit the Cherokees, for his message was not
welcome there, or needed. If you do visit the Cherokees, Ridge
told him, I will kill you.

Two more signs, ostensibly from the Great Spirit, did receive attention that year from Ridge and the other Cherokees. A
Cherokee named Charley forecast that big hailstones would fall
on a certain day, causing devastation to this errant people, but for
the top of a certain hill, which would be spared. Thousands left
their towns and stood all day on this hilltop, but no hail fell
anywhere.

The second sign was related to Tecumseh's prophecy. On
December 11, 1811, a month or so after he left the Creeks to
return home and stomp the ground, an earthquake struck the
Cherokee lands, a quake more powerful than any remembered by
the elders. Houses trembled, the earth groaned and shucked off
rocks, the rivers rolled and bolted as never before, and pits

opened, which quickly filled with greenish liquid. The Creeks living among the Cherokees claimed that it was proof of Tecumseh's power, of his and his brother's influence with the spirit world. That conviction flowed through the Cherokee nation and extended into the Creek nation and there young men came together to form revolutionary groups.

Perhaps influenced by his own power, Tecumseh's brother declared that the time had come for war. Indeed a war began in the North, but without sufficient arms or preparation, and without tribal unity.

Ridge was one of the Cherokee chiefs who visited the Moravians. In broken English they admitted their concern about the earthquakes. The earth was old, they realized, and they wondered if it was about to collapse. Some of the visiting chiefs felt that the tremors were warnings to the whites to leave the Indians alone. Was this likely to be so?

The Moravians told them earthquakes were sent by God and were forewarnings of the Day of Judgment, when God would judge all people and consume the Earth by fire.

Ridge wondered if God was so angry with the white man that he would punish everybody.

Some Cherokees, one chief reported, attributed the quakes to a big snake. Another asked the Moravians if the end of the world approached. Is God angry? How can we be better people and please him more? Ridge said he could not believe God would forgive people who spent most of their lives in evil, and he told them by way of example of an incident his light horse guard had encountered. A Cherokee had invited several friends to his house to drink and dance, and an old man got tired and lay down in one corner and slept; the host, for entertainment, beat the old man's head in, then killed a second man. All for sport, for a frolic. Would God forgive him?

One chief asked: Did the earthquake come from Tecumseh's brother?

The Moravians thought not.

Did it come as warning for sins of Indians or of whites?

Of Indians, the Moravians said, for their belief in shamans and false gods.

Ridge reminded them that the whites had often stolen land, had sold whiskey to his people, and induced families to go into debt and a type of bondage, had destroyed Cherokee customs. Even the ball games were no longer well attended.

The Moravians replied that those games and other forms of violence were sinful, and so was the players' nakedness.

More tremors came. One after another they shook hills and mountains and muddied waters; they confused the minds of friends and enemies. And in February 1812, yet another major quake shook all Cherokees, and Cherokee confidence.

Ridge attended another Creek council. It was at this meeting that he realized a Creek civil war was brewing, with upper and lower Creek towns aligning themselves against one another. The upper towns had a higher percentage of young militants, Red Sticks, so called because of their vermilion war clubs, and the red sticks, supposedly magic ones, used by their shamans. The council meeting Ridge attended issued a strong statement of support for the United States against her enemies, but this policy only further embittered the Red Sticks. In the middle of the hot summer of 1813, fighting broke out, not with the United States or the British or French: the young Creeks went to war with their own people. The Red Sticks conquered several lower Creek towns friendly to United States agents and burned them; the slaughtering was confined to hogs, sheep, cattle, such evidences of white agriculture, the burning of homespun cloth and clothes, and the destruction of the white man's pots and pans and dishes—of every white device except guns and knives. These skirmishes pitted brother against brother, young man against old, son against father, upper town against lower. The Red Sticks were Tecumseh-inspired, but did not coordinate their actions with him. As for Tecumseh, his Shawnees were still openly at war with the whites.

War with the whites touched the Red Sticks, too. A group of United States soldiers stopped a packtrain deep in Creek territory at Burnt Corn Creek, and found arms, powder, and bullets supplied by the Spanish at Pensacola, Florida. The whites became so frantic while looting what they found that the Creek Red Sticks, determined to save the munitions, were able to retaliate in a surprise attack. At that bloody spot the civil war became a war with the American whites.

On August 30, in the sweltering heat of Alabama, one thousand Red Stick warriors, accompanied by many shamans, their sticks red and waving, their faces painted black, their war bonnets flashing color, their throats hoarse from feverish cries, attacked U.S. Fort Mims, a day's hard ride north of Mobile. A white officer had left a gate open, and through it poured young Creeks seeking revenge for the indignity their people had suffered adjusting to the ways of the white intruders. Inside with the soldiers were white families and many mixed-blood Creeks who had fled from the Red Stick revolutionaries. The mixed-blood Creeks were the ones the Red Sticks came to get; but once blood was let, the Red Sticks' fever increased, man-to-man combat began, fires were set to the buildings, women cried out, children screamed, and in the sea of emotion both whites and mixed-bloods were killed, and more than five hundred people died. The corpses were scalped and in other ways mutilated, left for dogs and buzzards, exposed to rot in the Alabama sun.

Fort Mims. The news shot across the United States. Its ghastly spectacle was soon a household story, with dreadful meaning to the frontier white families and to the mixed-blood Cherokees.

The third Creek council meeting Ridge attended was held at Coweta. He found Big Warrior and his friendly chiefs in despair, their tribe's own body broken apart, their young men dancing to war drums. The elders had recently appealed to the United States government for help. Big Warrior also dictated a message for the Cherokee council asking for warriors to put down the Red Stick revolution, and gave it to Ridge to deliver. He sent a gift of tobacco to be smoked in the Cherokee council.

The message was delivered, and the Cherokee council solemnly smoked and contemplated, then voted to remain neutral, which did not set well with Ridge. Very well, then, he told them, the Tecumseh illness will spread and kill us, too. He would himself go help the Creeks fight the Red Sticks, and he called for volunteers.

Many council members volunteered at once, so many that the council meeting became bedlam, and out of it came renewed consideration of the Creeks' request. More tobacco was smoked. The second vote went in favor of sending an army of Cherokees to help the Creek leaders.

Meigs promised ammunition and suggested that the Cherokees join in with the Tennessee volunteers under a newly-appointed officer, Andrew Jackson.

At this time in the affairs of the young country, the "more perfect union" still retained features of the earlier confederation of colonies, and all of the states had volunteer armies that could be called upon by either their governors or the federal government. After Fort Mims, the Carolinas took up arms under Major General Thomas Pinckney, and the Georgian militia was organized under Brigadier General Floyd. Louisiana and Mississippi had a joint militia under Brigadier General Claiborne. The Tennessee militia, including the Cherokees and the friendly army of Creeks, was in three different contingents, one from the Nashville region under General Jackson and two from the east, each one having its own general. Of the three, Jackson had the highest rank.

Andrew Jackson had been born with gunpowder spicing his blood. He was one of the most quick-to-fight white men living on the Tennessee frontier. He was untutored, except for a brief apprenticeship at law in Salisbury, North Carolina, beginning at age seventeen, a period of study interspersed with gambling, horse racing, cockfighting, dueling, and fistfighting. He harbored an especially keen hatred of the English, who had imprisoned him during the Revolution.

He practiced law in Nashville, a town as tough and raw as fresh-cut hide. In the April term of 1790, out of 192 cases on the docket of the county court, Jackson was employed as counsel in 42 of them; in 1794, out of 397 cases, he was employed in 228. In addition, he was representing a number of Indians, some of whom had committed murders and thefts in the district. He served briefly in Congress. Appointed to the Senate, he resigned the next year to become a state Supreme Court judge; as a judge he was a failure, never wrote an opinion. He opened a store and went broke. He quarreled with almost everybody, and when a military man was needed by Tennessee, his name was mentioned because of his natural belligerence. He was elected major-general of the militia for the western district of Tennessee, even though he lacked any military experience or training; and in 1812, when war broke out between the United States and England, he organized a force of 2,500 Tennessee volunteers. To the north the Sioux and Shawnee were joining the English, fighting under Tecumseh, and in the south the Red Sticks were also falling in with the English; but he had somewhere a letter from three Cherokee chiefs offering to raise an army of Cherokees to fight for the United States.

He shared the white Tennessean's common opinion of Indians. As he saw it they were the festering sore that afflicted the settlers and limited the colonization of this great land, the progress of this newest and best nation on Earth, man's hope for freedom from kings and dukes and tyrants and priests, and also from the long-nosed, overeducated, weak-kneed sophisticates of New England who preferred an Atlantic Coast nation, and the northeastern states that had already slain their Indians and now pleaded every cause except that of the common white man, the average voting citizen, who was, thank God, patriotic and a fighter and a voter still.

He was convinced that Indians would not become civilized. He cherished all of his convictions, but most of all that one. The Cherokees were a roadblock in the way, isolating Tennessee. They made it blisteringly difficult for Tennessee to join the Union in any respect more than name. Cherokee: a blob of forests, burnt-off fields, and raging streams with savages robbing travelers and, often enough, torturing them to death. That was Cherokee to him.

Even so, he knew a few bits of history favorable to Indians in times of war. He recalled hearing that, when the pro-French Choctaws went on the warpath against the American whites in the 1750s, the Cherokee chief Oconostota with four hundred men had joined forces with the pro-British Chickasaws and had defeated them; he had heard that in the mid-1750s Chief Attaculla-

culla had led five hundred Cherokees against the Creeks to victory
at Taliwa, forcing the Creeks out of northern Georgia; he knew
that Virginia and other states had called on the Cherokees from
time to time to quell uprisings of even less dependable Indians
than Creeks. Also, he knew something of the reputation of the
three chiefs who had signed this new offer, especially the man
Ridge, a slave stealer turned patriot, the assassin of Doublehead.
He was reputed to be an honest Indian, whatever in hell that was
—which meant nobody had yet offered him enough of a bribe.
Jackson had purchased whites on occasion and Indians often.
There was no Indian above a bargain, not one he had known.

Let these three join in his army. He would commission them.
He would pay them what his Tennessee officers were paid. He
would feed them, give them guns, and expose them to the enemy
often. He would accept them, but he would not entirely trust
them. In fact, he would divide them among his three divisions.

So he reasoned. He called a clerk and dictated a reply accepting the Cherokees' offer. He claimed that he wished he had
time to write out the reply himself; it was embarrassing to him to
have such a young person wonder if esteemed General Jackson
could even write. One arm was nigh useless, that was true, it did
dangle at his side, the result of a wound received in a recent duel.
Now, this Ridge was a planter, Jackson understood, had flocks of
black slaves and even a few Creek slaves. How he persuaded Indians to work as slaves, Jackson didn't know. The blacks accepted it
more readily. He had heard that for generations in Africa blacks
had been taught to respect above all else those in authority, so
obedience seemed to be in their bones; they honored the chief
who sold them into slavery and wanted to do well by him, and
they respected the slave-ship crew, and they sought to help their
American purchaser. They wanted to succeed as a slave.

By contrast, an Indian would reject any and all authority,
had for generations been so taught. He made a damn poor slave.

Anyway, let the Cherokees come fight, Jackson agreed. He
ordered that there was to be no mutilation of the dead, by command, he claimed, of the War Department. Also, willing prisoners
were to be separated and protected. Whatever bounty a soldier
captured would be his property, including the Red Sticks' black

slaves. He had heard the Creeks had more and better black slaves than any other tribe. Also soldiers could capture the Red Sticks' women and children and sell them into bondage, if they wanted to go to the trouble. Jackson himself had dabbled in the slave trade and was willing to improve it. Cherokees were to be mounted and to wear white man's clothing, two white feathers, and a squirrel's tail, to distinguish them from the Creek enemy and his Tennesseans.

The autumn-colored leaves were still bright on the trees in northern Georgia when Ridge mounted the large horse he favored. Susanna had restitched his homespun breeches and shirt and had laced his buckskin leggings. He wore the two white feathers and a squirrel's tail, as ordered; he wore a knife and a sword. Behind his saddle was tied the army-issue blanket roll, that of a United States officer, and a government-issue rifle. He carried bearskin pouches for tobacco, powder, and bullets.

He stopped by Spring Place to show off his outfit and to say good-bye to John and Buck. He assured the boys that he had prayed last night with his favorite shaman and had been to the water; now he was here to accept the prayers of the Moravians, so that he would be doubly safe from all attacks. If not, he had lived a full life; better to be short-lived than a coward. Should he fall in the battles, let them all the more studiously apply themselves, grapple with every secret the white man knew, and learn to interpret them for the Cherokee people, who were brothers, sisters, our own. He believed he was looking at two great chiefs, destined to be greater than he, for even yet he carried heavy loads from the past. At the start he was a hunter, a warrior, a thief, and now he was a warrior for a while longer, to assure their right to learn.

After he left, Susanna came to the school and hugged her sons, both of them hers equally, she felt. They were both her husband's hopes, she knew. She had borne three sons; one had died and another, the most recent, was demented; therefore, the weight of her ambition and Ridge's fell on John and Buck, these children. Tears were in their eyes, as in hers as they thought of Ridge leaving for the war.

Ridge and the others, about two hundred full-blood and

mixed-blood Cherokees—most of them younger than he, some as young as sixteen—joined the thirteen hundred men under a General White. They camped side by side, these Tennessee volunteers from the Holston and other sections, every one of the whites suspicious of Cherokees, every Cherokee suspicious of these Holston people. More white men joined the army every day; their crops were in and they had time on their hands. The whites and Cherokees camped under the shoulders of the Great Smokey Mountains and learned the lesson soldiers need first to master: to wait. The food was good enough. The Cherokees ate only corn mush while at war, anyway, usually one meal a day; this army fare was more varied and plentiful. They made a camp. A drum—one drum was all General White could procure. Now and then the men moved their camp. That was the extent of the activity. In October they moved closer to the Coosa River in northern Georgia, into territory claimed by both Creeks and Cherokees. In November they reached the Coosa. Ridge and his men were always out front, but they were not going anywhere.

At camp dawn near Turkeytown, Alabama, the soldiers received word that Red Sticks were at Tallassiehatchee, twenty miles away, and Ridge was ordered to scout them out and, if he saw the chance, to take them. The date was November 4. A hard ride brought Ridge and his men to the village, but a company of white volunteers under another general had preceded them and had burned the place. The stench of the dead was sickening. The Cherokees rode near enough to view the charred wood and the scalped and hacked bodies. From horseback, his horse shying away from the smell of death, Ridge could see mounds made of mangled bodies; buzzards were feasting on the men, women, and children. His men raised a cry and flung themselves into the scene and began to scalp those corpses not already scalped by the whites. He watched this insane explosion of savage passions, vaguely hearing the reports of his own aides that they had counted more than 180 male corpses and would count the women and children later.

The Cherokees searched the woods all about and brought in nineteen Creek women and children, all terrified. Some of the Cherokee soldiers claimed the Creeks as slaves, but Ridge assured the Creeks of safety and took them to camp, where they were doctored and fed.

On November 9, the Cherokees met the Red Sticks at last, in a battle at Talladega. It was over like a stroke of lightning. After fifteen minutes of intense fighting, the Red Sticks fled. Their leaders were so totally demoralized that they sent an appeal to General Jackson for peace.

It was granted by General Jackson, but before the word was circulated other generals in the field attacked other villages. The Red Sticks, understanding that peace had been arranged, put up no resistance. At one town the Cherokees slaughtered 61 of them and took 250 prisoners, many of them women and children, without any losses of their own. Enraged, the Red Sticks furiously retaliated and the war continued.

Ridge and his men had taken so much booty that he ordered a detail of his men to take it to the soldiers' home towns. He sent a little Creek girl home to Susanna to help her at the house, along with several black slaves.

General Jackson called in an aide and told him to order Ridge to return those blacks to their owner. Surely he must realize that he took them from a Creek friendly to the Americans. Ridge had always been a slave thief, a horse thief, a Cherokee who would steal, Jackson told his aide. Admittedly he was a fighter; one had to admire a fighter.

His own white fighters were despondent. Most had seen less than enough action to justify their months of discomfort. The Creek war was winding down into a make-camp-here experience, with most men never having come upon the enemy. Men began to count the days till their enlistment was over. General Cocke, who had spent much of his time building a fort, realized that his men, once the fort was finished, planned to go home. He manned his fort with Cherokees and sent his whites on to Fort Strother.

Some of the white men were unruly and unkempt. Some were as mean as common sin and needed jailing. Gambling was rife, fighting was an everyday pastime, thefts were numerous. The three generals dreamed of fame, which each believed he deserved and would attain, if only he could find the enemy Indians.

Munitions were low. The generals vied for what was available. Food became scarce. Soap was gone. Whiskey was available for a price, and soldiers pooled resources for it. Tobacco was available and was the one remaining comfort in the wet and cold of the camps, relieving the forced marches, the searches of still more woods for yet another invisible Indian.

Jackson received reports of mutiny. He vowed to put it down ruthlessly wherever and whenever it appeared. He ordered the volunteers to patrol the militia. He set the militia to work policing the volunteers.

Georgia's militia under General Floyd marched into Creek country and was fortunate or unfortunate enough to find the enemy, who routed them. The Georgians fled, never to reassemble. Meanwhile, General Pinckney's forces were muddy and unmovable; he was able to issue orders and was good for nothing more, as Jackson judged him. Louisiana and Mississippi launched an expeditionary force, which found it could not ford the rivers.

The winter fell hard on the Tennesseans. They missed their families, too. In spite of threats and mandates, Jackson soon was down to fewer than two hundred whites. Of course, there were also his Cherokees, those busy looters, every man with three or four horses and his own herd of cattle. The Cherokees did not have a supply line feeding them in Creek territory; they had a supply line feeding everything to the Cherokee nation.

In January even the Cherokees went home, and General Jackson, the same one who had never fought a battle, who had dreamed of victories and glory, fell into depression. He aroused himself, called for fresh Tennessee troops, asked for more Cherokees. He promised to show his men honest combat.

Ridge from his home sent him a letter, penned for him by a child:

> This is a phew wordes from your friend the Rige. Sir when eye saw you last fall eye had taken up my gunn against the hostile Creekes but itt was because the[y] done bad and eye went against them and taken a good maney and have taken up my gunn to gow against them again and expect to have a lairg of my people with mee this time. Wee will gow with our oaldes brothers the whites like a band of brothers and Sir wee want to hear from you when Morgan our gide will bee ready to gow and when wee will see Ginneral Cock.

Jackson, still in the field so much longing to find an enemy, was down to 130 men when he received the letter. The governor of Tennessee had ordered him to retreat, to quit; Jackson had replied that he would die first. When the last of the Cherokee corn was gone—they had sent him most of what they had left—he ate acorns and recommended them to his men. His guts turned sour. He belched and farted and defied the enemy. Repeatedly he announced a need for soldiers and made promises of rank and wealth; he cajoled and pleaded. Men did respond, enough for two small regiments, and in addition there were two hundred white-feathered, squirrel-tailed mounted Cherokees and friendly Creeks. Disgraceful, he realized, that a general who deserved national fame and wanted it more than anything else on Earth, was reduced to penury.

7

Ridge had spent the winter at home with Susanna. When she became ill, he had brought the children home to be with her until the time of her recovery. Also, he brought her herbs recommended by Mrs. Gambold, and doctored her himself. She would not allow him to order a shaman: she trusted only to the Moravians' medicines, she told him.

Jackson had made him a major and asked him to raise a new troop of cavalry. Nobody rode better than the Cherokees, who were truly remarkable, Jackson admitted. Nobody fought more daringly. Major Ridge did seek to recruit men. He spent the winter traveling, convincing, and once his land was planted that spring, he led his recruits toward Jackson's headquarters, joining other groups. The total was two hundred Cherokees.

Jackson welcomed him in person and asked that the Cherokees make camp and wait. He was still trying to raise a larger white force, offering rank as an inducement. Ridge was one of the six or seven high-ranking officers, even though he spoke English only brokenly. Among the lesser officers was a scribe, whom Major Ridge needed, descended from both Scots and Indians: John Ross, one-eighth Cherokee—therefore, a Cherokee. He spoke Cherokee badly, but in English he was fluent, and of help to Ridge, who was, except for his language deficiency, favored by General Jackson.

Other Cherokees drifted in, along with the warmer temperatures. Five hundred finally came, almost all mounted. By March the men were ready to meet the enemy. Jackson drew them back the way a hunter draws a bow, told them to wait.

Cavalryman Charles Hicks had not seen a blinding light on the road or a messenger in radiant raiment; even so he was close to Christian conversion and was eager to discuss his soul's well-being with other soldiers. At camp his time was spent in reading the Bible and discussing Christianity with Major Ridge and his brother Watie, as well as other neighbors and friends. He was by nature a garrulous person, an acquirer and sharer of knowledge, inquisitive and talkative.

The Christian God had eyes, ears, a nose, a voice, a personality; man was made in his image. As Hicks explained to his friends, one can ask favors of the Christian God, but not of the impersonal Great Spirit. A man becomes part of the Great Spirit by living and can be what is natural for him to be; but to be one with the Christians' God, he must choose to be a Christian, must commit himself and change himself, become a new creature. Cherokees, and to a degree the Old Testament people, were by birth one with the Great Spirit, but Christians did not think of themselves as being wed simply by being born into a tribe or people. They were God's people by choice, their choice, and that choice must be made individually. A Christian chose to enter into a communion with God, and this conversion removed him from being a citizen of the present Earth: he was born again, became a new creature in Christ. All white men in these camps are not Christians, Hicks told his friends. Some are, most are not.

He told them that the Christian God was more of a comfort than was the Great Spirit. As he faced the Red Sticks, it was a source of confidence to believe God was watching over him and would take care of him. It was true that to remain a companion with God he must conform to a set of actions, and they were taxing. To the Christian believers sins were forgiven by God; nonetheless, the Christian must strive to improve, to grow toward being like Jesus, and that was difficult. The Old Testament had rules, and the New had goals, toward which men reached and grew, but which they could not attain.

It was all new to his listeners, and complex.

Hicks insisted that such basic truths must be accepted. I lie awake at night, he told them, thinking of all the mysteries.

He was repeatedly asked to reveal other secrets of the Bible, and he found himself repeating sermons he had heard at Spring Place, translating them into Cherokee; however, he was often at a loss to interpret New Testament thought into Cherokee. It was

easier to tell Old Testament stories, especially stories about battles and plagues and revenge. It was more complicated to convince Ridge, for one, that he must humble himself, deprive himself, and sacrifice.

Hicks found that the life story of Jesus did translate effectively: the baby born in a bed of hay, growing up in a carpenter's
family, questioning the priests, the shamans, in the temple, heal-
ing the sick and resurrecting dead people, sharing food with everybody—much of this was welcomed by the Cherokees. On the
cross Jesus had endured pain without protest or show of weakness. They liked that. He had risen from the dead victorious.
They marveled at that. Only the greatest shaman could do so,
Hicks told the soldiers.

On March 18, 19, and 20, 1814, every weary day and night the
army remained in camp. The Cherokee braves would go to the
water. The shaman chants came from every direction; some of the
men danced to the beat of the drum, and to such beat as could be
raised from hide stretched on kegs. The many sounds competed,
softened themselves against the mountains and came back, passed
on.

At long last General Jackson ordered the men to move out.
By now he had an army of five thousand in buckskin and homespun, with tobacco in their jaws and gunpowder in their pouches.
The Cherokees and the mounted whites rode as cavalry, the Cherokees out in front as scouts. Through forests and fields, crossing
rivers and marsh, the army moved, dyeing the trails with spit and
urine and horse manure.

They found no Red Sticks. They burned a few deserted
towns, but met no Red Sticks, nor any Creeks at all, and so they
moved farther.

Jackson divided his force, ordered out two thousand white
infantrymen to accompany four hundred whites and five hundred
Cherokee cavalry with about a hundred friendly Creeks. There
was a band of Cowetas to boot. Fifty miles they moved into Creek
country, and on March 26, late in the day, they camped near the
Tallapoosa River. The Cherokee scouts reported Red Sticks close
ahead at a bend in the river. They had breastworks in place, clos-

ing off the landward side of the bend. One thousand Red Stick warriors were there, well armed, and they had many women with them too.

Next morning the Americans took battle positions all along the river facing the breastworks. The army's two cannons were rolled forward and placed on a rise, commanding much of the enemy position. The cannons opened fire, poured grapeshot into the breastworks, while riflemen fired rifles and muskets at any Creek who showed himself.

For two hours the cannons fired; then they rested, and during the respite the Creeks came up from their hiding places, unaffected. Both white and Cherokee soldiers grew restless. Jackson appeared to have no plan beyond the volleys.

Major Ridge and his brother Watie, in position at the river, were considering the distant enemy; near them was Watie's brother-in-law, Charles Reese. All of them were impatient, and they began to speculate about how the river might be crossed. Reese said he would go get the Creek canoes, if anyone dared him to do so.

Directly he crept forward into the water and began wading and swimming toward the fleet of Creek canoes on the opposite shore. The Whale and another Cherokee followed. The Creeks began firing at the three of them, but they ducked under the river's surface and went on, as Ridge and Watie and others began firing at the Creeks.

Then the Whale was hit; he was near the canoes when he began to bleed in the water. Watie's brother-in-law freed a canoe and offered it to him, but by then the Whale was already dazed and weakened. He watched as the two others took two canoes to Ridge, and as these served to bring several more men to the fleet of canoes, and these men took many canoes to Ridge. They carried a number of Ridge's men onto the Red Stick side, bullets ricocheting off the river's surface all around. The Cherokees, with the Whale giving their battle cry, attacked. The Creeks were forced back toward the landward breastworks.

General Jackson ordered a major flank attack on the breastworks, and the Creeks were caught in the crossfire, the intensity from one side rising, then waning as the other side charged. For

five hours the battle was waged, the black-faced shamans of the
Red Sticks dancing wildly. Not one Creek surrendered, not one
shaman lowered his red baton. When half the Creeks lay dead,
when the breastwork was afire, many of the remaining Creeks
dashed for the river, and Ridge was the first man to leap into the
water in pursuit. With his sword he killed one Red Stick and left
the sword jutting up from another. He took the knife from a third
and butchered him with it. In all, in the bloodied water, he
slaughtered six Creeks before his passion ebbed and he was left
standing in the river among his men, satisfied.

Twilight. The small force of Red Sticks alive in the fort still
fired bullets at the Americans. Jackson sent messengers offering
peace. The Red Sticks shot them dead. Into the night the shooting
continued amid the howls of Cherokee warriors and the moaning
and screams of the wounded.

Hicks walked among the dead and dying, watching as if in a
trance as the whites and Indians robbed and mutilated the corpses
of Red Sticks. Don't smear the goddamned vermilion, a white
soldier cried out to another. They argued over retaining the patterns of color on the hide they cut. Colors won't stay on there
through tanning, one white was advised. If it's sun dried, it
might, another told him. Won't be soft, sun dried. Too prone to
stretch to make a belt. Now get on from me. Get your own to cut
on.

More vile even than usual, Hicks noticed. Less civil. Less
generous. They were in rapture wandering about gathering guns
and hatchets, powder and lead, the red batons of the shamans and
the red clubs of the Indians, collecting their knives, cutting with
those knives the straps and patches of Creek Indian skin, pausing
occasionally to survey the field of marauders: Indians and whites
taking scalps of Red Sticks, taking shirts, in the dawn light cutting bloodied shirts off the contorted, stiffening bodies, stealing
silver jewelry from dead ears, cutting through the neck to free a
necklace, the grinning-in-death head rolling away, stopping close
by an Indian working to free a moccasin from a cold foot. Men
quite busy, occupied, dedicated, concentrating, cursing, venting
rage and shame and multiplying excuses for their excesses.

Hicks took no scalps. He had, he believed, killed a man in the river. He didn't want the scalp. I baptized him with my own holy water, he thought. No way to find his body in this golden-lighted dawn, and what a sight I would be, floating him and pulling him out of the water for prayerful burial.

Major Ridge, a hulk of power, a moving blob in the dim light, stopped above him, then moved on, walking silently. He never stumbles, Hicks noticed. He makes not a sound as he moves.

A few men decided to sit near Hicks. One borrowed part of a fire and brought it on three sticks and set the fire near him, curious about him and his secrets, made more curious now that the exultation of battle had waned and the strangeness of this butchering took over, these feats of booty, robbery. Hicks began answering questions about the way "some white men" would act, meaning Christians, he supposed, a type not often encountered on the frontier or in battle. Do they fight? He addressed himself to that, saying they were under two dispositions. They had the Old Testament to authorize warfare as God's mission, and the New Testament, which said to forgive your enemies, do good to those who spitefully use you.

Nearby a wounded man, one not yet dead, cried out, a wavering howl; he had awakened to find he was being scalped. His cries ended in thuds of blows, then a few gurgles. No moans, either. Not like a Red Stick to cry out, a man said.

Drops of blood fell on Hicks's cheek, his hands. One of his listeners asked a passerby to be more careful.

Hicks left them, walked through the breastwork, stood near dead white men not yet robbed, heard himself talking to them: the meek shall inherit the Earth, he told them; and he spoke to them as brothers, felt warmed and rewarded by his speaking aloud the messages he had heard Brother Gambold preach.

An eerie confession: I think I killed a Red Stick in the river, he murmured. Ridge killed six, by Hicks's own count. The Red Sticks in the river were confused, with Ridge's men on both shores, other Cherokees coming into the river with them. No surrender; they would not offer it nor the Cherokees grant it. On to the Great Spirit's heaven and the celestial maidens. . . .

Hicks spoke to the dead in English. When he saw Cherokees listening, he spoke in Cherokee, translating as he recalled the English words, which he knew had once been Hebrew or Greek words, and which he supposed had been spoken on other nights, from the days of the disciples onward, after other battles. He told the black shadows the story of Jesus, which was of all Bible stories the one they most loved.

Jackson detailed men to count the dead. They decided in order to arrive accurately at the figure, to snip off the tip of each corpse's nose. By now the Cherokees were in the field also, calmly selecting what they wanted from the remaining stores of clothing, weapons, blankets, tobacco, food.

Several of the white soldiers continued to flay the Red Sticks' skins in order later to make belts or even reins for their horses. They made their initial incisions on the Creek's leg near the heel. They next made two parallel cuts, about three inches apart, all the way up the length of the leg and up the back to the shoulder blade, then across to the other shoulder, and from there down the other side of the back and down the other leg to the heel. The strip was then skinned out and would make about ten feet of belting.

How many noses? Jackson asked.

Five hundred fifty-seven here at the fort, and three hundred fifty in the water, but we can't find all that are in the water.

How many Red Sticks escaped?

Fewer than a hundred, and they were wounded.

There were dead squaws. Their corpses had been piled up but were not counted.

The white Americans had thirty-two dead and ninety-nine wounded. The Cherokees had eighteen dead and thirty-six wounded. The allied Creeks had five dead and eleven wounded.

Jackson asked that scribes be sent to him to take his report of the battle, which he called the Battle of Horseshoe Bend. One was Lieutenant John Ross, the white-looking Cherokee. For the press back home, Jackson dictated bare statements, the statistics, and a few observations. One of the great victories of the American frontier, he termed it, a major military success, with charge after charge against the breastworks defended by one thousand howling, painted savages. . . .

A chief of the Red Sticks, Menawa, had been wounded by the cannon fire. Unable to flee, he had stripped the clothing from a dead squaw, then had dressed himself in it and lain down among the dead squaws. Once the whites and Cherokees left, the breastworks deserted, he made his escape.

The principal chief of the Red Sticks, William Weatherford, appeared at headquarters at Fort Toulouse, which had been recently renamed Fort Jackson, and surrendered his forces.

The Cherokees returned home to find, to their dismay, that the eastern Tennesseans, preceding them, had stolen horses, torn down fences, taken corn and maple sugar, and terrified the old people and the children. Among the whites was a soldier by the name of Sam Houston. Another was Davy Crockett, who later wrote,

> The next day we marched on, and at night took up camp near a large cane brake. While here, I told my mess I would again try for some meat; so I took my rifle and cut out, but hadn't gone far, when I discovered a large gang of hogs. I shot one of them down in his tracks, and the rest broke directly towards the camp. In a few minutes the guns began to roar, as bad as if the whole army had been in an Indian battle, and the hogs to squeal as bad as the pigs did when the devil turned barber.

Meigs reported the losses to the Secretary of War in Washington, May 5, 1814.

> These depredations may at first sight seem incredible: but I have no doubt of the justice of the statements: they are well known to thousands. I received a letter from an officer of high rank in the army, in which he says, "The return of the Horse thro' their country has been marked by plunder & prodigal, unnecessary and wanton destruction of property: their stocks of cattle & hogs have been shot & suffered to rot untouched—their horses in some instances shared the same fate; their cloathing intended to defend them from the wet & cold in the present campaign has been stolen and in some instances where they remonstrated their lives have been threatened." . . . Some of the Cherokees have been deprived of all their cattle & hogs, others nearly all. The Cherokees cheerfully supported the army with Beef & Pork and nearly all the corn they had. General Jackson wrote me that on his route south . . . the Indians let him have all their corn.

General Jackson was enraged, not by the wanton destruction, which was contrary to his orders, but by the Cherokees having made the matter public. He denied it, all of it; not a cow had died in all Cherokee territory, the claims were lies, and what were not lies were exaggerated.

Meigs wrote him, giving details and listing witnesses, among them soldiers known personally to Jackson, Major Ridge among them. Jackson resisted admitting any error on his part, or on the white Tennesseans'.

The dramatic accounts of General Jackson's victory were excitedly discussed all across the country. He was made famous by the battle. Not long thereafter, in 1815, he became a second-time hero when he commanded the American army that defeated the British at the Battle of New Orleans.

This victory came about in spite of a magnificent British army, the men who had defeated Napoleon's. Their prideful British officers lined them up in columns and had them advance against bulwarks manned by Jackson's men, who were frontier riflemen, French pirates, dandies from Louisiana high society as well as soldiers. The British officers had no respect for unprofessional, civilian soldiers, so they picked that portion of Jackson's line manned by what appeared to be civilian rabble: they sent their soldiers toward the Tennessee volunteers, who shot the men dead. There were many ways to approach and occupy New Orleans without confronting Jackson's prepared fortification. It was a matter of honor for the British officers to prove the courage of their men.

This providential victory changed governmental control of the Mississippi Valley, ending British claims and securing those of the United States. Also, it enhanced the opinion of Europeans toward this rowdy, new, roughhewn country, this American republic. The victory set the tide of opinion against the view of many American citizens, who contended that the new country should be satisfied with its present territory and not spread thin its population and limited power. It strengthened the arguments of those who saw America as a larger territory, who believed the destiny of the new country did not lie only along the Atlantic

seaboard—a popular view in the Northeast and New England—
their new hero was the general from Tennessee, Andrew Jackson.

He basked in the glory. He needed it for his soul's sake. He
loved it. He could see great rewards ahead.

In the North Tecumseh had died in battle, his army defeated.
In the South the Creek Red Sticks were defeated and the Americans had conquered the British. Left living along the tributaries
of the greatest river in the world were eighty-five Indian tribes,
none, as Jackson saw, competently led, none with a constituted
government. Each had treaties with the various governments, including that of the United States, guaranteeing their rights to
portions of this valuable land; but Indians could be manipulated
and bought. He had bribed Indians all his life. Certainly, there
was no reason to allow them to handicap the new empire, to stand
in the way of his national goals, his dreams for the United States.
Involved were only 125,000 Indians in all, and most of them were
Cherokees, Creeks, Chickasaws, and Choctaws, the four tribes
close to Tennessee. Of the others, the Shawnee and Sioux were
defeated, and the Seminoles were under weak Spanish protection
in Florida. The Spanish in Europe were faltering and would fall
easily in America, if pushed. Any realist could see that the continent could be won.

General Jackson negotiated the peace settlement with the
Creeks. He stated his terms, thirty-six thousand square miles of
land, some 23 million acres. The Creek chiefs replied that they
had been fighting the Red Sticks, too, that it had been a revolution
within their tribe and should not cost the tribe anything. Jackson
said the war had been expensive for everybody.

The Creek chiefs left the conference, claiming they did not
feel well.

Part of the territory Jackson forced the Creeks to cede, some
1.9 million acres, was claimed by Cherokees as well as Creeks; it
had been used by both for many years, serving as a buffer zone
between them. There was no exact boundary. Jackson knew full
well that the Cherokees had equal claim to this area of three thousand square miles, but he wanted the land. The Cherokees had
done well in the war, he admitted. Now let them be helpful in
times of peace.

8

Mr. Gambold was opposed to the enslavement of other Indians or of blacks, and he dared to say so to the children. "Love all people, no matter what their color," he taught. He said God was the Creator and Father of all men. This was a remarkable, mind-awakening statement to John, Buck, and Nancy.

Another effective teacher was Sister Anna, wife of John Gambold, who taught the girls cooking, weaving, sewing, and instructed all the children, boys and girls, in English. Also, she taught music and found time for painting pictures and drawing with chalk. She was busy every waking moment but was the children's friend in work, encouraging their efforts. Her garden was a place of many marvels, with more plants discovered and transplanted every season, until twelve hundred varieties were flourishing there. A Portuguese abbé, Correa da Serra, on hearing about her garden came more than a hundred miles to see it and stayed a long while to marvel at it, to the immense pride of the children. They helped her collect seed for him—more than a hundred packets—and Sister Anna gave him specimens of dried plants, more than a thousand, and in addition many rocks containing the minerals of the region.

John Ridge would not admit to worshiping Anna, or to having any idols—which was forbidden—but he loved her.

Recently the Congregationalists, descendants of the Puritans, had founded in Massachusetts an interdenominational missionary organization named the American Board of Commissioners for Foreign Missions, and this organization was now ready to send teachers to the Cherokees. The board favored Indian rights and opposed slavery, and it had developed wide political influence. On the board sat business and political leaders, including Congressmen, and the financing of its missions all over the world came from wealthy merchants and industrialists, church members and pastors, most of them Congregationalists and Presbyterians. They saw the board as a chance to mold the evolving new United States, to influence it along New England lines, and to help slow down its growth and make government action more humane. Believing God had ordained them, as well as America, for great achievement, the board set out to educate and politically to influence the Indians of the South, and they saw at once that the tribe best able to advance was the Cherokee.

Only a few Cherokee leaders subscribed to church and national newspapers; among them were the young John Ross and Chief Hicks. Also, there was Meigs, for whom Ross now worked. Meigs knew of the new development through orders from Washington, instructing him to help their effort. Major Ridge heard it from his neighbor Hicks, and both came to welcome it.

Countering this new hope were increasing demands for President Madison and Congress to solve the "Indian problem" once and for all, forceably to move all Indians westward. These demands came from southern voices in the main, from land speculators such as Andrew Jackson and his friends, and from land-hungry farmers, southern planters seeking plantations for their sons and an oversupply of slaves, from governors and state assemblymen seeking votes, from congressmen and senators in the proslavery states, insistent that new slave states be formed. Most of them denigrated the notion that the Indians could be "civilized." They were not willing to wait to find out.

All the more urgent was the need for the powerful American Board to move quickly. In 1816 they obtained pledges of support from President Madison—a southerner who believed Indians would be well advised to move westward but should not be forced to do so—and his Secretary of War, William H. Crawford, who moved at once, without waiting for Congress, and set aside from his budget the necessary funds. Within weeks the American Board dispatched trained missionaries to the Cherokees.

The American Board's mission houses were paid for by the federal government, were equipped by the government, and a federal subsidy was provided for their first school, which was Brainerd Mission in eastern Tennessee, two miles north of the Georgia border, at Ross's Landing. No sooner had their doors opened than Major Ridge drove up in a white carriage, bringing his daughter Nancy and son John. A year earlier he had taken them out of Spring Place at Susanna's insistence and had hired a tutor, but the tutor had turned out to prefer whiskey to teaching. Consequently the major had his excuse to send his children to a better school away from home.

This was in May 1817.

Some of the board's students were from the families of white people. Meigs, for instance, entered two of his children. Most of the students were mixed-blood Indians. A few were full-bloods. In Cherokee territories at this time there lived between two hundred and three hundred children who spoke some English, most of them having learned it at home from white kin. The best of these young English scholars attended this new school, and among them John Ridge was soon the leader.

The new school had several buildings, including stables and storage rooms, and a log schoolhouse large enough to serve up to one hundred children taught on the Lancastrian plan: that is, the better students instructed the less advanced, and so on down the line. There were separate dormitories for boys and girls, a dining room, weaving and sewing rooms. There were forty-five acres of fields waiting to be used for crops or pasturage.

The new school proposed to teach "the rudiments of the English language, the principles of the Christian religion, and the industry and arts of civilized life." At once, as John observed, the missionaries got into trouble with parents who objected to the discipline being imposed on their children, especially whipping. The missionaries, therefore, devised a new form of punishment. Whenever a child revealed anger or told lies or in other ways sinned, he or she was required to stand in the middle of the floor and recite Bible verses selected by the teacher, most of them verses from Proverbs, chapters 12 and 14. One little girl told her parents that, whenever they brought her sweet potatoes and bean bread, if another child stole some, the young thief must repeat Bible verses for a long while, whether he understood them or not.

The children were put under threat of final judgment, too, just in case they persisted in sin. Parents complained that their children were being scared half to death with threats of eternal burning. Such a fire did not exist in their opinion, and they wanted no more reports about it. A knowledge of English and of numbers was what they wanted, not religion. "If they don't stop scaring people, I'm going to scare them," one elder Cherokee promised, who spoke for many. Of course, the shamans were set against the school in all its aspects, even its arithmetic.

The young Chief John Ross was particularly helpful to the new missionaries. He spoke and read English fluently, having been brought up by his Scots kin, and he understood Cherokee. He could translate and interpret for the missionaries and often did, serving them in much the same way he served the Cherokee council and Mr. Meigs. As a Meigs assistant and business associate—they owned a store together—he had influence, and he used it to obtain more help for the new missionaries. He even proposed selling some of the Cherokee land in order to endow this school and others, a proposition so intriguing and radical that the chiefs and Meigs were considering it only in whispers. He was personable, friendly, diplomatic, and well-to-do, with inherited wealth, a rich farm, excellent stock, and a complement of slaves.

Short of stature, his nickname was Little John.

Other supporters of the school included Major Ridge, his brother Watie, and Chief Hicks. Hicks was particularly important. Not only was he a Christian and leader of the most progressive Indian political party, but he was this year elected assistant principal chief, polite acknowledgment that the principal chief was too old and feeble to function dependably.

In this year, 1817, a sizable group of Cherokees migrated to the West, settling in northwestern Arkansas—the largest group in years.

Major Ridge talked often about Baltimore, the largest city he had seen. He claimed that its order was the result not of any one man's design, but of growth from human needs and wants too numerous to record. Baltimore was a success.

Washington City, designed by one man, was now a mud puddle ten miles square. When recently he had visited it, the capitol

building had been defaced, its marble walls having been fired
upon by the British, and the executive mansion had been left by
the British in ruins; however, the problem was that Washington
as a city was not yet working well. Its streets were too wide, the
distances from one place to another were too great. Washington
was a man's dream, while Baltimore was many people's home,
and at the time of his visit it was wonderful.

He did like the social life in Washington. His clothes, always
of the latest cut, marked him as a gentleman, and his knowledge
of English was growing apace. He was not inhibited. Even at
large parties he was confident of himself and was admired by both
the ladies and gentlemen. At one party, when asked to give an
idea of Indian music, he sang a song racy enough to cause the
interpreter to blush and hesitate. The ladies caught the drift and
wanted to have its meaning. "Oh, you don't want to know," he
told them. "It's just like a white man's song—all about love and
whiskey."

Often he talked to Susanna about President Madison, a short
man who had been dwarfed by Chief John Lowrey on the occasion of their meeting on February 22, 1816, seven years after the
visit by Cherokee chiefs to President Jefferson. Madison was fair-
minded, Ridge told her. He had granted every one of three re-
quests: to return the joint Creek–Cherokee land to the Cherokees,
regardless of General Jackson's effort to usurp it; to pay for the
losses caused by white soldiers to Cherokee livestock and possessions, in spite of General Jackson's contention that the losses were
fabrications; and to provide the same care for Cherokee wounded
as for white soldiers. The President did not wince at the most
critical remark in the paper the delegation had prepared, which
Lowrey read forthrightly: "Father, you have with you, as with us
red children, those who make crooked talks; they, like the serpent,
speak with a split tongue. Believe not their talks, for they are
false; nor their actions, for they are deceitful."

Ridge would reminisce about his trips, tell Susanna and the
children what the President looked like, what he wore: a brown
coat and knee breeches. Ridge could recite the opening remarks of
Chief Lowrey: "Father: I now have the pleasure to be in your
presence. I am directed by my national council to take you, Our

Father, by the hand. This day was appointed by the Great Spirit for us to see one another. It makes my heart as glad to enter your house as it does when I enter my own house."

The President had replied, "I was apprised of your coming before you arrived. It always gives me pleasure to receive my friends in my house, especially my red Brethren the Cherokees, who have fought by the side of their white Brethren & spilt their blood together."

The room in which they stood was inside an eight-sided house Madison was borrowing—the children laughed whenever Ridge got to this part of his story—which was angular and circular at the same time, a house little people might enjoy living in, and the doors were curved, the glass windows were curved, very like a doll house Ridge might have bought in Baltimore.

Visits of Indians to see the President were a tradition as old as the country. President Washington, when he was housed in Philadelphia, invited to visit him the chiefs of the Iroquois confederation. Fifty-one accepted the invitations. They were from the Iroquois, Mohawk, Seneca, Oneida, and other tribes. Each chief was issued on arrival a military uniform and a cocked hat, and all were entertained for two months, indeed so fulsomely that two died from overindulgence. One of them was Peter Jaquette, an Oneida chief who had been child protégé of Lafayette and was a graduate of excellent French schools. This batch of chiefs finally agreed to call a peace conference, including in the catch the Shawnee and Miami tribes, and went off well pleased with their gifts, leaving their hotel and bar bills. This had been the start, as Major Ridge understood it, of federal efforts to influence the Indians by means of entertainment.

President Jefferson had done as much, as well, with the Osage and other Plains Indians, the Cherokee and other southern Indians. At one time, in the autumn of 1805, twenty-seven chiefs from twelve tribes were visiting Washington, D.C. Chief Big White of the Mandan tribe, among other chiefs, attended the festive dinner Jefferson gave for explorers Lewis and Clark in the new White House early in 1807. After that banquet Chief Big White, when asked when he was going home, avoided commit-

ment. He stayed for three years. Stories of his delays made Major
Ridge roar with laughter. He gloried in all of this rich tradition
and told these stories, which the new federal Indian supervisor,
Thomas Loraine McKenney, had told him. McKenney had, he
said, pride in his assigned work and insisted on treating the Indians as ambassadors, which they were, Major Ridge among them.
There was only respect in McKenney's manner, and he insisted
on respect from the hotel keepers, too. No separate tables for
Indians because they were Indians, no discrimination of any sort.
If one became ill, the government at once sent a doctor. If one got
drunk, the government put him to bed as soon as was practicable.
When a group of Winnebagos sought to hug and kiss female
strollers on Connecticut Avenue, causing a certain amount of
fainting, the government apologized to the ladies as graciously as
the government could. That was all. If the press criticized Mc-
Kenney for excesses and excuses, he took the criticism manfully
and went ahead with his work. Of course, there had been, in
times past, fear of the Indians; both Washington and Jefferson
were aware that the Indians were one of two dangerous, explosive
problems, European empire-building being the other. Now that
the Indian was disarmed, perhaps Washington's lavish hospitality
would diminish, but it had not as yet. Going to Washington was
still a pleasure.

   Major Ridge was appointed to meet the three-man delegation
President Madison commissioned to discuss the disposition of 1.3
million acres south of the Tennessee River, claimed by both Cherokees and Creeks, the land Jackson still claimed as war reparations. One of the commissioners was General Jackson himself,
and Major Ridge, having already been asked by Jackson personally to intercede on his behalf, would not, could not bring himself
to enter the controversy. The other Cherokee delegates met with
the commission, their assignment being flatly to sell no land.
   Jackson presented evidence that the Chickasaws had once
claimed the land, and now they were willing to sell their rights.
He then presented affidavits saying that it belonged to the Creeks,
and they would have to give it up as part of the peace treaty. That
the land had been accepted as Cherokee in at least one past treaty

ratified by the United States was a fact he did not consider persuasive enough to delay his plans.

He offered bribes, saying it was polite to do so, and in effect he bought the Cherokees, body and soul, as Major Ridge told his children, his friends Hicks and Ross, and other chiefs. He bought them with new rifles and trinkets. Twelve of the fifteen signed to sell the land for five thousand dollars, plus six thousand annually for ten years.

Again, Ridge and Hicks boycotted the conference called to exchange eastern Cherokee land for western land occupied by those Cherokees who had migrated over the years. Jackson, appointed federal commissioner, sent his agents from town to town, arguing his points in 1817. Wholesale bribery was their method of choice. On June 20, in Calhoun, Tennessee, fifteen Cherokee chiefs from the West met with Jackson and his cohorts, and not one chief from the East attended until Jackson sent promises of further booty. One by one eastern chiefs came in to hear his arguments, until Jackson had enough to transact business. He proposed that the eastern land to be traded be equal in size to western land now occupied on the White River in Arkansas, and further—to the astonishment of his listeners—that the remainder of Cherokee territory in the East, all of it, be exchanged for equal lands west of the Mississippi. He promised that all who migrated would receive "a rifle gun, ammunition, a blanket, and a brass kettle or in lieu of the latter a Beaver trap." Should a Cherokee choose to remain in the East, he would receive a farm of his own and citizenship in his state of residence.

Jackson bought chiefs enough for his proposal to pass. As for the first part, two cessions of land were tentatively agreed to: one in Georgia, the other in Tennessee. No money was to be paid to the Cherokees. For this action the bribes were in the amount of $4,225. The second part, the inducements to encourage other Indians to go west, was entered into the treaty, along with the provision that the government would pay the travel costs for the people and their goods, including slaves; but there was no agreement that such removal must take place.

Ridge and Hicks were enraged. Under their leadership, on September 3 the council voted "to make a boy" of the leader of this Cherokee committee. They broke Chief Toochalar accordingly, and voted "forever [to] do away [with] all authority or commission with which he [had] been invested." A treaty negotiated by open bribes was fraudulent, but Jackson's widespread influence in Washington led to its ratification by the United States Senate, overcoming arguments against the policy of exchanging lands with Indians and the fact that only a few chiefs had signed it.

Jackson, however, was far from satisfied. He had got one million rather than two million acres, only half of the area he had wanted for development by land agents, who were friends and associates of his. He had doused the Indians in firewater and had won half a cake. He had not won the major prize: the mass movement of all of the Indians.

Jackson amused himself by thinking of Major Ridge dressed in a new suit, his face peeking out over his white collar like a red bull looking over a picket fence; and that little Scottish bastard, Lieutenant Ross, had been at Ridge's elbow as the two went about lobbying Washington. During their leisure they visited the best restaurants, ate like white men, went to receptions and danced with the wives of ambassadors. Major Ridge was a social triumph. They met with senators, with President Madison and his cabinet officers, insisting that this treaty be rescinded. Never in history, as Jackson recalled, had a United States treaty, once ratified, been rescinded. Damn fools, waste of time.

So Jackson had mused, and he had been ill prepared for the news soon received. The impossible had been done. The red bull and the little Scot had gotten the treaty rescinded. The two had traded away the Cherokees' South Carolina hill country, all right, but the northern Alabama land had been returned to the Cherokees; land designed by God for the use of southern planters was returned. There were bound to be disappointments in life, Jackson concluded, he had waded about in them for years.

Now that he was a national hero and the spokesman for frontier America, criticism of him was vehement, an uproar coming from the entrenched, safe, rich, fat citizens of New England and the Northeast who wouldn't know an Indian if one scalped them. They were safe in their beds. They needed no land to farm, only lots for their shops. They had never traded with Indians—not since they had cheated them and driven them away. Who in hell was the government of the Cherokees? Where is such a government located? Where are its courts? Its judges are still on horseback, they hold sessions under trees. There is no Congress; there are no standing committees. The laws are those of the witch doctors. Any treaty must be made with those chiefs who want to negotiate. One uses the chiefs who are at hand, who come when called. You can't negotiate a treaty with the chiefs who want no treaty, for God's sake.

To Major Ridge's surprise, agents and land experts began to move through the territory, offering wealth and safety and security out West for Cherokee immigrants who accepted Jackson's offer. These agents left a world of anxiety in their wake. Chief Hicks opposed accepting any such offer from the government. He pointed out that the federal government, starting about 1807 and for two or three years, had made a similar offer, and many people —perhaps as many as fifteen hundred Cherokees—moved to the West. But no land had been provided, and the western resident Indians did not welcome them, indeed went to war to protect their own homeland. Chief Pathkiller was also opposed to leaving the present country. Major Ridge, John Ross, all the chiefs who supported the education of the people, the work of the Moravians and of the American Board, were openly opposed to Jackson's new maneuver. The man seemed always to be at war, even with his allies, whether there was an enemy or not, and he never accepted defeat.

Jackson's main agent to encourage removal was Governor Joseph McMinn of Tennessee, and one of his tactics was to charge that the Cherokee leaders had made threats on his life. No efforts had been made to deprive him of his life, but he asked the Secretary of War to send troops to protect him anyway. He claimed that every white settler was afraid of an uprising led by the three half-breed chiefs, Hicks, Ridge, and that Little John Scot, and that the settlers also disliked missionaries stirring up trouble, teaching the savages what they had no need to know.

The government did send troops. They were present at the

next council meeting. The soldiers courted the Indian women and smoked tobacco and watched for dangers, and they found none.

The Tennesseans, though eager to have Cherokee land and needing road access to the rest of the Union, did not despise the Cherokees; many of them rather fancied themselves to be kinsmen in spirit. They admired their pride and confidence. By contrast, the Georgians did not know the Indians, had never even fought them successfully. Their few invasions had led to Georgian embarrassment. They despised the Cherokees, who occupied a large portion of their state, the northwestern corner above Atlanta.

The states had formed the Union, not the other way around, and had retained their sovereignty, Georgians contended: certainly enough of it to govern their own lands. The Cherokees were on Georgian land, as well as Tennessean, Alabaman, and North Carolinian lands. In Georgia, let them be subject to Georgian law, and let the law be written to the end that they cannot hire a white man, cannot testify in court against a white man, cannot enter into business or own property. Make the laws tough enough to drive them out of the state.

The only obstacle seemed to be the United States government, but even that could be managed, the Georgians reasoned, once Andrew Jackson agreed to stand for President.

The Tennessee school of the American Board was expected to be the first of several in the Cherokee territory. Others were planned for other southern tribes. However, the work was proving difficult at Brainerd. The half-breed children arrived knowing some English, so they held an advantage over the full-bloods. Not only were the full-bloods untutored in English, but they obstinately held to their own language and outmoded ways. Spite often erupted between the two groups. This school was not merely a place for English and cipher instruction; it was a place for building a new form of life, with some of the old customs, others new.

Mixed-blood children wrote papers about the burdens they felt:

As we often write to our teachers friends she has requested me to write a few lines to you. She wishes me to give you an idea of the customs of the Cherokees, as she has not time. I am willing to do it because I think when christians know how much we need the means of knowledge, they will feel the importance of sending missionaries. The unenlightened parts of this nation assemble for dances around a fire. The one that goes before sings; a woman follows after having herself adorned with shells which make a rattling noise when she dances. The others follow after, dancing around a fire in a ring, and keep up their amusements all night. In like manner the men dance the night before their ball plays. The next day when the two parties are collected at the ball ground, the side that excels receives horses, kegs, guns, clothing &c. from the other party. When they wish it to rain, they will send for a conjurer who will throw a black cat into the water, hang up a serpent &c.

Likewise when they are sick, they get one to blow and throw cold water on them and mutter over talk that cannot be understood. . . . Every year when the green corn, beans, &c are large enough to eat, they dance one night and torture themselves by scratching their bodies with snakes teeth before they will eat any.

When they go to each others houses, they will stand and peep through the fence, till some one goes out and inquires what they wish. Their living consist chiefly of pounded corn, sweet potatoes, and some meat. Their dishes are made by themselves of clay, first hardened by burning, then glazed by the smoke of meal bran; eight or ten will often get around one of these on the ground, with one wooden spoon, one will take a mouthful and pass it on to the other.

Many about this station are more civilized. Some come to meeting and appear as well as white people. Others dress in the Indian manner with maucassins for shoes, and handkerchiefs round their heads for turbans.

But I have learned that the white people were once as degraded as this people; and that encourages me to think that this nation will soon become enlightened.

I will tell you how the Cherokee live. They generally live in log houses and cabbins, though some have framed ones. Some of our neighbors go to the seat of government and to the neighboring states and see how civilized people build houses and they begin to live a little as they do. They have gardens and cultivated fields. Some of them have oxen, sheep, horses, and a great many swine. They have all kinds of fruits such as peaches, apples, pears, and the veggatables are sweet potatoes, beans, peas, corn, groundnuts, and turnips &c., which they raise for their family to live on. But a great many of the Cherokees are poor and ignorant and live so poorly that they have scarcely any houses or clothes. Then they often go to those families that can take care of themselves and if such families do not maintain them they think they are stingy.

Our cabins as I told you are built of logs and the open places are filled up
with mud. When they prepare the mud they pull up the turfs of the ground
then they hoe up the gravel and put water among it and put their children
in to mix it with their feet. Some have framed houses; some, but very few,
have brick. I suppose you heard of conjurers. They still have them but not
so many as they used to have.

I am now under the care of Mr and Mrs Fernal. They live down to the creek
where Mr Dean used to live. Catharine my sister stays there too. My parents come here to meeting on Sabbaths. My Father thinks is a great
privelege to learn to read. He can read but Mother cannot. I should like to
tell you how my Father's house is situated. It is surrounded with hills.
There are trees in the door yard. I take pleasure in sitting under them to
attend to my work. And an orchard back of the house. A road between the
house and field where the travellers pass. They very often call to stay all
night. I help Mother to take care of my Brothers and sisters. My Father
works in the field. Mother spins and weaves.

The missionaries gloried in the brighter young people who
were willing to accept the new culture, and they were dismayed
by those children who were unable or unwilling to budge. They
began to make code letters on student applications: Md, Fb,
mixed-blood, full-blood.

Most of the Fb children simply did not learn, did not seem to
realize that their people were in a new type of war, not one with
lead balls but with words and plows and thread and worship.
Dear children, we do desperately pray for you.

The full-blooded children were unable to wed the words, the
numbers, all the new concepts, and at the same time to abandon,
even repudiate all they had learned in life thus far. They sang
hymns but secretly decried what they knew of Christianity and
white people, and they were irritated by those mixed-bloods who
catered to whites and teachers.

Several girl students, Mbs, went so far as to raise money to
send to the American Board, to help pay for missionaries to go
save other peoples. They formed a society:

Our Society continues yet. We have not forwarded any money to Boston.
The regulations have lately been altered. When the Society was first estab-
lished we used to work in the hours that were given us to play on Saturdays.
Not long since when we met, Miss Ames asked some questions like these,

who are you sewing and knitting for? We answered for ourselves, then she asked who pays you? We answered the Board. Then she said do you think that you are doing the Board a great service to work for your selves and they pay you for it. She told us how they managed in charitable societies in civilized countries. I felt little mortified but I did not say any thing for several days and then I asked her if I could not do something to get some money for the Society myself. As the Cherokee women sometime wish her to do a little work for them such as making and fixing their bonnets and such things, she told us that she would learn us to do them and would set a price and we might have the pay for our society and she likewise said if she could get material she would learn us to make such articles as they keep to sell in societies at the North. She thinks that it may be that such things can be sent to some place where people do not know that Indian children can learn like white children and that the christian people will be so well pleased that they will purchase them. Then we shall have more money to send you. We have not worked in this manner but a little while, and we have not earned but two dollars.

The missionaries loved these girls. Their attitude was to be rewarded. The sullen resentment of some of the Fbs must be tolerated, regretted; one must try to understand.

John Ross and James Hicks helped. They would encourage the Fbs. Even though Chief Ross could not speak Cherokee well, he could communicate effectively enough with them, explaining the advantages of being able to trade with the whites and to protect the Indian rights and boundaries.

Many of the traditional customs upset the missionaries. For one, whenever full-blooded Indians were seen on the road, they would be in file, the man in front, the woman following. This was for reasons of protection, supposedly, but there were no dangers on the road now, not from animals, or Creeks, or whites. If ten Indians traveled together, they formed a single file, the women trailing along behind, nobody speaking—not a sound. They moved swiftly, concentrating on making rapid advance. If there were burdens to be carried, the women carried them. The excuse was that the men must be free to ward off attacks of animals and Choctaws and John Sevier. It was not unusual to see a woman trailing her husband with an infant tied to her backboard and a big load on her head, trying by might and main to keep up, while he hurried on unencumbered.

The Fbs' medicine was abhorrent to the missionaries. Their shamans—or conjurers or witchdoctors, as the missionaries preferred to call them—were of the devil, pure and simple Satan-possessed, stupid creatures. Several of those nearby claimed to be able to judge whether a sick person will get well. They would go into chants of gibberish, calling on denizens of the spirit world, whether of god or Satan the missionaries couldn't know, and they would, once in a trance, toss beads belonging to the sick person onto the surface of a stream, or of the river. If the beads swam, all would be better. If they sank at once, the patient would die. Assuming they swam, these men would prescribe medicine, claiming that the cure was revealed to them: soot and tobacco and spiderwebs and roots of herbs, most likely—no telling. Of course, they did not prescribe for the poor patients whose beads sank.

The Fbs were often lost in ignorance so deep that missionaries despaired. They had superstitions layered on one another and were given to self-satisfaction, self-gratification no matter what the vice or evil. It was unimaginable to the New England pastors that human beings in North America could have remained so near the state of purely sensual beings.

Yet, admittedly, they had dignity. They were hospitable without humbling themselves or making apology for their simple state of affairs. They were at the moment peaceable. Lord help us should they change that. They were tolerant of the mixed-bloods and usually supported them to be chiefs, to deal with the white men; but this did not seem to limit their own pride in their kind. They willingly gave to others the disagreeable tasks of governing and negotiating. This was not an admission of their own inadequacy, as much as an expression of pride in it.

They never harmed one another. The Fbs' disposition was to be content. One ate when hungry and would eat without complaint. One of their favorite foods was corn and bean bread. The missionaries found it to be an acquired taste, but they would cook some each day for the students. They would use lye ashes to strip the skins from grains of corn, then pound the meal and mix it with mashed, cooked beans; the dough, formed into small loaves, would be wrapped in corn husks and baked in hot ashes, or boiled.

The Indian ball games were strenuous, exhibitions of brutality, and decidedly sinful. So were their dances sinful. All that was needed to have a dance was for the town chief to announce one. Usually he gave several days' notice and might ascribe a reason for holding it. A dance was, the missionaries realized, another excuse for the men to drink firewater. On the appointed night, yelling commenced, shrill whooping as the people approached the council house; it was expected that on approaching any house a visitor would make his presence known by yells. For an hour or so, about dark, the people gathered and waited in the council house, stoically considering the walls of the building, until at last a leader walked all around the central fire and invited others to do the same. He began to sing, and to stamp his feet, and to prance proudly, still circling the fire. A drum began to accompany him. The leader set a faster pace, others following, and as he chanted, they replied. After a while one or two women fastened to their legs noisy contraptions, shells of land turtles with small stones inside them, and a clatter was set up.

Stamping with one or both feet at a time, in quick succession, constitutes the Cherokee mode of dancing. Any person wishing to dance, may now fall in ranks. Generally, an equal number of males & females are engaged at the same time; but strict regularity is not considered necessary.

The men and women do not dance alongside, or fronting, each other; but invariably preserve "Indian file." The rear is commonly filled up with boys and girls, who are thus initiated into the art at an early age. The leader generally sings extempore; the air is a combination of high and low sounds, used in quick succession, with but few variations, which renders it disagreeable and monotonous. He relates his love adventures, misfortunes and triumphs; boasts of his manhood, influence, with the fair sex, and dexterity in various performances. If he be an old man, he relates with enthusiasm the adventures of his youth, the exploits which characterized his movements in the field of battle, and the hair-breadth escapes through which he passed; he also boasts of stealing. He makes a great many grotesque motions, and contortions; slaps his hands together, and raises them alternately, one above the other, all the while turning and twisting, and bowing ludicrously. The motions and gestures of the leader are repeated by his followers; and sometimes they are simultaneous with his, for by much practice they are enabled to anticipate him. Any person can commence or leave off, dancing at pleasure. Frequently, a large concourse of people are engaged at the same time. Towards the close of the dance they interlock hands, and represent the figure of a serpent in its coil; and often, the whim of the leader causes him to make almost as many turnings and windings, and excentric evolutions, as are laid down in a figure of the walls of Troy. As the line of dancers is considerable in length, his (the leader's) sudden retrograde movements never fail in producing confusion, and the dance ends precipitously with bursts of laughter, hallooing and yelling. Repetitions of this dance, conducted by different leaders—drinking whiskey, sensuality, quarrelling and fighting, consume the night.

The missionaries considered such an affair passionate and sinful, and so they informed their students. Dances and ball games were not permissible. The emphasis on human nakedness and torso movement certainly was evil, as were the drinking, gambling, and frivolity. The result was effectively to disperse the spiritual attitude that one sought throughout life to enhance. A Christian atmosphere required invitation to prayer and contemplation and even adoration of God. Nobody—red, white, or black —could adore God at a Cherokee ball game or dance.

The missionaries who were upset by the common dances were altogether stunned by their first eagle dance. Men naked, or naked except for a kerchieflike diaper, the most handsome athletic men in the town, painted and decorated with eagle feathers, appeared before the tittering women in files four or five deep. This phalanx of war-whooping men came forward in quick steps and answered a leader in brief chorus. They used minced steps and halted frequently, issuing deafening whoops, the noise alone disruptive of compassionate thoughts. They seated themselves and sang a song, one that the missionaries were spared understanding, and after a pause for breath and to allow the eardrums to rest, one of the elders bounced up with a club and related the adventures of his life, in which he apparently clubbed several of the enemy. He ended by singing and dancing. Other elders, men and women, related their experiences, exploits in war, thievery, hunting.

I will now bring another company to view:—this consists of three or four men disguised in masks, made of large gourds, with openings for the eyes, nose, and mouth, and painted in a hideous manner. They represent mendicant travellers on a long journey; and their raiment and other equipments, remind me of the crafty Gibeonites, who appeared before Joshua as ambassadors from a distant land. I doubt whether Garrick ever acted a part on the

English stage, more in conformity to nature and reality, than I have seen low life, decrepitude and old age, acted by young Cherokees disguised, in a rude dance house. Some person advances & asks them various questions;—where they are from?—Where are they going? etc. The first they generally answer by saying they have come from a far distant land. Other questions are propounded, and answers given, which produce great merriment. They are invited to dance, and, accordingly, perform after the singing of the Eagle dancers. Their dancing, and accompanying gestures, are so ludicrous, and at the same time, so exactly in imitation of the characters they represent that the giddy multitude are almost convulsed with laughter.

Immediately after this comedy, the principal performance commences.

The performers, stripped, decorated with feathers, and painted in such a manner that their features cannot be easily recognized, advance into an open space in the central part of the house, dancing after the singing of an old man; and, in a stooping position, glide around the fire with a movement of the feet so rapid as to resemble the twirling of a top. It consists in a trembling or rapid vibration of the muscles, and, at the same time, a regular and brisk movement forward, requiring the utmost exertion of muscular power. But the sport appears to depend mostly upon a variety of obscene gestures and movements, which will not bear a description. The remainder of the night is spent in a common dance, etc.

Dancing, ball games, war, and hunting had been of vital importance to all previous generations of Cherokees, and all four were now to be avoided.

The students complained about the bread every day. They said it was too mushy. Asked for advice, an old squaw said the corn being used wasn't Indian corn and made poor flour. Also, the bread should be boiled an hour. Also, no salt should be put into it.

After that the squaw came in each morning for a while, to make bread for the children, balling the dough, then shaping it into "broadswords," and wrapping them in corn husks or, as sometimes happened, oak leaves.

It occurred to the missionaries that if the bread making had gone awry, which was a simple process, they must move slowly if they meant to change all of Cherokee life.

Another worry of the American Board was the slaves. The board opposed slavery. Among the Cherokees the federal policy was to encourage plantations. Subsidies were pushing toward a large-scale agricultural economy, and plantations needed more and more slaves.

The blacks were kept under deplorable conditions. The Indians, on average, were kinder masters than were the whites, but they had fewer resources to share. They accepted the prevailing attitudes that blacks were inferior to both whites and Indians. Blacks were not to be accepted as family, were not taken as wives or husbands, were not taught to read, write, or figure, were not allowed rights of citizenship, ownership, inheritance, personal decision.

The black children were filthy mouthed, the missionaries found, and were prone to steal and quick to lie. They were sexually promiscuous, too, and needed watching every minute they were associating with the Indians.

One Moravian teacher, Miss Sophia Sawyer, taught a few blacks to read; at least, she began such an engagement, but she was reprimanded by other missionaries, who valued the cooperation of chiefs. She went to the slaves' homes after that, taught them there. Their houses were hovels, filthy, fly-choking, vermin-infested.

A report arrived at Spring Place that a rite involving human sacrifice had been held, and the Moravians in distress appealed to the friendly chiefs, Major Ridge and Charles Hicks, to investigate. The report was unverifiable, but it served to alert the Christians to yet deeper secret places in Cherokee society that might erupt. There were no laws here against rites offering up lives of human beings; over the years captive men had been killed in such ceremonies, prisoners not wanted by any of the adult Cherokees, not as husbands or slaves, at least not enough to interfere with the frolic. Each town had an elder woman, usually the mother of a noted warrior, who had authority to spare a prisoner. She could do so out of magnanimity, or because he had been brave, or because she liked him, or for no stated reason. Failing to gain her pardon, the poor fellow fell sacrifice to the festive spirit of the town. The women tied him to the end of a vine, one fifteen feet long, long enough to let him dash about a pole as they approached him with flaming torches, scorching and burning him until he expired. If he fainted, they would revive him with doses of cold water, in order to continue.

The missionaries were horrified. They maintained that such practices should be made illegal. Astonishingly enough, there appeared to be no compulsion on the Indians' part to do anything of the sort. Indian women did not want changes, would not appreciate losing their entertainment. Let the men give up something they administered. The missionaries looked afresh at the women, to judge their characters anew—unassuming, easily smiling, kindly looking.

To Brainerd, in September 1817, came an American Board director, Reverend Cornelius, a tall, thin man with refined manners and a reflective nature and fire in his soul to save Indians. He decided at once that the hardships encountered by the missionaries were to be expected, were similar to those encountered around the world by other Christians. He was pleased by the quality of students, by the substantial building, the storehouses and smokehouses filled with vegetables and meat. Instead of retrenching, the American Board should push ever onward, and he told the local missionaries to arrange a meeting with as many Cherokee chiefs as could be assembled.

Chief Hicks agreed to invite a group of Cherokees and a few visiting Creek chiefs to his house to meet Reverend Cornelius, enough to fill the large ground floor. Present was an old man, the Pathkiller, who reclined on a rug to one side of the room. Cornelius spoke to them about the need for more schools.

On October 17, with Hicks interpreting, he spoke to the council, using, as one witness said, "tongue of silver and soul of fire." In his notes for the occasion, he wrote,

> I had travelled far from the North to see them on a subject of highest importance to them and their children; that in this I was not acting as a private man, but, as I had shown them, I had been sent to them by a society of great and good men at the North who loved them and wished to do them good; that it was their belief that in no way could they do the Cherokee so much good as by sending wise and good men among them to teach their children; to instruct them in the arts of agriculture; and in the knowledge of their great Creator; by means of which they might be made happy and useful in this life, and which would lead them to happiness when they

should die. I assured them that none but good men would be sent among them; that these would never seek to deprive them of any of their lands, but would be entirely satisfied if they could teach the Indians how to cultivate them in the best manner to themselves. I stated the plan, which would govern the society in the establishment of school; and according to which they had already, by the consent of the Cherokees, established one school at Chickamaugah [sic], and might yet establish more.

The visiting Creeks hesitated to cooperate, but the Cherokees did so unanimously, and Pathkiller asked Major Ridge to make the acceptance official. Ridge took his place near the council fire, facing the chiefs seated under the spreading council house roof, with other Cherokees standing around the outside railings, in number more than a thousand; and he, a hulk of strength, spoke, according to Cornelius, "with great animation, . . . in a loud tone of voice, and in true native style," while holding his big hands folded, motionless, across his chest. He spoke for fifteen to twenty minutes, punctuating his remarks with deep grunts.

I am going to address the council of the Cherokee nation, and each representative will inform his own town respectively the result of our deliberations on the subject of what we have heard from the northern good people who have sent this man to us; of their offer of pity to our people, and that we have taken hold of their offer. We have thought right to accept of their benevolent object, that our children may learn to act well in life, and their minds be enlarged to know the ways of our Creator. For we have been told that by education we may know, that at death our spirit will return to the Father of it. It will also promote our children's good to labor for their living when they come to years of manhood. I am sensible the hunting life is not to be depended upon.

These good people have established one school at Chickamauga and sent us teachers to educate our children. Whereupon the council requires all persons to treat them friendly, and not to disturb anything they have. And as there is now a deputation of warriors to start immediately to visit the President of the United States, the chiefs are also requested to instruct them to ask our father, the President, for his assistance to educate our children.

Reverend Cornelius was moved by the speech and encouraged by the standing ovation following. Here were men of war, recently conquerors of neighboring tribes. Among them were urbane, educated individuals seated beside braves who had severed their ear lobes so that their silver ear ornaments would more deeply dangle. Another had a silver disk hanging from a hole through his nose. All manner of chiefs were here, dressed in hunting shirts, vests, turbans, fur hats, felt hats, silk garters, moccasins, the differences in dress designed to show their individualism. Yet all stood, all made known their approval of this big man.

Reverend Cornelius left them to visit the Choctaws but later returned, and this time he invited several Cherokee students to attend a special, new school in Cornwall, Connecticut. Previously a few northern Indian boys had been accepted, along with children from foreign countries. He talked with Watie about his son Buck, and they agreed to have Buck attend. He also visited Major Ridge to invite John, who was the best student at Brainerd, but the major was away. Susanna said he was in the south fighting wild Seminoles for General Jackson, and John was not well enough to go on a long journey to a faroff place.

Therefore, in June of the following year, 1818, when several Cherokee students left for Cornwall, John was not among them. Making the trip with American Board ministers was Buck, Charles Hicks's son Leonard, a young man named Redbird, a student from Brainerd who had taken John's place, and a Choctaw boy named Folsom. The party, all mounted, rode through eastern Tennessee into western Virginia, where they stopped by Monticello to visit ex-President Jefferson. He was delighted to meet bright Indian students and to hear about the new mission schools. They visited nearby Montpelier, meeting with ex-President Madison, who invited them to dine with him. On reaching Washington the ministers took them to the War Department, where they so favorably impressed the Secretary that he gave a scholarship to each boy. They met the President, Mr. Monroe, who was gentle, friendly, and as unassuming as a common friend; he did appear to be genuinely impressed with them, and particularly with Buck, who was bright and friendly. Wherever the boys went in Washington, they were greeted and feted. Indians even here were novelties, living characters from romanticized, fictional stories and poems.

Moving on north, Buck was one who spent the night in the home of Dr. Elias Boudinot in Burlington, New Jersey. Seventy-

eight years old, he had been a member for many years of the
United States Congress, had even been its president. Also, he had
been director of the Mint under Washington, John Adams, and
Jefferson. A member of the American Board, he was pleased to
receive Buck, and the two at once became friends. Boudinot
promised to support the boy financially, and in turn Buck agreed
to accept the elderly man's name as his own. He entered the
school at Cornwall on Mr. Boudinot's personal scholarship as
well as the one from the federal government, under the name of
Elias Boudinot.

Arriving in springtime in Connecticut, young Boudinot was
impressed by the orderliness, the neatness of the roads and towns,
and the industriousness of the men and women, and even of children his own age, which was fifteen. The school was full of excitement for him, too. It had an advanced student body, with one
Malay, one Tahitian, two Mauis, two Hawaiians, one Maori, two
Choctaws, three Mohegans, one Oneida, one Tuscarora, two
Coughnawaugha Mohawks, and the Cherokees. Of the Cherokees,
Elias and young Hicks were judged on entry to be "able to read
and write and parse the English language . . . have made some
progress in arithmetic . . . speak the English language well, they
would not be suspected by their pronunciation of being any other
than English descent."

The name of each student was his native name, a rule insisted
on by the founder and director of Cornwall, Herman Daggett.
Elias's insistence on an English name did, however, intrigue him,
and with customary sagacity he listed him on his books as Kuh-le-
ga-nah Elias Boudinot. The master encouraged his young people
to retain their native differences, even as he was introducing them
to works of Vergil, to world history, to Enfield's philosophy, to
the rules of surveying and "trigonometrical concepts." And basic
to the school day was its hours of prayer and Bible study, and the
tenets of evangelical Protestantism.

General Jackson undertook to liberate Florida from the waning Spanish empire. Major Ridge enjoyed the sights of Florida
but had little fighting to do. The Seminole campaign was another
notch in Jackson's belt, and by publicizing the war as savage, he

was able to add luster to his reputation. The facts were that only two men were killed and no savage battles were fought.

On Major Ridge's return home, he was profoundly disappointed to find John at home with his mother, who had removed him from Brainerd because she was dissatisfied with the level of training. John's abilities went beyond those of the other students. He had tried a school at Knoxville but had left there, too. The major was beside himself, unable to bear his son's losing the opportunity for a great education. It was simply too much for Ridge to endure.

It was at this juncture that a family tragedy interrupted everyone's life. Daughter Nancy, who had married a Cherokee, died in childbirth. The day-by-day expectation had been for a celebration, and the reality was bitter as gall.

Susanna and Major Ridge buried their daughter near their home and took seats, Indian style, along with John, at the front door of their home, in grief receiving friends. One who came was a missionary from the American Board, a Reverend Butrick, who conversed with them about death and reunion beyond death, talking with them into the evening hours. Ridge asked him to meet with his household servants, ten black and Creek slaves, and Butrick found them more accepting of Christianity than was Major Ridge, who was courteous and attentive, but who spoke of Indian, not Christian affairs. The three did enjoy studying the heavens together. They spoke of the cluster of stars called Seven Sisters by whites, Seven Brothers by Cherokees. The Seven Brothers, he said, had made medicine to elevate them into the sky; but one, the seventh, had been pulled back to Earth, to become the father of all pine trees. Major Ridge and his son John knew the names of many stars, and had stories about them.

One morning Butrick was asked by the major to preach. Naturally, he agreed. The major decided that the congregation of friends should worship near Nancy's grave, and there he had them kneel. Reverend Butrick decided to kneel, too, and in that humble condition held services for about fifty Cherokees, along with the major's slaves.

Susanna herself asked Butrick to take John with him to New England. She could not keep him happy here, with nothing to occupy his brilliant mind, and his father was in despair and was upset with her. As she knew, the major expected John to be prepared to become the leader of the Cherokee people. Butrick found the boy aloof, somewhat proud and reserved, but he was certainly brilliant. With pleasure, he left with him for New England. Along with John, one of James Vann's sons, also named John, born to his wife Margaret, was traveling to Cornwall. The major and Susanna and little sister Sarah said good-bye, all in tears, standing under a great tree near their spring.

Assistant Principal Chief Hicks approved of John's going. He had always felt close to him, having watched his family's wealth grow from a small farm to an immense plantation; also, the boy's ailment was identical to Hicks's, the same debilitating, painful, scrofulous condition. From this one valley three boys had gone: his own son Leonard, Watie's son Buck, and John Ridge, three hopes for the future.

Butrick and the two Johns and a few other boys took three weeks of riding to reach Salem, North Carolina, where they made themselves comfortable for three days and where they heard their first organ music, their first chamber music, and their first church choir. The rich German music was, to John, beyond belief; he was simply overcome.

On the trip he succumbed to his longtime desire for a watch. He used his travel allowance to purchase one, which exhausted the account. It did not cost much, as Butrick told him, but it cost all he had, which made it expensive, and showed him to be gullible.

Once John recovered from the minister's criticism, he wrote a poem to commemorate his purchase:

> Little monitor, by thee,
> Let me learn what I should be:
> Learn the round of life to fill,
> Thou canst gentle hints impart,
> How to regulate the heart.
> When I wind thee up at night
> Mark each fault and set thee right,
> Let me search my bosom too,
> And my daily thoughts review,

> Mark the movements of my mind
> Nor be easy when I find
> Latent errors rise to view,
> Till all be regular and true.

A few weeks later John wrote a poem "On the Shortness of Human Life":

> Like as the damask Rose you see,
> Or like the blossom on the tree,
> Or like the morning to the day,
> Or like the Sun, or like the Shade,
> Or like the Gourd which Jonas had:
> Even such is MAN! Whose thread is spun,
> Drawn out and cut, and so, 'tis done.
> Withers the Rose, the blossom blasts,
> The flower fades, the morning hastes,
> The sun is set, shadows fly,
> The gourd consumes,—so mortals die.

John did not often write letters to his parents. After all, neither of them could read. He did write to the Gambolds, who were second parents, and Susanna on her trips to services would have the letters read to her. In mourning, with a daughter recently buried, Susanna went often to the services, and sometimes the major would accompany her.

Indians in the various states had not been given citizenship or the rights of freemen. The estrangement was based on their not being Christians. Whenever one, such as Hicks, became Christian, the rights were denied him because of his being an Indian. He was, in effect, a free citizen of color, the same status as a freed slave. He must live and work segregated from full citizens. The federal government would not define for the states qualifications for citizenship, each state being sovereign. The Cherokees knew this to be so; therefore, Mr. Jackson's highly promoted treaty proposal, offering them citizenship in their respective states should they choose to remain, in fact offered them a blanched citizenship, a false promise, a paper doll that crumpled on examination.

His treaty made them this fake offer along with ownership of their farm, which they could not protect. Of course, what the offer and its agents hoped was that the Indians would move to the Arkansas river country. It was true that the Osage Indians and others had claims on it, but that situation could be adjusted in the usual ways. Already many had moved, Creek, Choctaw, Cherokee. Admittedly, most had not, and the federal policy as represented by Jackson encouraged these others to go now.

Among the chiefs who felt that they should, that all Cherokees should, was John Jolly, who lived on an island in the Tennessee River. Jolly had taken in Sam Houston, a white boy, when Sam had run away from home, and had reared him as a son. Now, in 1818, this Sam Houston became a federal agent, a job negotiated for him by Jolly and Jackson. He was to register Cherokees for emigration.

In the work Houston met many deterrents, which obviously originated among the missionaries. Reverend Cornelius, for instance, had advised chiefs that any such removal treaty would not be given the two-thirds vote in the United States Senate required for ratification. Another had told prospective emigrants that the rifle offered would be old and useless. Then too, some missionaries suggested that the attitude of whites toward Indians was cruel and unjust, that Indian children were similar to white children and could be reared for citizenship.

Houston wondered what the federal government was up to, supporting removal to the West while at the same time building schools in the East, supporting removal to the West and urging land clearing and new plantations here. Please explain why our own government has sent to the savages here only instructors from far away, Germans and New Englanders, none of whom was present in the days of Indian cruelty. Where did the government find these pious, impractical preachers?

Jackson also steamed and roared. The government was a coward. It did not serve its own national interests. The government officers had no knowledge of Indians, except those chiefs who came to Washington and donned frock coats and told risqué stories at parties. The officials thought Major Ridge and Hicks and young Ross were representative of the Cherokees. Well, go down by the Tennessee River and watch them dunking their sick in the water, and hear their witchdoctors howling.

The American Board offered to open a school in the Arkansas territory for Indians who would emigrate, and their offer was gratefully accepted by the War Department, which saw it as an inducement for emigration. At the same time the board began to negotiate for payment of the value of their holdings in the Cherokee territory, once the tribe moved west. They requested ownership of a square mile of land and payment for improvements, even though, as the War Department pointed out, the government had already paid for the buildings and held title to them.

The board meanwhile was receiving criticism from pastors in the South, who wondered if the board really knew what in God's name they were doing with these Indians. The board tried to be reasonable and neutral. Its missionaries were told to be so, too, but to be neutral was to aggravate those very chiefs who had supported the mission, all of whom were opposed to removal. One missionary, Reverend Ard Hoyt, wrote the board as follows:

> We think with the Chiefs of this People that a general removal would greatly distress this people and in a great degree retard, if not ultimately defeat, the benevolent design of bringing them out of their state of darkness to the light of divine truth and the privileges of civilization: still, we hold ourselves bound not to interfere with state affairs or in any measure to become partisans in this business.

The board was advised that the Cherokees as a nation would soon yield to government maneuvers and go west. It was only a matter of time. The New England staff did not see in Congress any congressman or senator persuasive enough to change the pro-removal policy. Even so, fewer than two thousand of the thirteen thousand Cherokees had gone West or were enrolled to do so, in spite of Houston's and other people's efforts.

At the beginning of 1818, Cherokee farmers did not know whether to plan to plant crops, which they might not be present to harvest. As 1819 arrived, they again wondered what to plant. The council decided to send a delegation to Washington in January to try to resolve the uncertainty. The delegates were empowered to agree to move West, should that seem to them to be the best solution.

9

A silversmith, a mixed-blood, came to Charles Hicks and asked him to write his name on a piece of paper, in order that he could sign his own works of jewelry. Cherokee men, and they only, wore ornaments—crosses, spurs, gorgets, bracelets, earrings—and the wealthier ones decorated their horses. Chief Hicks asked which name the silversmith wanted to use, his English or his Indian one; the issue was difficult for the silversmith to decide. He wrote out both: "Sequoyah" and "George Gist."

His father, as Hicks knew, was a Virginian, Colonel Gist, who had deserted the boy and his mother years ago.

Subsequently, with a piece of pointed brimstone, Gist signed his pieces, did so for years. He was an excellent craftsman, but in time, weary of crafting ever so many copies of each piece, he began to be slack in his work, as his sharp-tongued Cherokee wife told him.

He found other women for entertainment. And he would drink whiskey. At first he merely supplied whiskey to his friends; he could always afford a bottle. Soon, however, he was drinking with them, and occasionally instead of a quart he supplied a three-gallon keg. When drunk, he became even more introspective than usual, content to utter reminders that his friends were not to become violent and were to love one another.

He was from childhood able to draw animals, human faces, almost any scene. In fact, to keep books at his shop, he would draw the picture of the person commissioning work to be done and enter a code for the amount agreed to. I^{0000} might represent four dollars, for instance. He found this method time-consuming and marveled at the ingenuity of the white man and his systems of communicating by writing. Two people by sending marks on paper to each other could communicate as if they were talking. One evening, a friend admitted that he did not know how writing was done, even though he had seen a man do it. Gist told him he saw no problem in conceiving how it was done: there was no secret to it. He said that in ancient times Moses, one of the early writers, had written down instructions from God by making marks on stone. I, too, can make marks on stone, he said; and he did, but they were not meaningful.

His friends laughed at him for saying he could make stones speak and told him he would not find stones to be entertaining company, anyway.

Not only can I make them speak, but I can make characters you can understand, he told them. One morning he took a pin, and on a stone he made many marks, each intended to represent a sentence, such as: "I made the journey," "I am well," "The children are well," "When arrive you here?" "I arrive before the snows." Within a few days there were too many marks to be remembered, even though he was not nearly through, so he began to make marks that represented words. Here again, the mass of signs overcame him, and their combination in sentences was complicated. Next he came upon the idea of devising a character for each sound. These sounds, when combined, would convey words. He decided that there were eighty-six distinct sounds in Cherokee use. He made a simple sign for each, borrowing them from a copy of the Bible, the McGuffey Reader, and a Greek text.

His wife, annoyed by this new strangeness and the lack of business, destroyed records of his marks, which set him once more to drink.

Major Ridge did not go with the delegation to Washington in January 1819, the one headed by Charles Hicks and empowered to negotiate to move the tribe West. Hicks took eleven chiefs with him, including both Ross brothers, John and Lewis. The missionaries were told in secret that there was authorization for these dozen men to trade all Cherokee land for a suitable, equal holding west of the Mississippi, should the government prove adamant. They were to negotiate proper payment and conditions. The Reverend Ard Hoyt wrote on January 11,1819,

For the information of those concerned in the mission, we are told, in confidence, that the delegates have full power to negotiate an entire exchange of country if they think best after a conference with the President. If they do not agree to a total exchange, a considerable part of the country must at all events be given up as the portion of the emigrants, perhaps this may be the best time to secure the property of the Board here; but if the whole country is now given up, it may be the only time.

John Ross visited Brainerd just before the delegation's departure. He wanted the missionaries to know that total removal, if agreed to, would leave the mission's property vulnerable to land speculators, and the delegation should try to except it from any treaty.

Reverend Hoyt later wrote from Brainerd:

Mr. John Ross, one of the delegates, without even a hint from any of us, has asked us how a portion of land can be secured for the benefit of the schools in the nation. He is not satisfied that the Cherokees should barely say they are *willing* to receive instruction; it is his wish that they should evince their ardent desire for it by *doing* something to promote it. He had not consulted the other delegates, but he did not doubt they would be all of his mind.

He thought the mission families must have a reserve at least equal to the Cherokees who choose to remain, i.e., 640 acres to each family—that the grant for Chickamaugah [Brainerd] must be sufficient to include all our buildings and improvements—but the great object of his inquiry was how a large tract of good land at some place where it would sell high, could be secured in the hands of some white people (as they had no law by which it could be secured among themselves) so that the nation should hereafter have the benefit of it for the support of schools.

The missionaries suggested to the board that Reverend Cornelius join the delegation in Washington, to mediate with the federal officers. Also, Reverend Samuel Worcester from Brainerd would try to make the trip, even though he must delay a few weeks.

The Secretary of War, Mr. Calhoun, was advised by Governor McMinn that the Cherokees were authorized to consent to removal; however, Calhoun knew that McMinn had given such assurances for a year and a half, and his efforts to register emigrants had been a failure. McMinn and Sam Houston, along with other agents had spent all the money appropriated by Congress for removal, eighty thousand dollars, without persuading 15 percent of the Cherokees to remove, and many of those had been drunk at the time. McMinn was a drunkard, too, Calhoun understood, and would when drunk issue inflammatory, illegal orders. He once even put up the Brainerd mission property for sale, in an effort to silence the missionaries, and he had offered for sale to the highest bidders, whites included, the improvements made by those Cherokees who had removed their families to the West. Now McMinn advised the government yet again that removal of all Cherokees could be achieved, if the government stood firm.

Secretary of War Calhoun did not believe him. He meant to stir up no further controversy. McMinn, Houston, and their ilk had managed to antagonize the American Board, their preachers, and allied congressmen and senators, and now they were telling the president what he must do. Better to take care. Also, McMinn had spent all the appropriation, which overspending would lead to embarrassment should there be a hearing. He had drunk it, he and his agents, Calhoun supposed. This damned fool, successor to the effective Meigs, had spent on himself and his cronies all of the funds for removal of the Cherokees. Calhoun did not even invite him to the meeting in Washington with the Cherokee delegation. He entrusted the matter to himself.

First he had a dozen delegates fitted out with fashionable clothing, which pleased the Indians every time, no matter what their tribe, and he saw to their comfortable housing. He met with them and was pleased to find Chief Hicks's offer reasonable. The Indians had twelve million acres of land, which Hicks admitted was more than Cherokee men, women, and children could cultivate. Many had moved west in an earlier wave of families dissatisfied and disinherited by the Revolutionary War and its aftermath, and others were moving by reason of the recent inducements and recruitment. But in the West Cherokees found they had no land at all, and no welcome from the Osage tribe. Therefore, the eastern Cherokees would trade with the federal government a sizable piece of eastern property, representing the birthright of these western Cherokees, for federal western lands of equal usefulness, which the federal government would guarantee as belonging to the western Cherokees.

The eastern Cherokees wanted in turn to be guaranteed ownership of the remaining eastern land and for the government to cease all efforts to obtain more land from them; also the government was to cease trying to persuade Cherokees to move westward. Hicks agreed that Cherokees who had agreed to move west, but had not yet done so, were free to do so.

The Secretary told them that he could not guarantee the future: "it will not be possible by any stipulation in the treaty to prevent future cessions." He did believe that if the eastern acreage agreed to were large, the government would itself be reconciled to a permanent Cherokee home in the East for those wishing to stay. He added,

> You are now becoming like the white people; you can no longer live by hunting but must work for your subsistence. . . . Your great object ought to be to hold your land separate[ly] among yourselves, as your white neighbors; and to live and bring up your children in the same way they do, and gradually adopt their laws and manners. . . . Without this, you will find you have to emigrate, or become extinct as a people. You see that the Great Spirit has made our form of society stronger than yours, and you must submit to adopt ours.

The delegation agreed to his conditions; all went smoothly. Indeed, the question of total removal never came up. There was no conflict of opinion, except that the amount of land to be traded did enter into a discussion of geography and arithmetic. John and Lewis Ross were expert in this area, as was Chief Hicks—and, of course, the War Department, which pronounced that there were fifteen thousand Cherokees, of whom six thousand had gone west or had enrolled to do so; they wanted one-third of the Cherokee eastern lands. Hicks and John and Lewis Ross said that there were sixteen to seventeen thousand Cherokees of whom three thousand, perhaps thirty-five hundred, had or would decide to emigrate, leaving by their count about thirteen thousand in the East.

This was a bargaining position. The Cherokee delegation had no accurate statistics. The government said it did, so the Cherokees, accepting the federal figures, agreed to give up four million acres; they also agreed that the government was henceforth empowered to give to the western Cherokees one-third of the Cherokee annuity resulting from previous treaties.

The lands to be ceded were 986,880 acres of mountain land in North Carolina, including the Black Mountain Range but not the Great Smokies; 536,000 acres in Georgia, all of it tillable farmland; 739,000 acres in Alabama, all rich land; 1,541,000 acres in Tennessee. This left an eastern Cherokee territory somewhat larger than the states of Massachusetts, Rhode Island, and Connecticut combined. It embraced the southeastern corner of North Carolina, the northwestern part of Georgia, the northeastern part of Alabama, and that part of Tennessee which lies south of the Hiwassee and Tennessee rivers.

Near the close of negotiations, John Ross, who had been almost as active a participant as Hicks, recommended approval of his education endowment, and to his joy it was approved; the government was to receive and to sell a portion of valuable Cherokee land, the proceeds to be used to support schools. There was some question regarding administration of the endowment funds —whether the American Board was to have them, or the Cherokees, or the government—but in any event the delegates agreed the money was to be used to expand Cherokee educational opportunities in the East.

Reverend Samuel Worcester arrived in Washington too late to attend any of the meetings. They had gone so well that they had ended quickly. There was some anxiety in the Senate, he was told, where the Jackson forces were disappointed that all Cherokee land was not ceded; nevertheless, the land speculators were eager to begin the new expansions and would help carry the two-thirds vote for ratification of the treaty. Worcester congratulated Chief Hicks in a letter of March 4, 1819:

I rejoice with you and thank the Great Spirit for his kindness to you and your nation. It was a day of darkness. . . . You feared that you would be compelled to give up your houses, your cornfields, your rivers, plains and mountains. . . . The Dark cloud has passed away. A good portion of your lands is secured to you; the wicked men who seek your hurt are to be kept from troubling you. You are to be allowed to sit quietly around your own fires and under your own trees and all things are to be set before you and your children. . . . Many have long been your friends and now many more

are coming to be your friends . . . hundreds of thousands of good men and
women in all parts of this country. . . . Brother, it is the morning of a new
and happy day.

On March 6, Secretary Calhoun wrote to Governor McMinn:
"You are requested, as no further encouragement will be given to
the emigration to the Arkansas, to take immediate measures to
wind up the business." Among the business was the unwinding
of many illegal sales and entanglements McMinn had made.

Surveys were completed in the East before the government
even began them in the West. Almost four million acres were
exchanged, eastern land for western.

Chief Pathkiller welcomed the agreement. He listened to the
reports and concluded that Hicks and the Ross brothers had saved
the nation. It was his view that his people were now safe forever
in their homes.

John Ross was little known before these negotiations. He was
the descendent of a Scot, William Shorey, and his Cherokee wife,
Ghigooie. Fluent in English and Cherokee, Shorey had been a
British interpreter at Fort Loudoun. On his death in 1762 of consumption, he left two children, Anna and William. Anna married
a Scot, a trader named John McDonald.

A family dispute arose in 1809 when Anna's brother, William, died. John McDonald produced a document, which he said
represented a will given orally by William to McDonald's grandson, John Ross. This will left a large portion of William's wealth
to Anna, much of it to become John Ross's on her death. John
Ross also inherited part of an island, located just below Tellico
Blockhouse. William's daughter Elizabeth insisted that her father
had never mentioned such ideas. She claimed that John Ross had
obtained the commitment when her father was drunk. Angrily
she challenged the purported will, but the judgment of the Cherokee principal chief, Pathkiller, and the United States agent went
largely against her.

This, John Ross's introduction to public life, was not propi-
tious.

John McDonald was an interesting figure, one who held

great influence over his grandson. Born at Inverness about 1747, he had come to Charleston and journeyed to Fort Loudoun. There he met Anna Shorey and married her. The two settled near Lookout Mountain. As three European powers converged on the Cherokees seeking support, McDonald sold his influence at times to each in turn—England, France, and Spain—and later to the United States.

McDonald had one child, a daughter named Molly. She married a Scots trader, Daniel Ross, about 1785, and they and their growing covey of children lived near old Mr. McDonald, who exerted his will over the family, particularly over John and his brother Lewis. They were brought up as Scots. John often cried piteously, begging to be allowed to wear Indian clothes rather than the clothes his grandfather favored. McDonald supplied the boy with books, maps, newspapers.

Private tutors were hired for them. Later they were sent to private boarding schools. They grew up in the world of white people, but they identified with the Cherokees, and John, though only one-eighth Indian by blood—the white man's method of establishing relationships—was through his half-breed mother, a member of the Bird clan, therefore as much a Cherokee as anyone, even though he would not trust himself to speak the language in public.

Sequoyah built a house near his wife and family, and he secreted himself inside to work on his syllables. He sympathized with his wife, admitted his faults, but he was required by his own sense of duty to complete this task. She, of course, could not be expected to go hungry without complaining. She said their children were laughed at by the offspring of sensible parents. Sequoyah admittedly was in a sort of trance; he might be insane, as she and her brothers decided. But he would, he said, do his work regardless.

Friends came to him. One told him, My friend, there are a great many remarks made about this employment that you have taken up. Our people are much concerned about you. They think you are wasting your life. They think, my friend, that you are making a fool of yourself, and will no longer be respected.

Gist replied:

> It is not our people that have advised me to this and it is not therefore our
> people who can be blamed if I am wrong. What I have done I have done
> from myself. If our people think I am making a fool of myself, you may tell
> our people that what I am doing will not make fools of them. They did not
> cause me to begin and they shall not cause me to give up. If I am no longer
> respected, what I am doing will not make our people the less respected,
> either by themselves or others; and so I shall go on and so you may tell our
> people.

Once he had a set, Sequoyah taught his six-year-old daughter
the symbols and sounds. Visitors began to come by to examine
the mystery as Sequoyah would send his little girl as far as the
woodpile, as far even as the road, a visitor accompanying her;
other visitors who remained with Sequoyah would give him a
sentence, which was known only to those inside the house. Sequoyah would make marks on paper, or on the face of a slate. It
could be paper supplied by the visitors, even that, and chalk or
ink they could supply. Back into the house would come the child.
Her father would show her the writing, and she would at once
call out the secret sentence.

Fearful of the tricks of witches and magic, some of the visitors fled, men as well as women.

Try as many times each day as anybody pleased, the girl
could always read the secrets.

Then another child learned to do the same. And another person, one of Sequoyah's nephews, the son of Mike Waters.

A brother of Chief John Watts came to consider the trick, and
was so impressed that the next morning at dawn he returned and
woke Sequoyah and admitted he had not slept for thinking of the
wonder. He asked if Sequoyah could write down anything he
chose, or only particular subjects.

Anything, Sequoyah assured him, as long as it was in the
Cherokee language.

The brother of John Watts recalled great speeches he had
heard at councils and believed they should be written down even
now, because often they were quoted in error; and Sequoyah
agreed to help him.

Sequoyah's first composition was on the subject of the boundary lines between Cherokee country and the states of Georgia and Tennessee. He had been called to speak on the subject at a court held at Chatonga, and he appeared and read his statement while people drew near to stare at the marks.

Sequoyah went to Arkansas in 1822, and carried with him letters from relatives in the East; he taught several bright children to read them. He returned to the East with letters, proving that Indians "could talk at a distance," which delighted everybody.

What Sequoyah saw in Arkansas attracted him, and he decided to emigrate there. His wife, basking in the family's notoriety, agreed. With him he took other letters, these from eastern to western relatives, and they served further to prove the worth of his syllabary.

John Ridge was ill each winter season at Cornwall, and the third winter was by far the worst. His sleeping quarters, under the gambrel roof with inadequate ventilation, were steamy hot in summer and cold in winter. Deep snow limited outdoor activity, and his scrofulous complaint became severely painful.

The Cornwall physician wrote to his parents, who replied that he should return home as soon as he could travel. The doctor felt that such a time was distant. Students met to pray for his health. His condition deteriorated, and the doctor moved him to a special room where he could be nursed efficiently.

There was speculation about his returning to the south by a boat leaving from Boston and going to Norfolk or Charleston. He might then register in a college in a southern state. Even travel by boat seemed impossible just now. In spring the doctor placed him under the care of a specialist in New Haven, and John spent almost a month there. The school was given such dire reports that the staff decided he might very well never see his home country again. During the summer he failed to gain against his illness, and the school informed his parents of the seriousness of the situation.

The major drove north at once, accompanied by a black man to serve as aide and interpreter—most black slaves could speak English. He carried letters from the missionaries and students at

Brainerd and a painting of Brainerd, all carefully packed. He rode overland, arriving in Connecticut in three weeks.

Near Cornwall he put up for the night in an inn providing baths, and in the morning rented, for use the rest of the journey, a coach and four, so he and his servant rode into Cornwall in "the most splendid carriage . . . that ever entered the town." He wore white topboots and a coat trimmed with gold lace. A resident of the town, one of the Beechers, wrote, "his tall and athletic form and noble bearing bespoke him as one of the princes of the forest." The son of Dr. Gold later wrote, "No memory of my boyhood is clearer than that of a visit to my house in my sixth year of . . . John Ridge and his father, Major Ridge, the Cherokee chief. The latter wore the uniform of a U.S. officer, and I was deeply impressed with his 'firm and warlike step.' I called him 'the nice, big gentleman.' My father exchanged presents with him, giving him a small telescope and receiving in turn from him an Indian pipe carved in black stone, with the assurance that it had often been smoked in Indian councils."

John had begun to recover before the major arrived, but his father's gallant and affectionate nature did help him, and throughout the two weeks of his father's visit he made progress. The major was often about on the streets and was in the school every day except Sundays, when he stayed in his room. He explained to those who asked after him that he would attract attention away from the worship of God, should he go to church.

In spite of improvement, John was not well enough to travel even by boat, but Charles Hicks's son Leonard asked if he might return south with the major. Leaving John in the care of kindly white women at the school, the major, Leonard, and the black servant boarded the *Caravan* in New York City, where the major at once, and for the entire voyage, was the main attraction, autographing cards whenever asked to do so, using his *X*, and everywhere winning friends—the most impressive Indian the crew and passengers had ever seen.

In Cornwall John basked in the attention of the school's staff, especially favoring that of an attractive young lady, Sarah Bird Northrup, nicknamed Sally. Blue eyes, auburn hair, gracious manner, she was a vision in his mind, and her presence in his room certainly did help to revive him.

When Dr. Gold discontinued the medicine, he mentioned to the school ladies that John appeared to be worried. He would not care to speculate, but could one of them—perhaps Sally's mother —talk to the boy? Mrs. Northrup had often visited his room, but always in a rush; one night she took her basket of sewing with her and sat for a while. She asked him if he had some particular worry, and he confessed to her that he was in love.

Well, we all go through that, life seems to hinge on it, she told him. Who is the girl?

Sally, he told her.

Mrs. Northrup, stunned, alarmed, irritated, amused, was devastated.

She was, however, confident of her God, who would intercede, and she knew Sally to be a level-headed, sweet lady-soon-to-be who was considerate of everyone, including those of foreign cultures. She was doubtless merely showing respect for John. Indeed, Sally was, in her childlike way, thinking of becoming a missionary to a foreign land.

When Sally returned home, Mrs. Northrup asked her at once, simply, directly, if she loved John.

Yes, Sally said.

Mrs. Northrup sent Sally to her grandparents' house in New Haven, with instructions to them to keep her there, to have "parties and introduce her to other gentlemen and try every way to get her mind off John Ridge."

Sally was not easily distracted. She did not care for the boys she met, she missed her noble friend, the beautiful, graceful, brilliant Indian, always the polite gentleman; she missed him and she was certain he missed her. She became quite ill, would not eat, lost weight, and after three weeks accepted her grandparents' offer to take her home.

John wrote his mother asking for her blessing should he ask Sally to marry him. Susanna took the letter to Reverend Butrick, who was as surprised as she by the words he found there. Susanna was simply struck down. Butrick agreed with her that John's marrying a white woman would make him a less effective leader of his people. She told Butrick that the major had planned for John to marry the daughter of a chief, not an auburn-haired New England girl.

With Butrick's help she wrote a letter to John, refusing him permission.

A second letter from John was more emotional. John confessed his love for Sally and required his mother to respect that. He pleaded for permission. Unable to deny her son what he wanted most in life, with his father's approval she had Butrick write a letter consenting.

The school term came to a close, the students prepared to go home. On crutches, John approached the Northrups and asked for Sally's hand. Her parents had expected it, but even so they were unprepared. They were aware of their own love for both John and Sally; they were also aware that the marriage of an Indian man and a white girl would alarm many citizens of New England and might very well threaten the support of the school. To refuse the boy, however, because he was an Indian was to deny the school its mission.

Mrs. Northrup put off the decision; she simply could not face it. She told John that Sally was too young to marry. John should go home and get well; if he got well, he had her permission in two years to return to ask Sally for her hand.

Sally and John agreed to the two-year separation, and at the moment of John's departure, Sally's tears broke Mrs. Northrup's heart.

Dr. Gold noted that Elias Boudinot, though not ill, was worried, with the same symptoms John had shown, which interested him. Who, he wondered, was his girl?

John took with him a copy of a letter he had written on behalf of Cornwall School to President Monroe on March 8, 1821, to show his father:

Honored Sir, . . . I am happy to understand that Doct. Morse is about to visit the seat of government, to exhibit to you, his report, relative to the Indians, whom he has visited. We their sons, who have the advantage of instruction in this seminary, hope that it may meet your cordial approbation, and that assistance may be profered to [our] long-neglected and despised people. . . . I rejoice that my dear nation now begins to peep into the privileges of civilization—that this great and generous government is favorable to them, and that ere long, Congress will give them the hand of strong fellowship—that they will encircle them in the arms of love, and adopt them into the fond embraces of the *Union.* . . .

It is a known fact, that those Indians who have missionaries among them, and who live on this side [of] the Mississippi, are coming up, with faster steps to civilization, than those who have been enticed to remove to the west. An instance of this may be found in viewing the condition of my dear people. I left them about two years ago; when they were at work the tools of the whites were used—some possessed large farms; cattle, horses, hogs, etc. Their women were seen at the wheel, and the weaver's shuttle was in motion. How different is the condition of that part of my nation, who have been enticed by their foolish imaginations, and particularly by the allurement of the white men, to remove to the Arkansas. The equipage of a hunter, viz. a brass kettle, gun and knife were offered to them, which mortified at the sight, we saw them eagerly receive and depart. They are now in pursuit of game, in which employment we have reason to apprehend, they would have continued, or perhaps have sunk into oblivion, were it not that teachers have been sent to them by Christian benevolence.

His letter ended with a personal example: "My father and mother are both ignorant of the English language, but it is astonishing to see them exert all their power to have their children educated, *like the whites.* "

In the fancy, refined city of Charleston, where their ship docked, the Cherokees were asked to speak at a local church, to address the subject of Cherokee progress. John was the one Elias Boudinot and the others voted to represent them. He had a portion of that talk with him, also, when he met with his father:

I question whether the gentlemen who support this argument would be willing to renounce the privileges of polished society and voluntarily adopt the manners of savages, and take their abode in the wilderness, far from civilized people. Will anyone believe that an Indian with his bow and quiver, who walks solitary in the mountains, exposed to cold and hunger, or the attacks of wild beasts, trembling at every unusual object, his fancy filled with agitating fears, lest the next step should introduce his foot to the fangs of the direful snake, or entangle it "amidst his circling spires that on the grass float redundant," actually possesses undisturbed contentment superior to a learned gentleman of this commercial city, who has every possible comfort at home? Can anyone convince me that the degraded Hottentot in

Africa, or the wild Arab in the desert of the Sahara, whose head is exposed to the piercing rays of a meridian sun, entirely dependent on his camel for safety, enjoys more real contentment of mind than the poorest peasant of England? Will anyone compare the confined pleasures of the Hindoo, whose mind is burdened with the shackles of superstition and ignorance, who bows before the car of the Juggernaut, or whose wretched ignorance compels him to invoke the river Ganges for his salvation—Will anyone, I say, compare his pleasures to the noble and well regulated pleasures of a Herschel or a Newton, who surveys the regions of the universe—views the wisdom of the Deity in forming the lights of heaven with all the planets and attending satellites revolving in their orbits, irradiating infinite space as they move around their common centres—and who demonstrates, with mathematical exactness, the rapid flights of the comet, and its future visits to our solar system!

I have made this contrast to shew the fallacy of such theories, and to give you a general view of the wretched state of the Heathen, particularly of the aborigines of this country, who are gradually retiring from the stage of action to sleep with their fathers. It is on the exertions of the benevolent that their safety depends, and only the hand of charity can pluck them from final extermination.

He also told his father about the money contributed by the congregation for that and another talk: almost four hundred dollars in cash, as well as a number of books.

Boudinot attested to John's prowess in stirring the congregations. John had his father's oratorical ability. As for himself, Elias had a way with words, too. His hopes were to attend a college, if money could be found even for a year—perhaps Princeton. He had his own style, his glowing personality, which shone all the brighter under the brand-new silk umbrella he had bought for himself while in Charleston.

From the March 7, 1821 issue of the *Franklin Gazette* of Philadelphia, Pennsylvania, this report was mailed to the newspaper from the West, from the Arkansas River country to which many Cherokees, including Sequoyah, had migrated:

The Osages and Cherokees have just commenced hostilities. The Osages, a short time since, made an attack on a party of Cherokee hunters, killed two, wounded some others, and took all their horses. This took place at the Oporto, and not far from the garrison. I understand the governor, who was then in that country, where he had been since the first of November, told the Cherokees to protect themselves. This is what they have been wanting for some time. I am told that the Shawnees and Delawares, now on their way to Indiana, to settle in this country, will join the Cherokees. It is very probable the Osages will be completely driven off. It is the intention of the Cherokees to possess their country, if possible, and I have no doubt they will effect their object. The missionaries to the Osage nation started from Little Rock on the 12th instant; but hearing of the hostilities between the Osages and Cherokees, they have stopped again; they are now waiting for the governor to come down, to get his advice how to proceed. It is probable I think, that they will not effect their object, as the Osages will either be driven off, or subdued, before they arrive. It would be rashness for them to proceed at present.

Creeks and Choctaws were also having skirmishes with the Osage, and it was believed that if a new Choctaw treaty with the government was ratified, calling for Choctaws voluntarily to emigrate to the West, an Arkansas war would break out as the Osage tried to protect land they claimed. The land the treaty granted Choctaw emigrants extended all the way to the Rocky Mountains.

10

The American Board had opened more schools, chiefly for students, though up to ten resident students were housed at each. The distances some of the children had to walk contributed to their tardiness and frequent absences, and the total number of young scholars was greater at the start of a school year than at any later time. By October 1, 1821, there were fewer than fifty remaining in these new operations.

At Brainerd ninety-six children attended, of whom just over thirty were girls. All of them boarded, the expense borne by the American Board, which also clothed them. Twenty-four were new scholars.

To the board, Reverend Ard Hoyt reported, "The children of the schools continue to manifest an aptness to learn, a willingness to labour, and a readiness to submit to all the rules of the school. The Cherokees, we think, are fast advancing towards civilized life. The[y] generally manifest an ardent desire for literacy and religious instruction."

The blacks were less promising. Progress was made whenever teaching was done, but it was done only surreptitiously. The love of humanity that made the missionaries feel deeply about wrongs done the Indians also made them unwilling that wrongs should be done to the less powerful blacks; but there was no power on Earth strong enough to change all the cogs and wheels at the same time. One prayed for forgiveness.

Slavery came naturally to the Cherokee masters: *Atsi nahsa'i* was the Cherokee term for slavery, and it referred to any creature that required care, whether beast, bird, pet, or human being not member of a clan needing to be fed and managed. If an Indian said to another, "I have an *atsi nahsa'i* for you," the gift could be a puppy or a turtle or a human slave or a milch cow, and to the Cherokees the enslaving of one of these was as ordinary as the enslavement of another. To tell a Cherokee slaveowner that slavery was wrong would be as surprising to him as telling him that any other commonplace activity was wrong, and the admonition was likely to be ineffectual. Such a statement would reflect on the peculiarity of the speaker.

Cloth was the most treasured innovation for the women. Of course, the men were fond of their new garb, too, especially when brightly colored; but to the women cloth was practical as well as decorative: the cover for the feather pillow, for instance, the cotton swab, the rag for washing up, the towel for drying, the diaper for the baby. Some women had two diapers only, some half a dozen—they were the wealthy ones. Half a dozen diapers for one baby! What a marvelous advance over the bygone days when there was no cloth diaper in an entire town.

Thomas Jefferson was in declining health at his Virginia home, Monticello. His six-foot-two-inch frame was weakening, but his mind was alert and busy with plans for the University of Virginia, including the selection and hiring of its faculty, most of them to journey from Europe to this remote Appalachian community. He was aware of the charge that he had set in motion inconsistent patterns of dealing with the Indians and their place in the nation. He made no explanations, no excuses, leaving the matter for public outcry and judgment. He had believed that removal to the West would benefit the Indians in some ways and would save everyone the human and financial costs of Indian wars. He did believe that the Indians had rights to land and life, but also that the citizens had a need for land. After all, the expansion of the nation's population was not under his control, or the government's.

Frontiersmen were in many cases rough, determined individuals, not known for tolerance. He had at times directed noble thoughts and praise toward the Indians, knowing that the character of the frontiersman made his views unwelcome. He had done so because he viewed the Indians as equals, capable someday of producing a nation.

Land. He was a planter. Whatever else, he was a planter, just now trying to hold off creditors to save this dear acreage of his own. The great Louisiana purchase was his doing, a chance to expand the new nation; even lacking congressional authority, he had grabbed it. Land was a hunger in every southerner, anathema to many northerners who wanted a country hugging the Atlantic.

What was it Tocqueville wrote about this Indian matter? To pay debts, Jefferson had sold thirteen thousand of his books, and Tocqueville's was one of them. Something to the effect that Indians have been entered into a competition they have not the means of sustaining. Isolated in their own land, their race becomes a little colony of troublesome strangers in the midst of a numerous and dominant people.

Much truth there. Hope did exist for a few tribes. For the Cherokees, more than the others.

Back in 1802 when President Jefferson, while negotiating with France for the Louisiana purchase, had tried to buy Georgia's western claims, Georgia had finally agreed to release to the federal government lands of Alabama and Mississippi for three to four cents an acre, provided the federal government would acquire from the Indians their claims to lands in Georgia and move these Indians to western lands at the government's expense, "as soon as the same can be peaceably obtained on reasonable terms."

President Jefferson had negotiated that contract. The next year he completed the Louisiana purchase and recommended the exchange of all Indian lands east of the Mississippi River for equal land to the West, which he believed would save the costs of Indian wars and in itself pay for the purchase of the Louisiana territory.

In 1821, John Ridge and Elias Boudinot, along with Vann's and Hicks's sons, returned home to find that Georgia was protesting that the federal government had not removed the Indians from Georgia. This failure, Georgia said, would ultimately require the sovereign state of Georgia to take action.

Half of the eastern Cherokees lived in Georgia. There also were located most of the Indians' wealthy plantations. Any threat from Georgia struck at the jugular vein of the Cherokees.

On the Georgia seal were engraved three promises: Justice, Wisdom, Moderation. All three were now to be tested.

At age fifty the awkwardness commenced, as Ridge realized, of looking at one's physical powers from the downhill side. He felt about as strong and agile as ever in his life, but even so was winded while hurrying up the orchard hills; and he became sleepy at night as soon as the sun set. Inevitably his strength, that of a giant, would be receding now, would be shading downward, bleeding off like blood from an open vein. John was with him, was educated, and would find a place to live near his father. The major was speaker of the council, one of the three highest positions, and he could help John gain authority of his own. John was already accepted by Hicks and John Ross as a person of influence. Ridge could see respect in their eyes whenever John spoke.

John saw it, too, and was surprised that at his young age his opinion carried weight with Charles Hicks and his father. The two even deferred to him. Also, his father deferred to Elias Boudinot and young Leonard Hicks. All three young men, only now in their teens, seemed to be hopes of the nation, as far as Major Ridge was concerned.

John's health improved. Strength seemed to come up from the ground through his moccasins and bathe his sick body. The home country healed him. So did being with his family, whom he had scarcely seen for many years. His father was jubilant, confident; the major smothered all doubts. And his mother doted on him. She gathered herbs to prepare for his use and selected good foods from the gardens and fields; there were storehouses full of onions, cabbages, potatoes, apples, pears, smoked bacon and hams; the streams were stocked with trout, the forest and meadows still afforded game. The plantation was immense, a living, growing, enriching creation. There was no end to its growth, either. As John knew, his father did not need to acquire more land through purchase, he invested not a dollar in land; he could take what Cherokee land he wanted, provided others were not using it.

John and Elias together visited their foster parents at Spring Place, the Gambolds, who were ecstatic to see them and turned the student body out—only six were present. The young chiefs translated English prayers and verses into Cherokee, and Elias led in a rousing prayer for the place and its good people. Elias was a confessed Christian. John still was considering it. He was surprised that so many Indian students had, indeed, professed Christianity; he met several at Spring Place. They were unashamedly, unabashedly Christian, which John couldn't help but feel was a repudiation of Indian ways and culture.

Spring Place was about twenty years old and had weathered nicely, seemed to belong to its setting. Several new buildings stood out starkly. It had Brother and Sister Gambold puttering about, she with heart trouble, recurring angina, but active every day. The girl students were studying the making of cloth, as well as academics. The boys' chores were fewer, due to the slackened farming operation. Brother Gambold was tired of farm work. He had decided the students could not work a large farm. For years Mr. Vann had let his slaves work on Sundays, which had helped. Vann was long since buried, however, and his slaves dispersed.

There were fourteen Cherokee members of the church at Spring Place, John found. Fourteen members in twenty years. Not many, but admittedly fourteen times as many as Mrs. Vann alone. Sixty-some students had been educated there, Brother Gambold said.

The new schoolhouse the missionaries showed off proudly. It had been built by contributions received from individuals and the Department of War. That department promised to pay two-thirds of any building expenses that might hereafter become necessary. It was unusual, he admitted, for Moravians to accept help from a government, especially money from a Department of War. Mr. Gambold grumbled, We don't believe in war, and don't believe in the church taking the government by the hand.

Among the changes made since John left here was his mother, Susanna, becoming a Christian. Major Ridge had helped as best he could with encouragement, even while candidly admitting that he could not resolve to devote himself to Jesus. He made himself useful to her by assisting with translations from spoken English to Cherokee, and he encouraged her to believe what the Bible claimed. When she converted, he expressed great joy and told her and the children he was fired with a hope that his own time would come.

Susanna took Catherine for a middle name. She was baptized the same day the new church house was consecrated at Spring Place. Major Ridge simply could not cast out all doubts, as she had, but he wanted instruction and invited the Gambolds, who were old and weakening, to open a mission near his house, which he would support financially.

Anna Gambold favored the move, but just at that time her heart gave out, a blow her husband could scarcely live through. After her burial, Spring Place became for him a lonely place, and his own body suffered, his hair turned silver. He lost his direction in life, and he supposed he must leave the house, the school. He agreed to move to Oothcaloga alone, if Major Ridge still wanted him.

Another change John noticed on his return was increased interest in church attendance. Some people walked thirty, forty miles to attend church, even though the services were in English. On Easter and Christmas, the church was sometimes filled.

John understood that many missed the special services, however, because they could not understand the numerical figures for the dates and times of day the services were to be held.

John and Elias together visited Brainerd, and there, too, the school turned out to greet two of its successful alumni. Sixty-two boys and forty girls were in attendance on this day. Not all were Christians, not by any means; but as Boudinot was assured by the missionaries, many were "hopefully pious."

Efforts were still being made by the American Board missionaries to start successful local schools, these to be affiliated with the central school at Brainerd: one local school was open at Taloney, one was being built for the Choctaws, soon to open, and one was being built for the Cherokees at Creek Path, with Reverend Butrick and his wife to take charge personally. The chiefs had been most helpful. The national council at its latest meeting, which was held near the homes of Chief Hicks and Major Ridge, passed a rule compelling parents to keep their children in school, when once entered, until they finished their education, or to pay all expenses the children had incurred for clothing, board, and tuition. They had also given the superintendents authority to take out of school such children as they thought were not learning, and with the consent of their parents to put those students to trades such as carpentry, farming, coopering, tanning, tailoring. Once they had mastered the trade they would be furnished with a set of tools at the expense of the nation.

Major Ridge spoke warmly, emotionally of the missionaries and their work and expressed thanks to them for providing a way for his son to receive an education, a great education. He said he hoped the Lord would give John a good heart, so that he might be very useful to his nation.

At the national council of 1820, other measures had been passed: one divided the Cherokee nation into eight districts, each with a court, judge, and marshal. Another levied a tax of fifty cents a year on every head of household and single person under the age of sixty. Yet another forbade bringing white families into Cherokee territory to live on land rented to them. Anybody doing so "shall forfeit and pay the sum of five hundred dollars and receive one hundred stripes on the bare back."

And another:

> Resolved, That any person who shall permit his negro or negroes to purchase spirituous liquors and vend the same, the master or owner of such negro or negroes shall forfeit and pay a fine of fifteen dollars for each such offence, to be collected by the marshals within their respective districts for the national use; and should any negro be found vending spirituous liquors, without permission from their respective owners, such negro or negroes, so offending, shall receive fifteen cobbs, or paddles, for every such offence, from the hands of the patrollers of the settlement or neighborhood in which the offence was committed; and every settlement or neighborhood shall be privileged to organize a patrolling company.

Often the population counts and other tabulations did not include the blacks, but Chief Charles Hicks prepared a letter to the Secretary of War late in 1821, which included them in several instances. He discussed his letter with Major Ridge and John, as well as with his son Leonard.

> The Cherokees may be considered in a progressive state of improvement, more particularly those in the middle part of this nation, for there is

scarcely a family but what understands the use of the card and spinning wheel, except those in the mountainous parts of this territory, who have not had the same advantages as those have had in the middle and lower parts of this nation. But the greater part of them understand the use of the wheel and cards. The arts of weaving and knitting have become part of the female attention of this nation. There are ten families within twenty or thirty miles of this place, who weave coverlets and double twilled cloth; a considerable number of persons besides these are provided with sheets to supply the wants of their families.

The agricultural labor of the male part of the Cherokees, it is hoped, will continue to advance with progress to the improvement of their farms, to supply the wants of their families and live stock, as the aid and labor of the advantage of the use of the plough are properly estimated as their best acquisition to their farms. Most families cultivate from ten, twenty, thirty, to forty acres of land, without the assistance of black people. The greatest number of whom might raise plentiful crops of corn, were they to get into the habit of plucking out one or two stalks in a hill in old ground. It is believed that there is not more than one eighth or ninth part of the families, but has either horses or cattle; and perhaps there is none without a stock of hogs. The art of making the spinning wheel and loom has been acquired by five or six Cherokees known in this neighborhood; and also making water vessels out of wood. Besides, there are six or seven others who work at the blacksmith's trade, though not to any extent, but only in repairing the plough, the axe, the gun, and shoeing of horses, some of whom even make the plough.

The convenience of mills is begun to be felt, and much wanted in different parts of the nation; as a considerable number of families that live ten of [sic] fifteen miles from any mill go to have their corn made into meal; as but five are in operation in this country, and lie scattered about in different parts. There are six grist and two saw mills owned by natives, and fourteen or fifteen grist and two saw mills owned by white men who are married into native families.

. . . The School at Brainerd commenced in the spring of 1817. Since that time, 29 boys and 18 girls have left the school, who could read and write; and the present number of scholars, including those absent, expect to return, is 100, which has been the usual number for some time, and as many as can be accommodated.

There have been baptized here ten Cherokees, two whitemen, and four African adults, and twenty-three Cherokee, and four white children.

The number of scholars at Tallony is twenty, at Creekpath eighteen. The number of adults baptized at Creekpath is seven, of children nine; of candidates for baptism four.

. . . The advances in christianization among the Cherokees, by the missionaries at that place, are twelve persons who have been baptized, and twenty-four children, of whom six are black, and five white children, and twelve are communicants; four other persons are received into the brethren's congregation from other denominations; and eight pair of marriages of the Cherokees. The present number of persons belonging to the brethren's Congregation is fifteen, including three white men married to natives; and the whole of the members, including the missionaries, is twenty at Springplace and Eukilloggee.

There has been no particular information received from Elder Posey himself, superintendent of the mission schools at the Valley Towns, as to the number of scholars belonging to that establishment, nor from the local school at Teneswattee, under his direction. The only certain accounts have been obtained, a few days past, from one of the people who had visited Elder Posey's school in October last, to satisfy his own curiosity, and to see the number of scholars there. He stated that there were fifty-four, of whom thirty-two were boys. Other accounts received last summer from the local school at Teneswattee, state that there were upwards of twenty. It is reasonable to believe that there is, at these two schools, upwards of eighty scholars, as Mr. Posey had written to the chiefs in October last, after the visit already stated, that his school was increasing, and there is good reason to believe the present number of scholars may be relied on to contain the number stated.

Hicks also said in the letter that at Brainerd four Africans had been baptized and four white children, and at Spring Place six black children had been baptized and five white children. He listed an inventory of the establishment at Brainerd, to indicate the extent of this center of successful missionary work:

The buildings at Brainerd are a dwelling house, dining room, kitchen, lumber house, meat house, a framed house for the girls, school house for the boys, framed barn, log stable, six cabins improved as dwelling houses, a grist-mill, a saw mill, smiths and carpenters' shops, a cabin used for a wash house, and five cabins occupied by the boys.

Other new laws passed while John and Elias were away at school pertained to the subject closest to their hearts, marriage; each boy wanted to marry, each prayed every night for ways to be found to marry his white girlfriend. The law was explicit about white men marrying Cherokee women, but the reverse situation was not covered:

Resolved, That any white man who shall marry a Cherokee woman, the property of the woman so married shall not be subject to the disposal of her husband, contrary to her consent; any white man so married, and parting from his wife without just provocation, shall forfeit and pay to his wife such sum or sums as may be adjudged to her by the National citizenship; and it is also resolved, That it shall not be lawful for any white man to have more than one wife, and it is recommended that all others should also have but one wife hereafter.

The American Board was pleased by Cherokee progress. The Reverend Jeremiah Evarts, their treasurer and leading writer, had given this opinion in 1822:

Encouraging prospects: It is very evident that the Cherokees are improving more rapidly at present, than at any previous time. There are more instances of laborious industry among them every returning year. There are more instances of serious inquiry after moral and religious truth. There is an increasing conviction, that many of the whites sincerely wish to promote the welfare of the Indians. The best informed and more intelligent Cherokees are very favorably disposed toward the mission and school at Brainerd. At several places in the nation, is found an earnest desire to have village schools, with regular preaching; and there is nothing to prevent the establishment of these, except what results from the want of pecuniary means, and of interpreters. It is hoped that the deficiency, in both these respects, will be removed, to such an extent, that the present generation may have lights kindled in all their borders; and that generations to come may be saved from the darkness and wretchedness of their fathers.

It used to be said, a few years since, with the greatest confidence, and is sometimes repeated even now, that "Indians can never acquire the habit of labour." Facts abundantly disprove this opinion. There are numerous instances among the Cherokees, of very laborious and long and continued industry; and, in some of these instances, the habit has commenced and become established, after the individuals had grown up in hereditary freedom from any thing like regular labour. In more instances, the habit commenced in youth, and is confirmed by practice. Som.. Indians not only provide an abundant supply of food for their families, by the labour of their own hands, but have a surplus of several hundred bushels of corn, with which they procure clothing, furniture, and foreign articles of luxury, particularly sugar and coffee, of which they are immoderately fond. Others manufacture their own clothes from cotton produced in their own fields. The current is now setting very strongly in favor of agriculture, and other laborious pursuits. All are convinced, that the very existence of the community must be preserved in this way, if preserved at all.

Notwithstanding these encouraging appearances, however, it is not to be disguised, that many things still remaining among the Cherokees are greatly to be deplored. Much poverty and wretchedness, ignorance of God,

his law, and the plan of salvation, need to be chased away, before the people generally can reach the proper standard of rational and immortal beings.
. . . The Cherokees, the Choctaws, and the other tribes, must either rise to the rank of intelligent men, and well instructed Christians, or they must melt away, destroyed by vices copied from unprincipled whites, having sold their birthright for a mess of porridge, and being left, in the land of their fathers, without property, without a home, and without a friend. Who would not be pained at so lamentable an issue?

The American Board made known to much of the country their sense of urgency. They were engaged, as Evarts said, in a battle against time.

The Office of Indian Affairs at the War Department was intended to keep track of treaties and commitments, to operate the government's trading posts, to serve Indian delegations visiting Washington, D.C., and to perform similar chores. Thomas Loraine McKenney—a tall, friendly man with blue eyes, a hawklike nose, and a clump of white hair—was prompt, courteous, punctilious, a detail-conscious administrator who liked Indians and gave his guests rein to go about and do as they pleased.

On almost any day in Washington, Mr. McKenney would have a number of Indian chiefs in tow—among them Pawnee, Sioux, Sauk, Fox, Menomini, Miami, Chippewa—guests in town to see the Secretary of War and President Monroe. He decided to have their portraits painted for his offices, actually to start a gallery of Indian likenesses. There was a respected portrait painter living in the city named Charles Bird King, a New Englander who had studied with Benjamin West in London, and he was willing to do a bust in oils for twenty dollars, or a full figure for twenty-seven. There would be criticism from the press and Congress for any expense for art, but McKenney, who made about two thousand dollars a year and had a family, was unable to spare the money to commission the artist himself. He was also unable to part with the opportunity to have the works done. The Pawnee chief had his feathered headdress, for instance, feathers all the way down to his waist. The Pawnee braves painted their faces with red from eyebrows to cheekbones. One of the chiefs had his entire face colored yellow, with ocher. All of them spent much time decorating, arranging, dressing.

Then there was Eagle of Delight, whose husband was a scowling, jealous elder named Prairie Wolf. She was a striking figure, beautiful, charming, and was one of Washington's social successes of the winter season. There was Generous Chief, son of the principal chief of the Skidi Pawnee, a six-foot-tall, handsome warrior who set the women to fluttering.

McKenney lodged his dignitaries at Brown's Indian Queen or at Tennison's hotels. They were there for weeks on end, one excuse being that Mr. McKenney had not been able to get an appointment with busy, busy, paper-inundated President Monroe. McKenney had taken his Indians to the President's Christmas ball. He had got them into the White House for that all right, had led them into the place at the height of the reception, and they were well received, too. The Pawnees wore buffalo robes painted with colorful birds and horses; in fact, most of the chiefs were covered with fur robes and were painted with thick red or yellow paint. Two wore buffalo horns. The other guests reached out gingerly to touch and cried out their greetings to the elusive Indians. Then—awesome sight, a visage as in a dream, a portrait unframed—entered Eagle of Delight, and all the guests became quiet. Her black hair, parted down the middle, had been worked into two braids, each carrying silver and beaded jewelry. She wore a green camlet coat and, marvelous to behold, a daring pair of scarlet pantaloons. Her little moccasins peeked through underneath, with decoration of colored beads.

Paint her? Of course McKenney was going to paint her. He was going to paint about twenty of them.

President Monroe simply could not grant them an appointment, even despite their success at the gala, until—and this struck McKenney as amusing—the *National Intelligencer* wrote a piece about a young Pawnee chief who had attended a Pawnee ceremony at which a pretty maiden was to be burned at the stake, in order to please the Sun God:

> The fatal hour arrived. The trembling victim far from her home and friends, was fastened to the stake. The whole tribe was assembled on the

surrounding plain to witness the awful scene. Just when the funeral pyre
was about to be kindled, and the whole multitude was on tiptoe with expectation, a young Pawnee brave, having gone unnoticed, had prepared two
fleet horses with necessary provisions, sprang from his seat and ran through
the crowd, liberated the victim, seized her in his arms, placed her on one of
two fleet horses, mounted the other himself and made the utmost speed
toward the nation and the friends of the captive.

The multitude, dumb and nerveless with amazement at the daring
deed, made no effort to rescue their victim or her deliverer. They viewed it
as an immediate act of the Great Spirit, submitting to it without a murmur
and returning to their homes.

The released captive was returned to her home after three days in the
wilderness with her deliverer. He then gave her the horse on which she
rode with the necessary provisions for the remainder of the journey and
they parted. On his return to the village such was his popularity no inquiry
was made into his conduct, no censure was passed on it. And since that
transaction no human sacrifice has ever again been offered in this or any
Pawnee tribe. The practice is now abandoned.

The brave was in Washington, one of McKenney's guests, a
handsome warrior named Petalesharro; and the story, published
on a Tuesday, earned for all the chiefs a presidential invitation to
appear on the following Monday afternoon, at which time other
guests were present, including the Vice-President, Mr. Calhoun,
the full cabinet, the justices of the Supreme Court, and several
leaders of Congress. The Indians were pleased to be so augustly
received.

One mistake McKenney had made, as he saw it, was to dress
the men in blue surtouts with red cuffs and capes, blue pantaloons, and black boots. They did not look authentic dressed this
way; they were neither whites nor reds. They did paint their
faces, which maintained an Indian air.

It was disconcerting when two of them removed their boots
and rubbed their feet.

All essential, McKenney decided, all part of the scheme arranged for the human players by a mirthful God, no doubt for his
amusement as he watched the tragedies and comedies played out
on this massive stage, America.

As usual, President Monroe spoke slowly and paused often in
order to gather his thoughts. He was glad his children were so

well attired and he hoped his children had enjoyed their visits to the ships and foundries of the War Department, and had come to see the might of their Great Father.

His statements were given assuring grunts, and one of the Pawnee chiefs, Sharitarish, spoke in reply, admitting the President's main thesis:

> But the Great Spirit made some men white and others he made red. The white man could make fine clothing, furniture and carry many guns while the red could make nothing. The white man lived upon the animals he raised at home while the red man hunted the buffalo whose skin he wore and whose meat he ate. Yet the Great Spirit intended that there should be both white men and red men and he looks down and regards them as both his children.

Turning to the President, he said,

> We have plenty of buffalo, plenty of deer and other wild animals, Great Father. We have an abundance of horses. We have everything we want. We have plenty of land if you will keep your people off of it. Before our intercourse with the white man we could lie down and sleep and when we awoke we would find the buffalo feeding about our camps. But now we are killing them for their skins and feeding the wolves with their flesh to make our children cry over their bones.

Gifts were exchanged. The President got a painted buffalo robe with beautiful pictures on it. Leaders of Congress Daniel Webster and Henry Clay, along with Chief Justice Marshall, were among the recipients of gifts, the justice now and then releasing his barking, nervous laugh. Cakes and wine were served.

An *Intelligencer* reporter present at the meeting made this observation:

> that these people are destined to soon vanish from the face of the earth . . . they still possess fine traits of character and we can never forget they were the native lords of the very soil which they are gradually yielding to their invaders. . . . Yet I firmly believe all our humane efforts to civilize them will prove to be unavailing. Whether it is [sic] they acquire our bad habits before our good ones or their course of life cannot exist under the restraints of civilization, I know not. But this I do know: it is certain that all the tribes

which have remained among us have, or are now dwindling to insignifi-
cance or [are] entirely extinct. . . .

You know that every experiment to rear the wild duck has failed, and
that they die as certainly by your kindness as your neglect.

That was much too gloomy a prospect to suit Mr. McKenney. Otherwise what a beautiful session, with hero Petalesharro
and tall Eagle of Delight making a brief talk and smiling win-
somely at the short president. What a match that, Eagle and
Monroe, McKenney thought.

Her husband, Prairie Wolf, confided in McKenney that he
could not service five wives; the management of five was too
much for him, for anybody, not to mention their maintenance.

McKenney told him about an Iowa chief who had brought all
his wives with him to Washington, including a new, young one,
and in the bar he listened to their squabbling in the rooms upstairs until, losing patience, quite drunk, he stalked upstairs to his
suite, set them all straight, smashed a few chairs, overturned a
table, then—not as yet being accustomed to living on an upper
floor—proudly stepped out of a window and fell into the street,
breaking his arm.

Georgia decided to confront the issue of Cherokee removal at
the annual Cherokee council, which was to be in October 1823 at
a new Cherokee capital, New Echota, Georgia, about four miles
from the homes of Ridge and Hicks. The state of Georgia was to
send a delegation, seeking to arrange clear ownership of the
northwestern sector of the state and to clear out the Indians.

Only two houses had been built at the new capital. The place
had been fields and woods and had been designated the capital at
the previous meeting of the council; it was an idea only, one of
Major Ridge's dreams. So far the place had a council house, a
large building open around the sides, two open pavilions facing
each other, and a log house for the clerks of the nation. The site
was at the confluence of the Coosawattee and Conasauga rivers, so
there were few water or waste problems, and for the session an
abundance of food was on hand, to be prepared by some thirty
cooks: cornbread, beef, pork, chicken and other fowl, and all man-

ner of wild game—venison, bear, opossum, raccoon, squirrel, rabbit. Thousands were expected, among them the Georgians and the federal commissioners delegated to work with them, other federal agents, delegations from other neighboring states, delegations from other tribes. Major Ridge usually led a Cherokee delegation to the Creek nation's council, and they had been sending a group to visit the Cherokees every year, the only time these old enemies, friends, and sometime war companions met.

Dozens of people wanted to stay each night with Susanna and the major in their big house, or with Watie or Chief Hicks, and dozens did so, all who could find room to lie down. There were hour-by-hour meetings of chiefs to prepare arguments, consider dangers, lobby for privileges and appointments. The federal allowance coming in for education was the biggest sum to be appropriated. Major Ridge was involved in everything, and he and Hicks and John Ross, the three leaders of the progressive chiefs and the three leaders of the council, met often in field and woods and woodlot (for there were no quarters elsewhere), in order to shape procedures. There were always dangers, though none from the federal people, none from the other tribes. Peace was now a comfortable, year-by-year luxury. The dangers came from Georgia legislators.

The major saw to it that his son met all the Cherokee chiefs. He had him appointed official translator to the council; those duties ought to bring him to the fore. Everything must be translated, English being the written language of the Cherokee government, and Cherokee the spoken language. The major, for instance, understood English but would not use it even in conversation. John Ross understood Cherokee but would not trust himself to talk to the council in that language. Hicks knew and used both and, having learned the new Cherokee syllabary, he wrote both. John and his classmates from Spring Place, Brainerd, and Cornwall both spoke and wrote English and were learning Sequoyah's syllabary. Communication was complicated.

Major Ridge still had his favorite, splendid, big horse, and he rode with the ease the Cherokees seemed to have from childhood until death. John, now recovered from the worst of his illness, selected the next most imposing mount for the trip.

John wrote an account of the meeting that appeared in a Boston newspaper:

> The appointed time for the commencement of business was the 1st of October 1823, whose dawn was the prelude of transactions the most essential and important to the Nation. . . . The whole confidence and talent of the Nation was now seated. The Agent of the United States was expected, and the Commissioners on the part of the United States and Georgia were to come. These arrived, and were received with a respect equal to the importance and weight of their commissions.

Major Ridge in friendly exuberance welcomed the commissioners representing the United States–Georgia delegation, and one of the federal commissioners replied to the welcome, complimenting Cherokee civilization. The commissioners at that point retired, to the surprise of the others—evidently assuming that time was on their side—and occupied themselves conversing with chiefs individually. John concluded that they were lobbying these individuals, trying to shake commitment to protect Cherokee lands and striking bargains. After a while the commissioners presented their objective in writing. John read it aloud, and later commented on it: "Its whole drift and motive was to impress the Cherokees with a conviction that the State of Georgia had just, but long-standing claims against this Nation, which they attempted to authenticate by quotations from some old treaties . . . entered into by the United States and this nation."

The council discussed the document and in a paper replied that the Cherokees would never part with another foot of land.

The United States commissioners then entered the discussion and, faced with Cherokee obstinacy, became harsh and threatening, which did not effect improvement. Ridge, Hicks, and Ross were unimpressed. At this point the agents became wheedling. Meanwhile, man-to-man efforts were being made by the commissioners to purchase votes. As John saw the situation: "Gentle, brilliant and forceful periods of eloquence, strongly backed by large sums of money as presents, were spent in vain."

The Creek delegation arrived. It was, as usual, headed by General McIntosh, a half-blood Creek and a relative of the Troup family of Georgia, an old friend and sometime adversary of Major

Ridge. McIntosh had brought along several Creek chiefs, all well dressed and mounted, and they received a handsome reception from the major. McIntosh was escorted to the White Bench reserved for special guests, those held in the highest esteem.

The chiefs were eager to hear him speak, confident that he would oppose cessions, particularly because the Creeks were under pressure, too; but he decided not to address the council immediately. Later, in private he told Major Ridge that he had become convinced Indians should take this opportunity to sell land and emigrate, sell while the white man was still willing to buy. The white tide rises, he said, we can't stop it; and if we don't sell, we will be cast aside homeless, and treated like animals without any place to go.

The major thought all that unlikely, and argued that recent treaties were protective of Indian rights. But McIntosh foresaw great dangers. He advised Major Ridge to urge the Cherokees to sell and emigrate to their new homeland.

The Cherokee chiefs sought to arrange their arguments, even while Georgian and federal representatives circulated freely, offering bribes. McIntosh, himself, sent John Ross an offer, a letter he had dictated to his son. In broken English it offered Ross two thousand dollars should he favor a treaty for cessions, the money a present. Another two thousand would be given the clerk of the council, Alexander McCoy, with three thousand to go to Chief Hicks, "for present." He wrote, "nobody shall know it." He wrote further that the money would be paid at once, before the treaty was signed, "and if you got any friend you want him to receive they shall receive the same amount."

Ross took the matter to Major Ridge and a few other confidants, and it was suggested that Major Ridge and Alexander McCoy talk with McIntosh, if possible that evening, and seek to find out whether the offer had the approval of the United States commissioners. The meeting was held, the two Cherokees pleading interest in knowing where so much money was originating, and McIntosh told them that the federal commissioners approved of the offer. He said, further, that he would be willing to address the council and say that he favored cessions. He ended the meeting by telling them about other bribes he had taken previously for treaties.

There was a central committee, with John Ross as chairman, and it was in this small body that McIntosh's proposition was reviewed the next day by Ross and Ridge, all in secret. The committee decided to invite the Creek chief to address the full council, and on his arrival there Major Ridge received him cordially. Ross asked to be recognized. He came forward with the letter McIntosh and his son had written. Ross handed it to the clerk, McCoy, who knew it well enough, of course, and read it out loud sentence by sentence.

When the letter was finished, after a long silence, the principal chief, Pathkiller, rose to his feet. Affected by rheumatism so severely that he could scarcely stand, he expressed his regret that a letter of this sort had been written.

McIntosh began explanations, excuses, but Pathkiller turned away. "Set him aside," he ordered.

Major Ridge took charge, began to soothe the hot tempers without condoning the bribes.

> I now address the Honorable Council. It is a talk which must spread and be universally heard. It is concerning a brother, who these twelve years has been considered a standing guardian of the interests of the rising generation. A plain maxim of this Nation is, never to trust a man who goes astray from duty, or corrupts the obligation of sacred confidence—This has been observed in McIntosh's conduct—He has stood erect, encircled with the generous confidence of the people and the authorities of his own Nation. I now depress him [sic]. I cast him behind my back. I now divest him of his trust, and put it firmly in my hand.—I do not pretend to extend this disgrace in his own Nation. He is at liberty to retire in peace. We are not advanced to public notice for confidence to make fortunes. Money is out of the question. We are not to be purchased with money. The trust placed in our hands is a sacred trust. The most distinguished chief of this Nation is liable to be disgraced, as this man, when found deficient of patriotism, that precious standard of moral excellence and political virtue.
>
> But let us not triumph in the disgrace. He may resort to the bosom of his family to spend his sorrows and revive his wounded spirits. He has been the concern of my warmest friendship and still carries my sympathies with him.

McIntosh left at once, swiftly rode south with his friends, stopping only when his horse dropped from exhaustion. The federal and state commissioners retired and decided to depart, as well.

As with other Cherokee engagements with Georgia, it was Georgia that retreated.

== 11 ==

When John wrote Sarah Northrup and her parents that he would be traveling east to Washington and would come to visit them, she was captivated by questions and excitement. He had told her in other letters that his health was improving, but she wondered if he had thrown away his crutches, which her mother would require as a condition for their marrying, and if he still loved her.

He was coming east with his father and sister Sally, aged thirteen, who had studied at Spring Place and now might qualify for a federal scholarship to a girls' finishing school. John was to leave them in Washington and travel alone to Connecticut.

Sarah saw his carriage as it rounded the last curve in the road, and she was on the stoop when he climbed down. As she ran to meet him, she noticed he had a limp, but only a slight one, and there were no crutches. She let out a yell of triumph.

The Northrups hesitated to announce the engagement. Their love for their daughter and John impelled them to approve, but even so they kept the decision private. Then the word got out. The reaction of the town of Cornwall was explosive. Fury exceeded any expectation. The newspaper, even that liberal voice, denounced the engagement as an outrage. Ministers preached sermons about female chastity, demanding that this white–Indian wedding not take place.

The Northrups steeled themselves and proudly, with grit, held to their course. They scheduled the wedding, invitations were sent out. Few attended the ceremony. Sarah and John exchanged their vows, then were rushed to a coach, and Mr. and Mrs. Northrup rode with them as far as the next town. There, and at almost every subsequent stop, crowds met the couple and angrily denounced them. At one station John replied; he admitted that he, a visitor from a far-off place, had stolen one of their prettiest flowers, but he did not feel he was inferior for that or any other reason. He came close to being fist-lashed by several men.

It was an unsatisfying start for a honeymoon, but distance proved kind, soon nobody knew or cared, and the two were left alone, John grateful that his father had not been present to meet his accusers.

False rumors were rife in Cornwall, one maintaining that Mr. Northrup subsequently lost his mind and fled. The editor of the Litchfield *American Eagle* attacked not only the lovers, but the Foreign Mission School:

> The affliction, mortification and disgrace of the relatives of the young woman, who is only about sixteen years old ["and who has thus made herself a *squaw*"] . . . will, it is believed, on examination be found to be the fruit of the *missionary spirit,* and caused by the conduct of the clergymen at that place and its vicinity, who are agents and superintend the school. And though we shrink from recording the name of the female thus throwing herself into the arms of an Indian yet, "daring to do all that may become a man or a christian," we hesitate not to name those believed to be mediately or immediately the cause of the unnatural connection; they are—[Here the writer named five men, beginning with Dr. Beecher and ending with Mr. Daggett]. . . . And the relatives of the girl, or the people of Cornwall, or the public at large, who feel indignant at the transaction, some of whom have said that the girl ought to be publicly whipped, the Indian hung, and the mother drown'd, will do well to trace the thing to its true cause, and see whether the men above named, or their system, are not the authors of the transaction as a new kind of *missionary machinery.*

There were further diatribes, and the school found it necessary to condemn mixed marriage publicly and to agree that no more would take place involving the school's people.

That stricture came before notice of the love affair of Harriet R. Gold, daughter of Colonel Benjamin Gold and John Ridge's personable cousin and friend, Elias Boudinot. When Harriet first told her parents of this other romance, her father exploded in anger. At once he wrote Boudinot a firm letter rejecting his suit.

Harriet became ill: always an effective line of defense. Harriet languished, declined, lost weight and color, until Dr. Gold, who was the colonel's nephew and Harriet's first cousin, declared that the girl was dying. He insisted on the accuracy of his diagnosis. The colonel was told his precious daughter had lost the will to live. Dr. Gold told him that he and his wife were fighting against God.

The colonel at once fired off a second letter to Boudinot, accepting him as a future son-in-law.

Harriet revived. Dr. Gold returned to routine practice of medicine.

The Gold parents did request secrecy. Nobody was to know. The colonel forbade even private conversation, except within the family. On hearing the secret, his brother-in-law did, however, feel called upon to mention the matter to the board of the school, which, as he later admitted, made the members "white as sheets."

The school felt called upon to announce that such an engagement had been formed and to denounce the human instincts that had brought them about. They branded any and all persons who had condoned it as "criminal; as offering insult to the known feelings of the Christian community, and as sporting with the sacred interests of this charitable institution."

The fever began to mount, and for her protection Harriet was hidden in a neighbor's house. On the village green, which could be seen by her and her parents, was unveiled "an enormous painting of a young woman and an Indian and, in addition, an older woman depicted as the instigator of Indian marriages." As evening fell, while church bells tolled, two young men of the town laid Harriet's effigy on a funeral pyre—a barrel of tar—and her own brother Stephen set it afire. The bells continued to toll till ten or eleven o'clock.

There is censure enough to chill the blood in the tolling hour after hour of the town bell. Pressure fell on Harriet to reconsider, to recant, to apologize, to tell her parents and brother and friends she had made a mistake.

That's not what Harriet did. She went to church on Sunday and took her place in the choir, and when she was told to leave the loft, she left proudly, head erect, still the colonel's child. "I have seen the time," she wrote, "when I could close my eyes upon every earthly object, and look up to God as my only supporter, my only hope; when I could say to my Heavenly Father with emotion I never felt before,'Other refuge have I none.'"

Back home, stories about Harriet's ordeal dismayed Major Ridge, who was still smarting from John and Sally's troubles. The major approached missionaries with a plain question, to which he wanted a plain answer: was there anything in the Scriptures or in church doctrine to forbid the marriage of an Indian man and a white woman? They assured them there was not, but the information did not appear to relieve his angry mood.

Boudinot and Harriet were married on the twenty-eighth day of March, 1826, at Colonel Gold's house, by a minister hired for the occasion, one new to all of them. The colonel himself rode with the two as far as Washington, Connecticut.

The school was forced to close its doors. After this second wedding, its support evaporated, and its board succumbed.

Poems were written commemorating the marriages of John and Sarah, Elias and Harriet. One was by Silas H. McAlpine:

> O, come with me, my white girl fair,
> O, come where Mobile's sources flow;
> With me my Indian blanket share,
> And share with me my bark canoe:
> We'll build our cabin in the wild,
> Beneath the forest's lofty shade,
> With logs on logs transversely piled,
> and barks on barks obliquely laid.
>
> O, come with me, my white girl fair,
> Come, seek with me the southern clime,
> And dwell with me securely there,
> For there my arm shall round thee twine;
> The olive is thy favorite hue,
> But sweet to me thy lily face;
> O, sweet to both, when both shall view
> These colors mingled in our race.
>
> Then come with me, my white girl fair,
> And thou a hunter's bride shalt be;
> For thee I'll chase the roebuck there,
> And thou shalt dress the feast for me:
> O, wild and sweet our feast shall be,
> The feast of love and joy is ours;

> Then come, my white girl fair, with me,
> O, come and bless my sylvan bowers.

Another came from the pen of Edward Coote Pinkney:

> Why is that graceful female here
> With yon red hunter of the deer?
> Of gentle mien and shape, she seems
> For civil halls designed,
> Yet with the stately savage walks
> As she were of his kind.

The Baptists arrived to help save the Cherokees. Reverend Humphrey Posey, the Baptist pastor in charge, opened four schools for Cherokee children and sought native teachers "to piece out instruction" while he continued his schedule of itinerant preaching. The schools operated hit or miss for about two years, then closed. After a hiatus Posey opened a single school and mission station on the Hiwassee River, below the Great Smokies. He and his assistant constructed buildings, bought livestock, imported a sawmill for lumber and a mill for corn. White Baptist volunteers joined them in December 1821, several bringing children—fifteen in all—and slaves. Soon the station had three women teaching forty Indian students in brand new quarters. Next year the size increased to seventy boys and girls, and a second school was started a five-hour hike away to the southeast.

Posey asked for a part of the federal funds for education, those annually dispensed by the federal agent, and he received five hundred dollars, enough for three teachers' salaries for an entire year, and he praised God for the government—a unique prayer for Baptists.

The mountain Cherokees were traditionalists, were devoted to the old customs, and watched the school suspiciously. Their children were intelligent, and according to Baptist Reverend Roberts learned "as fast as any Children I ever saw. They are kind, obedient, and industrious." He said their "mental powers appear to be in no respect inferior to those of whites." He wrote, "Though their skin is red or dark, I assure you, their mental powers are white—few white children can keep pace with them in learning."

The teachers at Valley Towns taught the more advanced students, who taught the others, rewarding achievement with tickets that would help buy clothing and books. The boys learned their lessons and worked at farming, the girls learned their lessons and made cloth. All heard the religious views of the pastors. The Baptists threatened to expel students who attended a ball game or a dance, who stole or got drunk.

No student was allowed to keep a horse at school. That was a rule.

The students' clothing was furnished by their parents, and each was required to bring a blanket.

On their arrival, some teachers sought to learn to speak the Cherokee language, but found it hard to master. Reverend Butrick at the Brainerd mission was having difficulties, too. In 1823 the conversion of a bilingual Indian at Valley Towns provided help with the Baptists' instruction there.

Some of the white settlers and traders discouraged the mountain Indians, telling them there was no truth in what the white preachers and teachers said. Also, the local shamans were upset by the Bible tales being circulated. The Baptists' emphasis on hell was particularly irritating; most Indians simply had no fear of death or of judgment. One Baptist ritual did bring instant favor, however: baptism by immersion in the river. This burial of sin, the cleansing of the soul "in the Savior's liquid grave," the rebirth of a convert's spirit so that a new life could begin, caused the Indians great pleasure. It resembled their own traditional ceremony of going to water. The Baptist missionaries would dress the converts in white robes and lead the march to the river, the students and congregation following, singing. The pastor would wade into the river, in the same way as a shaman, and one by one the converts would come to him, bolstered by the supportive cries and prayers of friends, and be dunked three times.

The Methodists also arrived, but they were less willing to occupy a remote and separate part of the Cherokee nation, and by 1825 they had taken so many converts that they had alienated everybody else, the American Board, the Moravians, and the Baptists. They showed no sign of caring. They brought joyfully into their fold all who would come and required little of them. The other denominations would not baptize a person simply because he claimed an awakening, or a spiritual palpitation; baptism came only after instruction and growth as a believer. In contrast, the Methodists baptized on any excuse and expected growth to follow. "Their manner of receiving members is directly calculated to lead souls to hell," according to one missionary, Isaac Proctor, of the American Board.

In giving totals of converts, the Methodists listed everybody seriously interested in the faith—white, black, and Indian. By 1828 the Methodists claimed seven hundred converts, of whom the furious Proctor believed that not more than a quarter were Indian, and he questioned whether one in twenty was a Christian.

The key to the Methodists' growing influence was the circuit rider, who slept rolled up in his blanket in a convert's house and otherwise lived in his saddle. People met him and his horse on specified days at crossroads or watering places, under ledges, near a named point; sometimes the faithful would throw up a shed roof, or even build a room for services. Between visits, the Methodist laymen would help one another and recruit others, as each sought "to grow in grace." Baptism was merely the entryway to the experience, did not require elaborate knowledge or even complete commitment. In this way, baptism could serve to encourage Cherokees who were willing to examine the new but not yet ready to break with the old.

The religious experience Cherokees liked best was the camp meeting, an experience resembling traditional Indian council meetings and all-night festivities. Hundreds of Methodists came from miles around to mill about in the woods greeting one another and seeking emotional release. Revival in the forest was familiar to the Cherokees. The Methodist emotional outbursts, annoying to the ministers from New England, pleased the Cherokees. They enjoyed sharing their spiritual and their physical feelings.

Education, either in academic subjects or in husbandry, was not of first importance to the Methodists. Their schools were described as slipshod. They called them itinerating schools, and each circuit rider—these men were at first white pastors, later were whites or Indians—had a school somewhere on his circuit. The students were children and adults who came together to learn basic language and arithmetic skills, often spending several hours a day there for months on end. The next year the circuit rider would locate the school at another place on his circuit, leaving the previous class to self-instruction or to none at all. This method taught basic skills to large numbers of people, children and adults, taught them cheaply, encouraged them to help one another, and did not require parents to send their children away from home. As the schools were not permanent and therefore did not qualify for federal monies—any one of them was likely to disappear before government action could be completed—the Methodists could claim that they alone of the denominations were in no way paid agents of the United States.

The Methodists would not stay in an assigned geographic area. They enjoyed, even gloried in, outright competition. Back home hundreds of Methodist churches contributed their mite each quarter, money to go to support the circuit riders, the itinerant preachers and their helpers, the interpreters and exhorters who were snatched from the ranks of the common people. Young, poor, dedicated, these helpers lived for the labor, lived with the people they wanted to help, ate their food, learned their language, and sometimes chose a wife from among them. Methodists baptized and taught, exhorted and encouraged, terrified and reassured, and had a great time. The pastors made their four-hundred-mile circuits, stopping at perhaps forty preaching stations. The circuit was made not once a year, not twice a year, but four to twelve times a year.

Major Ridge's dreams for the Cherokees grew in depth and breadth now that he had young people who had unlocked the box of white man's magics, who knew the Book, who could search inside all the works of the English language and speak with white men and merit attention. When he had been given audience recently with President Monroe in order to acquaint him with the Cherokee problem with the Georgians, he took John with him to translate. He had him present to translate when Secretary of War

John Quincy Adams asked about progress being made. He had
John with him at receptions and parties with Mrs. Adams and
Mrs. Monroe.

Now the major had a new dream, to start an academy in the
new Cherokee capital, where the streets were just being laid out.
One hundred lots for one hundred houses were being flagged,
with council houses for two legislative bodies, as in Washington,
and a building for the Cherokee Supreme Court and one for the
Cherokee administrative officers. The academy was to be nearby.
A library was to be part of it, with books contributed from all
over the nation and from England, and a faculty of great teachers
and writers. The main building was to be forty by forty feet
square, with four rooms downstairs and four up, with four chimneys and eight fireplaces, and many glass windows. Also the nation needed a museum, to be modeled after the Smithsonian—he
had enjoyed visiting it, a great success in Washington. The Cherokee museum would preserve artifacts of Cherokee life and history. For instance, one of his forefathers, Attacullaculla, was in no
place pictured—no artist had ever struck his likeness—and, of
more consequence, no record had been written of his negotiations
with French, English, Spaniards, and Americans, with Creeks,
Choctaws, Sioux, Shawnee, of his wars, of his ancestors, of his
views and prejudices and visions. Not even his bow, his axe, his
belt, his bridle were displayed as tokens proving there had been
such a person.

Ridge also dreamed of a newspaper printed in English and
Cherokee. Nothing could be more important than frequent no-
tices of fact, date, opinion, to unify and alert the Cherokee and to
exchange material and views with others. The council should buy
the presses at once. Use Sequoyah's characters to have type made.
Even now Cherokees in byways and in their homes were learning
the characters, learning to read, to write. Never in all the generations of all the Indians in America had any tribe had a way to
write its language; and now, here and now, the Cherokees were
prepared.

Hurry with the museum. Hire Sequoyah for the academy.
Get the type cast, order the type for the newspaper, and build a
little building for it. And lay out a capital city. A new city, and

there put all the evidences of Cherokee attainment, lay off streets and measure town lots and build houses, grow, preserve, save, change. . . .

Have I come to this, he wondered, from the place I began, from where my mother and father left me, from the going to water and the first stickball game, the hunts preceded by polite prayer, the killing of whites, the killing of Indians, even Cherokees, the thefts of slaves, the horse stealing? Have you, Major Ridge, grown into this different person, and are you growing, changing still? I scarcely know you.

Two or three of the young men should speak to the next council on experiences at Cornwall School and the immense value of education. Have David Vann speak, and John, and maybe Boudinot—dear Boudinot with his pretty wife, who has declared herself to be a missionary to the Cherokees.

He further enlarged the house for Susanna and himself and their visitors. Always there were visitors, mixed-blood, full-blood, pleading for one cause or another, one law or another, or merely wanting audience with Ridge, still elected speaker of the council. In the additions he included an apartment for John and Sarah. John, who knew New England houses, helped design the addition, which resulted in a Ridge mansion with front and back porches and balconies supported by Grecian-type columns. The house had brick fireplaces, four of them. The eight rooms had thirty windows, framed by the best available woodworkers. The paneling on the walls and ceilings was of excellent craftsmanship, as expert as John had seen even in the new White House; it was exact and was elegantly designed. In the front John had the workmen put an arched triple window, a bow window, overlooking the river and the ferry, which was one of the new commercial Ridge operations—the ferry, the store, the toll road the Ridge had caused to be built. In the back of the house, in separate buildings, were kitchens, stables, barns, hog pens, chicken house, and cabins for thirty servants. Standing around the house were the trees the Great Spirit had given this splendid site. The establishment was a testimonial: here lived a Cherokee, a civilized man. What we are trying to do here, the major believed passionately, is build a civilization.

Not the civilization of the missionaries, although their help was vital, but one of Cherokees. The missionaries were unable to see what Cherokees were, for their vision was limited by the sheen from the light of their faith. There was much in the Cherokee of value, including his knowledge of nature, his courage, his patience, his tolerance of other people, including the whites—all should be melded into Cherokee civilization. It should not be imported. The land was here, even yet saved—the high mountains, the pure rivers, the pastures, fields, forests, all here—the perfect setting for the liberation of body, mind, soul of a people.

For his part, John loved his father but found himself sucked into a vortex of his father's activities. And, of course, his mother had her home arranged as she liked, using fleets of servants who, in turn, had their schedules and preferences and who needed to be rewarded and chastised, so that his own wife, Sally, found her life fitted into small, spare, scarce openings. Once this problem was mentioned to Susanna, she began to talk to the major about a house apart for John and Sarah.

The major was frankly disappointed. John was the culmination, the fruit of his family. Argument could not persuade him; but Sally could, with gentleness, affection. She pleaded no cause except that of the very human, warm desire to live privately with her husband, and once the major understood this, he was at once launched on designs of a cottage for her and John off to itself, at least some way off to itself from his own house.

Six miles, Sally insisted. A small house, two-room.

The two-room cabin in actual fact increased, grew, spread out, as all the major's enterprises seemed to do, and it became a version of his own house, two-story, large rooms, set on a high hill among a stand of oak and hickory trees, with open fields about.

And slaves. Major Ridge gave them slaves. Sally was displeased, but how else could John expect to keep up so magnificent a place?

Always, according to the shamans, the Cherokees had owned slaves. The most powerful tribe in the Southeast, they had often managed to capture trespassers, raiders, and enemies and had made slaves of them. These were occasionally whites; more commonly they were other Indians and blacks in the eighteenth century, with the number of Indian slaves declining, that of blacks increasing.

In Europe intellectuals had agreed by 1825 that slavery was undesirable, untenable. On the American continents arguments and excuses were still given for it. The Cherokees were deep in the Southern slave region, carrying on this ancient practice along with the established whites and using, they contended, discretion and compassion. Slavery was necessary for the plantation system on which rich Cherokees depended. Rich Cherokees were, of course, the more educated Cherokees. They were chiefs—even John Ridge, a young man, a rich man, was a chief. Their wealth depended on their black slaves; their way of life required servants.

Newly arriving New England missionaries were shocked on encounters with the black slaves, whom they found to be hard-working, even-tempered people, living in squalor. Many missionaries had not at first realized that Indians owned slaves. They closed their eyes and ears to the tragedy, and even closed off their schools to blacks. Some of them did offer a Sunday school for blacks.

The Cherokee planters contended that slavery was accepted by the various nearby governments, that it was featured in both Old Testament and New, and that the slaves preferred their Cherokee situation to the more dire conditions imposed by some white planters in Georgia, South Carolina, and Alabama.

This smiling argument did not satisfy Sally Ridge and Harriet Boudinot. To their husbands' chagrin, the wives made repeated attacks on them and their system. The fact was, the ladies were upset, finding themselves in the role of slave mistresses.

At the next council meeting, John and David Vann spoke about education, and Major Ridge added his eloquent tributes. Authorization was given for the new capital's hundred lots. One way to get it approved was to suggest its name be Echota, which had been the ancient capital of the nation on the Little Tennessee River; this one should be called New Echota, the major suggested.

It would have a central square two acres in size—many wanted one acre, but the major two—and its main street would be sixty feet wide—though many wanted a more reasonable width. The lots, an acre each, would be sold and the money would build, he said, the National Academy, the Council House, a Supreme Court building, and the printing office.

During the debate the academy was for the time being eliminated, but the major and his lobbyists, among them John, Boudinot, David Vann, and young Hicks, won all the rest. Money was appropriated from the treasury for a press and type, to be struck at once, and Boudinot was elected editor and agreed to tour cities raising money for the project. The world was circling Ridge. His young men were taking their places. The fruit was on the limbs of the trees, the leaders to help him were on hand. They were more capable, better educated than he, well prepared, and he was ready to follow, to serve them.

In this year, 1825, John Ridge and David Vann were hired by the Creeks to be official negotiators, to help undo strings tied by General McIntosh and his fellow bribed chiefs. Major Ridge was also hired. He suggested a fee of ten thousand dollars for himself and fifteen thousand for each young man. The Creeks objected. The fees were exorbitant. Major Ridge reminded them that their tribe was in a most difficult situation, with millions of acres at stake, the best part of their homeland, so the fees were proper.

The Creeks realized that they had no negotiator equal to Major Ridge. They knew of the respect he had earned in Washington. He was a favorite in Creek council, too. They had no young men who could speak and write English with the facility of John and David. At a time when a schoolteacher made two or three hundred dollars a year, such fees as were suggested were outrageous; but they must be met, or at least promised.

In order to keep the Georgians from precipitously occupying Cherokee and Creek acres, the new President, John Quincy Adams, planned to send General Edmund Gaines and a sizable number of troops to secure the territory and protect Indian rights. John Ridge and David Vann were told to prepare a speech for Creek Chief Opothle Yoholo to deliver to General Gaines, a protest against the treaty signed by McIntosh and his associates. The speech was written by John and David, was delivered, and General Gaines reported its substance:

> They protest against the Treaty—they refuse to receive any part of the consideration money, or to give any other evidence of their acquiescence in the Treaty. But they have in the strongest terms deliberately declared that they will not raise an arm against the United States, even should an army come to take from them the whole of their country—that they will make no sort of resistance, but will sit down quietly and be put to death, where the bones of their ancestors are deposited; that the world shall know the Muscogee nation so loved their country that they were willing to die in it rather than sell it or leave it. This was their mode of expression, as interpreted in the presence of B. Hawkins and several instructed to state whether or not the public interpreter did his duty.

The speech impressed Gaines; the concept of a nonviolent nation was novel, without precedent in his studies. Late that year, in November, John Ridge and David Vann left for Washington with thirteen Creek chiefs. They passed through the Georgia capital, Milledgeville, accoutered in full Indian regalia. Most of the remainder of the journey was made by boat, the party dressed in white men's clothing. They took rooms at Brown's Indian Queen Hotel in Washington, while nearby, at Tennison's Hotel, settled a second Creek delegation representing the McIntosh faction, which was willing to sell all the eastern lands of the Creeks and move west. For the main group, its secretary, John Ridge, became spokesman and chief writer, preparing a Creek offer to sell land east of the "Chattahoochy River" for money, but not to cede any other lands:

> In our first letters, in the spirit of reconciliation & loyalty to the U. States, we agreed to surrender all the lands east of the Chattahoochy [sic] River. This ought to convince the genl. Government that we are not incapable of Reciprocating, in proportion to our ability, the Liberality of the U. States. Further concessions cannot be made and after the reasons first assigned, more you cannot demand. We now appeal to the magnanimity of the United States. We have travelled a long road to perform this duty. It is ordained by the Great Creator that we are so reduced as to be dependent on your power and mercy: and if in the hugeness of Strength you determine to decide by power and not by right, we shall return to our friends and live there, untill

[sic] you take possession of our country. Then shall we beg Bread from the whites and live the life of vagabonds on the soil of our progenitors. We shall not touch a cent of money for our Lands thus forced from our hands, and not a drop of a white man's blood will be spilled. And as fast as we are knocked in the head—the throats of our wives and children are cut, by the first tide of population that know not law, we will then afford the United States a Spectacle of Emigration, which we hope may be to a Country prepared by the Great Spirit for honest and unfortunate Indians.

Again, the commitment to nonviolent opposition was prominent, and most unlike the Creeks at any earlier moment in their history.

Several weeks were spent negotiating a treaty that was approved by John's and David's delegation, the Creeks giving up virtually all their Georgia lands in return for $217,600 and a perpetual annuity of $20,000. The government further agreed to pay for the removal westward of the McIntosh faction of the tribe. Finally, the only threat to a successful conclusion lay in the disposal of the $217,600. The Creek chiefs were apparently intending to divide it among themselves. Once he realized this, John was so shaken that he asked the Secretary of War to discuss the delicate matter with them. The Secretary did so, and he was told that this practice was not unusual: a Creek chief was expected to use such money for his people; nothing was underhanded, everything would be announced to the Creek council. The Secretary had no choice but to consent; however, once the treaty reached the United States Senate and word of this arrangement leaked out, speeches full of outrage erupted. Among the more fierce barrages were aimed at John Ridge and David Vann, who had been the spokesmen for the Creeks all along. Senator Littleton Tazewell of Virginia defended the young men: "And these two Cherokee boys sent here had completed a treaty on better terms for the Creeks, and worse terms for the United States, than all the diplomatic functionaries employed."

The treaty was ratified, and the chiefs divided the money, except what they paid to John and David, five thousand dollars each, one-third of the amount originally agreed.

Major Ridge was paid his full amount, even though he had not been active, had entrusted the delicate matter to his boys.

What influence he exerted with the Creek chiefs and the council is another matter. Also, earlier in the year he did meet with Andrew Jackson, with whom he had friendly relations and whom he certainly sought to influence. His warm relations with him were shown in his greeting to Jackson, translated and written down, earlier in 1825; the letter also demonstrates the emotional dramatic quality of traditional Cherokee address.

My heart is glad when I look upon you. Our heads have become white. They are blossomed with age. It is the course of nature. We ought to thank the Great Spirit who has taken care of our lives. When first we met we were taking the red path. We waded in blood until the murders of our women and children had ceased. In the land of our enemies we kindled our war fires. We sat by them until morning, when battle came with the yells of our enemies. We met them; they either fled or fell.

War is no more heard in our land. The mountains speak peace. Joy is in our valleys. The warrior is careless and smokes the pipe of peace. His arms lay idle; he points to them, and speaks to his children of his valiant deeds; his glory will not depart with him, but remain with his sons.

We have met near the house of our great father, the president. Friendship formed in danger will not be forgotten, nor will the hungry man forget who fed him. The meeting of friends gladdens the heart. Our countenances are bright as we look on each other. We rejoice that our father has been kind to us. The men of his house are friendly. Our hearts have been with *you* always, and we are happy again to take the great chief by the hand.

The artist Charles Bird King had a house on Twelfth Street NW, between E and F streets, in Washington, and he would sit under the shade trees and paint portraits for the government, as well as for other clients. He painted both John Ridge and David Vann. John was depicted with a piece of writing paper under one hand and a long goose quill in the other.

He did one of Red Jacket, the Iroquois Cicero, wearing the enormous medal President Washington had given him; one of the Creek Apauly Tustennuggee, who had the largest nose King had seen; one of the Creek Oche Finceco—he was the most handsome young Indian King had ever met—who received a ten-thousand-dollar annuity for his people, lost it gambling, and went to his loft and hanged himself; one of the Creek chief Yoholo Micco, a mild, generous person, who posed wearing a turban, a black scarf and sash, and a white coat, with a belt around his waist ten inches wide made of red, white, and blue ribbons; he had ornamented his face with red and blue lines. He made portraits of the Sioux Wanata, who wore eight or ten feathers in a sort of vest and insisted on keeping his rifle; of the Shawnee chief, the Flying Cloud, with a red handkerchief on his head; of Sauk and Fox chief Keokuk with his child, ornately dressed; and of Chippewa chief Ongewae, whose hair was as curly as a Roman emperor's. No two were alike. Each decked himself in furs and feathers and silver and medals: the Seminole Tuskosee Mathla and Neamathla, the Oto L'Ietan with buffalo horns, the Menomini chief Markomete, all different as summer and winter, each a stoic, patient model, holding the pose there in Georgetown, under the tree.

On a crisp morning in April, a large group of Creeks surrounded the plantation house and outbuildings of Chief McIntosh. They set fire to the buildings. The general's son escaped through a window, ran to the river, and swam to the far bank. All of the women and children, including his Cherokee wife, one of three wives, fled the house and slave quarters. The general, who guessed the purpose of this visit, could not bring himself to flee.

The Indians saw him at a window on the second floor and set up a cry for his life. He had a rifle but, seeing so great a number of executioners, did not bother to fire. They called to him to come down.

As he came down the stairs, which were in flames, men fired at him, many bullets striking him. Instead of allowing him to burn and thus losing their entertainment, the men entered the hallway and pulled him out feet first, propped him up in the yard, and began randomly firing bullets into his body. He stared at them until an Indian, Ockfuskie, sank his knife into his heart.

Then the Creeks plugged fifty bullets into his head.

12

The council meeting in July 1827 was one of mourning. Recently Charles Hicks and the Pathkiller had died. The old man's death had been expected; but Hicks, his principal assistant, had fallen ill from a cold he had caught by sleeping on the ground on his way home one night, and pneumonia had taken him suddenly.

Both losses came in January, and the Cherokee government for six months had rested on a wobbly arrangement, on Major Ridge as speaker of the council and his protégé, John Ross, as president of the national committee, the two of them elected chairmen of the bicameral legislative bodies.

Georgia welcomed the passing of the old regime, which had been able to nullify that state's efforts. They had reason for hope that a new administration would be more susceptible to influence.

To the council, President John Quincy Adams sent three commissioners to inquire politely among the Cherokees what changes might be expected. Many other observers were present when the first Indians began to arrive for the council at New Echota that summer. Thousands came, men, women, children, and made camp all about. Feasts were prepared and dances held as the opening sessions approached. There was no set day for opening deliberations; a council started once all the distinguished guests arrived.

Early in the session Major Ridge and John Ross presented a new constitution, a compilation of existing laws and methods. It imitated the United States Constitution, particularly its preamble:

> We, the Representatives of the people of the Cherokee Nation, in Convention assembled, in order to establish justice, ensure tranquility, promote our common welfare, and secure to ourselves and our posterity the blessings of liberty; acknowledging with humility and gratitude the goodness of the sovereign Ruler of the Universe, in offering us an opportunity so favorable

to the design, and imploring His aid and direction in its accomplishment, do ordain and establish this Constitution for the Government of the Cherokee Nation.

Significantly, the Cherokees committed themselves to a nation under God. Jefferson had mentioned God in the Declaration of Independence, but the United States Constitution, written by Gouverneur Morris, did not; neither did any seal or motto of the new nation. The Cherokee reverence was a significant addition to government and revealed John Ridge's influence.

The council's adoption of the new constitution alarmed the Georgians who were present. Accepting the Cherokee as a nation would further establish their rights to territory Georgia also claimed as its own, along with lands claimed by the United States. Even President Adams' delegates, who favored the idea of a Cherokee constitution, criticized the words "sovereign and independent," contending that the term was acceptable only in terms of Cherokee internal affairs.

The council, under the rules of the new constitution, was unable to elect a principal chief until the spring meeting. John Ross, who had assumed most of the work of the dead chiefs, was made acting chief, and Hicks's son William was given his father's title, was made acting assistant chief.

Major Ridge was in his mid-fifties when the political campaign for principal chief began. Better to elect a younger man, he believed, to serve in that post; new challenges needed new men. He was impatient with the threats of Georgians and Jacksonians, their chorus of hateful demands, the feverish dedication to their own nation sprawling, bawling, hacking its way westward, solving eastern problems of poverty and overpopulation by taking Indian land. As they saw it, all that stood in the way of a United States dominating the continent were the splintered, divided Indian tribes. Better to have young men in the top posts of government, who would have the patience to meet these opponents and who spoke and read English. The very progress he had encouraged had left Major Ridge behind—or so he admitted to Susanna; to John and Sally; to Boudinot and Harriet; to his other nephew,

Boudinot's brother Stand Watie, who was beginning to show out-standing ability; to David Vann; and even to John Ross.

Also, Major Ridge was burdened by business. He had en-couraged all manner of growth and found himself master of vast fields and many slaves. Once upon a time he and Susanna had planted a few apple trees. Now they had more than a thousand. Count the cattle on the hills, the swine, the wagons, carts, sleds, the horses. Count the slaves, these families of human beings, as Harriet and Sally so often reminded him, human beings in all respects, with hunger for food and affection; he had recently seen two of them holding hands, a man and woman, and the sight had moved him, the two seated on a bench, a log that had been axed and shaped, together discussing some crisis perhaps—an illness, or maybe they had received a threat of another sort—or they were accepting, that's all, they were acceptors of another orderly day, aware of the one step at a time of their lives. The incident, even though a small fragment of life, told Major Ridge that these two were nothing less than human beings, and that Sally and Harriet were in the right.

He had fifty human beings attentive to him, depending on him, and John had two score.

He was also busy with New Echota. He was overseeing com-pletion of the Council House: a log building, two stories, plank flooring brought from a sawmill, glass windows, brick chimneys and fireplaces, a stairway to conference rooms on the second floor.

Progress was Ridge's everyday attitude. Change occurred ev-erywhere he went, and the atmosphere became heady. Opposition grew up around him. It became thick and suspicious among the shamans and apprentice shamans and their followers. All this so-called progress was unnerving. One chief, Big Half-breed, merci-lessly drove his octogenarian wife out of their home when she confessed to wanting to join the Moravian church. Chief Big Cabin refused to permit his young Creek girl slave to attend church services and beat her whenever she did so. At the Ameri-can Board mission at Haweis, Reverend Elsworth had his service interrupted when he asked a girl of thirteen to interpret the ser-mon for the congregation; venerable chief Noisy Water came forward, criticizing the use of a child to instruct adults. When his interference was criticized, Noisy Waters, hurt, embarrassed, left the meeting, issuing angry threats, saying he would whip Elsworth.

Other missionaries were threatened seriously. One claimed his life had been threatened when he was accosted by two sons of Indian Thomas Pettit. A convert of the American Board, John Huss, was told not to return to Turkeytown. If he did so, the chief told Huss he would put out his eyes. Huss returned anyway, defying the threat.

Some of the resentment of change was vengeful, some amusing. Cherokee boys, revolting against the everlasting criticism of ball games, prepared a field in sight of one of the mission houses, stripped naked, and held their game there.

Preachers were interrupted by hecklers trained by shamans to ask questions during services. "Who made the Savior?" "Why did not God make man holy?" "Why did he let Satan tempt Eve?" "Why could God not lock out Satan from the garden?"

As the major well knew, every change in laws was abhorrent to the full-bloods. There were now more than one hundred new laws, some of them too complicated for even the major to master. It was easy enough to read the one outlawing polygamy in the future, but what business was it of the government, the decisions in marriage of its citizens? the shamans asked him.

And if a husband of two or three wives did join a church, he was required to enter with one wife only, which meant he must make two heartbreaking decisions. And why were there rules against conjuring, while almost all Cherokees, including church members, engaged conjurers as needed and trusted to the magic of the shamans to predict, to protect, to cure, to take revenge on others. Even the meetings in the town council houses were always opened by a conjurer equipped with a preparation of the black physic for all present, the medicine needed to purify the mind and spirit. The Cherokee had his own religion and customs, enjoyed his all-night dances, and was weary of the admonitions, restrictions, warnings of white people and their Indian friends. The new laws passed by the council at New Echota were like black seeds in a bowl, beyond translating and recalling, one as tough as another. The elders could recall the time when no laws existed, except the blood laws requiring revenge.

At the old council meetings, between 1808 and 1817, only three laws had been passed, while in the ones between 1818 and 1827, more than one hundred had been passed. Who wanted to clothe his life with so many garments? Was John Ridge, or John Ross, or the major to be the arranger, director of everybody's life?

Take this law. It's in English, of course. Can somebody translate it for the town council?

> Resolved by the National Committee and [concurred in by the] Council: That all lawful contracts shall be binding and whenever judgment or judgments shall have been obtained from any of the Courts of justice in the Cherokee Nation against any person or persons whatsoever on a plea of debt, it shall be lawful for such person or persons to stay such judgment or judgments by giving bond with sufficient security within five days after such judgment shall have been issued; and the stay shall not exceed for all sums under ten dollars, twenty days; for all sums from ten and under thirty dollars, sixty days; for all sums. . . .

Laws about the new national treasury; about marriage, requiring that Cherokee women who marry white men must be joined "by a minister of the gospel or other authorized person"; about alcohol, prohibiting its use at ball games, all-night dances, and other public gatherings; about rape, which had been virtually unknown in earlier times, when sexual relations between male and female were considered natural, marriage and divorce were easily arranged, and children were reared by uncles and aunts; but now a wife became the exclusive companion of one man. This law had to be passed to protect women, to make it unlawful for a man to lay violent hands upon any female in a forcible attempt to ravish her.

Consider the new oath of office, requiring a Cherokee to swear solemnly "by the Holy Evangelists of Almighty God"— which god? What god? The Great Spirit or the Christians' God? What Evangelists?

Nobody liked the poll tax levied on each head of a household. Nobody liked the law permitting loans to be made by the nation's treasurer to wealthy Indians.

The one national printing press was to be in the control of Christians.

The house lots at New Echota had been sold but all had gone to rich people.

The new constitution, what is the need of it? It was favored by John Ross, Major Ridge, John Ridge, George Lowrey, Elias Boudinot, Alexander McCoy—the very people who had no need of it, all of them peepers through the cracks of every white man's door. Did a Cherokee family living in their log house, cooking their corn and bean bread and rabbit stew, need a constitution? Did a woman trudging through snow carrying slop to her pigs need a constitution?

The animosities led to a special national council called by resentful chiefs. White Path and other chiefs, as well as hundreds of Cherokees, attended and enjoyed the quarreling and dances, took their tribe's leaders to task, passed resolutions, and broke into factions, some favoring a particular law, others opposing.

White Path, Kelechulah, Rising Fawn, Big Tiger, Big Cabin, Katchee, and Terrapin Head were major figures in this faction. The shamans were at work: Cherokee religious services multiplied as shamans told about their visions and interpreted dreams. One story making the rounds was of a Cherokee woman who gave birth to triplets, all three with teeth in place, and the firstborn spoke to her in Cherokee, criticizing her for venturing away from the Cherokee religion.

All night the critics of reform danced, and all day they talked in council, even after it was clear that no one trusted anybody else. Extremists hinted at killing all Christian Indians. Reports arrived at the meeting that slaves back home were burning the houses. Murders were reported. One report heard by missionaries was that Big Tiger had been elected king of this extralegal council. He was a known sorcerer and, according to rumor reaching Spring Place, a thief, as were his sons.

One resolution called for closing all the missions.

Another called for canceling all the new laws.

The council members finally returned home, their alliances in disarray. Their movement, recently led by many, came to be leaderless. As the day approached for election of members to the authorized, legal Cherokee council, the normal level of politicking began, the experienced politicians emerged, ones better organized and directed. Three months of open, disorderly rebellion began to recede into regular channels. The effort to destroy the government withered; its slogans were by now boring.

Nobody had kept written records of this emotional, nationwide rebellion of the full-bloods, the disillusioned non-Christians, and the shamans: nobody had thought to do so, even though Sequoyah's syllabary was highly regarded among them.

John Ross and Ridge had ridden the revolution out. Ross had been the one who had advised waiting. Urged by Major Ridge and others to defend the constitution and to explain the new laws, Ross chose not to do so. He would not feed the fire. It raged and in three months was only ashes, as he had predicted it would be.

Ross talked with Major Ridge about how much time either of them could afford to give to Cherokee politics. The major's businesses included a half-interest in a store, a toll road, a ferry, a plantation. John Ross and his brother Lewis were also planters and storekeepers, and John was the owner of the ferry at Ross's Landing. He was as busy as Major Ridge but was willing to leave much of the work to Lewis and to give most of his own time to the nation.

Ross told the major that Assistant Principal Chief William Hicks had sat down with an emissary from the President who had come to raise questions about removal to the West, and William had asked how much his own improvements—his house and sheds and clearings—would be worth to the government. William was obviously entertaining the idea of his own family's removal, if the price were high enough. Was such a man to be trusted with affairs of the nation? Obviously not, Ross concluded. It was clear, in the major's eyes, that Ross did not mean to retain his assistant principal chief.

Ridge supposed he must support John Ross for the highest office, but he wanted something for his son John, too. What was for John, for David, for the young, educated leaders?

The voting began. It was carried out in every town, and the voting was honest. Each town chose its representatives, as the

Constitution required. They were to elect the national officers at this autumn's council.

For that council the visitors arrived once more at the Ridge and Watie and Hicks homes, threatening to force the rooms to explode, Susanna claimed. Everybody who came was fed and given a bed. New Echota itself was filled too; the village and forest overflowed with people, food, politicking, speeches, proclamations written in the new lettering, which was used on every occasion. The votes were cast and counted.

In the race for principal chief, John Ross was elected overwhelmingly. For assistant chief, William Hicks—to his consternation—was passed over, and George Lowrey, kinsman of John Ross, was elected. For the newly created post of adviser to the chief, Major Ridge was elected. The major's previous position as speaker of the council was taken by Chief Going Snake, and clerk of the council went to Alexander McCoy—yet another descendant of Scots traders. Rumors were circulated, however, that McCoy had sat down with the emissary from President Adams, Colonel Hugh Montgomery, and had been curious about what price might be given him for his improvements; so there was a change of mind resulting in the cancellation of his election. The post went to John Ridge.

John Martin was elected treasurer of the nation, an office more honorary than practical, as there were no funds and there was no Cherokee currency. The Cherokees did receive $7,500 annually from the federal government as annuities on past treaties, but this year John Ross had already spent $5,000 of that on the council meeting. To be treasurer was an honor, a privilege, and not much more, as Martin understood.

Among those personally hurt by the elections were Hicks and McCoy. Defeated, their loyalties questioned, their offers to serve had been rejected by the Ridge–Ross political machine, which held no less than four of the top offices. That party also had the newspaper. It was in charge of the money, the words, the planning, the vision, and the dreams. William Hicks felt he had been raped by a system created and controlled by these former friends. His father had been one of their group, but he had been cast aside. Hicks wandered about as if in a trance, even his body tottery and his direction wavering, fury and hurt confusing his senses.

John Ross had moved from Ross's Landing to a plantation only a mile from Major Ridge's, to be near New Echota. He built a comfortable house on the Coosa River. His orchards were planted with all manner of fruit, and on his lawns were peacocks, symbols of his wealth and pride.

In Georgia a new song was making the rounds among the whites.

> All I ask in this creation
> Is a pretty little wife and a big plantation
> Way up yonder in the Cherokee Nation.

13

The printing press arrived in New Echota. Over the decades metal imports had created excitement—the gun, the pistol, the mill, the forge—each instrument had brought magic of its own, but none more than this black contraption brought to the Boudinots.

With this a writer, such as Boudinot, could make weekly reports to Philadelphia, Boston, Washington, London. . . .

Jeremiah Evarts of the American Board had seen to its selection and the casting of type. And here in New Echota in the new house made for it, a room twenty by thirty feet with doors at each end, the press was ensconced, was even now being cleaned of dust and polished to a shine by Harriet Boudinot.

Elias Boudinot, as editor, was paid three hundred dollars annually. A printer living in Tennessee had been hired, a Christian named John Foster Wheeler, and the council had agreed to pay him four hundred, which embarrassed Boudinot. Even so, paid more than the editor, the printer insisted that he must have an assistant.

Boudinot and Harriet had prepared an advertisement, which read, "To subscribers who can read English, the price of the paper is $2.50 annually, if paid in advance . . . to subscribers who can read only the Cherokee language, the price will be $2.00 in advance, or $2.50 if paid within the year." Subscriptions were coming in. A number of newspapers had agreed to exchange copies, among them the Washington *National Intelligencer*, the New Hampshire *Patent and State Gazette*, the Boston *Statesman*, the New York *Mirror*, the *Niles Weekly National Register*, and the *Journal* of Georgia.

Once the thousand-pound press was in place and its furniture and type were ready, the moment arrived to run a test. Printer Wheeler was present. So was his white assistant, Isaac

Harris, who entertained himself by muttering profanities. He tried setting a few words in the Cherokee type and dismissed that with a flurry of oaths, leaving the Cherokee work to Wheeler.

Where is the goddamned paper? Harris asked Boudinot.

The paper? The paper? Boudinot repeated.

The paper for printing on, Harris said.

There was none. It had been forgotten in the excitement of the press's arrival.

Boudinot often traveled in search of contributions. He spoke in churches and to clubs, and was adept at raising money. One such speech was delivered to the First Presbyterian Church of Philadelphia in 1826:

> You behold an *Indian*; my kindred are *Indians*, and my fathers sleeping in the wilderness grave—they too were Indians. But I am not as my fathers were —broader means and nobler influences have fallen upon me. Yet I was not born as thousands are, in a stately dome and amid the congratulations of the great, for on a little hill, in a lonely cabin, overspread by the forest oak I first drew my breath; and in a language unknown to learned and polished nations, I learnt to lisp my fond mother's name. In after days, I have had greater advantages than most of my race; and I now stand before you delegated by my native country to seek her interest, to labour for her respectability, and by my public efforts to assist in raising her to an equal standing with the other nations of the earth.

Using the recent census figures, he listed many impressive items: 22,000 cattle owned by Cherokees, 7,600 horses, 2,500 sheep, 46,000 swine, 2,488 spinning wheels, 762 looms, 2,943 plows, 172 wagons, 10 sawmills, 31 gristmills, 62 blacksmith shops, 8 cotton machines, 18 ferries, many miles of year-round roads, and 18 schools.

Boudinot was personable, able, himself an example of Cherokee advances, and he was successful. In all respects, his life was a success. He was happy. He had built for Harriet and himself a house near the printshop: two-storied, seven rooms, with a rock-walled cellar. The fireplace mantels were moulded, the chimneys were brick. Porches stood front and back. He and Harriet loved it, and they loved each other and their children—and their work.

The first issue of the *Phoenix* came off the press February 21,

1828, on paper brought by Harris from Knoxville, Tennessee. In size it was four superroyal pages, five columns on each. Printed in English and in Cherokee, it contained an editorial by Boudinot, part of the newly prepared Cherokee constitution, the Lord's Prayer in both Cherokee and English, and a thesis by Reverend Worcester praising Sequoyah's syllabary. It was the first newspaper ever printed by Indians, the first ever printed for them, the first ever printed—at least in large part—in an Indian language.

Missionary Worcester, who was an expert linguist, and his wife moved to New Echota to be near the Boudinots and the press, and they worked day and night translating religious literature into Cherokee. A hymnal was printed, about fifty pages of text, and they proclaimed it to be the first Cherokee, the first Indian book ever printed. They prepared a Cherokee edition of the Gospel of St. Matthew.

One of the frequent visitors was Boudinot's uncle, Major Ridge, who took the books in hand. Worcester told him that Cherokee was the most complicated language he had studied, that he and Boudinot had isolated 178 forms of the verb "to tie" in the present indicative tense alone. He praised Boudinot, which embarrassed the young man but pleased Major Ridge. Boudinot's devotion to playing Indian ball was his only sin, Worcester said; except for that, he was acceptable indeed.

At New Echota Major Ridge also saw to the completion of the Supreme Court building, with its elevated judge's bench and the benches for jurors, witnesses, and visitors.

Major Ridge liked Worcester. Tall, wiry, black haired, scholarly, a printer from Peacham, Vermont, a linguist of the Andover Theological Seminary, he was a minister who had dedicated himself to the mission fields and, instead of being sent to India, his preference, had been assigned to this place by the American Board.

The place did look like parts of New England, he and his wife, Ann, agreed. She was a pretty and spirited bride who had, she supposed, been picked by him to be a helper in his work. In the one-horse carriage during the fifty-day trip to New Echota, they had come to know each other well, and were—in her view of it—in love.

Fortunately, Boudinot met them, and they him, and never was a match more favorable for the printed word. They also met and liked John and Sarah Ridge. And now they met his father, this affable great bear of a fellow, this outright idealist, talking about the completion of the Supreme Court building.

Who is this Phoenix? Major Ridge asked Worcester. Boudinot had proposed the name. The weekly was named the *Cherokee Phoenix*, in that the Cherokees must rise like the phoenix from the ashes of the past.

On the newspaper's mast was printed, Worcester showed him, three words: "I will arise."

New Echota itself was rising, Major Ridge noted proudly. A visitor described the scene:

> The ground is as level and smooth as a house floor; the center of the nation —a new place, laid out in city form—one hundred lots of one acre each—a spring called the public spring, about twice as large as our sawmill brook, near the center. . . . Six new frame houses in sight besides the Council House, Court House, printing office, and four stores, all in sight. . . . The stores in the nation are as large as the best in our town in Litchfield County; their large wagons of six horses go to Augusta and bring a great load, and you will see a number of them together. There is much travel through this place. I have seen eleven of these large wagons pass by Mr. Boudinot's house in company.

Boudinot's first editorial was a criticism of white hunger for Cherokee land. Georgia, encouraged by success in removing the Creeks out of the state, was applying more pressure on the Cherokees. Boudinot promised "not to intermeddle with the policies of our neighbours . . . we will not return railing for railing, but consult mildness, for we have been taught to believe that a soft answer turneth away wrath, but grievous words stir up anger."

The Georgia Legislature passed a bill placing all lands in Georgia under Georgian judicial jurisdiction, which, as they interpreted it, included the Cherokees' territory. Also, in December 1828, they passed a resolution, intended to be a warning, a testing of the waters:

> That the policy which has been pursued by the United States toward the Cherokee Indians has not been in good faith toward Georgia. . . . That all

the lands, appropriated and unappropriated, which lie within the conventional limits of Georgia belong to her absolutely; that the title is in her; that the Indians are tenants at her will . . . and that Georgia has the right to extend her authority and her laws over the whole territory and to coerce obedience to them from all descriptions of people, be they white, red, or black, who may reside within her limits.

The resolution further said that Georgia would not use force to exercise her authority "unless compelled to do so."

Boudinot was annoyed but sought to be considerate in reply, as John Ridge and John Ross advised. He relied on the federal government to protect Cherokee rights. Harriet also encouraged the attitude of goodwill, of kindness—at least she did in the moments when her babies and relatives gave her quiet and her husband's schedule allowed her sight of him.

Not only did Elias and Harriet have children of their own, but they had many nieces and nephews who by Cherokee custom were theirs to rear. The nieces and nephews did enjoy living in the big Boudinot house. They constituted a family invasion, often bringing their blood parents with them. Harriet persevered, adjusted to living with twenty to thirty people; sometimes she even enjoyed it. She was running a home, a small school, a hospital, a Christian mission station, and, of course, helping Elias run a newspaper, one so far-reaching in success that now more than one hundred other newspapers sought to exchange copies with it.

Worcester helped with the newspaper. He and Boudinot conferred about subjects for articles; developing such topics as the Beneficial Effects of Laughter, Sunset in the Alps, the Excavation of Pompeii, Recipes for Insuring Health, the Evils of Alcohol. . . . For each issue Worcester contributed an article from his own hand.

Mail poured in. Previously federal post offices had been opened at Spring Place and Ross's Landing, and a new one had to be opened at New Echota to handle the *Phoenix* mail. Worcester, who had used the power of the American Board to help bring this new post office about, was appointed its postmaster.

The *Phoenix* had as one of its readers Governor John Forsyth of Georgia, who sent copies to President Adams and to Andrew

Jackson. What was to be done with the impertinence of these Indians? And who were these ever-present missionaries, these weepers from the North? Did anybody believe that Georgia, or any other state, would tolerate much longer Indians claiming national sovereignty, living within its borders with their own legislature, courts, and laws? Would the federal government take action to remove them as promised? Georgia was asking no more than had been promised by President Jefferson and the United States Senate, than was assured her in return for lands of vast size and fertility now comprising two states, Alabama and Mississippi. If the federal government still would not proceed, was Georgia expected to play invalid?

In 1828, in the United States national election, Andrew Jackson won the presidency. He and his wife, who was ill, were living at the Hermitage in Tennessee when the word was received. For years, since the battles of Horseshoe Bend and New Orleans and since his conquest of the Spanish and Indians in Florida, he had nurtured ambition to lead the country as president. *Mr. President.* Hear the words. They sounded like a bell. *Mr. President,* do come once more to Washington, and this time all of us do so want to be attentive to you.

Mr. President. An echo in the word itself, a resonance. But no fear in it. Very polite: pres-i-dent. There was more size and daring to *emperor. King* had a sting to it. Nothing in *president* to suggest that here was the final, the unnegotiable directive. The damned ruler.

Probably they'd try to bury him under papers and meetings. History does not roll on details, it sweeps the horizons.

One hundred seventy-eight votes in the electoral college, *Mr. President,* to only eighty-three for Mr. Adams. A grand victory.

His wife died two days after his election: after the elation, the new elevation, she passed away and brought to a halt the celebrating, stopped the loud music in his head. From a peak of elation, he was taken as close to death as he had ever stood, there in the room beside her.

Now, his political opponents had done this to them, to him, attacking him viciously, slandering, libeling, belittling him, kill-

ing her. At her funeral, he threw his body across her grave. Even
in the rain he prostrated himself over her, as near her precious
self as ever again he would be.

Jackson, President-elect, sent this message to a Georgia congressman: "Build a fire under them. When it gets hot enough,
they'll move."

Many blacks—perhaps most living in the Cherokee nation—
spoke and understood both Cherokee and English. They therefore knew much about the developments taking place under the
laws. For instance, they knew that even yet they were unable to
vote, to hold office, to marry or make love to a Cherokee or a
white, to sell whiskey, to own property in the nation. They had
no right to counsel, to testify in court, to protect themselves phys-
ically, even if attacked. Removed from citizenship, without repre-
sentation, denied freedom to leave, they had the stolen right to
teach one another, provided they did it unobtrusively, the right to
tell stories snatched from the Bible and to create stories and songs
of their own.

A sister of John and Lewis Ross married a Methodist circuit
rider, and directly her two wealthy brothers were signed up as
"seekers" by the Methodists. The other denominations stood by,
mortified. Why, the Rosses lived only a few miles from Brainerd
and had often encouraged it. The missionaries stationed there
could only assume that it was another John Ross political maneuver, that he saw advantages in identifying himself with the
church most popular with poor people and the full-bloods, the
religion just now sweeping the nation.

Harriet Boudinot had given birth to two babies and was carrying a third. It was the imminent arrival of the third that induced her parents, Colonel and Mrs. Gold, to come for a visit.
They would drive themselves in their buggy, trusting to their
favorite horse to see them all the way from Cornwall to New
Echota.

When they first reached Cherokee country, the Golds
stopped at Lewis Ross's house and were invited to stay a night or

two. He had a richly furnished home and food aplenty, as they found out. The Golds decided, if this were Indian life, they could adjust to it nicely.

The Golds found the Boudinots situated in their own pleasant house. Their larder, pantry, and cellars were well stocked. The colonel wrote, "They get their supplies of clothes and groceries—they have their year's store of teas, clothes, paper, ink, etc. from Boston, and their sugar, molasses, etc. from Augusta. They have two or three barrels of flour on hand at once." The three grandchildren won them over completely—little Mary, William, and Eleanor. They were bright and affectionate, and each had Harriet's light complexion and blond hair. Grandfather Gold walked with Eleanor, the oldest, to school each morning, a one-teacher operation run by a friend of the Worcesters, Miss Sophia Sawyer. Miss Sophia had become discontented at Brainerd and had migrated to New Echota under the Worcesters' protection.

The Golds received John Ridge and Sally for a visit. They again met Major Ridge, who arrived mounted on his great horse accompanied by a mounted black servant. Every day they were engaged by brilliant people who loved their daughter and her beautiful family. Harriet assured them that she envied the situation of no one in Connecticut.

From outside the courthouse, Colonel Gold could look through the windows at Miss Sophia's class: two black scholars were sitting with children of the Cherokee elite, Vanns, Hicks, McCoys, Martins, Fields, and the white Worcesters. He heard Miss Sophia discuss the geography of Europe and America, and when she told the children about the poverty of Greece, he marveled at their reaction. They decided to collect money for the little Greek children.

The next day the students brought to class their contributions, totaling three dollars and sixty cents, which was sent along to the American Board.

John Ridge became licensed as a lawyer. He also enlarged his plantation and bought the improvements on an adjoining one. In all, he had ninety-six cleared acres lying on both sides of the Coosa River. On the high ground he had apple and peach orchards and seven houses. His and Sally's own house now had a piazza running its entire length. He had two stables, three corn-cribs, a smokehouse, and many sheds, coops, and pens; he worked seventeen slaves in the fields.

Nearby at Turkeytown, he had bought the ferry from the estate of the Pathkiller. John had been executor of that estate, and he knew the ferry was a highly profitable venture, with an income of four dollars a day.

In July 1829, an event took place that shook the Cherokees' confidence in their ability to control their lands. It was more startling than an earthquake or a killing flood. The first inkling of the news was, rumor recalled, that a young black slave found a peculiar-looking stone and showed it to his white master, who showed alert interest at once. Where had the lad found it?

The slave told him; the spot was east of New Echota by about thirty miles.

Another later rumor attributed the discovery to an Indian youth living on Ward Creek who sold his pebble to a white trader, a Yankee, who recognized it for what it was.

Gold.

For a generation—at least since 1804—the gold mined in the United States came from North Carolina, with twenty million dollars' worth mined to date; but this new strike lay predominantly south of the North Carolina border, and much of it was within the Cherokee territory, within the boundaries of Georgia.

To Georgia now came the miners in droves, flinty, tough, certain of their rights, uncareful and uncaring men.

In 1829 there were few ways for people to become wealthy. There was no market in stocks or shares, no franchises to be bought or sold, few factories in the South, few opportunities. The most likely ways were gambling or finding gold. Gold was the great elevator of men's fortunes. Luck and gold. Gold and luck. Lucky gold. Golden luck. Gold was as close to an earthly god as a man could find, and with gold he could have earthly goddesses, would merit respect from brothers, partners, enemies. Gold opened all doors. Nothing else was as instantly persuasive.

Here are the scales, here are the gold nuggets. They weigh five hundred grains, enough to buy almost anything in Georgia, including you. You say I broke the law in getting it? There is no law above this five hundred grains. Gold makes its own laws.

It was the largest gold strike since North Carolina's. The gold was on the surface of the ground and in the streams, free for the taking. A man's fortune could change in a second, here in the Georgian fields. Every day more miners were arriving, discovering, crying out with joy. Communities of huts were going up on the muddy fields at Auraria, Dahlonega. One reporter wrote, "The dust became a medium of circulation, and miners were accustomed to carry about with them quills filled with gold, and a pair of small hand scales, on which they weighed out gold at regular rates; for instance 3-1/2 grains of gold was the customary equivalent of a pint of whisky."

The autumn of 1829 continued the invasion of men and mules, followed by the ravishing of the streams and banks, followed by thefts and deals, lies and purchases. Gold miners were not proper neighbors. The Cherokee council met, shocked and diminished by events too large to grapple with. They evaded the problem, delayed. William Hicks and Alexander McCoy, embittered, were still smarting from last year's defeats; the chiefs sought to mollify them and their friends. A few new measures were introduced. The full-bloods wanted a new law and John Ross, John Ridge, Elias Boudinot, and other mixed-blood leaders welcomed the chance to please them. Their initiative put into written form an age-old law, and strengthened it:

Whereas a Law has been in existence for many years, but not committed to writing, that if any citizen or citizens of this nation should treat and dispose of any lands belonging to this nation without special permission from the national authorities, he or they shall suffer death; therefore, resolved, by the Committee and Council, in General Council convened, that any person or persons who shall, contrary to the will and consent of the legislative council of this nation in general council convened, enter into a treaty with any commissioner or commissioners of the United States, or any officers instructed for the purpose, and agree to sell or dispose of any part or portion of the national lands defined in the constitution of this nation, he or they so offending, upon conviction before any of the circuit judges of the Supreme Court, shall suffer death; and any of the circuit judged aforesaid are authorized to call a court for the trial of any such person or persons so transgressing. Be it further resolved, that any person or persons, who shall violate the provisions of this act, and shall refuse, by resistance, to appear at the place designated for trial, or abscond, are hereby declared to be outlaws; and any person or persons, citizens of this nation, may kill him or them so offending, in any manner most convenient, within the limits of this nation, and shall not be held accountable for the same.

All who spoke at the council favored passing the measure. Aged Chief Womankiller spoke most eloquently:

My sun of existence is now fast approaching to its sitting, and my aged bones will soon be laid underground, and I wish them laid in the bosom of this earth we have received from our fathers who had it from the Great Being above. When I shall sleep in forgetfulness, I hope my bones will not be deserted by you. I do not speak this in fear of any of you, as the evidence of your attachment of the country is proved in the bill now before your consideration.

I am told that the Government of the United States will spoil their treaties with us and sink our National Council under their feet. It may be so, but it shall not be with our consent, or by the misconduct of our people. We hold them by the golden chain of friendship, made when our friendship was worth the price, and if they act the tyrant and kill us for our lands, we shall, in a state of unoffending innocence, sleep with thousands of our departed people. My feeble limbs will not allow me to stand longer. I can say no more.

Finally, nothing was done in council about the miners or Georgia. Depend on national influences to force Georgia to relent, missionaries privately advised. Take no rash action yourselves, either against Georgia or the miners. It's too big a problem for piecemeal measures or for resolutions.

Several weeks later, on December 8, President Jackson sent to Congress his first message, and in it he endorsed the removal of Indians from eastern America, "voluntary, for it would be cruel and unjust to compel them to abandon the graves of their fathers and seek a home in a distant land." He mentioned particularly, specifically, the Cherokees. Georgia's claim for jurisdiction would be upheld by the United States now, as in the days when it was established by President Jefferson. If they did not move voluntarily, the Cherokees would have to accept absorption by the state.

Georgia's legislature met in mid-December, a week after

Jackson's address; the members were encouraged by the President's assurances. They were uncomfortably aware of stirrings in the North critical of untoward actions against Indians, but the North was far removed from Georgian politics. Of more concern were a number of Georgians who cautioned against rashness. Georgia already, even without the Cherokee property, was the largest state of the twenty-seven, and its population numbered half a million. Begun as a British convict colony, it had in two or three generations earned rights to the respect of its neighboring states. Fewer than eight thousand Cherokees lived in Georgia, and it would be immoderate for half a million whites to smash, to smother them, or so these critical Georgians contended.

The legislature acknowledged the critics, but it overcame any and all hesitation. It passed laws forbidding any Indian to engage "in digging for gold in said land, and taking therefrom great amounts of value, thereby appropriating riches to themselves which of right equally belong to every other citizen of the state." They passed a law that further denied Indians rights in a court, declaring that an Indian cannot testify at a trial involving white men; that no Indian testimony was valid without at least two white witnesses; that no Indian contract was valid without at least two witnesses. They voted through a bill making it unlawful "for any person or body of persons . . . to prevent, or deter any Indian, head man, chief, or warrior of said Nation . . . from selling or ceding to the United States, for the use of Georgia, the whole or any part of said territory." The penalty was a sentence in the Georgia penitentiary, at hard labor, for up to four years. They passed a bill making it illegal for any person or body of persons to prevent, by force or threat, Cherokees from agreeing to emigrate or from moving to the West. They passed in this same bill a provision outlawing all meetings of the Cherokee council and all political assemblies of Indians in Georgia, except for purposes of ceding land.

These measures also were to take effect in June 1830—only six months away.

In southern Georgia was a pocket of territory for which the Cherokees had obtained Creek rights in 1821, in a trade made by

Major Ridge, and Cherokee ownership had been accepted by
treaty with the federal government in 1826. But Georgia had not
accepted it and took possession of the territory prior to the mid-
1830 deadline they had set. The Cherokees appealed to the federal
government, who sent a General Coffee, friend of President Jackson, to investigate. After holding hearings, he reported confiden-
tially to the Secretary of War, now a Mr. Eaton: "I cannot see any
reasonable or plausible evidence on which [Georgia] rests her
claim." He further advised Major Ridge and other chiefs that it
was the duty of the principal chief to throw the Georgians off the
land in dispute. He set in motion a series of events involving the
General Council, John Ross, and Major Ridge, which led to a
snowy morning in January 1830, when Major Ridge led a party of
thirty braves on just such a mission.

Earlier that morning Major Ridge had pulled on buckskin
trousers and, stripped to the waist, baring his powerful chest with
its ringlets of curly hair, he painted his body with red paint made
by Susanna and the servants from hematite. He pulled over his
head—to Susanna's and the servants' astonishment—a buffalo
head with horns. The major looked like a Christmas cake,
Susanna decided. He claimed he was trying to look fierce.

The war party rode into the disputed territory and rounded
up the white families, eighteen in all. They gave each family time
to leave their stolen house, usurped from Cherokees. Once everyone was safely out, Major Ridge set fire to the structures and
ordered the whites to leave Cherokee land, which they did, grateful to be spared punishment.

News of the Cherokee defiance startled the Georgian government. It published a version of the raid in which Governor Gilmer described Major Ridge as "the most active and malignant
enemy of Georgia" and wrote further that he had burned "all the
houses occupied by the whites on a day when the earth was covered with snow and sleet." He wrote that women and infants
were "deprived of shelter from the severity of the coldest and
most inclement weather." The Savannah newspaper, the *Georgian*, suggested a portrait be added to Washington's Indian collection, one of Major Ridge wearing his buffalo regalia and cutting

the air with his tomahawk near the suffering women and little children.

The mission was, from the major's perspective, successful, except for four of his men, who remained behind at the site of one house where they had found a keg of whiskey. They were drunk when next morning a party of twenty-five whites found them. The whites bound them hand and foot, beat them, and arrested them. On the trip to Georgia, one Indian who kept falling off his horse was roughly set back on, until the whites decided he was dead. His name was Chewoyee, and his corpse was left for wild animals and buzzards. As the white patrol proceeded, two of the other Indians escaped; one was stabbed as he fled. The fourth Cherokee was put in the Carroll County jail, where he was kept for months.

Armed white men seeking further revenge rode into Cherokee territory, but the Indians showed only politeness to them curiosity, and the whites' warning shots failed to terrify. The threats to burn down the home of John Ross and Major Ridge resulted in armed Indians congregating at both places to protect them and to visit the chiefs for a few days. Susanna fed the ones gathered at her place, Quatie Ross those at hers.

Susanna was incensed to think that her husband was doing his war dance again, old as he was. You are sixty, she reminded him.

He never knew his exact age, he said, and would not admit to having any certain number.

No, you won't admit to any age, she told him. A buffalo head!

With horns, he told her. Admittedly, a bad dream all around, but maybe it had shown the Georgians something. It must surely give them pause.

In the *Phoenix*, Boudinot was critical of the Cherokee raid:

It has been the desire of our enemies that the Cherokees may be urged to some desperate act—thus far this desire has never been realized, and we hope, notwithstanding the great injury now sustained, their wonted forbearance will be continued. If our word will have any weight with our countrymen in this very trying time, we would say, forbear, forbear—revenge not, but leave vengeance to him 'to whom vengeance belongeth.'

In New England the American Board's spokesman Jeremiah
Evarts wrote twelve essays on the Indian cause, which were circulated throughout the country and furnished evidence, arguments for the Indians' defenders. The opponents found the essays
galling, all the more bitter because of their eloquence and flagrant
claim to have all justice and reason on their side.

> If the agents of the United States purchase land for a public object, such a
> purchase is not a treaty. If the State of Virginia, on the application of the
> United States, cedes a piece of land for a navy yard, or a fort, a compact of
> this sort is not a treaty. If the State of Georgia cedes to the United States all
> its claim to territory enough for two large new States, and the United States
> agree to make a compensation therefor, such cession and agreement are not
> a treaty. Accordingly, such negotiations are carried on and completed by
> virtue of laws of the National and State Legislatures. Of course, compacts of
> this kind are never called treaties; and the idea of sending them to the
> Senate of the United States for ratification would be preposterous. One of
> the confederated States is not an independent community; nor can it make a
> treaty, either with the nation at large, or with any foreign power. But the
> Indian tribes and nations have made treaties with the United States during
> the last forty years, till the whole number of treaties thus made far exceeds a
> hundred, every one of which was ratified by the Senate before it became
> obligatory. Every instance of this kind implies that the Indian communities
> had governments of their own; that the Indians, thus living in communities,
> were not subject to the laws of the United States; and that they had rights
> and interests distinct from the rights and interests of the people of the
> United States, and, in the fullest sense, public and national. All this is in
> accordance with facts; and the whole is implied in the single word
> *treaty*. . . .
>   It is now contended by the politicians of Georgia, that the United
> States had no power to make treaties with Indians "living," as they express
> it, *"within the limits of a sovereign and independent State."* Thus, according to
> the present doctrine, General Washington and his advisers made a solemn
> compact, which they called a *treaty*, with certain Indians, whom they called
> *the Cherokee Nation*. In this compact, the United States bound the Cherokees
> not to treat with Georgia. Forty years have elapsed without any complaint
> on the part of Georgia, in regard to this exercise of the treaty-making
> power; but it is now found that the Cherokees are tenants at will of Geor-
> gia; that Georgia is the only community on earth that could treat with the
> Cherokees; and that they must now be delivered over to her discretion. The
> United States then, at the very commencement of our federal government,
> bound the Cherokees hand and foot, and have held them bound nearly forty
> years, and have thus prevented their making terms with Georgia, which

might doubtless have been easily done at the time of the treaty of Holston. Now it is discovered, forsooth, that the United States *had no power to bind them at all.*

Three-thousand Cherokees now lived in the West, migrants and their descendants. One of them was the adopted Cherokee Sam Houston, a friend of Jackson's since the days when he had been a successful Nashville lawyer. Jackson had helped him become governor of Tennessee. At this time of success and power, he had married Eliza Allen of a powerful Nashville family, and within two weeks, claiming he was "overwhelmed by sudden calamities, which from their nature preclude all investigation," he left Eliza, left the governorship, began to drink heavily, and made his way to the home of his foster father, John Jolly, who was chief of the western Cherokees. Houston admitted that his "feet like a weary wanderer returned at last to his father's house."

Jolly welcomed him, helped sober him up, and appointed him ambassador to Washington. Houston, refusing even yet to discuss his abandonment of wife and work in Tennessee, started for the federal capital in the winter of 1829–1830; he wore Cherokee buckskins, a purple robe befitting his new status, and a pair of comfortable moccasins.

14

Attorney William Wirt, a neighbor of Jefferson, offered his services to the Cherokees to represent them against Jackson's and Georgia's governments. He had served as Attorney General under Monroe and was familiar with the Indians' legal status and the treaties. An essayist, the anonymous author of a nationally popular book, *Letters of the British Spy,* he was conceded to be one of the most brilliant lawyers in the country and was one of many people offended by the new laws of Georgia. He also did not like the new Indian Removal Bill. In spite of the American Board's lobbying and intense debates in Congress, it had passed Congress and had been signed into law by Jackson on May 28, 1830, a featured issue of Jackson's administration.

President Jackson himself, respectful of the Cherokees, invited them to send delegates to the Hermitage to meet with him. How to respond to the invitation was one item of business put on the agenda for the general council meeting announced to begin the second Monday in July, 1830. At the council his invitation was announced, discussed, and refused. John Ross and Major Ridge saw no advantage in exposing themselves to offers of bribes and wasting their and the President's time.

Three days were spent going over Cherokee legal problems, as outlined by Mr. Wirt. Further days were devoted to worrying about the financial situation, Jackson's government having tampered with the annuity, the tribe's main income, by deciding it could be issued only in proportional bits to each Cherokee; this meant that the entire population must travel to one central place to collect fifty cents apiece. The council objected, of course. Further, it voted to retain William Wirt and Associates as principal council, along with Underwood and Harris, a Georgia firm.

Soon after the adjournment of the council, Mr. Wirt filed a case against Georgia before the United States Supreme Court.

The case was based on the situation of a Cherokee, George Tassels, who had been convicted in the Hall County Superior Court of murder and was to hang. Wirt appealed on his behalf, and Chief Justice John Marshall ordered the state of Georgia to appear before him and show cause why he should not issue a writ of error.

Georgia did not respond to the citation. The governor placed the matter before the state legislature, which ordered him to ignore the court and to hasten the execution of Tassels, which was done.

Mr. Wirt had also appealed to the Supreme Court for an injunction to stop Georgia from executing its Indian code, and this matter was on the agenda when in October, ignoring one part of the Georgian law, the Cherokees met in council at New Echota. Thousands attended. The men wore everything from blankets to frock coats; the women wore calico skirts with colorful prints. All visited with one another and prepared for days of feasting. The children took to the woods, the boys with blowguns and bows and arrows. New Echota became a city overnight, an overpopulated, crowded one, and the night air reverberated with drums and the beat of dancing feet and the voices of the chanters. With hundreds of torches lit, the Cherokee capital reminded Major Ridge of his visit years ago to beautiful Baltimore.

John Ridge, highly regarded for his work with the Creeks, took his seat on the national committee and was, to his father's immense pride, elected its president. Going Snake, wearing a frock coat and a hat with a cockade, was elected speaker of the council. Alexander McCoy won the clerk's post that John Ridge previously had held.

The federal government had its agents here present, among them Indian Colonel John Lowrey, who had been with Jackson and Major Ridge in the Seminole war. In his speech—in addition to the usual offer to trade lands in the West—he gave the council members to understand that Jackson's federal government would not interfere with the state of Georgia, even should Georgia proceed to survey, divide, and assign to white citizens the Cherokee lands within that state.

Responding to Lowrey, the council repeated that the Cherokees had "long since come to the conclusion never again to cede *another foot* of land."

The new Georgian senator in Washington was Wilson Lumpkin, age forty-seven, a surveyor who acknowledged friendship with several Cherokees. He claimed to have their interests at heart, and he believed their best interest lay in their agreeing to move West. Their fate was sealed in Georgia, as he saw the situation, and the other three states of Cherokee residence would surely sooner or later join in. The Cherokees had been dispossessed, he felt. It was not Jackson who was taking from them their soil and the graves of their forefathers—in his opinion they did not know where the graves were. It was Jefferson who had inaugurated the removal policy years ago.

Lumpkin had surveyed in Cherokee country and knew and respected John and Lewis Ross, the Vanns, Major Ridge and his son, and their families. For years as a United States congressman he had served on committees dealing with Indian matters, with slavery one of the two most heated and controversial subjects in American politics. Those two issues were almost life-endangering in the House of Representatives. During meetings he had shown respect for Indians. He believed himself to be fair toward them. Further, he had spoken out in the Senate concerning the missionaries' participation in this government matter. Why are these church representatives set against government policy? Why do they ask for money from the government, he asked, then bite the hand that feeds them? Are the pastors of the Presbyterian churches in the South, who are financial supporters of the American Board's missionary work, aware of the nature of its work in the South? Are their members in the South aware? Are the Baptists who send their dimes and dollars to support missions among the Cherokees aware that their money goes to oppose federal policy? Are the Moravians, who have always claimed to remain apart from politics, aware that their missionaries are involved in politics? Is it known to Protestants that this preacher Worcester and his wife, as well as others, are writing essays against federal policy, doing so weekly, while their own mission station takes federal money and one of their helpers openly teaches blacks in her classes in the Cherokee courthouse?

In his view, his own state of Georgia should take steps to relieve the missionaries of a weight they need not any longer carry, by sending them—book, bag, and baggage—home.

For his part, Worcester realized that the attack on missionaries would worsen. The rough ground of Indian rights was prepared for major change. The soil was being plowed and the seeds planted, either for the Indians successfully to be accepted by whites, which many of them did so much want, or for them to be rejected by whites, who would take their lands. It was a moral issue, a church matter; but it was a political one, too. The church dealt chiefly with the soul and hoped for heaven hereafter: a city not built by hands, a more perfect place ruled by God. It claimed no New Testament mandates to change this world's governments. The continuation of slavery had proved the impotence of the church once it entered a political arena. Religious institutions, whenever they had tried to act against slavery, had begun to stammer and bow; the whacks of rulers and of those institutions' own members struck at vital parts of the church itself. Even so, he felt a fire burning inside to help these people in their cause. The church must try—political or not, government or not, separation of church and state or not—the church must try.

Worcester and Boudinot received many reports from Cherokees in Georgia of beatings by white miners, a group who also beat and mauled one another. The Indians were not afraid of brawls, but they were outnumbered. The federal agent roused himself, called in federal troops, and ordered them to control the violence; but the troops were also outnumbered. They did take the side of the Cherokees whenever they were engaged.

The Cherokee world was turning awkwardly, the rumble threatening. There were so many irons in the fire, as Cherokee leaders knew, that it was difficult to choose which one to draw out and try to shape. Meanwhile, white settlers crisscrossed the countryside, laying out, selecting claims that they meant to file once the new Georgian laws governing the Indians and their land could be enforced.

John and Sally named their first son John Rollin. His Cherokee name meant Yellow Bird. Sarah admitted she would need a
while to get used to the name Yellow Bird, even though she found
yellow birds attractive in their place.

John read to her editorials from Georgian newspapers, berat-
ing his buffalo-headed father. One writer wondered whose houses
Major Ridge and his war-painted braves had burned. The houses
were Cherokee; therefore, the patrol had the right to burn them,
the writer admitted. All the same, the houses were soon to belong
to the white families who had taken possession. Could the Indians
burn down a house that was theirs, but was soon to belong to
another?

Senator Lumpkin tried to implement the President's Indian
policy by introducing a bill that would provide rich, good land
west of the Mississippi for the five southeastern tribes to be theirs
forever, in exchange for their eastern claims. The bill appropriated funds to go toward paying the cost of transportation, to re-
imburse the Indians for their houses and other improvements, to
pay any losses of livestock, and to give them subsistence for the
first year, while they prepared new fields for crops and built
houses.

As Lumpkin anticipated, the debate on the bill caused an
uproar in Congress. The measure broke apart all previous political alliances; it realigned the Senate. No bill had ever been more
heatedly attacked and defended, and the press joined in. The
Cherokees, because of their advanced society and their Georgian
problem, were the main topic, but the other four tribes—Creeks,
Chickasaws, Choctaws, and Seminoles—had defenders and attack-
ers, too.

Georgia did have a claim on the federal government. That
was one key to the affair, and many efforts were made to shake
Georgia's resolve. Edward Everett of Vermont gave as his view
that the move "cannot, as it professes, elevate the Indians. It must
and will depress, dishearten, and crush them." He called on Geor-

gia to yield: "If Georgia will recede, she will do more for the Union, and more for herself, than if she would add to her domain the lands of all the Indians, though they were paved with gold."

The Georgian senators simply did not agree with him. The northwestern portion of Georgia was the land they wanted.

Senator Theodore Frelinghuysen spoke for a few hours on the subject, a few hours each day for three days, describing the nation's policy toward the Indians from the American Revolution onward, dozens of broken treaties left behind.

Do not break the treaty between the United States and Georgia, Lumpkin replied.

Everett asked his fellow senators not to stain the country's name. "Our friends will view this measure with sorrow, and our enemies alone with joy." He asked how Americans of the future will view it "when the interests and passions of the day are past," and replied, "I fear, with self-reproach, and a regret as bitter as unavailing."

Senator Peleg Sprague of Maine compared Georgia's position with that of Shylock.

Senator Lumpkin focused on the poorer Cherokees who were, he said, being misled by rich rulers and missionaries, "the wicked influence of designing men, veiled in the garb of philanthropy and Christian benevolence."

The *Phoenix*, on May 29, 1830, reported that a certain Cherokee farmer was asked by whites to sell them his horses, and he refused. They turned the horses out of the corral. While the farmer chased after his animals, white men entered his house and beat his wife unconscious. Boudinot wrote, "Here is the secret. Full license to our oppressors, and every avenue of justice closed to us. Yes, this is the bitter cup prepared for us by a republican and religious government—we shall drink it to the very dregs."

The Choctaws, meanwhile, conceded. That very month they made known their willingness to treat with the federal government, to sell their present lands and to move west. President Jackson handled the negotiation himself.

Thomas McKenney was in trouble in Washington. President Jackson had replaced scores of federal employees with his own people, and McKenney felt the heat on his neck. Personally he was without savings, without another job, and his position as head of the Office of Indian Affairs was one he loved. He had been its superintendent and servant for sixteen years.

Publicly he was a strong supporter of the Indian Removal Bill. That was not the trouble. The trouble was his considerate feelings toward Indians, which ran counter to the usual attitude. Another was the federal trading posts his bureau had inherited, which sold goods to the Indians; the posts also policed the frontiers, keeping the whiskey sellers at bay. This system had been set up by President Washington, who knew the fur companies and had created the trading posts to protect the Indians "from scoundrels in the fur trade; and from the confrontation with the white man's civilization."

Most of the posts were located in the far West, at places like Green Bay, Prairie du Chien, Chicago. Mr. John Jacob Astor had a hold on the trading business, owned the American Fur Company, and through buying from the Indians he had become the wealthiest person in America; but he could become much richer if he could do away with these trading posts. Should he attain a monopoly, the northern Indians would be at his beck and call on whatever terms, whatever prices suited him. Only McKenney stood in his way. His bureau was the solid wall, staunchly defended against charges made by congressmen and senators who found it advantageous to represent Mr. Astor's cause: Senator Thomas Hart Benton of Missouri, for instance.

Even as early as the Monroe administration, attacks had been made in Congress. One criticism of McKenney was directed against his accounts. On one occasion his account books disappeared from his office and the accounts were at once called into question by Congressmen. McKenney happened to have a duplicate set, to his critics' surprise; he even had a second copy of every bill and receipt from every trading post.

What he chose to sell was also questioned. Jew's harps were one item, eight gross of them. Senator Benton got authorization for a public hearing to look into the affairs of the bureau, and Benton used the hearing to attack him, employing distortion, polishing his fluent oratory, his wit, his sarcasm, his remarkable memory for details.

McKenney replied in his perfunctory, competent, clerkish manner. As for the harps, they had been requested by the Indians. Which of the two, he wondered, Mr. Benton or the Indians, is best acquainted with the needs and wishes of the latter? As for Mr. Benton's estimate that the federal money expended by the Indian bureau must by now exceed $165,000, the actual amount was $50,185. And five cents.

The hearing brought forth affidavits and the testimony of any number of McKenney's business associates, and their calm presentations shot holes in Benton's declarations. The majority of the investigatory committee members exonerated McKenney. Even so, the attacks continued, and McKenney knew he could not stand forever against John Jacob Astor.

In fact, that had been the bureau chief's precarious situation before Jackson came to power. Now it was even more shaky, because the President himself was suspicious and alien. There was rumor of McKenney's replacement being imminent.

Meanwhile, tradesmen visited his office seeking government contracts to move the eighty thousand southeastern Indians, once the westward move took place. Sam Houston wanted the contract; he claimed a reestablished friendship with the President. He was planning on a rich profit, indeed—apparently counting, McKenney decided, on contacts and influence rather than budgetary competitiveness. Such manipulators would want McKenney out of the way.

Then there were the portraits. Over three thousand federal dollars had been spent on "paintings of those savages," as they were called, and many senators and congressmen were simply dismayed at what they considered waste, unauthorized waste at that.

Also, the hotel bills of the Indian delegations did appear to be exorbitant, with oysters on the half shell, gin slings, and broken furniture figured in.

McKenney was told that the President wanted to see him. Obediently McKenney waited in Jackson's office, his bones cold, his body tense. Mr. Jackson entered, sat down, and began to item-

ize the reports against McKenney that he had heard. Item, Mc-
Kenney had been the principal promoter of a famous pamphlet,
"We the People," which had scandalized Jackson's dear, dead
wife. Item, he had circulated handbills, so-called "coffin handbills," that had described Jackson as an incompetent general who
had suffered his troops to be killed. He finished the list and looked
up.

McKenney asked, "Well, sir, what else?"

McKenney later recalled that Jackson said, "I think that conduct is highly unbecoming of one who fills an office in our government such as you do."

"Are there any more charges?"

"There are."

"What are they?"

"I am told your office is not in the condition it should be."

"What else, sir?"

"Nothing, but they are all serious charges."

McKenney said he would like to reply while under oath. The
startled President apparently did not at once know what he
meant to do. McKenney raised his hand and recited aloud the
oath.

Jackson said, "You are making quite a serious matter of this,
sir."

McKenney said he was. He then denied all the accusations.
He had not had any connection with "We the People" or with the
coffin handbills. "As for my office, that is my monument and my
records are my inscription. Let it be examined. I invite a commission for that purpose, nor will I return to it to put a paper into
place or in any way prepare for an ordeal."

Jackson considered McKenney for a minute or so before he
nodded. "I am satisfied." He got up and took McKenney's arm.
"Come down and let me introduce you to my family."

That was all very well, a polite victory; but later Jackson,
with the help of Congress, transferred the Indian bureau from the
War Department and simply neglected to transfer Mr. McKenney, who found himself unemployed. His files and papers, his
paintings were removed from the old quarters. A new director,

one of Jackson's men, was appointed at three thousand dollars a year.

McKenney, bereft, cleaned out his desk. On leaving, in the hallway, he encountered the chief clerk of the secretary of the War Department, a Dr. Randolph, and he paused to inquire why he was no longer needed. Mr. Randolph said, "Why, sir, everybody knows your qualifications for the place, but General Jackson has been long satisfied that you are not in harmony with him, in his views in regard to the Indians."

15

Major Ridge had 250 acres of cleared land, with eight fields for crops, most of them native to America—corn, tobacco, indigo, potatoes, as well as oats for his many animals. There was quite enough of the indigo both to sell and to fill Susanna's dye pots. His ferry and store were prosperous. His orchard now had 1,141 peach trees, 418 apple trees, and a number of plums. He was wealthy beyond counting, but even so he was, day by day, spare and saving; he rarely spent on himself and had as luxuries only his big horse and his massive two-story colonial house, painted white. With its fences and outbuildings, it was startlingly impressive to travelers. He and Susanna had come from the other world, that of a smoking fire, a bit of bread wrapped in corn husks. They had escaped the pattern of retreat, of hiding, of skirmishes and thievery and were luxurious, with many friends.

They could glory in their elder son's successes, too. John was a greenbag—a lawyer—a writer much sought after, a powerful speaker, a negotiator for the Creek nation so successful that the federal government itself recently decided he could not be allowed to continue and refused to receive him ever again as a diplomat representing the Creeks: only by that means could they break his influence in Washington and with the Creek chiefs, and bring about a round of negotiations more favorable for the government. So he became the key member of the Cherokee delegation in Washington instead, meeting with President Jackson and his Secretary of War, writing a memorial for Congress, conferring with New England congressmen and senators.

While in Washington, John was living at the Brown's Indian Queen. Major Ridge told Susanna all about the place, even to the portrait of Pocahontas over the doorway. John was with the Cherokee delegation. Also staying in the hotel at this time, as John wrote to his parents, were delegations from other tribes that were also in Washington lobbying Congress. They were men from the Choctaw and Creek tribes, as well as the Iroquois, the Quapaw, and more. The chiefs often met to eat and drink together, and to crowd into the galleries and listen to the orators challenge the House and Senate to be fair to the native Americans. One senator spoke for three days, Susanna understood—three days. Then lost the vote.

She and Major Ridge discussed such reports day and night. They learned of the speech of dear Congressman Everett, which had made many of the chiefs in the gallery weep. Following his defeat, all the chiefs of the several tribes met at Brown's and sought to find another savior or solution to their problems, to find an escape.

On Sunday morning of March 6, 1831, they came together at Brown's for a sermon in English given by a native Indian pastor. The men fasted all day, and that evening at Gadsby's Hotel they held another service, the chiefs of all the tribes—Christians and otherwise—together begging God to help them, to guide them.

Susanna and the Major, Boudinot, Worcester, and John and Lewis Ross followed the rise and fall of action as the public, the press, and Congress debated Indian matters. They also watched the Supreme Court's activities. That month Mr. Wirt appeared before the court, along with another Philadelphia lawyer, John Sergeant. Their argument read, in part:

> We know that whatever can be properly done for this unfortunate people will be done by this honorable court. Their cause is one that must come home to every honest and feeling heart. They have been true and faithful to us and have a right to expect a corresponding fidelity on our part. Through a long course of years they have followed our counsel with the docility of children. *Our* wish has been *their* law. We asked them to become civilized, and they became so. They assumed our dress, copied our names, pursued our course of education, adopted our form of government, embraced our religion, and have been proud to imitate us in every thing in their power. They have watched the progress of our prosperity with the strongest interest, and have marked the rising grandeur of our nation with as much pride as if they belonged to us. They have even adopted our resentments; and in our war with the Seminole tribes, they voluntarily joined our arms, and gave effectual aid in driving back those barbarians from the very state that now oppresses them. They threw upon the field, in that war, a body of men

who descend from the noble race that were once the lords of these extensive
forests—men worthy to associate with the "lion," who, in their own language, "walks upon the mountain tops." They fought side by side with our
present chief magistrate, and received his personal thanks for their gal-
lantry and bravery.

On July 18, 1831, Chief Justice Marshall was to read the
court's opinion of the constitutionality of the recent Georgian
legislation. The chief justice was old, his body and voice feeble,
and John Ridge had to strain to hear him. For almost half an hour,
the chief justice expressed his sympathies for the Cherokees. He
admitted that he personally was moved by their appeal. The court
had been unable to accept, however, their claim to hold the status
of a foreign nation. They were not that. They were a separate
state, admittedly. The court found them to be "a domestic, dependent nation"; he said this domestic, dependent nation was "in a
state of pupilage." The court found that it had no jurisdiction
over a domestic, dependent nation.

In this opinion Mr. Wirt had been struck down by his old
friend. The defeat was galling, the plight of the Indians ever more
desperate. Both the Supreme Court and Congress had voted
against the Cherokees, and John Ridge's delegation now sought a
new meeting with the President, the one person who could help
them. John wrote Boudinot a long letter about this meeting,
when it took place.

Jackson was friendly. He received the group hospitably in
the White House drawing room, recalled his campaigns with the
Cherokees against the rebellious young Creeks and the Seminoles.
He was inclined to favor the Cherokees, he assured John and his
associates; he had a "disposition to do them good."

John noticed the lines in his face, put there by the stress and
restraints of office, and in his eyes was the watchful attitude of a
dangerous, deadly animal at bay, aware of being hunted. "I am
particularly glad to see you at this time," he told the visitors. He
said he had believed all along that the Supreme Court would not
support their claim. He blamed Wirt and the whole clan of Philadelphia lawyers; a strange wedding, the Cherokees and Philadelphia lawyers, anyway. The lawyers charge high fees. "I blame

you for suffering your lawyers to fleece you. They want your money, and will make you promise even after this, perhaps, that they can make you safe." He said, "I have been a lawyer myself long enough to know how lawyers will talk to obtain their clients' money." He paused.

One of the Cherokees—very likely John—replied, "We don't believe you would blame the Cherokees for their effort to maintain their rights before the proper tribunal."

"Oh no," Jackson said. A cough troubled him; his voice hacked the air for a moment. "I only blame you for suffering the lawyers to fleece you." He changed his tack, began to talk about being the friend of the Cherokees, remembered their fighting for the country—he very well knew they had shed their blood "with the blood of my soldiers."

John Ridge and his colleagues sought to bring him around to discuss the situation of the Cherokees and Georgia, but the President decided to discuss the treaty of 1783 with Britain, which was irrelevant, and he wandered off into considerations of the Catawba tribe who, when Jackson was a boy in Monroe, North Carolina, had been a violent, powerful people living nearby. "At one time they took some of the Cherokee warriors prisoners, threw them in the fire, and when their intestines were barbecued, ate them." So he said. He compared the Catawbas' former position of power to their present subservience, "poor and miserable and reduced in numbers, and such will be the condition of the Cherokees if they remain surrounded by white people."

A Georgia politician was announced, and to the Cherokees' chagrin he was invited to join them. The Cherokees rose to leave, thanking the President for their audience, each shaking the President's hand. He delayed them, holding their hands while he assured them of his friendship. He urged them to tell Major Ridge and the other chiefs, and the Cherokee people, of his high regard, and he told them, while the Georgian waited, "You can live on your lands in Georgia if you choose, but I cannot interfere with the laws of that state to protect you."

No hope there in the White House. None just now in Congress. None in the Supreme Court. A letter from John Marshall was received by the Cherokee delegation, expressing his sympathies. The letter confirmed his earlier view: "If courts were permitted to indulge their sympathies, a case better calculated to excite them can scarcely be imagined."

There were virtually no federal troops left in Georgia after the spring of 1831, due to orders from Washington. Increasingly the state troops assisted in the assaults and thefts, preying on the Indians, choosing the poorer ones, as a rule, avoiding the wealthy and powerful, who were only threatened. Boudinot was occasionally ordered to come forth from the *Phoenix* office and answer for his editorials before armed Georgia troops and civilians, but the fear they hoped to instill in him did not change his views or his writings—though they did instill fear, and it came to haunt Harriet, too, and the children.

New Georgian laws were passed to stop public dissent. One required all white men living within the Georgian portion of the Cherokee nation to be licensed by the state or suffer four years imprisonment. Some of the missionaries, realizing that this requirement was aimed at them, moved to the other side of the Georgia state line; but most remained, carried on their work, and awaited the consequences. The arrests began. From the *Missionary Herald at Home and Abroad* comes the following account:

They continued unmolested until near night, on Saturday, the 12th of March, when a colonel and twenty-five men, all mounted and armed with guns and bayonets, reached Carmel, and paraded in front of the mission-house. Three men dismounted, entered the house, and inquired for Mr. Proctor, the teacher of the school, and secular superintendent of the station. When he came into the room, the soldiers immediately told him that he was their prisoner; and after ascertaining that Mr. Butrick, the missionary at the station, was absent on a preaching tour, they conducted Mr. Proctor to a public house, kept by a Cherokee, about half a mile distant, where he was kept under guard till the next morning. He was then permitted, accompanied by a guard, to visit his family for a short time; and then, it being the Sabbath, he was carried to New Echota, about forty miles, where they arrived just before sunset and arrested Mr. Worcester, a missionary of the Board, together with Mr. Wheeler, the printer of the *Cherokee Phoenix*, and Mr. Gann, another white man residing at that place, who were all taken to the place where the troops were quartered, and kept under strict guard. Mr. Worcester, however, was permitted to visit his family in the evening, and the next morning, attended by a guard. The party then proceeded with their prisoners to Hightower, thirty miles, where they arrested Mr. Thompson, missionary at the station, and another white man of the same name, residing near the station. After proceeding on a few miles, the party halted for the night, and the next day arrived at headquarters.

All these arrests were made without a warrant from any magistrate, or any civil precept whatever. The proceedings were entirely of a military character. Upon their arrival at the headquarters, they were marched into camp with drum and fife, and a good deal of military pomp was displayed. The missionaries were all treated with as much civility as was consistent with their situation as prisoners.

After remaining at headquarters one day, Mr. Worcester, and Mr. Thompson, with Mr. Wheeler and Mr. Gann, were taken about thirty miles, to Lawrenceville, where the court for Gwinnett county was then in session. Their counsel, Messrs. Harris and Underwood, immediately applied for a writ of habeas corpus, and the case was argued before Judge Clayton. The grounds taken by the counsel was that the law was inconsistent with the constitution of the United States. The judge set this defense aside. He then declared Mr. Worcester an authorized agent of the government of the United States, by virtue of his office as postmaster. He next declared all the missionaries of the Board to be authorized agents of the government, because the government had made appropriations of money to aid them in instructing the Cherokees. This, the judge said, constituted them agents of the government for this purpose, and of course exempted them from the operation of the law. . . . Messers. [sic] Worcester, Thompson, and Proctor, were therefore discharged without delay. The others who were arrested with them, were bound over to the next term of the court. . . . Special acknowledgements are due to the Rev. Mr. Wilson, and Dr. Alexander, of Lawrenceville, who kindly came forward and gave security for the missionaries who were carried to that place for trial and obtained their release from under guard; and also to general Edward Harden, a member of the bar, who spontaneously made an argument before the court in their behalf.

Worcester returned home to his wife and to his writing, a more solemn, sober man. That was the main effect the Georgians were striving for, to intimidate, frighten, silence the critics; and Worcester was a prime target.

That spring he was relieved by the Jacksonian government of his postmastership, and about the same time, in May, he received a letter from Governor Gilmer himself:

Sir—It is part of my official duty to cause all white persons residing within the territory of the state, occupied by the Cherokees to be removed therefrom, who refuse to take the oath to support the constitution and laws of the state. Information has been received of your continued residence within that territory, without complying with the requisites of the law, and of your claim to be exempted from its operation, on account of your holding the office of postmaster of New Echota.

You have no doubt been informed of your dismissal from that office. That you may be under no mistake as to this matter, you are also informed that the government of the United States does not recognize as its agents the missionaries acting under the direction of the American Board of Foreign Missions. Whatever may have been your conduct in opposing the humane policy of the general government, or exciting the Indians to oppose the jurisdiction of the state, I am still desirous of giving you and all others similarly situated, an opportunity of avoiding the punishment which will certainly follow your further residence within the state contrary to its laws. You are, therefore, advised to remove from the territory of Georgia, occupied by the Cherokees. Col. Sanford, the commander of the Guard, will be requested to have this letter delivered to you, and to delay your arrest until you shall have had an opportunity of leaving the state.

Colonel Sanford of the Georgia Guard appended a note to this letter, giving Worcester ten days to leave the state. He sent similar orders to other male missionaries.

Again, from the *Missionary Herald*:

The Georgia guard have arrested Dr. Butler, . . . assistant missionary of the Board at Haweis, and the Rev. Mr. Trott, a missionary of the Methodist church, and the Rev. Mr. Clauder, of the Moravian church. Dr. Butler and Mr. Clauder were temporarily released for special reasons; but Mr. Trott was very severely used, having been kept in chains one night, made to sleep in the open air, and to travel on foot, though he offered to furnish his own horse, and all the guards who seized him were mounted.

The wives of these several men were not given notice to leave, were not subject to the law; but they shared the apprehensions of their husbands. Part of one mission house was requisitioned by the Georgia Guard, and the missionaries were given notice to vacate it by a Colonel Charles Nelson, who doubtless expected to use the accommodation for himself and nine companions; however, missionary John Thompson dared to refuse him:

Sir—I have been informed that you design to occupy the missionhouse this evening, with a detachment of the Georgia guard. In regard to this subject, we can only say, that we have not the accommodations desirable to entertain yourself and company, and for this, and other reasons, you will excuse me in saying, that if your design is effected, it will be without my consent.

Permit me to add, that if an interview with me on this or any other subject is desired, it may be obtained at this place at any time during the course of this day.

I am, Sir, very respectfully Your obedient servant John Thompson.

He was arrested and, deprived of a horse, was made to walk two miles to a Major Dawson's, where he was secured as a prisoner.

Catherine Fuller, another missionary, wrote to her superiors, asking for instructions:

Since Mr. Thompson is a prisoner, I suppose I may stay here without molestation as heretofore. Do you think, Sir, that it is improper for me to stay as I do? I know that in common cases it would not be proper, but I trust that in the present instance it is right. I am desirous to stay, for I think that as soon as it is known that the people have left the house, some base intruder, if not the Georgia guard, will take possession of it. As yet I have no fears which would prevent my staying, though thus unprotected. My heavenly Protector is ever near for my defence. I trust that whatever may come, I may not be greatly moved.

Cherokees were also arrested. One was arrested for digging gold. Worcester was arrested for a second time, along with a Cherokee who was "chained by the neck to a baggage wagon," as another prisoner, the Reverend D. C. McLeod, reported. He added, "I was made to run on foot to get up with the other prisoners. . . . I was told if I opened mouth, I should be run through with a bayonet."

Worcester put up bond and was released, to appear at the coming session of the Superior Court. At home, he and his wife faced the cold awareness that he must endure continuing harrassment should he remain. She urged him to go to Brainerd, in Tennessee, for a while, until the arrests ceased in Georgia; and he did so, leaving her and the children in New Echota until the date for his trial. He left her with Elias and Harriet Boudinot. He was able to resume his work at Brainerd; however, learning that his newest child, an infant, his thirdborn, had died, he returned to be with his wife. He was arrested. After a few days, he was released to return to Brainerd.

His trial was held in September 1831, as he wrote the officials of the American Board:

> Our trial took place yesterday. There are eleven of us in all. One besides myself, Rev. Mr. Trott, of the Methodist church is a preacher of the gospel; and six, I believe, including us, are professors of religion. The jury soon brought in a verdict of guilty against us all. The judge has not yet pronounced sentence. We are waiting—Just after I had written the last word we were called upon to go to the court-house, and have received the sentence of four years hard labor in the penitentiary. Many and grievous crimes had been laid to my charge by some of the counsel for the state, which I may safely say they could not prove. The solicitor general, however, paid a regard to our feelings, which entitles him to our esteem. The charges against us were repelled by our counsel; and when we were called upon to speak, if we had anything to say why sentence should not be pronounced agreeably to the verdict, I ventured, I know not whether wisely or not, to reply nearly in these words: "May it please your honor, if I am guilty of all or any of those crimes which have been laid to my charge, in the arguments before this court, but which are not preferred in the bill of indictment, then I have nothing to say why sentence should not be pronounced against me; but if I am not guilty of all or any of them, which I solemnly aver before this court and my God that I am not, then I have to say what I have already said, that this court ought not to proceed to pronounce sentence against me, because the act charged in the bill of indictment was not committed within the rightful jurisdiction of this court."

He was imprisoned as was the Reverend Dr. Elizur Butler, a kindly medical man. The others agreed to leave Georgia.

Worcester wrote a letter on October 6, 1831, from the state penitentiary in the state capital, Milledgeville:

> We have applied to the Supreme court of the United States, and expect a hearing next winter, but whether the decision will be in our favor, and whether it will be executed if it is, remains for futurity to disclose. You know how to appreciate the motives which have brought us here. We are happy. We enjoy I trust that light of God's countenance which can make man rejoice in affliction. Whatever the result may be as to earthly things, we

hope to realize the fulfilment of that precious promise, all things shall work together for good to them that love God.

I preached Sabbath before last to about twenty-six prisoners confined in the same room with me, and last Sabbath in a room to which about sixty had access. I hope for similar opportunities hereafter. Dr. Butler and I sleep in different rooms, and have worship in each every night. Whether any good will follow remains with God. To human view, it is a discouraging task to preach to men who, as the inmates of a penitentiary may of course be expected to be, are corrupt and corrupting one another. But God can bless the effort if he will.

The prison yard, about five acres, had a high wall around it, and he and Butler were among one hundred prisoners who had been sentenced for all manner of crimes. He and Butler were given cotton shirts and trousers bearing their initials, and the length of their terms was printed on the front of the shirts. The food was ladled out to them and it was wholesome and plentiful. During the day Worcester worked as a mechanic; Butler turned a lathe wheel. They were treated as kindly as could be expected, an observer reported, and he found them to be cheerful.

Worcester wrote his reasons for not recanting, and sent them to the *Missionary Herald:*

On the 15th of last month, as you have already learned, I was brought to trial, and the next day sentenced to four years imprisonment in this place, at hard labor. I arrived here on the 23rd. Since that time my health has generally been as good as I commonly enjoy. I have been able to labor every day, and hope I may continue to be, during my time of service. It would be a great trial to be afflicted with sickness here.

I have formerly been told, there was no need of my going to the penitentiary; that it was easy for me to avoid it, if I would; and some have even told me since I have been here; others, I have been informed, have said the same, I would by no means compare myself with any of those mentioned below; but you will doubtless understand my meaning. Nehemiah might have gone into the temple, if he would. Shadrack and his companions might have worshipped the images of Babylon, if they would. Daniel might have ceased to pray for a season, if he would. But not to pursue this train of thought farther—they could not conscientiously comply with these requirements. Others in similar circumstances could not conscientiously comply with other requirements. However easy it might appear to others, I could not conscientiously comply with requirements which would have kept me from this confinement. And now, dear Sir, I have to say that, through the goodness of God, I have yet had enough to support me; I have had even more than I anticipated. And I am led firmly to believe that any man contending for the rights of conscience and the liberty of spreading the gospel, will always find strength given him from above.

The Tennessee minister Reverend D. C. McLeod, visiting in Georgia, was journeying on the road when other missionaries, under arrest, passed by. He asked if he might walk along with them. The officer, Colonel Nelson, consented. Reverend McLeod asked one of the prisoners if he had been chained the preceding night. He had been, was the reply. Reverend McLeod then asked if it was legal to chain a prisoner who manifested no disposition to escape, to which a soldier replied that he ought not to be blamed, as the guards were under orders. Mr. McLeod retorted to the effect that they seemed to proceed more by orders than by law. Some of the guards took offense and said so, and Reverend McLeod made the error of replying to them, which resulted in a torrent of obscenity from the guards and an order from Colonel Nelson to "flank off." Reverend McLeod did so, but on the way delivered other opinions, which so inflamed the soldiers that he was ordered to return and dismount.

McLeod obeyed.

Are you a preacher? the colonel asked him.

A circuit rider, McLeod told him.

Take his horse, the colonel ordered. He placed McLeod under arrest and forced him to walk with the other prisoners.

After several miles McLeod asked the colonel for his horse, explaining that he had severe pain in his hips and knees. The colonel replied that another missionary had complained similarly but had walked on very well.

Five miles farther, camp was made and the other prisoners were chained together. That night another detachment of prisoners joined them, this one with Dr. Elizur Butler, who had a chain secured by a padlock around his neck, the other end of the chain tied to a guard's horse. He was suffering mightily, and explained that often he had fallen, especially after dark, and had been dragged by his neck until the horse could be stopped. As one point he was allowed to ride behind the guard's saddle, his chain still fastened to the horse's neck, but the horse fell from the weight. The two men were pinned for a time under it. At times he was not tied to the horse, though the chain remained around his neck.

The next day McLeod's feet became so sore that he could only hobble, but even so he was cursed and ordered to proceed. Later, however, another missionary was told to walk and to let McLeod ride, using a blanket and a bag of clothing for a saddle. That night the guards removed the prisoners' chains, except for the lone Cherokee's, a Corporal Glenn having come upon the scene and declaring that, in the absence of other officers, he had no orders to chain the pastors.

The following day this group reached the prison, Camp Gilmer, where they were shut inside two houses, each graced with an unpleasant smell. There were no beds, but they had the floor and slept soundly. They had no chairs, bench, or table. They had blankets. Of great importance to them, they were not in chains. They were not allowed to write letters, and their visitor, Mr. Thompson, was not allowed to talk privately with them.

Reverend McLeod was allowed to write to Colonel Nelson, requesting audience with him, and the colonel consented and took his case under advisement. Later in the day he ordered his release. McLeod was not allowed, however, to return to the houses to give solace to the prisoners or to take messages away.

Worcester, Butler, and two other missionaries, J. J. Trott and Samuel Mayes, wrote to Colonel Nelson from the penitentiary at Milledgeville, asking that they be permitted "to hold a meeting tomorrow evening at some place where such of the guard and of the neighbors as are disposed might attend." They themselves would like to attend, they added.

Colonel Nelson wrote his reply on the outside of the note:

We view within request as an impertinent one. If your conduct be evidence of your character and the doctrines you wish to promulgate, we are sufficiently enlightened as to both. Our object is to restrain, not to facilitate their promulgation. If your object be true piety you can enjoy it where you are.

The country became aware of Georgia's unfairness and cruelty, and newspaper editors were in the main vehement in their criticism of the state and its new governor, the same Wilson Lumpkin who had earlier introduced the removal act in Washington, D.C. One such protest comes from the New York *American*, New York City, January 13, 1832:

> The avaricious unprincipled father is stated indeed to have given his son this advice—'Get money, my son—honestly, if you can—but, at any rate, get money.' In opposition to this, however, is a saying as old as the stars, and as true as it is old—a saying worthy of all commendation—which teaches us, that 'honesty is the best policy.' Is it honest then to seize on, and take by force, a piece of property that pleases our fancy, but does not exactly belong to us? It is true, that we have a kind of reversionary claim to these Indian lands—our right and title is clear and indisputable whenever the Government of the United States can purchase, as she is bound to do, for our use, from its present occupants, the Aborigines of the country; who are supposed still to have some right in the soil of their native land, derived from the laws of nature and of nations—from being the first and only possessors. But 'might gives right.' This is the maxim of the ambitious unprincipled politician, but not of an honest, pious man. And here we may suppose our conscientious fortunate drawer in the Cherokee land lottery to turn his attention to the signatures to his grant. Most conspicuous among these stands his excellency the Governor, William Lumpkin, without whose name no grant for land can issue. The communer may be supposed to continue his self-examination somewhat in this way: [If] this thing were wrong, as it appears to me to be, our excellent pious Governor would not surely give his assent and approbation; how could [he] do so, consistently with his oath of office, his obligations to the Most High, to the Giver of all good?

Governor Lumpkin must have been particularly unimpressed with that editorial, because his name was incorrectly given. His first name was Wilson, not William.

Another blast appeared in the Vermont *Telegraph* of December 13, 1831: "Perhaps no event has occurred in the country, which has excited greater surprise and displeasure among good men, than the degrading manner in which the missionaries of the cross have been arrested, conducted in chains to trial, and consigned to the penitentiary."

The American Board wrote to President Jackson, pointing out that their missionaries were in the Cherokee country on authorization of a previous Secretary of War and of President Monroe, that they were under contract and had agreements; and the Board prayed "that the Attorney General be directed to commence a suit in the Courts of the United States against the offending officers of the State of Georgia, for the false imprisonment, and other injurious treatment of the teachers and missionaries, in violation of the treaties and laws of this Union and of their rights as citizens of the same."

The Attorney General replied that he had submitted the matter to the President, and he had satisfied himself he could do nothing.

Several hundred Choctaws boarded the *Huran* for transport to the West in February 1832. These Indians, having ceded their lands, were the first of the five major tribes to move west. Disconsolate, they stared back at the clutch of white Mississippians who stood on the docks watching them.

Their Chief Harkins moved forward to the railing and addressed the audience of whites:

> We are hedged in by two evils and we chose that which we thought the least. . . . Yet it is said that our present movements are our own voluntary acts—such is not the case. We found ourselves like a benighted stranger following false guides, until he was surrounded on every side with fire and water. The fire was certain destruction, and a feeble hope was left him of escaping by water. A distant view of the opposite shore encouraged the hope; to remain would be inevitable annihilation. Who would hesitate, or who would say that his plunging into the water was his own voluntary act?

The chief went on to criticize President Jackson, the man who had said that he "would plant a stake and draw a line around us, that never should be passed, was the first to say that he could not guard the lines, and drew up the stake and wiped out all traces of the line."

Wirt went to the Supreme Court with a test case based on Reverend Worcester's arrest. John Ridge traveled to Washington to be present at the hearing, then left the city soon after to respond to an appeal for help from his friend Boudinot, who was in Philadelphia trying to raise money for the *Phoenix.*

While in Philadelphia, the two decided to try to arouse a storm of protest against Georgia and federal inaction. The welcoming toast of the publisher Mathew Carey, delivered one evening at dinner, acknowledged their purposes. In his Irish accent, he proposed "Confusion to the Councils of Georgia and the administration in relation to the Cherokees."

John Ridge was an eloquent speaker. A newspaper described him as rather tall and slender, erect, with a profusion of black hair, a complexion less swarthy than that of western Indians, and with less prominent cheekbones. "His voice is full and melodious, his elocution fluent, and without the least observable tincture of foreign accent or Indian. Even his metaphors were rarely drawn from the forest, and he had little or none of that vehement action that characterizes the orators of uncivilized tribes."

In his speeches, John Ridge called for fairness:

> You asked us to throw off the hunter and warrior state: We did so—you asked us to form a republican government: We did so—adopting your own as a model. You asked us to cultivate the earth, and learn the mechanic arts: We did so. You asked us to learn to read: We did so. You asked us to cast away our idols, and worship your God: We did so.

He reviewed the list of treaties and promises broken by the federal government, Georgia's raids against the Cherokees, the punishment meted out to missionaries. A reporter wrote:

> We only wish that we could adequately report the feeling narrative and convey to the reader the unaffected manner of the speaker. His narrative of the brutalities of the Georgia Guard towards the Missionaries . . . was sufficient to fire the blood and rouse the indignation of every American deserving the name of Man.

Six thousand people signed a petition to Congress, supporting the Cherokee cause. John and Elias achieved further successes in New Haven, Hartford, and Boston. As Thurman Wilkins describes the scene,

Ridge and Boudinot were at the missionary rooms of the American Board in Pemberton Square when news arrived of the Supreme Court's decision in the case of Worcester and Butler *vs.* Georgia. A friend who had just arrived from Washington City inquired if they were prepared to hear the worst.

No, they were not, Ridge replied.

Then the friend revealed the true nature of the decision—how the Supreme Court had ruled as unconstitutional the law which had imprisoned the missionaries and along with it the whole Indian code that Georgia had enacted. "The Cherokee Nation then," the decision had read, "is a distinct community, occupying its own territory, with boundaries accurately described, in which the laws of Georgia can have no force, and which the citizens of Georgia have no right to enter but with the assent of the Cherokees themselves or in conformity with treaties and the acts of Congress."

John Ridge called the news "glorious." Sympathizers rushed to congratulate him and Boudinot.

Over the subsequent days, the elation was dispersed, dampened by the realization that Georgia had not released the missionaries after all, that President Jackson was not enforcing the Supreme Court ruling. He was quoted as remarking: "John Marshall has made his decision; let him enforce it now if he can." John saw three possible meanings in the statement: let him enforce it if he is able because I don't see a way to do so; let him stay well clear of invading the President's authority; or simply, I don't want to enforce it, and I won't.

After making the speeches already scheduled for Salem and Newburyport, John Ridge hastened to Washington, called at the White House, and at once was admitted to see the President. John asked him whether he planned to stop the Georgian intrusions.

Jackson replied that he would not. Seeing the pain his answer caused, he at once assured John of his friendship for the Cherokees and his conviction that John should go home and advise his people "that their only hope of relief was in abandoning their country and removing to the West."

John offered the arguments about broken treaties and promises, but even to his ears the words now had a ring of melancholy defeat. The lanky President with the deeply lined face was not going to bother with broken pieces and bits; the momentum of his administration was established.

Jackson later wrote to his friend, General Coffee, "I believe Ridge has expressed despair, and that it is better for them to treat and move."

John left the White House much the same man who had entered it, and could even on demand have made the same speeches he had made days earlier in New England; but they would no longer ring so true, now that his lawyer's instinct had told him that he and the Cherokees might indeed be wise to accept their role in this stark play. One must prepare for what one sees as coming and make the most of it. The alternative was to be unprepared.

He talked with Boudinot, guardedly mentioning that it might be time to reassess the Cherokee interests.

Boudinot thought so, too.

It was possible that more could be gained in a treaty, provided the Cherokee nation negotiated now. Protest was not a solution.

Boudinot agreed.

The two ventured in whispers into these dangerous waters. Yes, Boudinot agreed, they would at once lose influence, lose the power to bring about the change, if they were to make known their views.

Two tortured souls, they wrestled with their demon.

In the coming days, even their supporters in Congress advised them to make the best possible bargain with President Jackson.

John, with two other Cherokees then in Washington, John Martin and William Shorey Coodey, sought out John McLean, a Supreme Court justice known to be sympathetic to the Indian causes. McLean admitted that the Supreme Court was prostrate before the President's refusal to act. He advised a treaty, seeking the best possible terms, and offered to serve as a commissioner at a treaty council to help achieve fairness. Ridge, Martin, and Coodey asked him to write to John Ross, giving him his advice and offer, and the three left the impression with McLean, as he reported, that they were prepared to return home and work to bring about such a treaty.

News of their change of mind reached Georgia congressman

Daniel Newman. Apparently he was privy to the McLean meeting. Jubilantly he released the news to the public, claiming, "the Cherokee Delegation have at last consented to recommend to their people to make a treaty with the government upon the general basis that they shall acquire a patent for lands over the Mississippi, and, at a proper time, be allowed a delegate in Congress." This letter, as printed in the press, was reprinted in the *Phoenix* by Boudinot's brother, Stand Watie, who was filling in as editor while Boudinot was away. He did so with his brother's knowledge. At once John Ridge and Coodey moved to deny the story.

On April 16, Secretary Cass summoned the two of them and Martin to the War Department offices. He suggested to them the terms of a treaty, offering extensive and fertile land west of the territory of Arkansas, where hundreds of Cherokees now lived. The Cherokees would be allowed to conduct their government there. They could appoint an agent to the federal government and a delegate to Congress even now, before their country had "territorial" status. White people would be excluded from their lands. The Cherokees would be allowed to choose the mode of travel to the West that suited them best, severally or individually: some might prefer to go by land, others by boat on river routes. The government would give the Cherokees subsistence for the first year they lived in the new land. The Cherokees would receive an annuity equal to improvements left behind, and would receive all annuities due from treaties negotiated over the past years. They would be given an annuity for the value of the lands left behind. In the new land schools would be subsidized, blacksmiths supported, and supplies, including iron and steel, furnished for building churches, schoolhouses, council houses, and homes for a few of the principal chiefs. Each male adult would receive a rifle. Each family would receive blankets, axes, ploughs, hoes. There would be wheels, cards, looms. Livestock left behind would be paid for. Orphans would be provided for. The United States would guarantee protection from hostile Indians. "It is the wish of the President," the Secretary said, "that all of your people should remove, and he is therefore unwilling that reservations of land should be made in the ceded territory." He stipulated that, should Cherokees remain in the East, they must become citizens of the states in which they lived and not look to the federal government for protection.

John Ridge was won over. He, Martin, and Coodey confided in the Secretary that they personally favored negotiation of such a treaty. They preferred, however, not to say so publicly, and asked that he send the terms to the Cherokee council by his own emissary. He agreed to have it delivered by Elisha Chester, an attorney retained by the missionaries.

In May, while still in Washington, John received a letter from David Greene of the American Board, who had just met with Chester. He was convinced that all political parties in Washington thought further defense of the Cherokee was impossible. "It makes me weep to think of it," he wrote. "But if your friends in Congress think that all further effort in your behalf will be useless . . . then, for aught I can see, you must make the best terms you can, & go."

When John returned home, the news of his conversion was out, retracted, affirmed, denied. He met first with John Ross, who was cool toward him. He was certain that his parents would be, as well as Sally. Relief was immense when he came upon his father and received a big welcome. He and the major settled down to confer. Major Ridge encouraged him to speak; after all, John was the one chosen and educated to lead the Cherokee people. Whatever his own doubts, regardless of the dangers, facing the loss of the home he and Susanna had made here, the land cleared and enriched, fenced and worked over the years, the orchards and roads and ferry and store—all to be sold off, in a sense discarded.

His son was recommending as much. It was John's and—as he claimed—Elias's decision after reviewing the Cherokee situation. Tearfully John confessed.

Very well. Major Ridge concurred. He enlisted to stand behind his boys. He gave them his support.

16

John Ross was furious. Not present at the last spate of negotiations in Washington, with no sense of the current popularity of Jackson and his immense power, of the waning support from Congress and even from the American Board and other missionary offices, he regarded John Ridge as having led "one of the most consummate acts of treachery towards his country that the annals of any nation affords."

He politely received the emissary, Elisha Chester, and the offer he brought, and shelved it.

At the next national council, in July 1832, the council under his guidance decided to forego its national election and retain the present leaders in office. One obvious purpose, as the Ridges decided, was to keep John Ross indefinitely as principal chief. John Ridge and the major argued before the council that a national election, with its inevitable debates, not only was required by law, but was needed. They judged that Ross's action was intended to deny them a hearing and to deny John the chance to run for the highest office. The rumor was even passed around the council that the three delegates had accepted bribes, had sold out their own people for money. The emissary, Chester, was also embarrassed by Ross's maneuverings to deprive John Ridge and his colleagues of influence:

> Their influence, on which I calculated largely, was thus entirely prostrated, and the clamor raised upon the subject was well calculated to prevent all calm reflection upon the real situation and interest of their nation. It was in vain that they demanded an inquiry into their conduct; no opportunity was conceded them for making their defence. Thus circumstanced, they thought it would be worse than useless for them, at this time, to press the subject of a treaty upon a people who have long been accustomed to regard the advocating a sale of their country as the blackest crime.

Boudinot was also overwhelmed by Ross. He received from Ross instructions not to print any detailed account of the federal offer. Offended, Boudinot threatened to resign. Ross remained adamant. On August 1, Boudinot wrote to Ross:

> I could not consent to be the conductor of the paper without having the right and privilege of discussing these important matters; and from what I have seen and heard, were I to assume that privilege, my usefulness would be paralyzed by being considered, as I have already been, an enemy to the interests of my country and my people.

Ross accepted his resignation and appointed as editor Elijah Hicks, Ross's brother-in-law.

Meanwhile, Georgia was surveying Cherokee land within the state. Three hundred fifty surveyors were at work, marking off plots of 40 acres each in the gold fields, and elsewhere 160 acres each, about half a mile square. As the Georgia politicians had promised the voters, these were to be assigned to white Georgians by lottery.

The Cherokees living on the land did not understand what the blazes and numbers meant and were bitterly amused by the efforts to divide, to measure off forests and streams. To Major Ridge and his boys, the surveyors were taking the first step toward the expulsion of most Cherokees from their homes and land, without a countervailing Cherokee plan to make the most of the process.

Harriet was incensed at her husband's dismissal as editor. Boudinot had given birth to the newspaper, had guided it and raised money for it, had made it lively and successful. Beyond his and her personal loss, she believed that to deny the Cherokees fair, full consideration of a subject affecting the nation's life was undemocratic and dangerous.

As if in reply to her objections Elijah Hicks, Ross's mouthpiece, wrote an editorial attacking Boudinot's patriotism. Boudinot, who continued to live a few feet from the *Phoenix* building, walked into the office and demanded space to present his views, which Hicks granted. Boudinot wrote his article with care, so as to touch on the main issues of the removal debate. He discussed his own definition of patriotism, which included both "the love of country and the love of people," and continued:

> In applying the above definition of patriotism to my conduct, I can but say that I have come to the unpleasant and most disagreeable conclusion . . . that our lands, or a large part of them, are about to be seized and taken from us. Now, as a friend of my people, I cannot say *peace, peace,* when there is no peace. I cannot ease their minds with any expectation of a calm, when the vessel is already tossed to and fro, and threatened to be shattered to pieces by an approaching tempest. If I really believe there is danger, I must act consistently, and give alarm; tell our countrymen our true, or what I believe to be our true, situation. In the case under consideration, I am induced to believe there is danger, "immediate and appalling," and it becomes the people of this country to weigh the matter rightly, act wisely, not rashly, and choose a course that will come nearest benefiting the nation.

In October, the traditional annual meeting of the council was held at Red Clay in Tennessee. John Ross set the tenor with an antiremoval speech. He spoke in English, pausing for the "linkster," the translator. Emissary Chester was again present with the federal proposal, but it was tabled for a week or more while other matters were discussed. Finally it was rejected.

John Ridge then made an appeal for reconsideration of the vote, and successfully proposed that the council send a delegation to Washington. He suggested that John Ross and three of his people go, trusting that they would learn there, as he had, that a removal treaty was inevitable.

While this mission was being voted through the council, to the south the first of the Georgia lotteries was being held. Titles to certain sections of Cherokee lands were parceled out. Soon, however, the lottery's wheel of fortune stopped, fraud having been uncovered on the part of Shadrach Bogan, the commissioner in charge. He had been taking care of his relatives and friends with choice plots. For instance, one relative had been given the house and 160 acres of John Ridge's plantation.

The prizes awarded by Bogan were drawn again, and this time John Ridge's house and land, plot 67 of the 23d division of the 3d section, went to a Mr. Griffith Mathis.

Major Ridge's home, plot 196, was won by a Revolutionary

War widow, Rachel Fergason. The major and Susanna were, however, granted by Governor Lumpkin the right to live in their
house for the time needed to negotiate a treaty, and the governor
granted the same right to John and Sally, as well as to Elias and
Harriet; their home in New Echota had on this first drawing been
given to others.

The rumor mill began to grind once more, claiming that
these three leaders of the so-called Ridge party had been given
favored treatment by the state of Georgia, further proof of their
connivance.

It was true that the privilege to remain in homes was not
generally extended. Many Indians were evicted. John Ross himself did not escape a subsequent drawing and a harsher enforce-
ment. In April 1833, he returned home to find his house and
ferry, and even his peacocks, owned by a stranger. His wife Quatie and their children were permitted by the owners to live in two
rooms. On being refused help by Lumpkin, Ross moved across
the river into Tennessee, to a small cabin near Red Clay.

By signing up to go west, John Ross would receive payment
for his losses; however, by moving to Tennessee he might have
forfeited his Georgian rights.

Worcester and Butler remained in prison. In Worcester's
case, Wirt wanted to file an appeal with the Supreme Court that
would force the executive branch of the federal government to
move in the matter, or refuse to move, now that the constitutional
question was decided; but both Worcester and Butler were placed
under pressure from friendly educators, clergymen, lawyers, and
statesmen of Georgia, who feared for the federal union, as well as
for the state's reputation, should the federal courts issue an order
for release that the state of Georgia would not obey and the president would fail to enforce.

Governor Lumpkin himself called on Mrs. Worcester at New
Echota and sought to convince her to persuade her husband to ask
for a pardon, which Lumpkin said he wanted to give. She told
him that the decision was her husband's.

Indeed, she did want him home. The New Echota community was in a state of division and dissention, and was frequently

harassed by militia. Elias Boudinot, with whose family she was living, was persecuted and often insulted for having a white wife. All the arguments between Indians, between Indians and militia, and between Indians and whites, seemed to involve him and might at any moment erupt into violence, and Harriet and the children needed a united family.

As for the two ministers who were serving time, more than a year had passed of boring daily chores, nothing the least bit mind-stimulating. Worcester and Butler missed their families and church duties; still, they were prepared to appeal their case and remain longer in prison if given support from their own American Board. The board was having second thoughts, however, apparently brought about by Jackson's popular support in all regions of the country. This was not a political administration in the usual sense; rather, it was an American revolution, a rush into politics by the common people.

Indians were not allowed to visit the penitentiary, but as far as Worcester and Butler could learn, the Cherokees favored further protest, appeals, and further incarceration, if necessary. Indians wrapped in blankets were often in sight at the edge of the woods, waiting, attending, assuring the prisoners they were not forgotten. The Indians would sometimes send food: a wild turkey roasted, a cooked haunch of venison, a brace of pheasants.

For thirteen months, Worcester and Butler stayed in the prison, then for another day, then day by day. A year and three months passed, and even so, day by day. . . .

The siege was broken finally. The American Board wrote John Ross to advise him that Worcester was withdrawing; there would be no further action. In turn, Worcester and Butler wrote Governor Lumpkin the letter he had been requesting.

Penitentiary, Milledgeville, January 8, 1833, to his Excellency Wilson Lumpkin, Governor of the State of Georgia:

Sir—In reference to a notice given to your excellency on the 23rd of November last, by our counsel in our behalf, of our intention to move the Supreme Court of the United States, on the second day of February next, for further process in the case between ourselves individually, as plaintiffs in error, and the state of Georgia, as defendant in error, we have now to inform your excellency, that we have this day forwarded instructions of our

counsel to forbear the intended motion, and to prosecute the case no further. We beg leave respectfully to state to your excellency, that we have not
been led to the adoption of this measure by any change of views in regard to
the principles on which we have acted; or by any doubt of the justice of our
cause, or of our perfect right to a legal discharge, in accordance with the
decision of the Supreme Court in our favor already given; but by the appre-
hension that the further prosecution of the controversy, under existing circumstances, might be attended with consequences injurious to our beloved
country.
    We are respectfully yours, S. A. Worcester, Elizur Butler.

The following day, after hearing of Governor Lumpkin's displeasure, the two ministers wrote again:

Sir—We are sorry to be informed that some expressions in our communication of yesterday were regarded by your excellency as an indignity offered
to the state or its authorities. Nothing could be further from our design. In
the course we have now taken it has been our intention simply to forebear
the prosecution of our case, and to leave the question of the continuance of
our confinment [sic] to the magnanimity of the state.

They remained in prison, working at their assignments. No
reply was received. It was five days later that the keeper of the
penitentiary came on Lumpkin's orders to release them. They
had been in that place a year and four months.

The missionaries to the Cherokees, in their efforts to play a
political hand, had been defeated. They could preach in the other
three states, they could teach, but they could not influence political action in Georgia.

The American Board wrote to John Ross early in 1833, advising him that "they think in the present posture of the affairs in
this Nation, it would conduce to the best good of the Cherokees
for them to accept terms proposed to them by the Government of
the United States and remove to the Country west of the Mississippi."

17

Ross returned from Washington, his mind unchanged. Two conferences with President Jackson and many with Secretary Cass had not shaken his resolve. Even Senator Frelinghuysen had told him that he advised the Cherokees to emigrate, but Ross was determined to defeat removal and to extol himself. President Jackson had offered to designate good land in the West, plus three million dollars to boot, but Ross had rejected all offers out of hand and on his return cared not to discuss any of it in his home country, or to allow discussion in the *Phoenix*. He had made the decision for the Cherokees. The gold on Cherokee land alone was worth twenty million dollars, he contended.

He did not discourage circulation of a rumor that he had turned down a bribe of fifty thousand dollars while in Washington, which John Ridge doubted.

At the May council meeting, Ross's nephew Cooley circulated a petition protesting his uncle's course, one signed by twenty-five leading Cherokees, including Major Ridge, Elias Boudinot, and his brother Stand Watie. The petition demanded that Ross explain why he was following a course of delay, which offered less than "a speedy and favorable adjustment of existing difficulties." The petition resulted in a two-day debate, Ross on one side and his nephew and Major Ridge on the other. Ross, suffering in the debate, promised a more adequate explanation if he and his followers would wait for the October council. John Walker, Jr., son of a distinguished chief, objected to delay, that being the very malady being criticized; but John Ridge and the Major decided to grant Ross's request for time.

The council meeting ended with a speech from Major Ridge. Emissary Benjamin Currey described it in a letter, referring to him as "the greatest orator in the nation" and saying further, he dismissed the meeting, after giving it a concise and well arranged history of their present condition compared with what it had been; the probability of their being called upon in a few months, for the last time, to say whether they will submit always to the evils and difficulties every day increasing around them, or look for a new home, promising them freedom and national prosperity; advising them to bury party animosity, and in case they should conclude to seek a new home, to go in the character of true friends and brothers.

John Walker, Jr., was despondent about John Ross and his leadership, as he was about Ross's delays, and when invited to accompany a delegation of western Cherokees on a trek to Washington, he packed his best suits and went along. A handsome man, a fancy dresser, he made a favorable impression everywhere he went. With Walker was one other Cherokee, James Starr.

They had no official position with the Arkansas Cherokee delegation, but they were entertained by President Jackson, who flattered Walker about his father's part in the War of 1812. Walker enjoyed the trip, and on his return home was surprised to find that a rumor had been started to the effect that he and Starr had signed a treaty ceding all the eastern lands to the federal government. Of course, he denied it.

In 1833 the President invited him to return to Washington, this time to discuss the issue of Cherokee removal. He did so, and repeated the visit the following year, this time along with David Vann. They found two delegations already there—the western Cherokees trying to get the government to remove the Osage from the Osage homeland, and the eastern Cherokees under Ross trying to get the government to stop Georgia from removing them from theirs.

Ross worried about Walker. Though without official position, he was personable and able. Ross feared the man might go ahead and treat with Jackson. He worried about his own brother, Andrew Ross, becoming more friendly with him, too. John Ross was smarting even yet from Walker's arguments at the council meeting in 1833 criticizing Ross for losing the best chances to negotiate.

John Ridge also worried about Walker and refused to lend him his support. He so informed Ross. He said he attached no consequence to Walker's movement "so far as that individual is concerned, but it affords to my mind a clear view of the extent that Jackson will go to divide our nation."

On June 19, 1834, the Secretary of War began negotiating a treaty with Andrew Ross. This Ross—who had little authority— was willing to cede all Cherokee lands in the East in return for modest allowances and advantages. This treaty had had its birth the previous winter when two delegations were in Washington, one headed by John Ross, the other by this younger brother, a leader among the so-called "Kitchen Chiefs," who said they spoke for the emigrating faction. On the Secretary's recommendation, the President welcomed Andrew and two of his associates; but Jackson found them lacking in the wiles of government, so he sent them home to fetch more chiefs. He agreed that the government would pay travel expenses for all.

Back home, Andrew sought out Major Ridge and Boudinot. Both agreed to return with him to Washington to see what the President had in mind. They were with him there in June when he began serious discussions.

Senator Gilmer of Georgia wrote,

Major Ridge spoke English so badly that he conversed . . . through an interpreter. He was a very large man, with features indicative of clear perceptions. His conduct was dignified, and his whole demeanor distinguished for propriety. He was the noblest specimen I ever saw of an Indian uncrossed with the blood of the whites.

The major sat for a bust portrait with painter Charles Bird King, while wearing a vest and a high-collared, ruffled shirt. By now his curly hair was gray.

John Ross, in Washington, found the presence of his brother's group so worrisome that he decided to discuss a treaty with Secretary Cass. Could the Cherokees give up part and retain the other part of their land? Could they expect eventual citizenship?

Cass answered in the negative: the President would negotiate only on his terms, as previously outlined.

John Ross suggested that the Cherokees remain on a part of

their land, subject to state jurisdiction, and amalgamate with the whites.

He also suggested his solutions to Major Ridge and others, and the major told Ross he thought that such an approach would result in the Indians being cheated, oppressed, reduced to beggary, becoming miserable outcasts, and as a body the Cherokees would dwindle to nothing. He said he feared the whites' whiskey, and was concerned that poor Indian women would be contaminated, become wretches. The major pointed out that Ross really had no solution, and even if his ideas had been good ones he carried no authorization from the council to negotiate a treaty, any more than his brother Andrew had.

Andrew cared nothing for all that. He offered to sign a treaty, and the War Department cooperated; however, the major and Boudinot would not go along with him. John Walker and David Vann, also in Washington being entertained by the President and Secretary Cass, were off developing their own strategy, and did not sign. John Ross would not sign.

Andrew Ross went hell-for-leather ahead, submitting a treaty with only three other signatures. The treaty was rejected later by the Senate; it came to nothing, except that it created anger, which John Ross managed to direct toward Major Ridge, his son, Walker, and his supporters, even though it was one of his own brothers who had, in spite of them, developed the treaty.

Fire and punishment seethed and simmered at the council meeting of August 1834. John Ross controlled the first day or two, taking up routine business and addressing the delegates with a speech opposing the removal policies of the United States government. Late on the second day, a fiery John Ross supporter, Tom Foreman, addressed the council and angrily called treaty advocates enemies of the Cherokee nation. He denounced the Cherokees who had agreed to move west and those who recommended this course to others. Foreman recalled that Major Ridge had in years past traveled widely urging the Cherokees "to love their land and in his earnestness stamped the ground. The ground was yet sunk where he stamped and now he was talking another way. Yet these man have good clothes on—why could they not be satisfied with their property and not try to suck for more in the veins of their country?"

The words and threats created a dangerous situation—or so John Walker, Jr., declared—and he left for home before plots could hatch. A friend, Dick Jackson, rode with him. Foreman also walked out. John Ridge and Major Ridge remained at the meeting, scarcely noticing that two other John Ross men rode out soon after Foreman left. John Ridge was concentrating on the challenge that had been made here in the session. He rose to defend his father. Replying to Foreman's speech, he said,

Major Ridge [has with] distinguished zeal and ability served his country. He saw that it was on the precipice of ruin, ready to tumble down. He [has] told of their danger. Did he tell truth or not? Let every man look at our circumstances and judge for himself. [Is] a man to be denounced for his opinions? If a man [sees] a cloud charged with rain, thunder and storm . . . [and urges] the people to take care . . . is that man to be hated or . . . respected?

Foreman [has] told untruths to prejudice your minds against certain men to gratify his malice. The Delegation [has] given us a candid report—I believe they [have] hid nothing from us. It offered no hope of relief against our suffering country. Why should we embitter each others feelings. But, if the presence of Major Ridge and myself in [this] Council, which we thought was ours also, is disagreeable to you we know how to stay away.

What would become of our Nation if we were all like Tom Foreman? Could any good grow out of our Councils? We should now fall together and twist each others noses. Our eyes would not remain in their sockets, but in general we [would] gouge them out.

Major Ridge also spoke:

It may be that Foreman has better expectations and that he should, in slandering men, establish his fame among you. But I have no expectations that he will enjoy it long, for we have no government. It is entirely suppressed. Where are your laws! The seats of your judges are overturned. When I look upon you all, I hear you laugh at me. When harsh words are uttered by men who know better . . . I feel, on your account, oppressed with sorrow. I mourn over your calamity, and fatal delusion in which you are bound. You can never stand on Freedom's ground again. This man will not reap my harvest of glory if he expects to be a great man in your estimation. It is past remedy. I am not angry at the people. I know how to feel for your condition —But—as for you who know better and hold your law to yourselves, I tell you that you shall not make a treaty by yourselves. You shall be carefully watched in your movements.

The appeal failed to win concessions or earn approbation among the John Ross party, and there were even threats made privately "that if some men did not take care they would drop from their ponies," as Major Ridge reported. He saw it as "a plan devised by Ross to divert the people's mind from Ross' failure and raise their indignation against the advocates of a treaty."

Elijah Hicks, John Ross's brother-in-law, chose this time to introduce a petition, one he had circulated for signatures while the council was assembled here at Red Clay; 144 Cherokees had signed, calling for the impeachment of Major Ridge, John Ridge, and David Vann because they favored removal. John Ridge recalled the event:

> The Council unanimously, except for George Chambers who made a speech against it found us guilty and impeached us. The Committee laid it upon the table to be taken up the 2nd meeting in October next when we come to be tried for our grievous sins. The Committee will of course set as a high court of Impeachment on oath. William Rogers and Boudinot will be our counsel.

Such disownment was to the major a life-jarring blow. The overwhelming vote humbled him. Not so John, who saw it as a political maneuver that could be negated by the other body of the council in October.

John Walker, Jr., and Dick Jackson were by this time riding near Muskrat Springs, the first fingers of night about them. The usual questions were asked, whether to go on home, traveling a few hours more to the north of Cleveland, Tennessee, or to camp, and whether to stop to eat the bread and meat they had brought. In both cases the argument weighed in favor of going on without delay, reaching home and their own wives and children. Indeed, John Walker had two wives, one the daughter of former agent Meigs, and it was to her house he wanted to go, to report to her the political travails of the council.

A bullet smashed into his back, knocking him from the saddle. In the confusion he and Dick Jackson managed to free their

own rifles and almost got shots at the fleeing assailants, who resembled James Foreman and his half-brother, Anderson Springston. It was a few moments longer before John figured out that
the bullet had passed through his body, leaving two wounds. The
one in his back was neat, Dick told him, but the other wound was
ripped outward and ragged. The two men tried to bandage both
of them tightly, but Walker was impatient with delay, was all the
more certain that he must reach his wife and not stay here to be
prey to these madmen.

By the time John Walker reached home, he was weakened by
the loss of blood. The wounds had been aggravated by the ride.
He accepted Emily Meigs's greeting, then collapsed on the floor
at the door. She and Jackson carried him to bed and sent word to
neighbors and to his father. The Walkers had many friends, and
almost at once armed men arrived to protect the house, the men
making camp, setting constant guard. The father, Chief Walker,
issued a torrent of accusations against John Ross, who was, he
said, implicated personally; he threatened to kill him.

The next day Ross left Red Clay with bodyguards and took a
new route to his house, where guards continued to attend him.

John Ridge, Major Ridge, Elias Boudinot, Stand Watie, John
Ross and his advisers, John Walker, Jr., and his advisers, Andrew
Ross—all of them and others knew they were now in danger from
Cherokees even more than from the whites. Several factions were
maneuvering, no one cleanly, clearly, legally in control. The
bankrupt government was tottering. John Ridge wrote, "Our Nation is crumbling into ruin."

John Walker, Jr., died, leaving two widows and seven children. He had been a Mason, and two funerals were held, one
Cherokee, the other with full Masonic rites. Emily Meigs had him
buried near her house. It so happened that President Jackson was
at his Tennessee home, the Hermitage, when the death was announced. He had liked Walker, as had many others, and in grief
and rage he wrote the federal agent, Benjamin Currey, on a piece
of pea-green paper:

I have just been advised that Walker has been shot and Ridge and other Chiefs in favor of emigration and you as agent of the United States government threatened with death. The Government of the United States has promised them protection. It will perform its obligations to a letter. On the receipt of this, notify John Ross and his council that we will hold them answerable for every murder committed on the emigrating party.

Major Currey had warrants issued for the arrests of James Foreman and Anderson Springston, and both were apprehended and indicted for murder. They were scheduled for trial at Athens, Tennessee, at the Criminal Court of McMinn County. Foreman's attorney claimed he could not be tried in the Circuit Court because he was a Cherokee and because the shooting had taken place in Cherokee territory. The Circuit Court agreed; however, the Georgia Supreme Court remanded the case for trial on its merits.

John Ross raised a large sum of money for the defense. He even called a meeting at Red Clay for this purpose, but before a trial took place, Foreman somehow obtained his release from prison in Athens. Nobody knew how this had been done, though a cousin of Walker, Jack Hilderbrand, reported that Foreman stated after his release, "By God, sir, I was let out with a silver key."

At the October council meeting, many rumors were released into welcoming, listening ears promising that the federal government would back down if only the opponents would stand with John Ross. Ross had decided not to prosecute the impeachment charges against the major and John and David Vann; however, he also declined to allow the charges to be withdrawn, and by that means he avoided an open hearing, which the three defendants earnestly solicited in order to clear their names.

Embittered by the refusal to try them, believing justice could not be expected from Ross, the major, John, and Vann resigned and subsequently announced by courier that in a few weeks they would call a council meeting themselves.

That meeting, held at John Ridge's house, lasted for three days. Boudinot served as chairman. It resulted in the election of officers and the formation of a Treaty Party. Only eighty-three Indians were present, admittedly a small number, but among them were most of the well-educated Cherokees. The council instructed a delegation to travel to Washington and present the Treaty Party's case. Chief of the delegation was John Ridge, and among the members were Boudinot, McCoy, W. A. Davis, Archilla Smith, Samuel Bell, and John and Ezekiel West.

The council further authorized John to write out a memorial for Congress, containing the intentions and beliefs of the Treaty Party. John wrote it, and in fact Congressman Edward Everett summarized it before the House of Representatives the following January.

And on February 4, 1835, Henry Clay of Kentucky read the statement to the Senate, with solemn and reluctant admission that the Cherokees must, indeed, move west.

> "Sir," the senator from Kentucky rumbled in the direction of the presiding officer, "it is impossible to conceive of a community more miserable, more wretched. Even the lot of the African slave is preferable, far preferable to the condition of this unhappy nation. The interest of the master prompts him to protect his slave; but what mortal will care for, protect the suffering injured Indian, shut out from the family of man?"

John Ross was again in Washington with a delegation, and he also had a proposal to make to Congress. Its terms called for the United States to purchase Cherokee land in Georgia, then to grant a portion of that land to the Indians residing there, along with the rights of Georgia citizenship.

The memorial was ignored or, whenever noticed, was dismissed.

On February 8, the members of the Ridge delegation moved a step further. They suggested to Secretary Cass that they negotiate "a preliminary treaty," to be signed by the Ridge delegation and submitted to the Cherokee nation for ratification. The War Department discussed the offer and decided to treat with the Ridge group; so they appointed a negotiator, a retired minister from New York State, the Reverend John F. Schermerhorn.

The negotiations were well underway when John Ross announced to Secretary Cass that his group had another proposition. At once the Ridge group set aside its discussion and waited.

Everything stopped while for ten days John Ross mulled over his offer, preparing it. His proposal, when it finally came, was to sell the Cherokee lands outright for twenty million dollars.

Secretary Cass rejected this out of hand, but he did agree to mention the offer to President Jackson, who stormed against Ross, accusing him of filibustering.

Ross, who had hoped to purchase, perhaps in Mexico, a new homeland, made a further offer; he was willing to let the dollar amount be set by the Senate. He and the members of his delegation signed this offer on February 28, 1835, and sent it to Secretary Cass: "We are prepared, so far as we are concerned to abide by the award of the sense of the American Senate upon our proposition, and to recommend the same for the final determination of our nation."

Pounced on at once by Jackson and Cass, the request was sent along to the Senate. There the senators deliberated, then recommended five million dollars. Ross, when told of this, began to try to extricate himself from his contract. On March 9 he suggested that the entire problem should be returned to the Cherokee council:

> And in order to insure harmony and good feeling among ourselves, it [is] greatly to be desired that the Cherokee people and their representatives should not be trammelled by any premature act on our part, and that the whole subject should be brought before them free from any suspicion or unjust imputations against ourselves or others.

The plea was denied by Secretary Cass and President Jackson, and their negotiations with the Ridge party resumed. The terms discussed were generous by treaty standards. The Cherokees were to receive $4.5 million for their land in the East and, further, 13 million acres of good land in the West; in addition, they were to receive 800,000 particularly choice acres, worth on the market $500,000. They would receive a perpetual annuity for schools. They were to receive subsistence, travel, and other benefits, as well as remunerations for losses incurred. The western acres were to be in addition to those already possessed by the western Cherokees.

John Ridge wrote on March 10 from Washington:

> Ross has failed before the Senate, before the Secretary of War, & before the President. He tried hard to cheat you & his people, but he has been prevented. In a day or two he goes home no doubt to tell lies. But we will bring all his papers & the people shall see him as he is.

The draft of the treaty, which John Ridge and his group believed would be endorsed in council, he prepared to take home with him. As he left Washington to face the battle with Ross, he suggested to Secretary Cass that the President should send a letter of friendship to the Cherokees. On request he outlined the letter for Jackson.

The letter, signed by the President, was printed in newspapers on April 7, 1835. A powerful statement, it was perhaps more than merely outlined by John Ridge. Indeed, it refers at times personally to the plight of the Cherokee people:

> To the Cherokee Tribe of Indians East of the Mississippi river:
> My Friends: I have long viewed your condition with great interest. For many years I have been acquainted with your people, and under all variety of circumstances in peace and war. Your fathers were well known to me, and the regard which I cherished for them has caused me to feel great solicitude for your situation. To these feelings, growing out of former recollections, have been added the sanction of official duty, and the relation in which, by the constitution and laws, I am placed towards you. Listen to me, therefore, as your fathers have listened, while I communicate to you my sentiments on the critical state of your affairs.
> You are now placed in the midst of a white population. Your peculiar, customs which, regulated your intercourse with one another, have been abrogated by the great political community among which you live; and you are now subject to the same laws which govern the other citizens of Georgia and Alabama. You are liable to prosecutions for offences, and to civil nations for a breach of any of your contracts. Most of your young people are uneducated, and are liable to be brought into collision at all times with their white neighbors. Your young men are acquiring habits of intoxication. With strong passions, and without those habits of restraint which our laws inculcate and render necessary, they are frequently driven to excesses which must eventually terminate in their ruin. The game has disappeared among you and you must depend upon agriculture and the mechanical arts for support. And, yet, a large portion of your people have acquired little or no property in the soil itself, or in any article of personal property which can

be useful to them. How, under these circumstances, can you live in the country you now occupy? Your condition must become worse and worse, and you will ultimately disappear, as so many tribes have done before you.

Of all this I warned your people when I met them in council eighteen years ago. I then advised them to sell out their possessions east of the Mississippi and to remove to the country west of that river. This advice I have continued to give you at various times for that period down to the present day, and can you now look back and doubt the wisdom of this counsel? Had you then removed, you would have gone with all the means necessary to establish yourselves in a fertile country sufficiently extensive for your subsistence, and beyond the reach of the moral exile which are hastening your destruction. Instead of being a divided people as you now are arrayed into parties bitterly opposed to each other, you would have been a prosperous and a united community. Your farms would have been open and cultivated, comfortable houses would have been erected, the means of subsistence abundant, and you would have been governed by your own customs and laws, and removed from the effects of a white population. Where you now are, you are encompassed by evils, morals and physical, and these are fearfully encreasing.

Look even at the experience of the last few years. What have you gained by adhering to the pernicious counsels which have led you to reject the liberal offers made for your removal? They promised you an improvement in your condition. But instead of that, every year has brought increasing difficulties. How, then, can you place confidence in the advice of men who are misleading you for their own purposes, and whose assurances have proved, from the experience of every year, to be utterly unfounded?

I have no motive, my friends, to deceive you. I am sincerely desirous to promote your welfare. Listen to me, therefore, while I tell you that you cannot remain where you now are. Circumstances that cannot be controlled, and which are beyond the reach of human laws, render it impossible that you can flourish in the midst of a civilized community. You have but one remedy within your reach. And that is, to remove to the West and join your countrymen, who are already established there. And the sooner you do this, the sooner you will commence your career of improvement and prosperity.

A number of your brethren, who have been delegated by that portion of your people favorable to emigration, have repaired to this place, in the hope of being able to make some arrangement, which would be acceptable to the government of the United States, and which would meet your approbation. They do not claim the right of making any arrangement which would be binding upon you; but have expressly stated, that whatever they did would be utterly void, unless submitted to and approved by you.

The whole subject has been taken into consideration, and an arrangement has been made which ought to be, and I trust will be, entirely satisfactory to you. The Senate of the United States have given their opinion of the value of your possessions; and this value is ensured to you in the arrangement which has been prepared. Mr. John Ross, and the party who were with him, expressed their determination to accept, so far as they were concerned, such sum as the Senate might consider just, and promised to recommend and support the same in your general council. The stipulations contained in this instrument, are designed to afford due protection to private rights, to make adequate provision for the poorer class of your people, to provide for the removal of all, and lay the foundation of such social and political establishments in your new country as will render you a happy and prosperous people. Why, then, should any honest man among you object to removal? The United States have assigned to you a fertile and extensive country, with a very fine climate adapted to your habits, and with all the other natural advantages which you ought to desire or expect.

I shall, in the course of a short time, appoint commissioners for the purpose of meeting the whole body of your people in council. They will explain to you, more fully, my views, and the nature of the stipulations which are offered to you.

These stipulations provide:

1st. For an addition to the country already assigned to the west of Mississippi, and for the conveyance of the whole of it, by patent, in fee simple. And also for the security of the necessary political rights and for preventing white persons from trespassing upon you.

2nd. For the payment of the full value of each individual, of his possessions in Georgia, Alabama, North Carolina, and Tennessee.

3rd. For the removal, at the expense of the United States, of your whole people; for their subsistence for one year after their arrival in their new country, and for a gratuity of one hundred and fifty dollars to each person.

4th. For the usual supply of rifles, blankets, and kettles.

5th. For the investment of the sum of four hundred thousand dollars, in order to secure a permanent annuity.

6th. For adequate provision for schools, agricultural instruments, domestic animals, missionary establishments, the support of orphans, &c.

7th. For the payment of claims.

8th. For granting pensions to such of your people as have been disabled in the service of the United States.

These are the general provisions contained in the arrangement. But there are many other details favorable to you which I do not stop here to enumerate, as they will be placed before you in the arrangement itself. Their total amount is four millions five hundred thousand dollars, which added to the sum of five hundred thousand dollars, estimated as the value of the additional land granted you, makes five millions of dollars. A sum, which if equally divided among all of your people east of the Mississippi, estimating them at ten thousand, which I believe is their full number, would give five hundred dollars to every man, woman, and child in your nation. There are few separate communities, whose property, if divided, would give to the persons composing them such an amount. It is enough to establish you all in the most comfortable manner; and it is to be observed that besides this, there are thirteen millions of acres conveyed to the western Cherokees and yourselves by former treaties, and which are destined for your and their permanent residence. So that your whole country, west of the Mississippi, will contain not less than thirteen millions eight hundred thousand acres.

The choice now is before you. May the Great Spirit teach you how to choose. The fate of your women and children, the fate of your people to the remotest generation, depend upon the issue. Deceive yourselves no longer. Do not cherish the belief that you can ever resume your former political situation, while you continue in your present residence. As certain as the sun shines to guide you in your path, so certain is it that you cannot drive back the laws of Georgia from among you. Every year will increase your difficulties. Look how their young men are committing depredations upon the property of our citizens, and are shedding their blood. This cannot and will not be allowed. Punishment will follow, and all who are engaged in these offences must suffer. Your young men will commit the same acts, and the same consequences must ensue.

Think then of all these things. Shut your ears to bad counsels. Look at your condition as it now is, and then consider what it will be if you follow the advice I give you.

Your friend, Andrew Jackson—Washington, March 16, 1835.

18

Major Ridge was ailing. He had left Washington early, trusting John and Boudinot with the negotiations because of his health. He found that Susanna was ailing, too, and she was depressed about leaving, abandoning to a lottery winner all she had loved and built and tended to.

Now in their sixties she and Ridge would plant new peach and apple trees, as years ago they had here, even though they might not live to see the trees bear.

For two years the discussion about moving had continued. For all those months she had been preparing to move, not sure of the date. Was the garden to be planted this year or not? She had wanted to know in April. She had been told yes, go ahead, take a chance.

All up and down the countryside it was the same, people were undecided. Do we plant the fields, do we transplant the tobacco plants from the beds, do we sell the old sow or hold onto her for a while longer? Do we move the loom onto the porch for the summer, or leave it broken down? Shall we mend the wagon, the kettle, the scythe, the cradle, or leave them as they are for the white inheritors? Do we bottle the cider?

No answers.

The major disconsolately walked the rows of his trees, his heavy shoulders bent, his face gray as a corpse, his hands chopping the air now and again, emphasizing a thought. He had been voted out, broken by his people, ostracized from his national government which he had helped design. Major Ridge had supported John Ross all these years, and now he was no less than an enemy.

The next meeting of Ross's council was in June this year. Somebody reported this to Susanna. Major Ridge was not invited. Of course, any Cherokee could attend and stand outside the Council House, she realized. No doubt the major would await

John and Boudinot. Already John Ross was issuing incorrect information about the new treaty John and Elias had negotiated in
Washington and were bringing home for consideration.

John Ridge and Elias Boudinot came home that April. They
called a council at John's home, and though only a small group
came, they made up in optimism for their short numbers. The
major spoke with his usual eloquence, extolling the advantages of
the proposed treaty. The council resolved to have another meeting the first Monday in May, to which everyone was to be invited
and at which a vote would be taken.

John Ross meanwhile was personally stirring up mischief for
them, opposing with all his considerable might the Ridge party's
offerings. He had couriers in day-long motion, urging people to
stand firm, saying that Jackson would be defeated soon; if not, he
would change his own mind. In any event, do not go to the Ridge
council in May.

Only one hundred did attend. The Ridges had expected more
than a thousand.

It was planting time, they reasoned, there were heavy rains.

Only one hundred came—too few to take the vote. Set another date: the third week in July.

Meanwhile, John Ridge from his windows at Running Waters could see Indian sentries at the edge of the woods, over there
and over there.

Boudinot noticed sentries at his place, too. So did his brother,
Stand Watie. So did Major Ridge. Susanna noticed them even
before he did. They were Indians wrapped in blankets up to their
eyes, patiently, silently standing. They were haunting sights, reminders of the ancient blood laws.

In order to increase attendance in July, the federal agent,
Benjamin Currey, suggested that the annual federal annuity
might be discussed at a Ridge-called council meeting, and the
method of dispersal be decided. The people would come to get
their portion; meanwhile, the council could air the need for a
treaty and announce the terms being offered. This was a welcome
idea and was heartily approved.

John Ross at once realized the purpose of the tactic. He had
reason to believe that John Ridge might secure control of the

entire year's annuity, which Ross wanted for the treasury he controlled. He decided that his followers must attend the meeting at Running Waters, but not to discuss the treaty, only to vote on disposal of the annuity.

On July 18, 1835, the Cherokees of both parties began to arrive at John Ridge's plantation, camping out in his rooms, in his barns, and in the open spaces alongside the river; the dance drums sounded far into the night and the sides of beef and pork sizzled. Reverend Schermerhorn was present, as were Currey and other federal representatives. John Ross turned down John Ridge's offer of a bed and slept in the open, "with his people," as he said.

The Indians—men, women, children—on foot, in wagons, by horseback, four thousand gathered in inclement weather, the largest crowd in Cherokee history. Nearby the bugles and drums of the Georgia Guard could be heard; the guard was present to keep order should they be needed, but none of the soldiers appeared and not one disquieting incident occurred among the Indians.

Currey was one of the first to speak to the thousands of men sitting in session. He spoke especially to the Ross faction, as he later reported:

> I took occasion to say . . . that let them vote the money in what way they would, it could not save their country; that their party had been invited to express their views and wishes freely; instead of doing this they had withdrawn themselves from the ground and been counselled in the bushes. Why was this so? Were their chiefs still disposed to delude their people, when ruin demanded entrance at the red man's door, and the heavy hand of oppression already rested upon his head?

Next, John Ross spoke. He was friendly, seemed to be considerate even of the Currey criticisms, but admitted he was sorry that the agent had been personal in attack. He claimed he was "not disposed to quarrel with any man for an honest expression of opinion."

John Ridge followed Ross and declared that he, too, wanted to discard party isolations and selfish party motives. He said he and his friends had isolated themselves from Ross and his friends because of "an honest conviction that it was the only way in which the integrity and political salvation of the Cherokee people could be preserved." He would accept Ross, he said, as principal chief, once the treaty matter was negotiated.

The cliff-hanger on the July agenda was the method by which the annuity was to be received; the Ridges, in order to keep the money from Ross's government, which was without funds, contended that the annuity should go to each male citizen. The treaty was not on the agenda, but Reverend Schermerhorn wanted to speak about it. The Ross faction, which had nicknamed him "the Devil's Horn," told him they were not present to listen to treaty talk, but to settle the matter of the annuity. Their people had not brought provisions for a protracted meeting, Ross told him.

Schermerhorn offered to provide food from a federal larder, if he might be heard at length, and Ross had no choice but to agree to a speech from him. Schermerhorn chose to wait till the next morning, when everybody would be fresh.

He spoke at nine o'clock, discussed at length the proposed treaty while the mass of Indians solemnly listened, scarcely an eye blinking.

Afterward the vote was begun on the motion to have the annuity payment given to each Cherokee. The Ridges required that each vote be recorded by name, a tactic yielding more time to lobby for the treaty with those present. Early in the voting Ross proved that he had influence enough to defeat the proposal of parceling out the money, and after that many members of the Ridge party refrained from voting or cast votes his way. The measure was defeated by a large majority, and a Ross man at once moved that the total amount be paid to the treasurer. Major Ridge offered an amendment to the motion, to the effect that none of the money go to lawyers, and John Ridge seconded his father's motion to amend. This playful maneuver allowed each to speak on the subject and, of course, each spoke mostly about the need for a treaty.

Currey reported:

They went into the most pathetic description of national distress and individual oppression, the necessity of seeking freedom in another clime; the importance of union and harmony, and the beauties of peace and friendship; but said if there were any who preferred to endure misery, and wed themselves to slavery, as for them and their friends, they craved not such company.

But when the Ridges were speaking, all the previous prejudices so manifestly shown by looks appeared to die away, and the benighted foresters involuntarily broke the line and pressed forward as if attracted by the power of magnetism to the stand, and when they could get no nearer they reached their heads forward in anxiety to hear the truth. After the Ridges had procured the desired attention, they withdrew their amendment.

The Ridges had taken full advantage of the opportunity to set the record straight about the treaty. Even so, by the close of the council there appeared to be little support for it—especially among the full-bloods—far less than had been expected.

Schermerhorn called a meeting of the leaders of both parties, suggesting July 29, to restore harmony and discuss modification of the proposed treaty. The day came. Ross's people did not attend. The next day a courier brought Major Ridge an apology— Ross had suffered from diarrhea, had not been able to travel, but invited both Ridges to meet him soon, to promote the common good.

At once John Ridge wrote a letter accepting the invitation, and he and his father delivered it in person, leaving at daybreak and arriving at Ross's cabin as Ross was having breakfast. Ross invited them and their companions to eat with him, had their horses fed, and was congenial in every respect. Nobody mentioned his suggestion of a meeting until the Ridges, on leaving, asked when it might be.

Ross wasn't just now sure of a date. He would need to consult others. There were crops to be worked, and he knew John Ridge was having a corn dance in August. It must not conflict with that. He would need to find a time convenient for everybody.

Learning of this breakfast, Currey wrote, "Ross holds out the olive branch of peace to Ridge, while his confidential friends speak of slaying him, because they say he has forfeited his life by

the laws of the nation." That John Ross had himself bargained for
sale of the eastern lands was not held against him by his followers; he had not returned with any treaty, had not moved even one
step closer to selling the eastern lands, while John Ridge and the
major had.

While the two Ridges negotiated and waited, their wives became more disturbed by the blanket-wrapped sentries. Harriet
Boudinot was unnerved, too. Harriet and Sally talked of their
"white" feelings, unable to shake free of apprehensions, afraid of
the full-bloods, recalling in mind and bones the stories about Indians as savages. They assured each other that Indians were no
more prone to violence than other people, and that the old laws,
which always seemed to call for death, were merely that: old,
outmoded, no longer enforced laws, replaced by those of the
evolving civilization.

They heard about an Indian named Hammer being beaten to
death by Ross men. They heard of another Ridge man, named
Crow. Chosen to keep order at a dance, he was obliged to remain
sober while others drank. When the dance ended, he was called
on to speak, and he used the opportunity to remind the dancers of
the beseiged state of the Cherokee and the need to free themselves
by ratifying the proposed treaty as negotiated. At once he was
attacked by a Ross man and stabbed sixteen times. He bled to
death. The two wives knew of two Indians, Ridge followers
named Murphy and Duck, both knifed to death at a dance. They
knew that a man named James Martin, formerly a Cherokee
judge, had threatened to kill John Ridge, which had caused Martin's arrest by federal agents.

In spite of the dangers, John and his father and cousins
moved about in public without guards. So, indeed, did John Ross,
who claimed his life had been threatened.

The Ridges were to come together for the public green corn
dance at John's place. This celebration was to last for four days,
the dancing and hilarity setting the hills to ring. There would be
talk about politics and the harvest. John Ross's people tried to
preempt the celebration by announcing dances of their own to be
held nearby, but the Georgia Guard under Currey's or
Schermerhorn's influence broke them up, claiming they were po-

litical meetings; so most of the dancers came to the Ridge frolic, and it was an enormous crowd, a success.

Many were beginning to accept the Ridge treaty; Major Ridge heard that Ross leaders were becoming frustrated with the stalling tactics he used and had given Ross until the October council to show them an alternative to the treaty.

The Creeks during this same period had been receiving their annuity, too. In June of this year, 1835, they had assembled at Setelechee, Alabama, and their meeting was attended by Indians and whites bearing accounts against Indians. Among the Indian claimants had been John Ridge and David Vann, who wanted the remainder of their hefty fees. The half-starving Creeks, their land infected by white settlers, their meager last year's crops stolen by whites, were in no mood for paying anybody anything, much less five or ten thousand dollars. Tempers flared. One Indian stabbed another on the council ground; the relations of the dead Indian immediately took the murderer, tied him to a tree and stabbed him to death and left his body hanging to the tree. Many white persons were on the ground, but neither they nor the chiefs took any notice of the affair.

The Creeks were being cruelly treated, their systems torn apart by white intrusion and the preparations for removal. It was a fate they had agreed to, as had the other southern tribes—except, as yet, the Cherokees. Hostilities between Indians and Indians, Indians and whites broke out. Fifty Indians led by a white man attacked a mail stage twenty miles west of Columbus, robbed the stage, burned it, and killed some of the passengers, which caused many whites to flee to Columbus, carrying pots and pans and babies and hoes and clothing. Starving Indians appeared at the gates of Fort Mitchell, where they were fed.

News arrived of fighting between whites and Seminoles in Florida, as the Indians were gathered up and penned. Rumors of war increased.

Alabama's Montgomery *Advertiser* protested the situation:

Is this country never to enjoy a season of repose? Are interested land speculators from Alabama and Georgia longer to palm off their deception on the public? Who believes that the Creeks are about to assume a hostile attitude towards the whites? We answer, no one.

The war with the Creeks is all a humbug. It is a base and diabolical scheme, devised by interested men, to keep an ignorant race of people from maintaining their just rights, and to deprive them of the small remaining pittance placed under their control, through the munificence of the government. We do trust, for the credit of those concerned, that these blood suckers may be ferreted out, and their shameful misrepresentations exposed.

We have lately conversed with many of the settlers of the nation, and also the Superintendent of Indian Affairs, and the unanimous opinion is, that there is nothing like a system of hostility meditated by the Creeks; that the chiefs are utterly averse to a war fare with the whites; that it is foreign from their intentions to resist the Treaty; that they are now preparing to remove, and will, in a short time, commence emigrating west of the Mississippi.

The Red Man must soon leave. They have nothing left on which to subsist. Their property has been taken from them—their stock killed up, their farms pillaged—and by whom? By white men. By individuals who should have scorned to take such mean advantages of those who were unprotected and defenseless. Such villainy may go unpunished in this world, but the day of retribution will most certainly arrive.

Reports continued to alarm, alert. A company of volunteer whites attacked Lutcapoga, chased the Creeks into the marsh, and burned the town. Hundreds of Creeks joined the company of Chief Eneah Emathla.

On May 19 the federal government ordered in troops. One company of Indians tried to cross the Chattahoochee River to get to Florida; some of them, riding stolen horses and mules, succeeded. In early June Chief Eneah Emathla was captured, and a thousand of his people, including women and children, surrendered. Mounted on ponies—most of them—they rode into captivity and were duly imprisoned. Two other chiefs, Jim Henry and Eneah Micco, were conquered soon after. On July 2 the hundreds of revolutionaries were dispatched to the West. Moving slowly, the men were manacled and chained, even Chief Eneah Emathla, who was about eighty-four years of age. His head was high, his eyes blazing; he was uttering not a word of complaint as he faced the western, setting sun.

Behind the men came a train of wagons and ponies, the women and children riding and walking, the women moaning, wailing. As the trail approached the town of Montgomery, where boats awaited them, one warrior cut his own throat. A brave killed a guard, using a hammer, and was shot and killed on the spot. An Indian for some reason was bayoneted by a guard and, wounded, moved on to the docks. There, on July 14, 2,498 Creeks, including 800 warriors who were now unchained, were ordered onto two riverboats for the voyage south to New Orleans, then north up the Mississippi to Little Rock, Arkansas, on the steamboats, *Lamplighter, Majestic,* and *Revenue.* Along the way the hated chains and handcuffs, packed in barrels, were rolled to the edge of the boat by Yuchi Indians on board and were pushed over the side, to be lost to the government forever.

When reports about the Creeks' experiences came to the Cherokees, lost was any doubt about whether force would be used to work President Jackson's will. For the Ridges, wisdom clearly suggested adaptation, compliance, treaty. All the southern tribes were now on their way west, except the Cherokee.

John Ross remained firm, dead set against going.

Major Ridge had available a brand new carriage to take him to the October council. The carriage, ordered from New York City, was hung with leather swings attached to large C springs. The driver's seat was on top. After examining it on its arrival, shaking the wheels to test them, Major Ridge assisted his family up the folding steps, then walked around to the driver, dismissed him, swung his big body onto one of the carriage horses, gathered the reins, and drove to church.

Major Ridge traveled in style to Red Clay. Streams of Cherokees were walking and riding, filling the road. An eyewitness wrote,

> The woods echoed with the trampling of many feet: a long and orderly procession emerged from among the trees, the gorgeous autumnal tints of whose departing foliage seemed in sad harmony with the noble spirit now beaming in this departing race. Most of the train was on foot. There were a few aged men, and some few women, on horseback. The train halted at the humble gate of the principal chief: he stood ready to receive them. Everything was noiseless. Their dress was neat and picturesque: all wore turbans, except four or five with hats; many of them, tunics with sashes; many, long

robes, and nearly all some drapery: so that they had the oriental air of the
old scripture pictures of patriarchal procession. . . . The salutation over,
the old men remained near the chief, and the rest withdrew to various parts
of the enclosure; some sitting Turk fashion against the trees, others upon
logs, and others upon the fences, but with the eyes of all fixed upon their
chief. They had walked sixty miles since yesterday, and had encamped last
night in the woods.

The autumn meeting was always the largest of the year; this
had been so for all time. The harvest was in, another year's supply of food secured; therefore, plans could be laid for the next
cycle. The weather was crisp but not cold and was usually dry.
Often the session lasted two weeks, and for days before and after
many families were traveling, camping out along the way, the
men and boys most likely taking time for hunting.

A graceful stream, the Cooayhallay, ran through the council
ground at Red Clay, which was just north of the Georgia state
line. A street was lined with huts, booths, and stores all hastily
built, made using forest timbers. The street was at the foot of
hilly ground upon which the Council House was built, the structure a parallelogram made of logs and having open sides, with
benches inside for the council members. There were several bold
limestone springs near the creek, which supplied a mild, cool water. The trees were large and beautiful, and the undergrowth had
been cut away, giving the area the appearance of a park. Paths led
in all directions, crossing and entwining, and the Cherokees
moved about in the greatest order. Fires were visible in every
direction. A wind was usually busy in the trees, wafting leaves
and carrying the sound of hymns being sung in the Council
House and of the drums and chants of Cherokee dancers and
shamans.

The autumn councils always had a target date announced for
opening. This particular council opened on schedule with a
prayer, then dawdled with incidentals for several days, Ross delaying Reverend Schermerhorn's proposed address. The poor fellow would lie sleepless every night, anticipating his appearance
next morning. John Ross suggested on October 19 that the conference between him and the Ridges, the one he had proposed in
July, be held now, with five members of each party—for instance,

John Ridge, Boudinot, David Vann, and two others might represent the Treaty Party.

The party representatives met for two days without consensus. It was on the third day that they reached a compromise, and a jubilant John Ridge wrote to a Georgian,

"I consider that the Indian controversy is now closed. The Ross party and the Treaty party have united, and have agreed to close the Cherokee difficulties by a general treaty."

Ross next wrote out the agreement, delegating full powers to a proposed negotiator, who would be authorized to treat with federal officials, with the stipulation that they should not accept the five million dollars voted by the Senate. This was the provision of the treaty now most difficult to change in the Cherokees' favor. The committee of ten—the five Ross and five Ridge men—voted to accept the compromise, a majority favoring it over no agreement at all, and Ross read the terms to the assembly of some two thousand. John Ridge described the presentation:

> The question was, Are you willing to take five millions of dollars for your country? No, no, was the cry of the people. Some few of the better informed were placed in different positions to lead the way, and the Indians, without knowing the difference between 5,000 and five millions, said No! They did not understand. Then the question was put, Are you willing to give full power to these twenty men to do your business? The answer was, Yes. They were then dismissed, and they scattered that very night. There was no deliberation. . . . A vast majority . . . were of the opinion that they had rejected the propositions of the Government altogether, and had instructed their delegation to make no treaty, and consequently, *had saved the land.* This was the result of a manifest equivocation and double dealing with an ignorant people. None but the committee of negotiators remained with John Ross's council to reject [Schermerhorn's] propositions.

Elias Boudinot and Charles Vann were asked to sign the resolution. They hesitated to do so, because it did effectively provide a way to defeat the making of a treaty. Boudinot admitted his hesitation to John Ross, explaining that he could in conscience sign as a member of the ten-man committee, because they as a majority favored the rejection of the five million dollar offer, but as an individual he could not. Ross asked Boudinot to go ahead, sign as member of the committee, which he did. John and David Vann followed suit.

Schermerhorn was upset with the terms, as well as with Ross's plans to send twenty men to Washington instead of dealing with him personally here and now. He suspected another delaying tactic, another John Ross effort to wall out a treaty. He speculated about calling a meeting at New Echota for December 21. John Ridge advised him that few would show up, but the pastor proceeded with plans and on November 3 formally invited the Cherokees to a council meeting to be held there. The notice contained the message that those failing to attend gave consent and sanction to everything done.

Boudinot, as requested, translated the notice into Cherokee, and copies were printed in Cassville, Georgia, presumably using *Phoenix* type that Boudinot's brother, Stand Watie, had borrowed from the home of Elijah Hicks.

His wife recently deceased, his temperament further tortured by the delays and maneuvers, Boudinot decided not to be one of the twenty to go to Washington, as John Ross had invited. Ross appointed Major Ridge, but he also declined. John Ridge nominated Stand Watie, and Ross agreed. There were planned simultaneously: the delegation traveling to Washington and Schermerhorn's proposed meeting, the two conflicting with each other.

On November 7, in the evening, John Ross's cabin in Tennessee was surrounded by Georgia Guards and he was arrested, rudely, threateningly, and illegally. With him, also arrested, was a houseguest, John Howard Payne, an American editor returned from Europe after twenty years, touring the country to gather material for a magazine he planned to publish in London. Payne had already met the Ridge family and liked them, and had then sought out John Ross. He was at Ross's house transcribing Cherokee documents in his possession. Among Payne's many accomplishments was a plaintive little song he had dashed off, titled "Home, Sweet Home," which he was proud of, and tired of listening to, and tired of hearing about.

Payne was arrested along with Ross, the guards operating on orders from a superior, perhaps Ben Currey, who was known to have objected to a powerful letter Mr. Payne had written for the Knoxville *Register*, one influenced by Ross. Payne had actually been at work on the evening of the seventh when "there was a loud barking of dogs, then the quick tramp of galloping horses, then the march of many feet." He wrote that the armed men who invaded the little house had bayonets fixed. No charges were made against either him or Ross, and when he asked what they were, Payne was struck across the mouth. "You'll know that soon enough," the sergeant said, and proceeded to gather up the papers Payne had written.

There was a heavy storm outdoors, with driving rain. Even so, the pair of prisoners were told to mount. They rode in the freezing cold into Georgia, to a military encampment at Spring Place, where they were imprisoned in the log cabin that served as a jail. Two bodies were in the same room, a son of Cherokee Chief Going Snake, speaker of the council under Ross's administration, who was chained to a table, and the corpse of a Cherokee hanging from the rafters, the remains of an execution weeks ago.

At one point the distressed editor heard Colonel Absolom Bishop humming "Home, Sweet Home." Hoping to strike up a conversation, Payne admitted that he had written the song.

"Oh yeah?" Bishop said.

The Georgia Guards, none of them chosen on the basis of literacy, thumbed through the papers of Ross and Payne. The Cherokee letters were, they decided, a code, and to Payne's bafflement they further decided that the code was a variation of the French language. One officer found in Payne's writing a reference to the Georgia Guard. He had called them "banditti," and the guard suspected that this epithet was unfavorable.

John Ridge was away from home when the Ross arrest took place; the day following his return, November 14, he rode to Spring Place, to the headquarters of Colonel Bishop, and asked to see Ross. The request was denied. Colonel Bishop told him that Ross and the editor were abolitionists and were plotting insurrection among the Negroes, who were to join the Indians against the whites.

John persisted in his effort to see Ross, and finally Bishop consented. The interview was short and ended with Ross being returned to jail.

John Ridge reasoned with Bishop further and was allowed to meet with Ross again that evening. On Monday, the sixteenth, he and Ross and the colonel met for several hours, at the close of which session the colonel returned to Ross his papers, which were judged to be harmless. After dinner he curtly told a sentry, "Mr. Ross is discharged."

Payne remained in jail. There were plenty of suspicions clinging to him and his writings, including one accusation that he was a French spy. After three and a half days, he was released with rude orders to get out of Georgia—which he was pleased to do—and at John Ross's house in Tennessee he returned to his writings, turning out blistering attacks on Georgia.

One of his pieces subsequently appeared in newspapers, an address to the American people on the Cherokee subject, which he said came from the Indians. John Ridge first read it while traveling to Washington with Ross and the delegation, and became upset. Payne had written that the Cherokees wanted to remain in the East and become citizens of Tennessee and Alabama, that only a small group had been seduced by the United States into spreading lies about the Cherokee officials. When Ross confirmed that the Payne views were valid in his own mind, John resigned from the delegation, with a written message to Ross: "That address unfolds to me your views of policy diametrically opposed to mine, of my friends, who will never consent to be citizens of the United States, or receive money to buy land in a foreign country."

Ross asked John to stay with him, to come with him to Washington and preserve the unity so long advocated.

John at last agreed, though he had little confidence now in Ross's sincerity in agreeing to negotiate a treaty. On arrival in Washington the hopelessness was deepened by the refusal of the President and his Secretary of War to receive the delegation. Go home and negotiate with our emissary, they were told.

John Ross was defeated. So, for that matter, was John Ridge.

19

Reverend Schermerhorn was characterized by the Ross people as a buffoon, and the women called his efforts at seduction numerous and hasty enough to be ludicrous. Even so, as emissary he was determined to succeed, to get a treaty, and he enlisted Major Ridge's help. Obstinately, hopefully, he made his plans for an open-air council in winter at the Cherokee capital the major loved so much, New Echota, Georgia.

On December 19 of this same busy, critical year, 1835, shivering Indians began to assemble there—a disappointing count of between three and four hundred. Schermerhorn waited for the large contingents expected from the valley towns and the mountains, and finally attributed their absence to John Ross's efforts to keep them away.

John Ridge was in Washington. Boudinot was present. So was Major Ridge. In the swept-out Council House, the elders, wrapped in blankets, sought places near the fire. A young visitor wrote:

> I mixed freely with the assemblage, smoked pipes and ate connahany, a kind of hominy, and laughed and chatted with the young folks. . . . The Indian men of the crowd sat around and smoked for hours, plunged into deep meditation and reflection. Occasionally one would say something in the Indian language, very little of which I understood, in reply to which a number would give a guttural grunt. That would be followed by another long silence. So the time wore on, nothing being done, and if the affairs of Europe had been under settlement, they could not have been more deliberate.

On the twenty-second, the other hundreds still absent, the session was launched with election of officers, and the next morning bright and early Reverend Schermerhorn launched himself on a sea of language extolling the treaty. The day after, Ben Cur-

rey went through the proposed draft of the treaty sentence by
sentence, everything being translated and recorded. Only occasional grunts responded. When, however, Major Ridge rose to
speak, there arose an expectant hum of interest.

> I am one of the native sons of these wild woods. I have hunted the deer and
> turkey here, more than fifty years. I have fought your battles, have defended
> your truth and honesty, and fair trading. I have always been the friend of
> honest white men. The Georgians have shown a grasping spirit lately; they
> have extended their laws, to which we are unaccustomed, which harass our
> braves and make the children suffer and cry; but I can do them justice in my
> heart. They think the Great Father, the President, is bound by the compact
> of 1802 to purchase this country for them, and they justify their conduct by
> the end in view. They are willing to buy these lands on which to build
> houses and clear fields. I know the Indians have an older title than theirs.
> We obtained the land from the living God above. They got their title from
> the British. Yet they are strong and we are weak. We are few, they are many.
> We cannot remain here in safety and comfort. I know we love the graves of
> our fathers, who have gone before to the happy hunting grounds of the
> Great Spirit—the eternal land, where the deer, the turkey and the buffalo
> will never give out. We can never forget these homes, I know, but an un-
> bending, iron necessity tells us we must leave them. I would willingly die to
> preserve them, but any forcible effort to keep them will cost us our lands,
> our lives and the lives of our children. There is but one path of safety, one
> road to future existence as a Nation. That path is open before you. Make a
> treaty of cession. Give up these lands and go over beyond the great Father
> of Waters.

The speech was successful. The words in English and Cherokee had gone out to the listening hundreds; the honesty and sim-
plicity of the utterance brought tears even to children's eyes. Elders crowded around the major, to "take him by the hand" with
respect.

Elias Boudinot rose to speak, and his speech, too, moved the
group:

> I know I take my life in my hand, as our fathers have also done. We will
> make and sign this treaty. Our friends can then cross the great river, but
> Tom Foreman and his people will put us across the dread river of death! We
> can die, but the great Cherokee Nation will be saved. They will not be
> annihilated; they can live. Oh, what is a man worth who will not dare to die

for his people? Who is there here that would not perish, if this great nation may be saved?

Both speakers had mentioned their own deaths as a price they were willing to pay for taking this stand, and Boudinot appeared to believe that his death was actually approaching. The two of them were put on a committee of twenty to negotiate with Schermerhorn.

Christmas was celebrated with whiskey, brandy, cider; there were oceans of laughter about this crass way of observing the birth of Jesus, but only the Devil's Horn seemed to be chastising, criticizing. The Indians welcomed Christmas to New Echota and had days of feasting, drinking, and hangovers.

On the twenty-eighth, the men were willing once again to be attentive. At least by evening they were well and sober enough to hear the negotiated terms, as their committee reported them. They were the same terms, in essence, as had been offered before, including the five million dollars in money and choice land, and they were acceptable. There was then the need to agree on who would carry the treaty to Washington. Fifty offered to go; twenty were appointed by a panel. Major Ridge was in charge of the delegation.

The twenty met on Tuesday evening, December 29, 1835, at Boudinot's house. Candles and the hearthfire supplied light. On a table was displayed the written treaty, ready to be signed. Nobody offered to be first, until John Gunter, from Gunter's Landing, Tennessee, came forward, took the pen, and dipped it in ink, declaring that he was not afraid. Andrew Ross signed next. The others, including Boudinot and Major Ridge, signed, the major even yet using his mark.

He was heard to say, as he made an X, that he had signed his death warrant. He justified his action with the argument that an intelligent minority has a moral right and duty to save a blind and ignorant majority from inevitable ruin.

The council in session on the next day, December 30, by unanimous vote, approved this treaty of New Echota, and the signators were asked to seek ratification by the Senate in Washington.

John Ridge signed the New Echota treaty as soon as his father brought it to Washington. So did Stand Watie. The New
Echota treaty group sought to involve Ross and his delegation
with their own efforts, but Ross was bitterly opposed. Boudinot
was caustic in his analysis of Ross:

> In this state of things, utterly unable himself to consummate a treaty which
> he may think preferable, Mr. Ross is using his influence to defeat the only
> measure that can give relief to his suffering people. . . . He says he is doing
> the *will* of the people, and he holds their authority; they are opposed, and it
> is enough. The will of the people! The opposition of the people! This has
> been the cry for the last five years, until that people have become but a mere
> wreck of what they once were; all their institutions and improvements ut-
> terly destroyed; their energy enervated; their moral character debased, cor-
> rupted and ruined. The whole of that catastrophe . . . might have been
> averted, if Mr. Ross . . . had met the crisis manfully as it became him to do,
> and unfolded to his confiding people the sure termination of these things;
> they might now have been a happy and prosperous community, a monu-
> ment to his forecast and wise administration as an Indian chief. But, no sir,
> he has dragged an ignorant train, wrought upon by near-sighted prejudice
> and stupid obstinacy, to the last brink of destruction.

The treaty went to the Senate, where debate was heavy.
Often quoted was a paper written by John Howard Payne, who
was still on fire against Georgia. Ross supplied a petition bearing
sixteen thousand signatures. There were not sixteen thousand
Cherokees in the East, and of those actually living there, half
were children; nevertheless, the petition was entered. Ross opposed ratification on the grounds that the Treaty of New Echota
did not carry the signatures of the principal Cherokee officials
and was not backed by the people. Most senators were convinced
that this was so; however, President Jackson was pressing hard,
and on May 17, 1836, the treaty was ratified by a margin of one
vote. Jackson proclaimed it law on May 23.

Along with his father and Elias Boudinot, John Ridge viewed
the treaty as a deadly friend: sooner or later it would require his
life as a penalty for signing. He returned home in June, too late to
plant; Sally had seen to it anyway. She and the blacks had put in
the field crops as well as the garden. The major found that

Susanna had overseen the planting of their crop lands, helped by the servants—she would not use the word slaves. Good crops were in prospect in spite of the heavy rains that had made the ground soggy in spring, in spite of the theft by a white man named Cox of one of the fields across the river. The man had planted it himself, and there was no legal action available to the major.

John's ferry had been taken over by one John H. Garrett, a boastful major-general in the Alabama militia, who had thrown the ferryman off the property. He had taken over the tenant farm located there in Alabama, as well. Alabama was modeling its laws on Georgia's, and there was nothing legally John and Sally could do. Sally had asked for Ben Currey's help before John returned, and Currey had ordered Garrett to leave. Failing that, Currey had gone to Alabama's governor, but that apparently had failed. The general was still running the ferry and the tenant farm.

Two weeks after his return home, John wrote President Jackson a letter, which he showed to his father, who signed it too. It reviewed the situation they found on their return:

> There was a strong warlike excitement in the minds of the whites, and rumor, with her thousand tongues, filled the land with Cherokee hostility or intentions of war. We have examined into the truth, and find the reverse of all these stories. A great many of the Cherokees have been disarmed of their rifles by the Georgians . . . , greatly to the injury of the Indians, as they are in a wretched condition for food. The appropriations demanded by the treaty have been so long delayed that we have, on our own responsibility, issued provisions, as far as our individual means allowed.

There followed a cheerful view of the treaty's reception, and then John returned to a dark picture of the Cherokee situation:

> But now we come to address you on the subject of our griefs & afflictions from the acts of the white people. They have got our lands and now they are preparing to fleece us of the money accruing from the treaty. We found our plantations taken in whole or in part by the Georgians—suits instituted against us for back rents of our own farms. These suits are commenced in the lower courts, with the evident design that, when we are ready to remove, to arrest our people, and on these vile claims to induce us to compromise for our own release, to travel with our families. Thus our funds will be

filched from our people, and we shall be compelled to leave our country as
beggars and in want.

Even the Georgia laws, which deny our oaths, are thrown aside, and
notwithstanding the cries of our people, and protestation of our innocence
and peace, the lowest classes of the white people are flogging the Cherokees
with cowhides, hickories, and clubs. We are not safe in our houses—our
people are assailed by day and night by the rabble. Even justices of the
peace and constables are concerned in this business. This barbarous treatment is not confined to men, but the women are stripped also and whipped
without law or mercy. . . . Send regular troops to protect us from these
lawless assaults, and to protect our people as they depart for the West. If it is
not done, we shall carry off nothing but the scars of the lash on our backs,
and our oppressors will get all the money. We talk plainly, as chiefs having
property and life in danger, and we appeal to you for protection.

This description of the wretched conditions and tortures was
based on incidents reported mainly in Georgia, although Tennessee and Alabama had also passed laws incorporating Cherokee
lands—only North Carolina had not. His letter might have exaggerated dangers in order to make its point, and his optimistic
view of the treaty was based on hope more than fact; a ground-
swell of resentment toward the men who had mandated removal
was swelling like a tidal wave.

By summer the major and Susanna were almost out of food,
having slaughtered their stock in order to feed the wandering
hungry; John and Sally were purchasing beef to serve the families
flocking to them and had only three shoats remaining. Many families were displaced, wandering about.

The missionaries at Brainerd had the best gristmills and sawmills, and the whites, arriving throughout 1835 in increasing
numbers to take over their lottery-won holdings, brought them
their logs to be made into planks in order to build or repair barns
and houses. Brainerd's cooperation displeased the Indians. The
missionaries were charging the whites, but, even so, they were
helping them and ought to stop doing so, the Indians argued.

These days the reasons for quarreling seemed to be endless,
and once the United States government moved troops into the
area, tension increased; the troops were there to protect the Indians, but were nonetheless viewed skeptically.

The missionaries had their own set of worries and persecutions in Georgia. Replacement teachers refused to take jobs there, so the vacancies were not filled, even after Georgia repealed its antimissionary law. The American Board closed several Georgia mission stations, those at Hightower, Haweis, New Echota, and Carmel. A new one was opened in Tennessee, at Red Clay, to hire some of the converts and missionaries leaving Georgia. The staff of all the board's mission stations combined, which had been thirty-four in 1830, was ten, including three ministers, one doctor, five women assistants, and one farmer. In addition there were four wives in residence.

At the board's missions the converts were half as many as eight years earlier.

The Moravians were reduced by half, too. They sought to serve Spring Place from positions in Tennessee, and were only partially successful. The Methodists were also reduced by half. Unlike the governing bodies of Moravians and Presbyterians, they had never for a moment supported removal or any other government activity; but most of the full-blood Cherokees now viewed all Christianity, all denominations, as the white man's religion. Also, the Devil's Horn was a minister, wasn't he, and he had been the architect of this final judgment issued by Washington and the Ridge family.

The Baptists, in spite of the hostility to whites, increased 500 percent, for many reasons. The denomination's strength was greatest in the western North Carolina mountains and in the strip of mountains in northern Georgia, where the whites were not pushing in. The Baptist leader there, Reverend Evan Jones, was the only missionary to have mastered the Cherokee language. He had on staff several exhorters, natives who preached and taught, using the circuit-riding system of the Methodists. One was Reverend Bushyhead, who was a powerful Cherokee preacher. Jones and Bushyhead also followed the Methodist practice of holding camp meetings.

Jones was not influenced by boards or overseers living in faroff places who supported removal; his superiors did not know what he was up to and did not want to know. He was converting Cherokees and that was enough. In fact, he was a John Ross man, an opponent of removal, as were Bushyhead and the other native preachers he had trained. He was against Indian enslavement of any kind, and spoke out in plain words about the evil of black enslavement. On a day designated by Ross for humiliation and prayer for the nation, Jones was preaching at valley towns, but he did not lead his congregation into remorse about personal sins of drunkenness, profanity, sexual misconduct, nor did he deal with the sins of the Andrew Jackson government. Instead he dwelled on the sins of the Cherokee nation, claiming that "if providence does not favor a nation, it cannot prosper." God's anger, his sense of justice, was now being visited on the Cherokee, and what were the sins that God was punishing the Cherokee for? Why, black slavery. That was the worst one. It was the one hidden from the mind, not discussed. It was the deepest scar on the body of the Cherokee nation, and while that nation pleaded with God for deliverance from its own enslavement, it allowed the enslavement of another people. God is not mocked. Onto your knees before the throne of justice.

That was Jones's notion of a call to repentance. He wanted Cherokees to free their two thousand blacks.

No Baptists had signed the Treaty of New Echota. No chief of the western North Carolina mountains had signed the treaty, either. On one occasion Schermerhorn had come into the mountains seeking, needing their signatures, and Jones had hounded him. Schermerhorn complained, "I visited the North Carolina Indians in order to explain the treaty to them and obtain some of their signatures to it, but through the influence of the Baptist Missionary, who was under the influence of Ross, I did not succeed in getting any of them to sign."

General Wool had been sent to quell any possible Indian uprising, such as those erupting among the Creeks and Seminoles. One of his first orders to the Cherokees was to surrender all guns. Of course, the Cherokees needed their guns for hunting, particularly in a year of only scanty crops; wild game sustained the mountain Indians. They did not comply. Wool knew of Evan Jones's influence among the Cherokees, so he ordered the Baptist to have the guns brought in. Not only was Jones to do that, but Wool told him to try to sell the Treaty of New Echota and to persuade the Indians to register now for removal. Reverend Jones reported:

> When I was introduced to him he used many arguments to induce me to advise the Indians to submit to the treaty. I took the liberty, respectfully, to state to him the plain truth with regard to the injustice practised on the Cherokees in the making of this Treaty and that the whole body of the Cherokees were opposed to it. He agreed to the truth of all this, but said the Treaty was ratified and must be executed. I, however, declined taking any part in the business.

Wool arrested him, along with his assistants. In all he arrested four Indian men, two of their wives, and one white man married to a native. He took them to his headquarters, where he decided to release all except Jones and one Indian assistant, David Foreman. The general ordered the two to accompany him on his treks through the mountain area collecting guns. Jones and Foreman bargained with him, offered to send out an appeal for arms, if that appeal would relax this dangerous situation; and their offer was accepted.

Jones's rationale was that troops should not go into the homes of the people; also, he reasoned that, given a choice between his old, broken gun and a better one, an Indian could choose the inferior one to send to the government.

He was warned by Wool not to preach any more of his inflammatory ideas, but Jones rented a house just outside the Tennessee boundary of the Cherokee nation; there he and his wife opened a school for Cherokee children, and from that base he rode on his circuit. On one circuit he and Bushyhead preached twenty-six times, held six conference meetings, received twenty-nine candidates for baptism, examining them about their understanding of Christianity, and of these baptized four men, two Cherokee women, and one black woman at Coosawattee, one man, four Cherokee women, and one black woman at Still's place, one man and one woman at Long Swamp, and three men and four women at Deganeetla. All the while he was avoiding arrest. Wool threatened to find him and his assistants and dispatch them at once to the West; but the Indians scouted for him, walked the roads and trails with him, their friend, Ross's friend.

At first Wool was suspicious of the Cherokees. A soldier, an officer to the core, he arrived expecting to find trouble that he would need to regulate, even anticipated uncovering the seeds of an Indian uprising; but he found a people whose young had never known war and knew nothing of fighting.

He became rather humane, this general, his military bearing softened.

September 10, 1836. General Wool to the Honorable Lewis Cass, Secretary of War:

> New Echota:
> . . . The duty I have to perform is far from pleasant. . . . Only made tolerable with the hope that I may stay cruelty and injustice, and assist the wretched and deluded beings called Cherokees, who are only the prey of the most profligate and most vicious of white men. . . . The whole scene, since I have been in this country, has been nothing but a heart-rending one, and such a one as I would be glad to be rid of as soon as circumstances will permit. . . . If I could, and I could not do them a greater kindness, *I would remove every Indian tomorrow, beyond the reach of the white men,* who like vultures, are watching, ready to pounce upon their prey, and strip them of everything they have or expect to have from the government. . . . Nineteen-twentieths, if not 99 out of every hundred, will go pennyless to the west.

President Jackson was in no mood for sentiment. Almost eight years of the presidency had left him weakened in health and lacking portions of his famous vengefulness. He was damn tired of the Indians, anyway. Take Sam Houston, the Tennessee Cherokee sonofabitch who was now president of the so-called Republic of Texas: "the Raven" was showing all the Cherokee traits of defiance, was telling the United States government what to do.

And here was John Ross back in Washington again—did he, Jackson wondered, now reside in Washington? Consider his last petition, a plea signed by babes in arms and dead Indians, almost everybody using an *X*. What the hell did a petition mean, signed by sixteen thousand *X*es?

Anyway, the question is settled. They have two years from the date of Senate ratification to go peacefully. Otherwise, they'll go by force. God help them if they diddle away that time and have to be taken west by the military, even such sweet-singing friends as Wool.

Ralph Waldo Emerson at long last learned that an injustice was being done in his own country, and he fired off a letter from Concord to the new President, Martin Van Buren:

> Sir, my communication respects the sinister rumors that fill this part of the country concerning the Cherokee people. . . . Even in our distant state some good rumor of their worth and civility has arrived. We have learned with joy of their improvement in the social arts. . . . And not withstanding the unaccountable apathy with which of late years the Indians have been sometimes abandoned to their enemies, it is the understanding of all humane persons in the Republic . . . that they shall be duly cared for; that they shall taste justice and love from all to whom we have delegated the office of dealing with them.

He went on to refer to the "Treaty of 1835," which was, he said, made by the country with some persons appearing on the part of the Cherokees. . . .

> Such a dereliction of all faith and virtue, such a denial of justice, and such deafness to screams for mercy were never heard of in times of peace and in the dealings of a nation with its own allies and wards, since the earth was made.
>
> Sir, does this government think that the people of the United States are become savage and mad? From their minds are the sentiments of love and a good nature wiped clean out? The soul of man, the justice, the mercy that is that heart's heart in all men, from Maine to Georgia, does abhor this business.

Emerson admitted that he had a gloomy opinion of the government's character. The current economic panic that the public and legislators were so concerned about was but a "mote" when compared with the report he had received of the Cherokee outrage. In oversized letters across the paper he concluded his letter: "In the name of God, sir, we ask you if this be so."

Harriet Gold Boudinot was ill, with complications from pregnancy, and for that reason Boudinot was not at the green corn dance. He was beside her bed, as were Worcester and his wife, along with Sophia Sawyer and others of the New Echota community who loved her. Medicine did not effect its promised miracle. The complications, as the doctor termed them, grew worse. Boudinot wrote two letters to her parents, the second on August 16, 1836:

> My Dear Father and Mother—By the last mail I addressed a hasty letter to brother Swift, apprising him of the dangerous [condition] of Harriet, and requesting him to communicate the same to you in such a way as he might think best, to lessen the weight of affliction the same which a future letter would in all probability inflict upon your parental hearts. In fact, in order that you might be saved from conflicting hopes and tears, in regard to her recovery or death, I stated to him that her case was a hopeless one, and that you need not look for any other information but that which would apprise you that she was no more. Presuming that you have, by the help of God, prepared your minds to hear what was too plainly to be expected, I now perform the sad office of communicating to you the death of your daughter and my dear companion. Yes, Harriet is no more—she died yesterday morning, 19 minutes after 1 o'clock, and about 3 o'clock in the afternoon, we consigned her mortal remains to our mother earth, there to lie until God shall raise the dead. As a last duty, therefore, in fulfilment of the promise I made in the letter alluded to, I undertake to give you some account of her sickness and death. . . .

Sequoyah enjoyed living in the West; so did many hundreds of other Cherokees who during recent years had gone out there, some in groups of a hundred or more, some with their families only. Here he made ornamented silver buckles and silver plates for horses' martingales; however, most of his time was spent in teaching his written language as adapted for use by the Choctaws, and musing while he smoked his long-stemmed pipe. The eastern council had voted him a medal back in 1824; to his knowledge it was struck a year or so thereafter, but John Ross apparently had not wanted to send anything to the West, even that. Sequoyah had not received it till recently, when it was finally sent to the "country where you dwell," as Ross phrased it. Of course, Sequoyah was proud of being honored by his own people. Two of his uncles were chiefs of distinction, Taluntuskee, the Overthrower, and Kahn-Yah-Tah-Hee, the First to Kill, once the principal chief of old Echota, the town of refuge, a special haven. The latter was called the beloved chief of all the people, a preserver of peace. As Sequoyah understood the story, during a public assembly he had been told that the whites were coming. All the people fled except him and one other Indian chief. He waited in the Echota square and met the whites. He was carrying, waving a white flag. He was murdered at once; as was the other chief. Days later, when the people returned, the carion birds had devoured the corpse of the other man, but this uncle, the beloved of all, was untouched; and, even more remarkable, he was not deteriorating. His hand was even yet as smooth as silk, clutching the flag of peace. And on his face was a benign smile.

His father's people were Virginian white planters, wealthy aristocrats who had not admitted they had Indian kin until Sequoyah's fame came to their attention. One of his grandfathers had pulled George Washington from an icy river. Now that was a Virginia blueblood, indeed.

Sequoyah would smoke his pipe and contemplate such heroics, accepting the affection of Cherokee and Choctaw and talking with his daughter and his grandchildren. Over sixty years of age now, crippled, he was best as a thinker, a muser—or so he had decided.

When his medal finally arrived from the East, it was accompanied by the following message from John Ross:

Head of Coosa, Cherokee Nation

Mr. George Gist, My friend—The Legislative Council of the Cherokee Nation in the year 1824 voted a medal to be presented to you, as a token of respect and admiration for your ingenuity in the invention of the Cherokee Alphabetical Characters; and in pursuance thereof, the two late venerable Chiefs, Path Killer and Charles R. Hicks, instructed a delegation of this nation, composed of Major George Low[e]ry, Senior, Elijah Hicks and myself, to have one struck, which was completed in 1825. In the anticipation of your visit to this country, it was reserved for the purpose of honoring you with its presentment by the Chiefs in General Council; but having been so long disappointed in this pleasing hope, I have thought it my duty no longer to delay, and therefore take upon myself the pleasure of delivering it, through our friend, Mr. Charles H. Vann who intends visiting his relatives in the country where you dwell. In receiving this small tribute from the representatives of the people of your native land, in honor of your transcendant invention, you will, I trust, place a proper estimate on the grateful feelings of your fellow countrymen. The beginning, the progress and the final completion of the grand scheme, is full of evidence that the efforts of all the powers of a man of more than ordinary genius were put in action. The present generation have already experienced the great benefits of your incomparable system. The old and the young find no difficulty in learning to read and write in their native language and to correspond with their distant friends with the same facility as the whites do. Types have been made and a printing press established in this nation. The scriptures have been translated and printed in Cherokee and while posterity continues to be benefited by the discovery, your name will exist in grateful remembrance. It will also serve as an index for other aboriginal tribes, or nations, similarly to advance in science and respectability: in short, the great good designed by the author of human existence in directing your genius in this happy discovery, cannot be fully estimated—it is incalculable. Wishing you health and happiness I am your Friend—John Ross.

The medal was made at Washington and of silver, to the value of twenty dollars. One side was thus inscribed:

"Presented
to
George Gist
by the
General Council of the Cherokee Nation
for his ingenuity in
the invention of the
Cherokee Alphabet:
1825."

Under the inscription were two tobacco pipes. Crossed.

When Major Ridge signed up, ready to move west, he registered his daughter Sally along with the other family members and slaves. Sally had recently been attending Salem Academy, operated by the Moravians in North Carolina. She had been "finished" there, and the result was a charming, graceful maiden with dark complexion, about the tone of her father's, "a lady of superior talent . . . very interesting in her person & appearance" as a missionary described her. One acquaintance wrote,

> She was a most accomplished rider, and her roan pony was known far and wide in the country. She was venerated by her father's allies as a kind of divinity. Many white men aspired to her hand. . . . A remarkable incident is related of Miss Sally's power of horsemanship. . . . Once her lover, the man she at last married, "bought from a Tennessee drover a nag for Miss Sally to ride on." He presented it to her, saddled and bridled, and begged the pleasure of riding with her. She mounted on the pony gaily, but something about the bridle needed adjusting, the lover slipped it off the pony's head to fix it. No sooner loose than the pony bounded off unfettered, and he and Miss Sally, for thirteen miles, tried for the mastery of the situation. "Miss Sally rode him down," it is said, and ever afterward the pony seemed a dispirited animal.

The major told Sally and the other members of the family to prepare to leave for the Arkansas territory. He had his coach made ready, his wagons packed. His slaves prepared themselves to move; sixteen of them were to be taken. The major, one of the three richest Cherokees—along with Joseph Vann and John Ross —had received a fortune, more than $24,000 for his property here. He assigned his family members their seats in the coach; then, to his surprise, his daughter Sally told him that she and Lieutenant George Paschal wanted to have his and her mother's permission to marry.

The major cancelled all plans. He told his family to unpack. They were to wait with him and prepare. He wanted to give the bride away. He was like a boy with a new toy. Later he would go west. All of them were to wait—John and Sally, too.

Ridge's family was to have been part of a large party traveling together. The party proceeded without them, some seven hundred pro-Treaty individuals, including their slaves. First they gathered in New Echota. They prepared their own march. Mounted chiefs wearing skins and furs headed the cavalcade. Following were the carriages carrying the women and children and the wagons filled with possessions, followed by the herds of cattle to be used for meat. It might have been a holiday excursion.

The federal agent, Benjamin Currey, fell ill. General Wool thought it might be well if he died, for all the ill he had done this patient tribe of people. He didn't care for Currey or any of the others in New Echota who were talking Indians into moving. John Ridge was all right, he supposed—a bit haughty. One of the two commissioners had had to ask John to stop feeding hundreds of Cherokees and billing the government for costs. Also, this commissioner thought the Indians' houses and barns and goods might not all be as valuable as John represented them to be. Of course, he had to represent his clients. And of course the commissioner was a Georgian, and was therefore untrustworthy around Indians. Lumpkin was his name. He was one of two commissioners, but the other was bedridden with arthritis, so he had everything his way. Wilson Lumpkin, the one who had years ago introduced the removal bill in Congress, had later become governor of Georgia, and was now the sole active commissioner. He was hoping to become a senator.

In fact, the other commissioner resigned. The replacement was to be John Kennedy, a Tennessean. That arrangement might prove to be much better, Wool thought.

The Indians coming to see the two commissioners often camped alongside the roads and waited patiently for an audience, and Wool couldn't help feel sorry for them. Damn insult to ask them to present their property for evaluation to the Georgian who had devised their turmoil and he sitting alone with nobody to check his actions. The Indians came from every part of the Cherokee nation, in carriages, wagons, ox carts, sleds pulled by steers, on horseback, by foot. They brought cooking pots and their wooden spoons. The commissioners had requisitioned blankets from General Wool, and Army rations. Some of the Indian women had brought salt and connahany. The women built fires and the men smoked pipes, and all of them waited, Ridge and Ross advocates together. General Wool had troops in New Echota, but the only trouble came when Indians became drunk. Then some of them were quarrelsome, prone to get into scuffles and fights.

A military man, Wool did not work easily with civilians, par-

ticularly when he did not know what his authority was. In a war
a man knew, but what would this type of registration be called?

6 November 1836.—Gen. Wool to Hon. B. F. Butler, Act. Secretary of War.
Ft. Cass:
. . . Your instructions of 20 June contemplates the application of military force only in the event of hostilities. . . . The treaty provides that
they shall be protected in the peaceable possession of their country within a
two year period. . . . This communication deprived me of all power, except in the event of hostilities. . . . Nothing was left for me to do but to
stand and look on until the Indians had raised the Tomahawk. . . . The
people as soon as they knew I was divested of all discretionary power would
relax into the arms of John Ross. . . . I can only say that I cannot be recalled too soon from this command. . . . For a military commander to be
held responsible for the peace and defense of a country, at the same time to
be placed under the control of civil officers, has no parallel in the whole
military annals of our country. . . . If I am culpable let me be arraigned
and tried, but do not degrade me until I am proved guilty.

Later that month he returned a communication from Commissioners Lumpkin and Kennedy, with the note that it appeared
to have been issued as an order when it should have been issued as
a request.

This was merely one more nail in Wool's coffin, as Wilson
Lumpkin and his co-commissioner viewed it.

30 January 1837.—Commissioners Lumpkin and Kennedy, New Echota, to
C. A. Harris:
In attempting in the *most humble and modest manner* to avail ourselves of
the services of the military, in the execution of civil duties, we have found
ourselves repulsed and insulted at every attempt which we have made to
obtain the co-operation of General Wool. When we politely requested . . .
an escort to guard public funds . . . the communication was sent back, in
contempt, accompanied by a written insult to ourselves *and the President of
the United States.*

Wool was particularly harsh with whiskey peddlers; they sold
to Indians and soldiers alike. And he was hard on gamblers and
other riffraff.

12 March 1837.—Gen. Wool to John R. Delany, Commanding at Ross' Landing:

The prisoner Bridgemaker, can be released on his promising not to oppose the execution of the treaty. . . . In relation to gamblers, or black-legs, you have all the authority necessary to prevent them from establishing themselves in your neighborhood, and to drive them out of the country. There is no State or United States Law to protect them within the limits of the nation. Gambling and selling them ardent spirits must be prevented.

His attitude toward the Cherokees became ever more pater-nalistic:

15 March 1837.—Gen. Wool to Col. Joseph Byrd, 2nd Regt. of ETV. Fm New Echota:
     You will proceed without delay and take command of the troops under Major Cunningham, at or near the mouth of Valley River. You will treat the Cherokees kindly and give them all the protection guaranteed by the late treaty. . . . You will inform them that rations, blankets, shoes and other articles, will be furnished the poor of the nation on application.

30 March 1837.—Gen. Wool to Lt. Deas:
     . . . You will take charge of collecting refugee Creeks scattered through the Nation. . . . You are authorized to purchase clothing for cov-ering the nakedness of the Indians, if needed.

30 March 1837.—Gen. Wool, New Echota, to Major Delany:
     Proceed to Red Clay to collect Creeks in the neighborhood . . . furnish them provisions. When you have a sufficient number . . . conduct them to Ross' Landing. After they are taken, they must be treated with kindness, and on no account must the soldiers be permitted to offer any insult to them, or allowed to commit any depredation on their property.

3 April 1837.—Gen. Wool, New Echota, to Col. Byrd near Valley River:
     Furnish Lt. Deas with military aid to apprehend Creeks in the moun-tains of North Carolina. If not able to purchase provisions in your neigh-borhood, get them at Camp Huntington, in charge of Lt. Montgomery, without interfering with the depot for the poor Cherokees. No doubt fresh beef can be procured, and corn from Hunter or Starritt.

20 April 1837.—Gen. Wool to Poinsett, Secretary of War:
     . . . 300 Creeks apprehended, these with the 150 at Gunter's Landing will be sent to Arkansas. Those found in Cherokee country generally in wretched condition. I ordered sufficient clothing to cover their nakedness. . . . The period is approaching when the term of the East Tennessee Vol-unteers will expire. I have requested a regiment of United States infantry. . . . I would prefer 500 disciplined troops to 2000 undisciplined and unin-structed volunteers.

Perhaps his kindly attitude toward the Indians was responsible, or maybe the co-commissioners finally got him ousted; for one reason or another, in midsummer he was relieved of his command. The indoctrination of a new general began.

The government men regularly opened John Ross's letters, in order to follow the course of his efforts to thwart their work. They would read some of his incoming mail, too.

12 August 1837.—War Department to John Ross, Chief of the Cherokees, Red Clay:

You are too well acquainted with the character of the white people by which the Cherokee people are surrounded to desire, or expect them to remain where they are now, and too well aware of the power of this Government, not to be convinced of the utter hopelessness of that nation being able, for any length of time, to evade the execution of the treaty.

The economic panic that struck the United States in 1837 was in part due to a law Congress passed distributing to the states some $35 million remaining in the federal treasury after the national debt was paid off. Panic ensued when the eighty banks in which the fortune was lying were told to produce it. Most of the banks had considered the money a type of permanent loan and had used it. That crisis, along with the decline in the price of cotton and overstrained credit between the United States and Europe, prostrated the entire financial, industrial, commercial system, with no hope for relief in sight, even as Jackson turned the reins of the presidency over to his protégé, Van Buren.

John Ross had been given notice in General Order 74, as publicly posted, that the treaty would be "fulfilled in all its parts, terms, and conditions, within the period prescribed," and that any further contraventions similar to the resolution at the last council "will be considered as indicative of a design to prevent the execution of the treaty, even at the hazard of actual hostilities, and they will be promptly repressed." Ross, as anybody could tell by stealing his mail, was ignoring these commands, and the government, including President Van Buren, was now ignoring him.

On his big black horse, one provided for him by the council, comfortable in the ornate saddle, Ross traveled the countryside, and everywhere he went he told his people to stand firm, to trust him and all would be worked out. Tears in their eyes, the frightened, angry citizens gratefully gathered round to take him by the hand.

In his home, as in the hotel room in Washington, Ross wrote numerous drafts of substitute treaties, even hundreds; but none of the stack was ever finished. One recurring variation started out by yielding up the Georgia lands in return for full citizenship for the Cherokees in Alabama, Tennessee, and North Carolina; that offer never came to fruition.

An English gentleman, George W. Featherstonhaugh, came through, a geologist whose interest in the pebbles and rocks amused the residents. He was, in fact, conducting a survey of the mineral riches. According to William E. Lass, his "greatest scorn was lavished on the political changes wrought by Jacksonian Democracy, for he was openly contemptuous of 'Republican America.' "

The following excerpts are from that book's section on his travels in 1837 among the Cherokees:

August 4.—This morning, whilst we were at breakfast, a company of Georgia Mounted Volunteers rode through the place on their way to the Cherokee Council. All had their coats off with their muskets and cartouch-boxes strung across their shoulders. Some of the men had straw hats, some of them white felt hats, others had old black hats on with the rim torn off, and all of them were as unshaven and as dirty as they could well be. The officers were only distinguished by having Cherokee fringed hunting shirts on. Many of the men were stout young fellows, and they rode on, talking, and cursing and swearing, without any kind of discipline. Upon the whole it was a picturesque sight, and brought to my recollection the descriptions of the condottieri of ancient times.

Having engaged the stage to take us to Red Clay, we left Spring Place at 8 A.M., passing for twenty-five miles through a wild country with a rolling surface, pleasingly wooded, and sufficiently open to admit of the growth of various beautiful flowers. We crossed the Connesawga, which is a beautiful mountain stream, and were frequently gratified with the sight of fine fat deer bounding across the narrow wood road with their magnificent antlers. The quail, too, were numerous, and the young birds large. The soil being derived from the lower Silurian limestone is very fertile, and certainly I never saw heavier Indian corn than in two or three settlements that we passed, especially at one Young's, about fifteen miles from Spring Place.

Towards the close of our journey we called upon Colonel Lindsay, who commanded the United States troops in this district, a detachment of which was here for the purpose of preserving order. His accommodations were rather humble, and every body seemed to be aware of it but himself, who appeared too intent upon the delicate duty he had to discharge to think of indulgences. The Colonel's quarters were upon the edge of an extensive rich, dry, bottom of land, thickly covered with young trees, most of them not more than from twenty to thirty years old, through which a graceful little stream, called Cóoayhállay, ran meandering. Advancing through the grove, we began to perceive symptoms of an assemblage of Indians. Straggling horses, booths, and log tenements were seen at a distance through the trees, young Indian boys began to appear running in the woods, and the noise of men and animals was heard in the distance.

Hearing that a half-breed Cherokee named Hicks, whom I had formerly known, had put up some huts for the accommodation of strangers, we found him out, and he assigned us a hut to ourselves, the floor of which was strewed with nice dry pine leaves. It contained also two rude bedsteads, with pine branches as a substitute for beds, and some bed-clothes of a strange fashion, but which were tolerably clean. Chairs we had none; and our first care was to get a sort of table carpentered up, and to place it in such a position that we could use our bedsteads for chairs when we wrote. Our log hut had been so hastily run up that it had neither a door, nor bore evidence of an intention to add one to it, and its walls were formed of logs with interstices of at least six inches between them, so that we not only had the advantage of seeing every thing that was going on out of doors, but of gratifying every body outside who was desirous of seeing what was done within our hut, especially the Indians, who appeared extremely curious.

Having refreshed ourselves with a cup of tea, we walked out with General Smith, the Indian agent for the United States, to see the Council-house. Crossing the Cóoayhállay, we soon found ourselves in an irregular sort of street consisting of huts, booths, and stores hastily constructed from the trees of the forest, for the accommodation of Cherokee families, and for the cooking establishments necessary to the subsistence of several thousand Indians. This street was at the foot of some hilly ground upon which the Council-room was built, which was a simple parallelogram formed of logs with open sides, and benches inside for the councillors. The situation was exceedingly well chosen in every respect, for there was a copious limestone spring on the bank of the stream, which gave out a delicious cool water in sufficient quantities for this great multitude. What contributed to make the situation extremely picturesque, was the great number of beautiful trees growing in every direction, the underwood having been most judiciously cut away to enable the Indians to move freely through the forest, and to tie their horses to the trees. Nothing more Arcadian could be conceived than the picture which was presented; but the most impressive feature, and that which imparted life to the whole, was an unceasing current of Cherokee Indians, men, women, youths, and children, moving about in every direction, and in the greatest order; and all, except the younger ones, preserving a grave and thoughtful demeanour imposed upon them by the singular position in which they were placed, and by the trying alternative now presented to them of delivering up their native country to their oppressors, or perishing in a vain resistance.

An observer could not but sympathize deeply with them; they were not to be confounded with the wild savages of the West, being decently dressed after the manner of white people, with shirts, trousers, shoes and stockings, whilst the half-breeds and their descendants conformed in every thing to the custom of the whites, spoke as good English as them, and differed from them only in a browner complexion, and in being less vicious and more sober. The pure bloods had red and blue cotton handkerchiefs folded on their heads in the manner of turbans, and some of these, who were mountaineers from the elevated districts of North Carolina wore also deer-skin leggings and embroidered hunting shirts; whilst their turbans, their dark coarse, lank hair, their listless savage gait, and their swarthy Tartar countenances, reminded me of the Arabs from Barbary. Many of these men were athletic and good looking; but the women who had passed from the maidenly age, had, owing to the hard labour imposed upon them by Indian usages, lost as usual every feminine attraction, so that in my walk I did not see one upon whom I had any desire to look a second time. In the course of the evening, I attended at the Council-house to hear some of their resolutions read by an English missionary, named Jones, who adhered to the Cherokees; a man of talent, it was said, and of great activity, but who was detested by the Georgians. These were afterwards translated, *vivâ voce*, into Cherokee by Bushy-head, one of the principal half-breed Cherokees. A most refreshing rain fell in the evening. About 8 P.M., somewhat fatigued with the adventures of the day, I retired to our hut, from whence, through the interstices of the logs, I saw the fires of the Cherokees, who bivouacked in the woods, gleaming in every direction; and long after I laid down, the voices of hundreds of the most pious amongst them who had assembled at the Council-house to perform their evening worship, came pealing in hymns through the now quiet forest, and insensibly and gratefully lulled me to sleep.

August 5.—The voices of the Cherokees already at morning worship awoke me at the dawn of the day, and dressing myself hastily, I went to the Council-house. Great numbers of them were assembled, and Mr. Jones, the Missionary, read out verses in the English language from the New Testament, which Bushy-head, with a singularly stentorial voice and sonorous accent, immediately rendered to the people in the Cherokee tongue, emitting a deep grunting sound at the end of every verse, resembling the hard breathing of a man chopping trees down, the meaning of which I was given to understand was to call their attention to the proposition conveyed by the passage. This I was told is an universal practice also in Cherokee oratory. When they sang, a line or two of a hymn printed in the Cherokee language was given out, each one having a hymn book in his hand, and I certainly never saw any congregation engaged more apparently in sincere devotion. This spectacle insensibly led me into reflection upon the opinion which is so generally entertained of its being impossible to civilize the Indians in our sense of the word. Here is a remarkable instance which seems to furnish a conclusive answer to scepticism on this point. A whole Indian nation abandons the pagan practices of their ancestors, adopts the Christian religion, uses books printed in their own language, submits to the government of their elders, builds houses and temples of worship, relies upon agriculture for their support, and produces men of great ability to rule over them, and to whom they give a willing obedience. Are not these the great principles of civilization? They are driven from their religious and social state then, not because they cannot be civilized, but because a pseudo set of civilized beings, who are too strong for them, want their possessions! What a bitter reflection it will be to the religiously disposed portion of the people, who shall hereafter live here, that the country they will be so proud of and so blest in was torn from the Aboriginals in this wrongful manner. God be thanked, that in acquiring the dominion of India, Great Britain protects and blesses the people whose country owns her sway! . . .

About 10 A.M., a deputation, consisting of members of the Cherokee Council, and some aged persons, formerly chiefs of some celebrity, came in procession to our hut, to pay a visit of ceremony to my companion, the United States special agent; but he being at Colonel Lindsay's, I received them in his stead, gave them seats at our bedsteads, and immediately sent a messenger for him, who soon after arrived with Colonel Lindsay and a military escort. An ancient chief, named Innatáhoolósah, or the Going Snake, addressed him, and complimented him upon his arrival. This old warrior had led a large body of his people in former times to assist General Jackson against the Creeks, and contributed much to the victory he obtained over them at the battle of the Horse Shoe, where he received a wound in the arm. He was a fine old man, with a good deal of Indian dignity. Nothing appears to have stung the Cherokees more deeply than the reflection, that after serving General Jackson so effectually, it should have been under his administration of the Government, from which they had so much right to expect protection, that their independence had been broken down, and their territories appropriated without their consent. There was also another old chief remarkably cheerful and light of step, although seventy-six years old, called Nennenóh Oonáykay, or White Path. After an interchange of compliments they retired. This day we dined by invitation with Mrs. Walker, a fine old Cherokee lady, who spoke a little English; and met John Ross, the principal chief of the Cherokees. Our hostess received us in a very polite and friendly manner. The dinner was good, we had boiled beef, chickens and bacon, with excellent vegetables. Coffee was served with the dinner, and we retired as soon as it was over, according to the custom. Large wooden bowls of *connaháyny*, or Indian corn boiled almost to a *purée*, with a small quantity of ley in it, were placed on the table. This is a favourite dish with the Cherokees, and I observed the young people ate it with great avidity; indeed, when mixed up with the broth of the boiled beef, it makes a capital soup; something like peas-soup.

The expense of feeding this multitude, which was defrayed by the council, was very great. Fifteen beeves were said to be killed every day, and a proportionate quantity of Indian corn used. Twenty-four native families were employed in cooking the provisions and serving the tables which were set out three times a-day. . . .

August 6.—Rising at day-break, and taking a cup of tea, I went to the Council-house to attend divine service. From a rostrum erected near it, a native Cherokee preacher delivered a very long sermon to a very numerous assemblage of Indians and white people who had assembled from various parts. The discourse came from him with great vehemence both of action and voice, gesticulating and grunting at every instant, and never stopping to take breath, as it appeared to me, in half an hour. It was like a continual stream of falling water. All the Cherokees paid great attention to the sermon, and the most perfect decorum prevailed. After the sermon we had a psalm, led by Bushy-head, the whole congregation uniting in it. Mr. Jones then preached in English, and Bushy-head, with his stentorian voice, translated the passages as they came from the preacher, into Cherokee. During all this time, the ardent beams of the sun were pouring upon our bare heads. I felt at length as if I could not bear it much longer, and therefore went away before we were dismissed, rather than by covering my head to appear to offer any irreverence.

At noon Colonel Lindsay called at our hut with an escort of cavalry; he had been kind enough to provide a horse for myself and we proceeded to a place called Red Hill, the residence of Mr. John Ross; here, on our arrival, we were shewn into a room and remained there two hours before dinner was announced, when we were taken to a room, upon the table of which a very plentiful dinner, singularly ill-cooked, was placed. Neither our host nor his wife sat down to eat with us, the dinner, according to Cherokee custom, being considered to be provided for the guests; a custom evidently derived from their old savage state. I was helped to some meat, but could not tell what it was, or whether it passed for roast or boiled. It was afterwards explained to me that it was pork, first boiled in a pot with some beef, and then baked by itself afterwards. Mr. Lewis Ross, the brother of our host, presided, and Mr. Gunter, a very intelligent and obliging half-breed, sat at the other end of the table. I sat on his right and obtained a great deal of information from him. . . .

The rock here was a grey crystalline limestone, very much inclined, (it is vertical at Red Clay), and contained no fossils; in many places, there was a strong bed of red clay upon it, like that at Tuscumbia, and the soil here was quite red. . . .

On my return, I went to the Council-house, and heard an excellent sermon delivered to the Cherokees in English, by the Rev. Mr. Buttrick, which received great attention as it well deserved to do, being admirable both in matter and manner. The indefatigable Bushy-head, in translating this sermon, almost surpassed himself, rendered every passage into Cherokee with the most enthusiastic energy at the very top of his noble voice, and marked every sentence with one of his deep-toned, sonorous *uh-húnghs*, that came from him like the lowest note from a bassoon. On my return to our hut, I got into a conversation with our landlord, Mr. Hicks, one of the most intelligent of the Cherokees. He told me, he had once seen some China men at Philadelphia, and that, from the strong resemblance to them in their faces and eyes, he thought it probable the Cherokees were descended from that stock. The remark is, at least, founded in fact, for the Cherokees resemble the Tartars very strikingly, both in the general expression of their faces, and in the conformation of their eyes. . . .

August 7.—The rain had been falling incessantly for thirty hours, and our hut being roofed with nothing but pine branches gave us very little protection; the bed-clothes were wet through, and we were thoroughly nonplussed what to do. It was impossible to remain long in this state without becoming sick. The Indians, at the numerous bivouacs were all wet through, and apprehensions were beginning to be entertained by the Council, that a serious sickness might fall upon them if they were detained twenty-four hours more in the uncomfortable state they were in. The chiefs, therefore, were desirous that Mr. Mason should deliver his "Talk" immediately; but the gentleman, supposing the "Talk" would be deferred, was gone to Colonel Lindsay's for shelter. . . .

At 4 P.M., Mr. Ross conducted Mr. Mason, Colonel Lindsay, Colonel Smith, and myself, into a stand erected near the Council-house, open at the sides, and from whence we could view an assemblage of about two thousand male Cherokees standing in the rain awaiting the "Talk" that was to be delivered. The special agent now advanced to the front of the stand, and read his address which was translated to them by the interpreter; after which, Mr. Gunter addressed them, requesting them to remain until the Council had taken the "Talk" into consideration, and informing them that plenty of provisions would continue to be provided for them, upon which they gave him a hearty grunt and dispersed. The scene was an imposing one; the Cherokees were attentive and behaved very well, but it was evident the "Talk" made no impression upon them. If the special agent had declared, in the name of his Government, that the Cherokee nation should continue to enjoy their native land, it would have been most enthusiasti-

cally received; but anything short of that was a proof to them that there was
no hope left for justice from the whites, nor any resource for them but in
the wisdom of their National Council. The "Talk" itself was full of friendly
professions towards the nation, and dwelt upon the advantages it would
derive from a peaceful compliance with the policy of the Government; but
there was a passage in it which showed that the United States Government
were determined to enforce the treaty which the minority had made with
the Government, and even insinuated that the resistance to it was factious.
This gave offence, and even Mr. Ross objected to it.

The Government now could only carry its policy out by gaining the
chiefs, or by military force. From what I observed, the chiefs, if not incor-
ruptible, were determined not to come to terms without securing great
advantages, whilst it was their intention not to precipitate things, but to
gain time and make another appeal to the Congress. Many of them who had
heard of me through Mr. Buttrick, and who saw the interest I took in their
affairs and in acquiring some knowledge of their language, spoke to me on
the subject; but I invariably advised them to submit to the Government, for
a successful resistance was impossible. I gave it also as my opinion that it
was a very possible thing that if they procrastinated, a collision would soon
take place betwixt them and the Georgians and Tennesseans, which would
involve the destruction of the nation. These opinions, it was evident to me,
were very unwelcome to them; and after the delivery of the "Talk," I declined saying anything on the subject. The rain continued to pour down,
and on reaching my quarters, I found the hut a perfect swamp, and full of
people all wet through, as many as could get there sitting on my bed. A
more uncomfortable place I certainly never was in; everything was wet and
smelt ill. All I could do was to lie down upon the wet bed, and keep the
crowd off with my feet and arms. It was late in the night before we got rid
of them: the rain still coming down in torrents.

In Washington, John Ross finally decided that preparing a
new treaty was futile. So was lobbying in Congress; he visited the
same representatives and senators, received the same sympathy,
and the advice that nothing could be done. Go west to the Arkansas territory, he was advised. The President did receive him on
occasion, but the meetings were without benefit. President Van
Buren agreed at one point to postpone the removal deadline from
May 1838, to May 1840, but when Georgia objected and put an
army of two thousand in the field, the President recanted.

John Ridge, Elias Boudinot, and Reverend Worcester left for
the West. They chose to take the water route. Ross did not cheer
them on their way but was pleased to have them gone. Once all

the treaty people were on the boats, he would have no Indian opposition at home.

Lumpkin also left. He had been elected to the United States Senate. His place was filled by Thomas W. Wilson. Wilson and Kennedy, the two commissioners, issued a joint statement at the close of the year.

December 28, 1837

Friends:

Our official relations to the Cherokee people imposes it upon us, as a duty, to make you acquainted with the true state of your affairs, and with what the Government of the United States will require at your hands. We have long since been convinced that many of you are laboring under a dangerous error, and that you have been duped and deluded by those in whom you have placed implicit confidence. In the 16th article of the Treaty of Dec. 29th, 1835, it is stipulated that the Cherokees *"shall remove to their new homes within two years from the ratification of the treaty"*—and this having occurred on the 23rd of May, 1836, you have now, after wasting opportunities, only the short period of less than five months for the settlement of your affairs here, and the preparation for your removal to your new homes. Do not deceive yourselves into a belief in the false hope held out to you that longer time will be given. The treaty will be executed, without change or alteration, and another day beyond the time named, cannot or will not be allowed to you. Your own safety, your own interests, require that you should abandon all idea of change, and set at once about the settlement of your affairs, and make your arrangements for speedy emigration. Rely no longer on the specious promises of Delegations at Washington—they have known for more than a year that no exertion or artifice of theirs could effect the slightest change in your position—and even if they *have* entertained a hope *heretofore*, on the subject, they can *now* be no longer in doubt. The Government has distinctly informed Mr. Ross that *no alteration* whatever would be made—and that the Cherokees *must* abide by the terms of the treaty of 1835; the Executive has formally declined all further intercourse or correspondence with Mr. Ross in relation to the treaty, and an end has been put to all negotiation upon the subject. . . .

You have been told by some that Mr. Ross would get back so much of your country as is situated in the States of Tennessee, North Carolina and Alabama, and that you would be required to give up only such of your lands and possessions as are within the State of Georgia. Mr. Ross may have been sincere in his belief that he could effect this alteration—but he was mistaken. He has *asked* the Government to make this change in the terms of the treaty—and he was *answered* with a positive and unqualified refusal. Mr. Ross, in his zeal upon the subject, may have deceived himself—but he is now fully convinced of his error; and in a letter written by him to Col. Mason, an agent of the Government, dated at Washington the 6th of the present month, he says *"we have nothing now to do but patiently to submit ourselves" to the requirements of the government.* He says this, after acknowledging that the Government has plainly told him *That the Cherokees must at all events remove to the lands set apart for them in the west. . . .*

We are not your enemies—we respect and regard you as the citizens of a great and honorable nation—and our solicitude for your prosperity and respectability, impels us to urge you to avail yourselves at once of the great and exalted privileges held out to you, and to be no longer false to your own interests as a nation and as men. Shake off the influence of treacherous advisers and counsellors—do not believe the stories they put in circulation to deceive and ruin you—but be men, and accept the advantages which the Government offers to you. Place confidence no longer in men who boast of their ability to do impossible things—but as you value your lives, the lives of your families, and your existence as a nation, fail not to take the advice we now have given to you.—JOHN KENNEDY, TH: W. WILSON, U. S. Commissioners. NAT. SMITH, Sup't. Cherokee Removal. Cherokee Agency, Dec. 28th, 1837.

Spring of 1838. Not a snip of cold weather after March 1 this year. The Indians began working the fields, preparing to plant. John Ross's slaves, and those of his brother Lewis, broke the skin of vast tracks alongside the rivers. The buds, the blossoms were joys to witness, their pretty assurance welcoming all to the start of another year. Field corners and hedgerows were cleaned out, vines and bushes were cut away from the fences.

By May 23, 1838, the deadline for voluntary removal, the corn of the Cherokee was knee high and doing nicely. The thousands of Indians and their slaves were pleased with it.

The Baptist Indian preacher, Reverend Jesse Bushyhead, one of the Jones men, had a daughter named Jane who, like her father, bitterly regretted the Indian upheaval. The preachers had gone with John Ross to Florida recently, to advise the fugitive Seminoles that an arrangement was possible with the federal government if they would only hold out, delay. Now Ross was in Washington appealing yet again for mercy, for more time, for a change of policy. Hopeless? Perhaps so. She was packing her things, would be as ready as she could be. She was writing those she might never see again, including white friends.

Red Clay Cherokee Nation March 10, 1838
>   Beloved, Martha,
>   I have delayed writing to you so long I expect you have relinquished all thought of receiving any thing from me. But my Dear Martha I have not forgotten my promise. I have often wishes to enjoy your company once more but it is very uncertain whether I shall ever again have that pleasure. If we Cherokees are to be driven to the west by the cruel hand of oppression to seek a home in the west it will be impossible. My father is now in Washington City. He was one of the delegates who went to Florida last Oct. We do not know when he will return. Not long since Mr. Stephen Foreman received a letter from father. He was absent when the letter came home and before he arrived the troops had been there and taken it to the Agency given it to General Smith and he handed it round for all to read. It is thus all our rights are invaded. About two months ago my youngest brother died. He was sick almost two months. I was not at home when he died but they sent for me to attend his funeral. He was burnt very badly last fall and it is very likely his death was occasioned by it however we do not exactly know.
>   It will not be long before our next vacation. Then we expect to go home. Perhaps it may be the last time we shall have the privilege of attending school in this nation. But we are not certain.
>   If we should remove to the Arkansas I should still hope to continue our correspondence. Please to present my best respects to your father & family Miss E. Jones and Miss Betsey Tirtle write with me in love to you.
>   Your, Sincere friend,
>   Jane Bushyhead

20

Something less than a thousand pro-Treaty people had recently left, going in three groups. Four to five thousand Cherokees had traveled west earlier on their own. Some had gone by riverboat, others by land, and there had been suffering, fatigue and illness and even death. Over the years, the roads to the West had been made and worn by many feet, white, red and black, booted, moccasined, and bare; the roads were burial grounds, particularly preying on the weak, the very old, the infants.

Federal removal agent General Nathaniel Smith, knowing of the difficulties of land travel over long distances—in this case almost a thousand miles—had assembled a fleet of keelboats constructed by the government, and they were on the Tennessee River awaiting use. The boats were 130 feet in length, each with a house one hundred feet long, twenty feet wide, and two stories high, with banister rails around the top deck. Each floor was partitioned into rooms fifty by twenty feet, and each room had windows and a stove. For cooking, there were five hearths on the top deck. The fleet could carry more than a thousand Cherokees and blacks, returning for others, so that the entire tribe could be moved in this way by winter.

For the first voyage, however, only three hundred Indians voluntarily registered. Others drifted in, but fifty deserted on feeling the shifting of the keelboat's deck under their feet and hearing stories of shipwreck and cholera along the river. Cherokees attached mystic powers to rivers and both feared and respected them. More than four hundred persevered, but once they reached Ohio, waves pounded the boat and the passengers all swarmed onto the small smelter, believing the big one to be sinking. They would not, even after the storm, return to quarters, so the big boat was cast adrift and the little boat steamed on, reaching Arkansas before its increased draft threatened it with grounding. Lieutenant Edward Deas, the government conductor, led the passengers onto a steamer with less draft, and for a week that boat chugged along, negotiating shallows. Once it could go no farther, Deas led the Indians ashore, hired wagons and oxen, and moved them overland to their property in the Arkansas territory. The trip took twenty-one days. Two infants, who were ill at the start, died. One was Cherokee, the other black. It had not been an easy trip, and it was certainly eventful and dangerous, but it was fast and easy when compared to land travel, which might take three months.

General Smith had received reports from Deas occasionally and was pleased. Before Deas had arrived in Arkansas, Smith had sent out a second group by water, Indians and slaves leaving on the seventeenth of June, 1838. All of these passengers had registered to go west, had sold most of their possessions, and had packed the remainder, and they had come voluntarily with their families to the dock. They were not in that respect typical of the Indians who remained.

For those recalcitrant ones, it was decided that soldiers would be needed. The government put General Winfield Scott, a six-foot-four-inch, big-bodied veteran of wars and skirmishes, in command. John Ross, who was in Washington at the time of the appointment, rushed to meet him and discussed the impropriety of the mission. Scott listened politely, but did not change his plans.

He arrived at New Echota in early May, established headquarters, and converted the Council House into a barracks. In the four states he assembled an army of seven thousand men, regulars and volunteers, infantry, cavalry, artillery. He was respected by President Van Buren and ex-President Jackson. In fact, some years previously, he had accepted Jackson's challenge to a duel. He appeared at the grounds, where the two shook hands and returned home, each satisfied with the other's courage. After that they were friends. General Scott had met Indians in three campaigns, one in 1812 when he was in his mid-twenties, in the Black Hawk war of 1832, and during a conflict with the Seminoles two years before.

His soldiers' nickname was "Old Fuss and Feathers."

He divided the Cherokee territory into three parts—western, central, and eastern districts—and in each he ordered his men to construct several immense collection camps affording shade, water, and security, to which in the next little while the Indian families could be brought; whenever a small number was gathered in a camp, they would be led to one of three river ports: Ross's Landing on the Tennessee, Gunter's Landing on the Tennessee, and the Cherokee Agency on the Hiwassee, where new federal boats would transport them to the Mississippi, down that river to the Arkansas, and thence upstream to their destination.

His first proclamation to the Cherokees proved to be jarring. As he said, it was the message of a soldier:

MAJOR GENERAL SCOTT, of the United States Army, sends to the Cherokee people, remaining in North Carolina, Georgia, Tennessee, and Alabama, this

ADDRESS.

Cherokees! The President of the United States has sent me, with a powerful army, to cause you, in obedience to the Treaty of 1835, to join that part of your people who are already established in prosperity, on the other side of the Mississippi. Unhappily, the two years which were allowed for the purpose, you have suffered to pass away without following, and without making any preparation to follow, and now, or by the time that this solemn *address* shall reach your distant settlements, the emigration must be commenced in haste, but, I hope, without disorder. I have no power, by granting a farther delay, to correct the error that you have committed. The full moon of May is already on the wane, and before another shall have passed away, every Cherokee man, woman and child, in those States, must be in motion to join their brethren in the far West.

My Friends! This is no sudden determination on the part of the President, whom you and I must now obey. By the treaty, the emigration was to have been completed on, or before, the 23rd of this month, and the President has constantly kept you warned, during the two years allowed, through all his officers and agents in this country, that the Treaty would be enforced.

I am come to carry out that determination. My troops already occupy many positions in this country that you are to abandon, and thousands, and thousands are approaching, from every quarter, to render resistance and escape alike hopeless. All those troops, regular and militia, are your friends. Receive them and confide in them as such. Obey them when they tell you that you can remain no longer in this country. Soldiers are as kind hearted as brave, and the desire of every one of us is to execute our painful duty in mercy. We are commanded by the President to act towards you in that spirit, and such is also the wish of the whole people of America.

Chiefs, head-men and warriors! Will you, then, by resistance, compel us to resort to arms? God forbid! Or will you, by flight, seek to hide yourselves in mountains and forests, and thus oblige us to hunt you down? Remember that, in pursuit, it may be impossible to avoid conflicts. The blood of the white man, or the blood of the red man, may be spilt, and if spilt, however accidentally, it may be impossible for the discreet and humane among you, or among us to prevent a general war and carnage. Think of this, my Cherokee brethren! I am an old warrior, and have been present at many a scene of slaughter; but spare me, I beseech you, the horror of witnessing the destruction of the Cherokees.

Do not, I invite you, even wait for the close approach of the troops; but make such preparations for emigration as you can, and hasten to this place, the Ross' Landing, or to Gunter's Landing, where you all will be received in kindness by officers selected for the purpose. You will find food for all, and clothing for the destitute, at either of those places, and thence at your ease, and in comfort, be transported to your new homes according to the terms of the Treaty.

This is the address of a warrior to warriors. May his entreaties be kindly received, and may the God of both prosper the Americans and Cherokees, and preserve them long in peace and friendship with each other!

> WINFIELD SCOTT.
> *Cherokee Agency,* ⎫
> *May* 10, 1838. ⎭

General Scott was busy with the paperwork. Couldn't fight a war or move an Indian tribe without it.

18 April 1838.—Office of Commanding General of Subsistence, Washington, to Gen. Scott:

To ensure to your command in the Cherokee country a full supply of hard bread and other subsistence stores, I have dispatched Lieut. A. E. Shiras to Pittsburgh, Cincinnatti, and Louisville. He will procure supplies and accompany them up the Tennessee river to their destination. . . .

Issue to Captain Connelly's Company 2 wall tents, 12 common tents, 12 camp kettles, 24 mess pans, 6 axes.

Oh yes, and 4 spades.

Scott issued many orders specifying just how the roundup was to take place, and with what respectful attitude. He directed

the soldiers to be polite and kind. The work itself would be per-
ceived as treacherous by a people unwilling to leave their homes.
In Order 25, May 17, he set up the various district commands and
gave his view of the Indians:

> The Cherokees, by the advances which they have made in christianity and
> civilization, are by far the most interesting tribe of Indians in the territorial
> limits of the United States. Of the 15,000 of those people who are now to be
> removed—(and the time within which a voluntary emigration was stipu-
> lated, will expire on the 23rd instant)—it is understood that about four fifths
> are opposed, or have become averse to a distant emigration; and altho' some
> are in actual hostilities with the United States, or threaten a resistance by
> arms, yet the troops will probably be obliged to cover the whole country
> they inhabit, in order to make prisoners and to march or to transport the
> prisoners, by families, either to this place, to Ross' Landing or Gunter's
> Landing, where they are to be finally delivered over to the Superintendant
> of Cherokee Emigration.
>
> Considering the number and temper of the mass to be removed, to-
> gether with the extent and fastness of the country occupied, it will readily
> occur, that simple indiscretions—acts of harshness and cruelty, on the part
> of our troops, may lead, step by step, to delays, to impatience and exaspera-
> tion, and in the end, to a general war and carnage—a result, in the case of
> those particular Indians, utterly abhorrent to the generous sympathies of
> the whole American people. Every possible kindness, compatible with the
> necessity of removal, must, therefore, be shown by the troops, and, if, in the
> ranks, a despicable individual should be found, capable of inflicting a wan-
> ton injury or insult on any Cherokee man, woman or child, it is hereby
> made the special duty of the nearest good officer or man, instantly to inter-
> pose, and to seize and consign the guilty wretch to the severest penalty of
> the laws. The Major General is fully pursuaded that this injunction will not
> be neglected by the brave men under his command, who cannot be other-
> wise than jealous of their own honor and that of their country.
>
> By early and persevering acts of kindness and humanity, it is impossi-
> ble to doubt that the Indians may soon be induced to confide in the Army,
> and instead of fleeing to mountains and forests, flock to us for food and
> clothing. If, however, through false apprehensions, individuals, or a party,
> here and there, should seek to hide themselves, they must be pursued and
> invited to surrender, but not fired upon unless they should make a stand to
> resist. Even in such cases, mild remedies may sometimes better succeed than
> violence; and it cannot be doubted that if we get possession of the women
> and children first, or first capture the men, that, in either case, the outstand-
> ing members of the same families will readily come in on the assurance of
> forgiveness and kind treatment.
>
> Every captured man, as well as all who surrender themselves, must be

disarmed, with the assurance that their weapons will be carefully preserved and restored at, or beyond the Mississippi. In either case, the men will be guarded and escorted, except it may be, where their women and children are mainly secured as hostages; but, in general, families, in our possession, will not be separated, unless it be to send men, as runners, to invite others to come in.

It may happen that Indians will be found too sick, in the opinion of the nearest Surgeon, to be removed to one of the depots indicated above. In every such case, one or more of the family, or the friends of the sick person, will be left in attendance, with ample subsistence and remedies, and the remainder of the family removed by the troops. Infants, superannuated persons, lunatics and women in a helpless condition, will all, in the removal, require peculiar attention, which the brave and humane will seek to adapt to the necessities of the several cases.

All strong men, women, boys & girls, will be made to march under proper escorts. For the feeble, Indian horses and ponies will furnish a ready resource, as well as for bedding and light cooking utensils—all of which, as estimated in the Treaty, will be necessary to the emigrants both in going to, and after arrival at, their new homes. Such, and all other light articles of property, the Indians will be allowed to collect and to take with them, as also their slaves, who will be treated in like manner with the Indians themselves.

If the horses and ponies be not adequate to the above purposes, wagons must be supplied.

Corn, oats, fodder and other forage, also beef, cattle, belonging to the Indians to be removed, will be taken possession of by the proper departments of the Staff, as wanted, for the regular consumption of the Army, and certificates given to the owners, specifying in every case, the amount of forage and the weight of beef, so taken, in order that the owners may be paid for the same on their arrival at one of the depots mentioned above.

All other moveable or personal property, left or abandoned by the Indians, will be collected by agents appointed for the purpose, by the Superintendant of Cherokee Emigration, under a system of accountability, for the benefit of the Indian owners, which he will deliver. The Army will give to those agents, in their operations, all reasonable countenance, aid and support.

White men and widows, citizens of the United States, who are, or have been intermarried with Indians, and thence commonly termed, *Indian countrymen;* also such Indians as have been made denizens of particular States by special legislation, together with the families and property of all such persons, will not be molested or removed by the troops until a decision, on the principles involved, can be obtained from the War Department.

A like indulgence, but only for a limited time, and until further orders, is extended to the families and property of certain Chiefs and head-men of the two great Indian parties, (on the subject of emigration) now understood to be absent in the direction of Washington on the business of their respective parties.

This order will be carefully read at the head of every company in the Army.

By Command:
WINFIELD SCOTT

In Order 34, issued May 24, 1838, he set dates for the roundup to begin, the twenty-sixth in Georgia and ten days later in Tennessee, North Carolina, and Alabama:

The commanding officer at every fort & open station will first cause to be surrounded and brought in as many Indians, the nearest to his fort or station, as he may think he can secure at once, & repeat the operation until he shall have made as many prisoners as he is able to subsist and send off, under a proper escort, to the most convenient of the emigrating depots, the Cherokee Agency, Ross Landing, and Gunter's Landing. . . .

AFTER Orders,
To each Indian prisoner will be issued daily without regard to age or sex, one pound of flour and half a pound of bacon.

In Order 35 General Scott decreed that in lieu of flour, a pint of corn could be issued.

He was in command of every detail. And he was distrustful of many of his soldiers' attitudes. The Georgia state militia was made up of volunteers temporarily on duty, composed in part of the same men who had come to the gold fields or who were awaiting their portion of Cherokee land; Scott was watchful of the Georgians particularly. As a general rule, North Carolinians and Tennesseans were evenly disposed toward the Indians; the Alabamans were less so. He was aware that some of the white Georgians on arrival at New Echota were vowing never to return home without killing at least one Indian. Their ferocious language surprised him, coming from supposed Christians, and he decided to remain personally with the Georgian division of the operation in order to control it. Georgians seemed to deny, Scott noticed, that Indians were human beings, an attitude he found reprehensible.

Tens-Qua-Ta-Wa, or The One That Opens the Door, Shawnee prophet and brother of Shawnee chief Tecumseh, who dreamed of uniting all Woodlands Indians, in lithograph printed by J. O. Lewis in 1823. (COURTESY: Library of Congress)

John Ross, mixed-blood Cherokee leader, and second wife, Mary Bryan Stapler Ross, photographed after the Cherokee removal to Oklahoma. (COURTESY: Archives and Manuscript Division of the Oklahoma Historical Society)

Left, Quatie Ross, John Ross's first wife, who died during the trip to Cherokee lands in Oklahoma. (COURTESY: Museum of the Cherokee Indian). *Right*, Lewis Anderson Ross, son of wealthy merchant John Golden Ross and nephew of Cherokee Chief John Ross. John Mix Stanley painted the child Lewis at Fort Gibson in 1844, on the occasion of the International Indian Conference at Tahlequah. (COURTESY: The Thomas Gilcrease Institute of American History and Art, Tulsa, Oklahoma)

John Jolly (Col-le), principal chief of the Western Cherokees, painted by George Catlin in 1834. His adoptive son was Sam Houston. (COURTESY: National Museum of American Art, Smithsonian Institution, Gift of Mrs. Joseph Harrison, Jr.)

Sam Houston as an Indian Agent, dressed in Cherokee attire. Houston's Indian name was Kalanu. (COURTESY: San Jacinto Museum of History, Deer Park, Texas)

"Granny" Houston, second wife of Sa Houston, Cherokee, photographed at a 109. (COURTESY: Campbell Collectio Western History Collections, University Oklahoma Library)

Left, John Sevier, leader of the white Tennessee settlers, opponent of the Cherokee nation, later governor of Tennessee. (COURTESY: Courtesy of the Tennessee State Library and Archives)

Below left, David Crockett of Tennessee. (COURTESY: Culver Pictures, Inc.)

Andrew Jackson, Indian fighter, native of Tennessee, President of the United States during the period of the Cherokee removal. (COURTESY: Culver Pictures, Inc.)

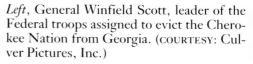

Left, General Winfield Scott, leader of the Federal troops assigned to evict the Cherokee Nation from Georgia. (COURTESY: Culver Pictures, Inc.)

Below left, Samuel Austin Worcester, American missionary to the Cherokee Nation, friend of the Ridge faction. Worcester was jailed by the military during the Cherokee evictions. (COURTESY: The Houghton Library, Harvard University)

Below right, Wilson Lumpkin, governor of Georgia during the Cherokee evictions. (COURTESY: Museum of the Cherokee Indian)

Building housing the printing press for the Cherokee newspaper *The Phoenix* at the Cherokee capital of New Echota, Georgia. (COURTESY: Historic Preservation Section, Georgia Department of Natural Resources)

House of Chief James Vann, Spring Place, Murray County, Georgia, built in 1805, later home of Vann's son Joseph. Vann's holdings included: "1 fine brick house, 800 acres of cultivated land, 42 cabins, 6 barns, 5 smokehouses, a grist mill, black smith shops, 8 corn cribs, a shop and foundry, a trading post, a peach kiln, a still, and 1,133 peach trees." (COURTESY: Photograph by Van Jones Martin)

Top, Rose Cottage, home of Chief John Ross, at Park Hill, Oklahoma. Ross's house was destroyed by Confederate troops under Stand Watie during the Civil War. COURTESY: The University of Oklahoma Press, Courtesy of the Archives and Manuscript Division of the Oklahoma Historical Society). *Middle*, Joshua Ross's shop at the corner of Broadway and Cherokee, Muskogee, Oklahoma. COURTESY: Archives and Manuscript Division of the Oklahoma Historical Society). *Bottom*, Home of Sequoyah, near Sallisaw, Oklahoma, built in 1829. COURTESY: Ferguson Collection, Western History Collections, University of Oklahoma Library)

One of the young officers, L. B. Webster of Company C, First Artillery, was a bridegroom in Florida before ordered to this duty, and he did so want to go back home. He wrote, on May 23, 1838:

My dear Wife.

Here I am safe and sound, this far on my way to the Cherokee country. It is from this point that the most fatigueing part of the journey commences, and I have made up my mind to foot it as far as I can, and then to purchase a horse. As this is the first march I have made, I hardly know how I shall stand it, but hope to acquit myself well. We arrived here yesterday morning, without any serious accident abscuring on the way though the men have given us a good deal of troubles by their beastly drunkenness. Tomorrow morning we take up the line of march, and I shall no doubt leave some more of the beauties of soldiers life before you hear from me again. I presume we shall not have any fighting, at least such is the general impression; and I have no doubt but the business will be over in July. And then God grant that I may be able to pay my personal respects to your ladyship. I am in much better spirits than when I wrote you from Charleston. Indeed I am determined not to give way to my feelings, and besides I have so much to do that I have but little time to think. But those thoughts are all turned to one little spot, in the sunny lives of Florida, occupied by my lady love. It is now quite late at night, and I am to be up by day light tomorrow; so you must not expect a great deal of nonsense from me in this letter. The principal object of which is to inform my sweet Fanny that a letter from her, directed to his lordship at Calhoun Ten. with my official title, will most likely be received by her unworthy husband.

At any rate you must write me there as soon as you receive this. I am prodigiusly anxious to hear from you already, but notwithstanding I do not intend to give you a scolding. Good night my dear Frances, and do take care of yourself for the sake of your devoted husband.

My love to all the family

Every Thine

L. B. Webster

P.S. Major Kirby is well. He is remaining in town, and I have the immediate command of the six companies with the arsenal.

Scott appealed to his men on the basis of Christianity to deal gently with this assignment. He was present in the camp on the Hiwassee all the first day of the roundup. Thousands were brought in before nightfall. Men, women, and children—sick and well were brought in, many of them half-starved, but even so they refused food from the government. At length the children consented to eat, and next their parents, and the general noticed that the waiters serving them were these Georgia Guards who had claimed to hate them. He was moved, and believed that the guards were, too; he even reported seeing some of them in tears.

True grief or not, the roundup was proceeding expeditiously, with no blood shed—that of Indian or white. It was cruel work, no question of that, made more difficult by fleets of opportunistic whites, human scavengers, following the troops, lurking at the edge of lots waiting to loot possessions that the Indians could not carry away. The soldiers objected, but could not control the situation. Later the Indians could put in claims to the government for the value of their losses, but much loss was of a personal sort. It was agonizing to be told to bring what one could and leave the rest. And what was the rest? A favorite cow. A pet dog. The tree that had been a sapling when Mother married and now shaded the house and spring. The field Papa and my brothers cleared with fire and then beat the roasted roots with clubs and stone. The hearth, where the bread has been baked for many years, every day; the apple house; the smokehouse with five prime, golden hams and three sides of bacon. The gourd still tasting of salt, though the salt is gone. The cider barrels. The clothing that used to fit Charley, and might again if this world does not soon right itself. The cat. The little pony that has back sores that don't seem to heal, but we kept her anyway. The flowers paled with brush. The fences made of split chestnut rails. The pots and pans. The trunk Uncle Rabbit left till his return; that was in '84, just before he went west. The billy goat: well, good riddance, he did smell up the place whenever he was in his rutting season, and he knocked over the children, seemed to entertain himself that way—no going to the west for you, mister. That bag of sassafras root. Do they have sassafras in the West? Take the small bags of herb roots for the journey. Leave the piece of beef, but bring that hunk of salt-cured bacon. No, leave the doll. Leave the old leggins.

The human vultures grew impatient as they waited. One of

them might venture close enough to bargain for choice pieces; he would pay a pittance.

This was sordid, demeaning, grief-stricken labor. Much here was being left, a type of family burial.

The Indians asked why it had to be decided now, all in an hour.

Two years and a month and an hour, the soldiers said.

Leave the corn in the fields for another family to harvest. Latch the door, soldier?

Or leave it open.

Can we come back to get more stuff?

It won't be here, now, will it? the soldier said.

We can't go till my boy gets home.

Where'd he go? To the mill? You come now. I'll leave men to bring him.

Ah, it'll scare him to death, finding us gone.

He won't die. We'd never get this work done, if we waited for everybody. It's pieced together. You wouldn't believe this, but every family has pieces of itself missing, somebody's always at the mill or the store or off in a far field.

Would you help us carry, if we bring more bowls?

No, we don't carry.

It's so sudden.

Two years, a month, and an hour.

A soldier waiting in the yard said, When I went into the army, nobody told me this is what I'm supposed to do, cattle people along.

Slow, most people moved slowly as they left their houses. It did not matter whether they were wealthy or the poor, whether the house had three rooms or two or one. Bundles of clothing. A pretty piece of cloth the mother had wanted to make into a dress. A pouch of tobacco. A round of butter. Don't know when we'll see butter this sweet again. A copy of Sequoyah's lettering. A leash, in case we ever get another dog.

Along the creek paths, from back in the hollows, the women and girls carrying the pick of their possessions, the men carrying little. One man carried a hatchet.

Here, let me take that there ax, buddy. No weapons allowed.

Down from Whitetail Branch, from Singing Creek, from the place Papa killed the young bear to the valley road, where the dust was loading itself into the air. Gets in your nostrils, makes a white man sneeze, all this dust stirred up by foot and hoof and wheel.

Drive them on. Let 'em weep. Hell, that's not against the law. But loitering is. Come on, old woman, we got to get the day's work done.

Rich and poor. Of course, the rich rode. Now and then a rich man took an old man or woman, or a sick man or woman along in his wagon.

Well, she won't ride, either; she won't walk, won't leave, not another foot. Just rests there on that there rock and cries.

Listen to that dog yelp. Wants to go with them. Have to shoot him, to have any peace.

What do we do with that old woman who won't leave that there rock?

She will, when she gets hungry. Move the others on, best you can.

Makes our work hard.

You're being paid.

Get fifty cents a day, all for me. Is this what the government calls soldiering?

Stop your talking; move them Indians along. Move the goddamn Indians down this here road.

Voices grow harsh as evening comes. Food is waiting in another three miles. Only an hour more, if the old would keep up.

That there pony is pretty as day, Indian, you want to sell me that pony? No? I can't keep it, anyway. Let me tell you something, sergeant, they got no way to understand most of what we say. You know why?

Yeh, I know why.

Because they're Indians.

That's the reason.

They look like people, walk like you and me.

Walk quieter.

Yeh. They don't stomp. They shuffle. See the shuffle on that boy.

He can't understand what you say.

Would think by now they'd speak as well as I do.

Would think so.

Tomorrow—you know what we're going to get to do tomorrow, boy? We're going to have our big chance to round up more Indians. That's the story of your life, boys.

Dust.

Please, mama, get your ass along, we got to arrive. Can't spend our lives going, have to arrive. Have to leave it farther behind, foot by foot. No, hell no, you'll never see it again.

The meanest work I'll ever do, men, is moving these Indians. . . .

28 May 1838.—From the Officer in Charge, Fort Hetzel, Georgia to HQ:
. . . I commenced on the 26th securing the Indians. I have made prisoners of 425 or perhaps 450. I think by the time I get in the outstanding members of the families that I have broken up I will have as many as I can manage. . . . They run in every instance where they have the best opportunity. . . . It will take me a few days to collect their little plunder as we captured them in the mountains I could not bring off their property at the same time.

3 June 1838.—Col. Bynum, HQ Cheowa Valley. Order No. 2:
. . . In pursuance of orders from Gen. Scott and from Brig. Gen. Eustis, the collection of Cherokee Indians preparatory to the emigration will commence in Cheowa Valley on tomorrow morning. . . . Each detachment will take with them as many horses as can be provided—and gather up all the Indian ponies on their march which can be of use.

4 June 1838.—Col. Bynum, HQ Fort Montgomery [to Gen. Scott]:
. . . I have this morning set a large number of hands at work upon the picketing . . . I have also commenced a hospital for the accommodation of our sick. . . . I think I was mistaken as to the number of Indians within this valley. . . . I am desirous of knowing whether there are particular instructions to be given as to the manner of disposing of the property of the Indians, whether the prisoners are to be detained until their property is gathered up or whether they are to be marched off . . . and their property taken care of afterwards?

6 June 1838.—Nath. Smith, Ross' Landing to Gen. Scott:
. . . This morning I started a party of near 1000, and there are now over 900 in camps, and a thousand more expected within the next two days.

The Indians were a step higher on the ladder than the blacks. Which of these blacks are to go to the West, which to the auction block? These are not worth the trip or are so independent they'd try to run off. Break up the black families, as needs be, choose for travel the best ones, the strongest, and sell the others. Have to make choices in this world. No wagon for the sick blacks, the old blacks. Now what does that nigger girl have with her? What's them spider webs going to do for you? What's that wooden cross for? Do you mean to carry them baby clothes all the way to the West, when you don't even any longer have a baby?

Not any room in the wagon for a slave or a slave's things. Of course, they can certainly walk all the way. My Lord, what are they wanting, pampering?

One in eight of the people on the road are black, marked by Cain's sin. Have you heard what Cain done, soldier?

Cain who?

All his descendants are to serve the others.

Cain who?

Moses's son.

Don't know him. He an Indian?

Along the road, Indians and blacks and soldiers, getting the harsh work done.

Or Abraham's son, one or the other.

Lieutenant L. B. Webster was ordered to take part in the roundup of Cherokees in western North Carolina, and there, on June 19, he was told to move eight hundred Cherokees from North Carolina to the encampment in Calhoun, Tennessee, a distance of eighty miles.

John Ross capitulated. For months he had held to his confidence that the federal government would relent, an attitude all the more remarkable when viewed against the experience of the other four southeastern tribes. The Choctaws had moved first to the West, the Chickasaws more recently, both suffering privation, robbery, disease. The portions of the Creek tribe that had resisted violently had been subdued by force and the men—some sixteen hundred of them—dispatched to the West. Another 776 Creeks were persuaded to help the federal government's troops ferret out

Seminole warriors in the Florida swamps; the captured Seminoles were being dispatched in boats to the Arkansas territory. For months John Ross had insisted that the practice, the experience, the momentum built up involving these other tribes, would be alleviated in the case of the Cherokees.

Now Chief Ross decided to consider placing Cherokee removal under Cherokee management. He called a meeting of the council. Some members had to be released from the camps in order to attend. In July the council met, and John Ross, Elijah Hicks, and four others were "hereby authorized and fully empowered on the part of the Cherokee nation: to make and enter into any & all such arrangements with Maj.-Genl. Winfield Scott on the part of the United States, which they may deem necessary and proper for effecting the entire removal of the Cherokee people from the east to the west of the Mississippi River." The six were further empowered to deal with the negotiations of payment connected with such services.

Whatever he had hoped to gain by delay had not come about. His promises to his people had been unveiled: nothing was there. His promises were washed down the creeks and streams of 1838.

Was he sincere now? Were his agreements to be believed, or was he plotting another stalling operation? John Ridge and his father and Boudinot had already moved west. Ross was left unchallenged, fully in charge. Better Ross, General Scott believed, than soldiers. The Indians would do whatever Ross told them. They had believed him when he urged them to stay in the East; would they believe him that their future lay in the West?

Go ahead and send the next group, Scott decided, while Ross bargained. Ross was a Scottish trader, as Scott knew, and would negotiate down to the last cent. What Ross apparently now intended was to give the contract to his brother. Lewis, who was, as Scott realized, John Ross's partner in their trading businesses, was to handle contracts and purchases of all supplies, wagons, and horses.

Bargain with Ross. One must do so. Old Andy Jackson would object, once he heard of it; but he would have to accept a fait accompli.

Still in charge of hundreds of Indians at the massive camp in Calhoun, Tennessee, lonely to his bones, aggravated by summer heat, by flies, by odors, by not knowing when this cursed line of duty would be up, L. B. Webster wrote again to his bride.

Calhoun, Tenn
July 19th 1838
My Dear Wife
 . . . Last night I dreampt about you all night long. I thought I have traveled a long journey on horse back to see you at last I arrived—hitched my horse at the post—and was running up stairs to meet you at the house of which I saw you standing to receive me. But alas! before I could embrace my dear wife I awake and found it all a dream.

I have not heard a word from you since your letter of the 2nd of June. The first letter you directed to me here arrived in due time—and why should not the others? Therefore I *will* not suppose that you have not written—at least once a week. I am weary of conjecture. Indeed I am not very well, and have not been for a number of days; and I feel miserably down spirited. But you must not chide me my dear Frank. I have almost made a vow never to leave you again, if Heaven will grant my constant prayer that we may soon be united in each others arms. I am encamped five miles from town. But shall go there tomorrow morning, as we then have a mail, when I hope & pray I may hear something from you. . . .

My dear Frances:
 I feel quite happy this evening, and beg that you will congratulate me on my good fortune. In the first place I have received a letter from you, which though not very recent affords me infinite satisfaction. It is dated the 22nd of June, and came by the hands of Lt. Thomas. This is the only one I have received from you since the one dated the 2nd of June; and I find the fault lies with North Carolina Postmasters who do not appear to know where Fort Butler is situated.

I have seen Bushy Head & some others of your Cherokee friends. I gave them your envelope.

My love to all the family. God bless my good dear little wife, and keep her from all harm, and grant that no evil on her thoughts on any subject should even enter her mind—Such is the prayer of your very unworthy but devoted husband.

I am afraid your health is not good—do take care of yourself my sweet girl, and I will give you some sugar plums when I come to see you.
 Goodby
 L. B. Webster

The camps were wretched and full of angry, sullen Indians. The river was too low in its banks to be ideal for moving them by water, but the Indians did have to be moved. Scott called in Lieutenant Deas and told him to take a thousand or so of these unhappy creatures on flatboats, going as far as he could by water, the best and by far the fastest means of travel.

On June 6, in the morning, a sizable company was brought in army wagons to the Ross's Landing docks and put aboard the flatboats. At noon this fourth drive was ready to cast off and did so. The six flatboats were lashed together, three on each side of the steamer, and the conglomerate moved at about five miles an hour into the Tennessee River.

Deas kept notes on the journey. As they approached the first rapids, called the Suck: "The river here becomes very narrow and swift and the banks on either side are rocky and steep, it being the point at which the stream passes thro' a gorge in the mountains." Upstream from the rapids, the flatboats were unlashed, and the steamer took two through at a time. Then they steamed onward to somewhat less dangerous rapids, the Boiling Pot, the Skillet, the Frying Pan.

> The steamboat, with one Flat on each side passed through, the most of the people on board, but after getting thro' the most rapid water, it was found impossible to keep her in the channel, and in consequence was thrown upon the north Bank with some violence but luckily none of the people were injured although one of the Flats was a good deal smashed. The other four boats came thro' two by two and the party was encamped before dark as it was too late in the day to reach the rapids in the daylight.

After three days, on the ninth the group reached Decatur. Here the river was unpassable for some distance, but Deas was able to hire passage on a railroad to the deeper water at Tuscumbia. He hired thirty-two cars and two engines, which could carry half the group at a time, except for the guards, whom Deas dismissed. While he was with the first half of the group, the other half was drenched with whiskey, "much drunkenness resulting," and more than one hundred of the emigrants escaped in order to return home. He gathered up those he had left, and he found back at Tuscumbia that many of the male Indians were gone. Above

Waterloo he loaded his Indians and blacks aboard a double-decker keelboat pulled by the steamer *Vesper*. The Indians, hung over, still bitter, refused to answer rollcall, so he was not certain that the count, 489, was correct. He believed about 311 had left him.

The boat kept moving day and night, stopping for wood. Nobody got to go ashore. They moved along the Mississippi to the Arkansas River, where sandbars and shallows hindered night navigation, so the Indians camped ashore after dark. Once the Cherokee passengers saw Cherokees waving to them from shore, they promptly joined them, the entire journey having been made by water and train. Nobody had died in this company.

> Deas issued a sufficient quantity of Cotton Domestic to the Indians for Tents to protect them from the weather. I have done so in consideration of their destitute condition, as they were for the most part separated from their homes in Georgia without having the means or time to prepare for camping and it was also the opinion of the Physician of the Party that the health of these people would suffer if not provided with some protection from the weather.

Behind Deas came another group, this one of more than eight hundred, under Lieutenant R. H. K. Whiteley. These Indians were also uncooperative and embittered, would not even give their names, refused to accept clothing and provisions offered them. In the first two days, during the fight with the rapids, one child died and one was born. Twenty-five Indians escaped before the steamer *George Guess* and its flatboats reached Decatur. The Indians were unfamiliar with trains; most had never seen one before. Many hours were spent contemplating the engines, staring at them, or at the horizon line just beyond them. An aged woman died and a man was killed by the train when he tried to retrieve his hat from beneath it.

Four more children died before the group reached the Arkansas River. The boats could not navigate the river much beyond Little Rock, so Whiteley sought enough wagons to carry the children and the sick Indians, of whom there were about a hundred. Before them lay an overland journey through Arkansas.

The weather was extremely hot, a drought had prevailed for months, water was scarce, suffocating clouds of dust stirred up by oxen and wagons, and the rough and rocky roads, made the condition of the sick occupants of the wagons miserable indeed. Three, four, and five deaths occurred each day. To avoid the heat the marches were started before sunrise and ended at noon. Before the end of the month there were between two and three hundred ill.

On August 1, the party was at Lee's Creek, near the Indian territory. Lieutenant Whiteley wrote in his journal,

Did not move this day, the party requiring rest and being more than one half sick; notwithstanding every effort used, it was impossible to prevent their eating quantities of green peaches and corn—consequently the flux raged among them and carried off some days as high as six and seven.

In three weeks, seventy died from this feasting, and others moved away from the group to seek their own comforts. Of the 875 who had left Tennessee, 602 remained at the arrival, the others dead or fleeing. The brutality of the land marches was marked by suffering, losses to families, exhaustion of soul and body.

Meanwhile, the grisly work of rounding up Indians and slaves continued in the eastern Cherokee territory, continuing to mid-June when, on the seventeenth, General Scott dismissed all the remaining volunteer troops.

The camps were hot and smelly, and General Scott dispatched on June 17 yet another group to the West, this one estimated to number 1,070 people. The upper Tennessee was so low that they traveled by wagon and foot 160 miles to Waterloo, Alabama, to reach the flatboats, and in that journey the ill-clad people, who refused clothing and blankets and other aids, lost four children and one adult to death. The group boarded the flatboats at Waterloo, their condition so desperate that the federal agent, Nathaniel Smith, was petitioned by a committee of Cherokee leaders to stop their march, to let them camp in Alabama till cool weather returned and water, enough water for boat passage. Many of the wells and springs were dry, and the river was shallow. The petition was signed by Assistant Chief George Lowrey

—John Ross was in Washington—and Lewis Ross, Hair Conrad, Thomas Foreman, and Chief Going Snake. The appeal was soulful and eloquent:

> Spare their lives; expose them not to the killing effects of that strange climate, under the disadvantages of the present inauspicious season, without a house or shelter to cover them from above, or any kind of furniture to raise them from the bare ground, on which they may spread their blankets and lay their languid limbs, when fallen prostrate under the influence of disease.

Superintendent Smith traveled to see the Indians for himself and found their health improving,

> and they well provided with transportation and subsistence, I determined they should go on and so informed them. Shortly after which about 300 of them, threw a part of their baggage out of the waggons, took it and broke for the woods and many of the balance refused to put their baggage into the waggons, or go any further and shewed much ill nature.

The Indians, as Smith himself wrote, "were about naked, barefoot and suffering from fatigue." They refused shoes, clothing, tents. Smith went with them as far as Little Rock, keeping track of the number of deserters as best he could, deciding that 722 of the original 1,070 remained. At Little Rock a light steamboat was hired to take them on.

Diarrhea and dysentery were gut-twisting in the camps. Two of the immense problems of any army, as General Scott viewed a soldier's life, were excrement and urine, and there was no healthy solution for them. Necessary they were, one might say; no plan thus far devised by man had properly disposed of the tons of excrement produced by an army or by thousands of Indians and blacks under confinement.

Confinement, not arrest. Or were they arrested, too? Legal niceties were absent from this operation, Scott realized. Oh, he was within the law, yes, certainly, but was the law within the law? A few doctors—not enough to go around, and shamans popping up by the score on every encampment's hillside, literally appearing out of the earth, with chants and charms and teas and tobacco cures. Whiskey was being drunk every damn night, and how it was getting into the compounds, Scott could not find out.

A deaf-mute Indian was shot. Repeatedly ordered to turn left, he turned right, did not hear the orders, and a stupid soldier shot him.

All such soldier crimes must be punished.

More testimonials were arriving on the subject of the soldiers' cruelty. Damn the army. Some reports were about the slobs who were revenging their ancestors' death at Indian hands, or the men showing off their toughness, callousness. Some were about the scavengers, fighting each other and stealing from the Indians. Then there was the matter of the Indians, deserted by John Ross who was just now on another trip to Washington, where yet again he would be told there was not to be not one whit more bargaining. What a strange leader, to handicap all these people, to deny what was surely predictable, to encourage them not to make ready, to hold out false promises and hopes, to continue to do so even while negotiating for the sole, absolute contract to move them to the West. Scott admired—one had to admire his audacity, his single-mindedness, his self-assurance. What a mixture of traits he was, this overlord.

Reports of more violence.

Reports of trading at the gates of the stockades, ponies being sold, a few women selling themselves to soldiers. Was this to become like a war campaign, with women bare-assed on the muddy ground, gonorrhea men pumping away?

The world is revolving, round and round we go, the same world over and over.

A hundred prominent Cherokees petitioned General Scott to send no further summer detachments, to await cold weather.

We your prisoners wish to speak to you. We wish to speak humbly for we cannot help ourselves. We have been made prisoners by your men, but we do not fight against you. We have never done you any harm. Sir, we ask you to hear us. We have been told we are to be sent off by boat immediately. Sir, will you listen to your prisoners. We are Indians. Our wives and children are Indians and some people do not pity Indians. But if we are Indians we have hearts that feel. We do not want to see our wives and children die. We do not want to die ourselves and leave them widows and orphans. We are in trouble, Sir, our hearts are very heavy. The darkness of the night is before us. We have no hope unless you will help us. We do not ask you to let us go free from being your prisoners, unless it should please yourself. But we ask that you not send us down the river at this time of the year. If you do we shall die, our wives will die or our children will die. Sir, our hearts are heavy, very heavy. We want you to keep us in this country until the sickly time is over, so that when we get to the west we may be able to make boards to cover our families. If you send us now the sickly time is commenced, we shall not have strength to work. We will be in the open air in all the deadly time of sickness, or we shall die, and our poor wives and children will die too. And if you send the whole nation, the whole nation will die. We ask pity. Pity our women and children if they are Indians—do not send us off at the sickly time. Some of our people are Christians—They will pray for you. If you pity us we hope your God will be pleased and that he will pity you and your wife and children and do you good. We cannot make a talk, our hearts are too full of sorrow. This is all we say.

Scott agreed to wait for cooler weather and set September 1 as the target date for the fourth march.

18 June 1838.—Nathaniel Smith, Supt. Cherokee Emigration, to Gen. Scott:
I had the honor to receive your note of this date communicating your opinion that further emigration of the Cherokees ought to be stopped until the 1st of September. . . . [I] most cheerfully give my assent to their remaining until that date, and I have no doubt the Department will approve of the proceeding. *I also discover that it will be impossible to get teams at this season, so fearful are the teamsters of their health. . . . I do not believe that 100 teams could be procured at $6 per day, each and found [with board]. . . . Every Physician, with whom I have spoken on the subject, is of the opinion that emigration ought to be suspended until September.*

Calhoun Tenn.
June 28th 1838
My dear Frances:
I do not intend to say more than two or three words to you in this, I feel so very bad at having missed a letter from you, which was sent from here to Fort Butler the day before I arrived here, and I do not expect to get it for two or three days to come. In the mean time I shall feel very cross & must grumble a little; but I will not scold my sweet wife, so do not be frightened.
I left Fort Butler on the 19th in charge of 800 Cherokees. I had not an officer along to assist me, and only my own company as a guard. Of course I have as much to do as I could attend to. But I experienced no difficulty in getting them along, other than what arose from fatigue, and this toughness

of the roads over the mountains; which are the worst I ever saw. I arrived with about one hundred more than what I started with. Many having joined me on the march. We were eight days in making the journey and it was pitiful to behold the women & children, who suffered exceedingly, as they were all obliged to walk, with the exception of the sick. I am to remain here and await the arrival of the remainder of the regiment, which is expected in about two weeks. After which, (and I have it from very good authority, Gen. Scott himself), two or three regiments of artillery will be ordered onto the northern frontier, about Plattsburgh & Sackettshaboun, and there is no doubt but our regiment will be one of them. How would you like to go on to Brownsville and Geneva my *dear girl?* I know you would like it; and I am in hopes that six weeks will find you on the way. As soon as Gen. Eustis arrives here I shall apply for a leave of absense and if I should be so fortunate as to obtain it, it will not take me long to fly to you; and we will then soon be on our way to the north. But should I be obliged to march with the Troops, and they will probably go through Ken. and up the Ohio to the Lakes, I hope you will find some means of joining me, say at Brownsville, or is this asking too much from your soldiers life? I am sure you will be a widow if I do not see you in two or three months—I can't stand it much longer, though I am now in excellent health. It appears to me that I have hardly been with you a week since we were married. Is it not abmoniable? Christopher 2 is here, and I am now writing in his tent. He desires particularly to be remembered to you, as also Major Whitney. Capt. Vinton is at Ross'es Landing. . . .

I suppose you have heard that the emigration of the Cherokees is suspended till September, and that they are to remain in depot about here till that time. They have all been collected with the exception of those to be brought down by Gen. Eustis. We have seven or eight thousand encamped about us, and they are the most quiet people you ever saw. I ommitted to mention that I have three regular ministers of the gospel in my party, and that we have preaching or prayer meetings every night while on the march. And you may well imagine that under the peculiar circumstances of the case, among those sublime mountains and in the dark forests with the thunder often sounding in the distance that nothing could be worse soldiers & [word cut out] and I always looked on with a [word cut out] lest their progress which I felt [word cut out] ascending to Heaven and calling for [word cut out] to Him who alone can & will grant [word cut out] fall upon my guilty head as one of the instruments of oppression.

My love to your father & mother & little kats. & remembrance to all friends. I have only received one of your letters, but shall write you again when I get halve of another.

I have written now more than I intended.

Do my dear wife take care of yourself, & I know Heaven will protect you. You must forgive your very bad Husband for deserting you so long. I feel guilty on account of it. God bless my dear good wife.

On July 5, Captain Connelly's company turned in their gear to the quartermaster: twelve camp kettles, twenty-four mess pans, four axes, three spades.

> 13 July 1838. Captain John Pope, Indian Agency, to Gen. Scott:
> Report on the number of Cherokees on hand: In the vicinity, 6853; that draw rations at Fort Payne, 800; at Ross' Landing, 2300; at Camp Ross, 2000; total, 11,953 . . . The above statement is as correct as it is possible for me to make at this time.

July 14. General Scott discharged twenty companies of Georgia volunteers.

July 21. Sick report, Indian camp near Ross's Landing. July 1–21. Twenty-three hundred Indians. Ten died. "They obstinately refused to take medicine . . . they were all old persons and small children."

Measles, whooping cough, pleurisy, bilious fever romped across the forty-square-mile encampment on the Hiwassee. Scott provided doctors, provisions, blankets. The Indians refused most of them.

The dead numbered in the scores. Burials became an everyday occurrence. The weeping, sobbing of women, the death chants of the shamans, were common sounds. A hundred dead.

> 13 June 1838. Col. Bynum to HQ:
> I collected yesterday about 80 Indians. They had all received orders from Welch on Valley River to leave home and take to the mountains. I have sent a large number of runners, if in their first alarm they have not gone too far, I think most of them will come in tomorrow. Big George, the chief of this valley has promised me that they shall. . . . A great deal of sickness prevails among the children . . . *I permit the females to remain at home with these sick children and the Indian physician to attend them.*
> They are desirous of selling their own property and I have promised them that liberty, provided some officer of this post witnesses the contract. . . . Almost every child and many grown persons in the valley are sick with the whooping cough.

On July 13, John Ross and his latest delegation returned from yet another visit to Washington, where he had beat his head against the federal wall, to find death set loose among his people. Three to four hundred dead, Indians and blacks. Soldiers, too.

Ross brought back a promise from the War Department to contract with him for the removal. The terms were to be worked out with General Scott, who welcomed the release from his awesome responsibility. Ross wanted more than twice the budgeted amount to move the remaining Indians and slaves. He wanted $65.88 per head, with eighty days expected on the land route.

The water route was safer and better, once the water level rose, Scott believed.

Eighty days, with extra pay for extra days. The contract to go to Lewis Ross, who would be the sole contracting agent for transportation and supplies. The land route would take longer by many weeks, it's true, but Indians prefer the land.

Scott told the Rosses he had an offer from Alfred Iverson, who had been moving Creeks to the West. For half the Ross price he would move the Cherokees by land, supplying one wagon and five horses and transporting 1,500 pounds of baggage for each group of seventy-five Indians. The rate of travel would be fourteen miles a day.

The Rosses had their own plans and price.

The cost, admittedly, was high—perhaps totaling a million dollars or more. The excess above the appropriation could come, if necessary, from the Cherokees' $4.5 million.

So at any rate, at last, John Ross and Scott agreed.

Two soldiers were killed in the North Carolina mountains. They were bringing in the last remnants of those Indians who were living within the Cherokee nation. The soldiers were on their way home, having finished the roundup, Smith reported, when they heard of this old man and his wife and their family, an illiterate full-blood named Tsali, or Charlie. They apprehended them. On the way to the compound two soldiers were struck down with an ax and the Indians fled.

A letter from John Ross arrived pertaining to the deaths.

4 November 1838. Chief John Ross to General Scott:

Sir: With much regret, I have this moment been informed by Major Anderson, your Aid-de-Camp, that the reported tragical act, has proved too true, in the death of two of your soldiers at the hands of certain individual Cherokee captives, under the charge of Lieut. Smith. . . . This melancholy affair, as I am informed took place at some point on the road from Valley River to this post—as to the particulars which gave rise to it I am wholly uninformed—but be they what they may, the act can only be viewed as one of those unfortunate individual occurrences which often take place among men of every nation, and for which the perpetrators alone can be held responsible to the laws of the land and to their Gods—I am sure you will believe me when I tell you that I sincerely hope that the offenders may speedily receive their award at the bar of justice—and that no effort shall be wanting on our part to carry on the orderly and peaceable Emigration which has commenced and is on the eve of being completed.

The 1835 census had listed Tsali as living with two males, perhaps his sons, and three females above the age of eighteen, all full-bloods. He had fourteen acres under cultivation, and owned two ponies. He was sixty.

Interesting complication, this matter of North Carolina Cherokees, as Scott realized. Four hundred of them did not live within the boundaries of the Cherokee nation, itself. Rather, they used some of the lands that they had apparently bought with the help of a white man named William Holland Thomas, their presence in accordance with a treaty negotiated from 1817 to 1819. They did not have to go west because they were not on tribal lands. These Qualla Indians were merely one more complication in an already complicated puzzle.

Now two soldiers dead—though not by Quallas, for Tsali lived within the nation.

[Sick Report. July 31. Ten weeks at the Cherokee Agency camp, three to four thousand Indians and slaves.] . . . Remittent fever, 11; "diarhea", 60; dysentery, 100; wounds, 25; measles, 63; whooping cough, 40; dead, 6.

[Sick Report, July 17 through August 17. Four weeks.] Camp Ross, for about 600 soul: 7 dead, seen by the physician; 9 dead, who were under the care of native doctors.

[Sick Report, July 17 through August 17.] Camp at Red Clay, 3 are listed as having died.

CHEROKEE ALPHABET.

Characters as arranged by the inventor.

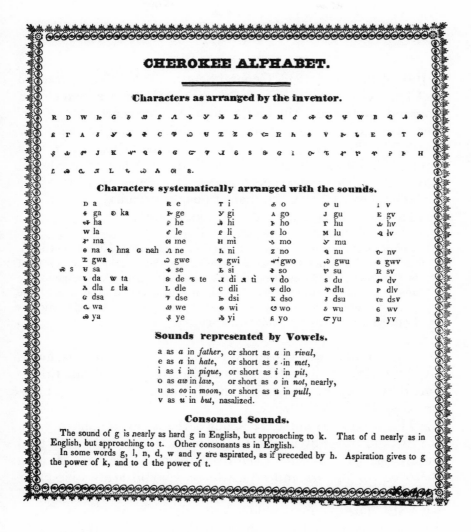

Characters systematically arranged with the sounds.

	D a		R e	T i	ꭲ o	Ꮎ u	i v
	Ꮜ ga	Ꮒ ka	Ꮆ ge	Ꭹ gi	Ꭺ go	Ꭻ gu	Ꭼ gv
	Ꮝ ha		Ꮯ he	Ꭿ hi	Ꮏ ho	Ꭺ hu	Ꮠ hv
	Ꮃ la		Ꮄ le	Ꮅ li	Ꮈ lo	Ꮇ lu	Ꮉ lv
	Ꮉ ma		Ꮊ me	Ꮋ mi	Ꮌ mo	Ꮍ mu	
	Ꮎ na	Ꭲ hna	Ꮐ nah	Ꮑ ne	Ꮒ ni	Z no	Ꮔ nu	Ꮕ nv
	Ꮖ gwa		Ꮗ gwe	Ꮘ gwi	Ꮙ gwo	Ꮚ gwu	Ꮛ gwv
Ꭷ s	Ꮞ sa		Ꮞ se	Ꮟ si	Ꮠ so	Ꮡ su	Ꮢ sv
	Ꮣ da	Ꮤ ta	Ꮥ de	Ꮦ te	Ꮧ di	Ꮨ ti	Ꮩ do	Ꮪ du	Ꮫ dv
	Ꮬ dla	Ꮭ tla	Ꮮ dle	Ꮯ dli	Ꮰ dlo	Ꮱ dlu	Ꮲ dlv
	Ꮳ dsa		Ꮴ dse	Ꮵ dsi	Ꮶ dso	Ꮷ dsu	Ꮸ dsv
	Ꮹ wa		Ꮺ we	Ꮻ wi	Ꮼ wo	Ꮽ wu	Ꮾ wv
	Ꮿ ya		Ᏸ ye	Ᏺ yi	Ᏻ yo	Ᏼ yu	Ᏽ yv

Sounds represented by Vowels.

a as *a* in *father*, or short as *a* in *rival*,
e as *a* in *hate*, or short as *e* in *met*,
i as *i* in *pique*, or short as *i* in *pit*,
o as *aw* in *law*, or short as *o* in *not*, nearly,
u as *oo* in *moon*, or short as *u* in *pull*,
v as *u* in *but*, nasalized.

Consonant Sounds.

The sound of g is nearly as hard g in English, but approaching to k. That of d nearly as in English, but approaching to t. Other consonants as in English.

In some words g, l, n, d, w and y are aspirated, as if preceded by h. Aspiration gives to g the power of k, and to d the power of t.

21

In July of this year, 1838, General Scott awarded the contract to the Cherokee council to conduct the removal of more than eleven thousand Cherokees still in the East. Consequently, the Cherokees were under tribal management and were no longer under guard. They were free to go and come as they chose—to return home, if they had a home to go to. Early in August the council convened, gathering near the Aquohee District camp south of the Hiwassee. Only a small number of people attended.

The council agreed on a statement of intent:

> *Resolved* by the National Committee and Council and people of the Cherokee Nation, in General Council assembled, that the inherent sovereignty of the Cherokee Nation, together with the Constitution, laws and usages of the same, are, and by the authority aforesaid, hereby declared to be in full force . . . and shall continue so to be in perpetuity subject to such modification as the general welfare may render expedient.

A committee was chosen to oversee the autumn movement, with John Ross as chairman. He was also given a duplicate title to United States agent Nathaniel Smith's: superintendent of Cherokee removal and subsistence.

The parties would have about a thousand people in each. They would travel by land. Appeals to use river rather than land routes were turned aside. Each detachment would have its own Cherokee conductors and police force. Should army officers or soldiers travel with the groups, they must serve as observers and that only. The groups would take cattle, to supply beef. Other food would be picked up at designated locations on the route.

Ross appointed his brother and business partner, Lewis, to handle the contracts for wagons, horses, rations, and provisions. Half of the appropriation would be needed to lease horses and wagons for the trip west and their return.

Soap. One must remember to put soap on the list of provisions.

The first detachment was to leave about September 1, the last about December 5. Questions about the advisability of land travel in winter were shunted aside. As to use of the federal boats tied up at the three river ports, they would not be needed.

General Scott had anticipated that there would be howls of outrage about his agreement with John Ross. One came from the War Department, which had not granted the right of self-administration to the Creeks, Chickasaws, or Seminoles, much less the complete freedom of action Scott had granted; and the budget far exceeded any figure the department had contemplated or had appropriated from Congress. Conceivably costs would go higher, with added days. Yes, and the soap: who had added the soap to the list of issued provisions? Would not the travelers have their own soap?

The other complaint came from ex-President Jackson, from the Hermitage. On August 23 he wrote the United States Attorney General, Felix Grundy, a fiery letter in a feeble hand:

> The contract with Ross must be arrested, or you may rely upon it, the expense and other evils will shake the popularity of the Administration to its center. What madness and folly to have anything to do with Ross when the agent was proceeding well with the removal on the principles of economy that would have saved at least 100 per cent from what the contract with Ross will cost. . . .
>
> I have only time to add as the mail waits that the contract with Ross *must be arrested*, and General Smith left to superintend the removal. . . . Why is it that the scamp Ross is not banished from the notice of the administration?

General Scott weathered the protests. He had expected all he got, would have been surprised with less. He saw that the attitude of the Indians had improved under their own leadership: they were cooperating, and he and his men were relieved of the responsibilities. Soldiers were meant for battles, not for chasing civilians and imprisoning them. Let the Indians take themselves to the West; let them decide how they wanted to go, and let the government pay what they charge, from the appropriation and the monies due to go to the tribe.

Let the War Department look to the sale of this eastern land to recoup the money John Ross's leadership would cost.

He wrote that the Cherokees had a "unanimity of feeling . . . an almost universal cheerfulness since the date of the new arrangement."

As for Old Andy—he had been twenty-five at that duel he never fought—he was too near the grave now to fight this.

White traders offered Lewis Ross forty thousand dollars for his contract to supply the transportation and provisions; he refused.

Most of the blacks were wary of new trails. They attached religious significance to making a journey; any departure or change or variance opened a way for menacing spirits. This proposed journey to the distant West was to them a dangerous event, threatening death. The blacks, on the whole, were willing to settle for what was present and known rather than risk unseen, invisible terrors.

Most of the Cherokees were of similarly superstitious mind. They considered rivers, even small creeks, to be ways to the underworld; pools were basins of the Uktena, a serpent with supernatural powers. To take a river trip was every hour threatening; to undertake any journey might annoy the spirits left here at home and would certainly alert new ones, with prospects of torture and terror.

Also, west was the direction taken by the spirits of the dead.

William Shorey Coodey, a nephew of John Ross, was a witness to the start of the first of the thirteen drives, and he described it in a letter:

To John Howard Payne, Esqr.

The entire Cherokee population were captured by the U.S. troops under General Scott in 1838 and marched, to principally, upon the border of Tennessee where they were encamped in large bodies until the time for their final removal west. At one of these encampments, twelves miles south of the Agency and Head quarters of Genl. Scott, was organized the first detachment for marching under the arrangement committing the whole management of the emigration into the hands of the Cherokees themselves.

The first of Septer. was fixed as the time for a part to be in motion on the route. Much anxiety was felt, and great exertions made by the Cherokees to comply with everything reasonably to be expected of them, and it was determined that the first detachment would move in the last days of August.

I left the Agency on the 27th, after night, and watched the encampment above alluded to, early the following morning for the purpose of aiding in the arrangements necessary to get a portion in motion on that day—the remainer to follow the next day and come up while the first were crossing the Tennessee River, about twelve miles distant.

At noon all was in readiness for moving; the teams were stretched out in a line along the road through a heavy forest, groups of persons formed about each wagon, others shaking the hand of some sick friend or relative who would be left behind. The temporary camp covered with boards and some of bark that for three summer months had been their only shelter and *home*, were crackling and falling under a blazing flame; the day was bright and beautiful, but a gloomy thoughtfulness was depicted in the lineaments of every face. In all the bustle of preparation there was a silence and stillness of the voice that betrayed the sadness of the heart.

At length the word was given to "move on." I glanced along the line and the form of Going Snake, an aged and respected chief whose head eighty winters had whitened, mounted on his favorite pony passed before me and led the way in advance, followed by a number of young men on horse back.

At this very moment a low sound of distant thunder fell on my ear. In almost an exact western direction a dark spiral cloud was rising above the horizon and sent forth a murmur I almost fancied a voice of divine indignation for the wrongs of my poor and unhappy countrymen, driven by *brutal* power from all they loved and cherished in the land of their fathers, to gratify the cravings of avarice. The sun was unclouded—no rain fell—the thunder rolled away and sounds hushed in the distance. The scene around and before me, and in the elements above, were peculiarly impressive & singular. It was at once spoken of by several persons near me, and looked upon as omens of some future event in the west.

In several letters written to my friends on the same evening, I alluded to the circumstances, so strong was the effect on my own mind at the time.

W. Shorey Coodey

This first Cherokee-administered march began on August 28. The second began a few days later, on September 1, and the third only two days after that, the three having a count on departure of

710, 859, and 846 people, as tabulated by an army officer, Captain Page. Ross had a higher count, 729, 858, and 950. The differences created immediate argument, Ross insisting on his accuracy and his superior ability in counting members of his tribe.

The routes for all of the Ross marches were substantially similar. The Tennessee River was crossed at the mouth of the Hiwassee, at Blythe's Ferry. The Cherokees and blacks, unguarded, journeyed to McMinnville and thence to Nashville. After crossing the river there, they went to Hopkinsville, Kentucky, and crossed the Ohio River at Golconda, proceeding through southern Illinois to Green's Ferry on the Mississippi. Crossing the river took days, considering the number of people and the horses, wagons, oxen, mules. Generally one of the detachments would camp well away from the river, awaiting the crossing of other Cherokees ahead. There was considerable plain fear shown during the crossing, while part of the detachment was on the west side, part on the east, waiting. After the crossing the people moved through southern Missouri by way of Springfield and from there to the Cherokee land in what would in time be Oklahoma, to a placed named Park Hill.

The thirteen detachments sought to retain their own identity and members throughout, but there was intermingling of people, and often Cherokees would drop out of one march and join another; sometimes they were looking for friends or relatives or better food, or they were tired to death and needed a rest, or they were changing their mind about going west. The men would leave a march to hunt game, needing meat to relieve the diet of salt pork and flour. They would hunt with shotguns or blowguns or bows and arrows, but because there were so many travelers with the same thought, it was rare that they found any.

There were 645 wagons, one for every eighteen to twenty people. Each was pulled by a double span of oxen, or by mules or horses. The wagons carried a family's supplies, equipment, and clothing. Rebecca Neugin recalled that she and her family numbered eleven people, and with them were two, sometimes three widows. Her elder brother, Dick, walked along with the four oxen and continually popped a whip over their backs. Her parents walked all the way.

There was scarce room in the wagon for the weary and the ill, once the sickness fell. Walking day after day was torture for the elderly, and the babies were weakened by the trip, too. The main enemy was not exertion, but disease, which chose the weaker Indians and blacks and humbled them. Dysentery, diarrhea, head and chest colds were common. It was rare for any of the travelers not to have intestinal cramps and other pains, and the diet provided by Lewis Ross—admittedly typical travelers' fare—was cheap and lacking in variety or nutrition. The campsites were not clean. The cooking utensils and bowls were wiped clean, in the Cherokee manner, but the wiping rag would become laden with grease and bits of bread and raw pork, and become contaminated.

Then too, there was the sun torturing the people by day. The cold of night caused their teeth to chatter, their tongues to stutter. Camp was whatever a family could arrange. Rarely was any shelter provided, except that the sick might be congregated in a church or school, placed on pallets on the floor in rows, little children on one side, the elderly on the other, Indian and black together, shamans chanting, with a single white doctor making inspections, crouching beside each patient, asking a few questions in English, struggling to understand the Cherokee or African or English replies, doing a little for each person. The white doctors, one per thousand refugees, were likely to fall asleep as they rode their mount, awakening whenever called or prodded to attend a sick person. The doctors were likely to fall ill, too, but they had to keep working anyway, and moving on. An Indian could pull out of one march, wait a day or so, then join another, and many did; but the doctor for a detachment must stay with it; he and the blacks were enslaved. So were the leader and the assistant leader of each detachment, who assigned policemen to keep internal order, confiscated whiskey, received the food waiting at various stops and junctions, found water, ordered the slit trenches dug, the firewood gathered—it was usually scarce—got a few fires built and the cooking taken care of, the sick taken care of, the blankets of the dying burned. The people must be asked to be quiet so others could sleep, then they must be awakened again. The slit trenches must be mounded over with earth, the garbage buried to prevent rats and wild dogs from congregating, to keep them from invading the campsites. There were broken wheels to mend; there were men and women without any moccasins to wear, or enough clothes to wear. Babies fouled their blankets. Nursing mothers went dry.

No rain. The drought lingered until September 23, and then only a light shower occurred. On September 28, at last the Indians and blacks could turn their faces upward into the pelting, refreshing drops, drench themselves with water's deliciousness, let it saturate their hair and clothing. The drought was broken.

Thank the little people. Thank the shaman. Thank Jesus. Thank the magic cast by the black witch doctor.

Oceans of mud. Every wheel and hoof and footstep now made mud. The road was used by thousands—whites' trains as well as those of the blacks and Indians—hordes used it, moving tortuously along the same road, so that one wagon's ruts would be the welcome waiting for other wagon wheels, to jar the passengers' teeth loose: a jolt to be remembered. The hooves of the animals, the feet of the people made a pudding out of the earth in the damp places, and the mud would splatter over everything, everyone.

Then they would come to a stream. The people would joyously cry out, several hundred people muddying the water; then a storm might break. Then and finally in winter the sleet and snow. So it was mud and rain and snow, slit trenches and firewood to be found somewhere, and a rabbit to be found somewhere, and puke and excrement of Indians, blacks, and whites. It was waiting at the fords and ferries, and standing in the road with foreboding in their faces.

And death. Graves along the way. First to go were the ones who might have died anyway. Many babies were expected to die even at home, from one mystery or another, and the very old approached death daily in whatever place; but sleet and mud and filth hastened the arrival. Also of weight was the hurt in the minds and bones of people taken from their homes, removed from their way of life, their will broken like a twig, their friends dispersed, their family ill.

Busted wagon. Can't mend what keeps breaking. Wheels cost dear in this part of the country, especially to an Indian.

Sometimes the Indians and whites were overcharged at the river ferries, too. There were hordes of people, finally a continuous stream of people. If ferry workers worked full speed and crowded the ferries, they could scarcely get all of the people and their gear and animals across. Always there were Indians and blacks, alongside white settlers, waiting at every ferry.

John Ross packed up his family for the trip west. He chose a water route for Quatie and their children and himself. They boarded a boat at Ross's Landing and waved to the hundreds of Indians who saw them off.

Fifty days on the land trail and not halfway there yet. Almost five hundred miles to go. Suppliers weren't at the drop yesterday to meet us. Supply merchant says we were due week before last.

Seventy days on the trail. Are we three-quarters of the way?

Eighty days. The sick load down the wagons, too little room for equipment or possessions, or even hay. We were supposed to be arriving at the destination about now.

A hundred days. The land trails continue to unroll five, six miles a day.

One hundred twenty days. Five miles yesterday. Five miles today. Can walk five miles in two hours' time. Slow as a lame horse. Delays getting all these people and mules moving.

Six hundred forty-five wagons on the trail now. Five thousand horses, twelve to thirteen thousand Indians and blacks. See this mournful procession. Well-nigh continuous ribbon of people and wagons and horses, clumps of people. This thousand-mile snake has eaten all the setting hen's eggs, thirteen eggs; see the lumps in her body, one by one; count us in this lump, the one Reverend Bushyhead commands.

Nights were cold and full of shaman chants.

A pretty woman lay down on the bare ground and received her lover, held him with her legs and arms, needing the promises and reassurances of life.

A pretty woman lying beneath a wagon spread her legs and

the black-haired head of her baby appeared, the head was seen by the midwives as the shaman put fresh sticks on the fire, chanting all the while.

A shaman led the line of measle-sick children into the river, and after bathing in the cold water they did seem to be better, somewhat better. An hour or so later, most of them began to shiver and chatter and quake.

Sing me a song, wife, hold me and sing me a song, mother. Who will dig the graves? No, not there. That place recently was dug. It's a buried slit trench or a lump of buried bodies. Either way, it's not for us to dig into.

Will the stain ever come off?

The stain on your hands?

The smell comes off, will it?

The smell of bodies?

Can't be clean. Oh my Lord, it's going to rain again. Get those children under the wagons.

Salt pork, cornmeal. Not even a blade of grass left anywhere. No hay or feed tonight for the horses or oxen. Wish I had a ewe to milk, indeed I do. I'd suck her tit, if that was the only way.

No food worth eating. Remember how the bread would fill the room with smells when I unshucked it?

Hush the shamans. Do they never hush?

An Indian man sits staring at the grave of his wife. He tells his shaman that two great figures, half raven and half human, flew down to the grave. They shone in the dark, were the pale blue of *skili*-fire. They dived into the ground and brought the coffin to the surface, opened it, and most mournfully looked into his wife's face. They lowered the coffin into the ground and flew away.

The shaman sits before a fire, reciting chants and formulas invoking the aid of the fire, which he says is as an old woman, able to serve others. The shaman waits to feel the presence of a witch. Occasionally he scans the sky. He rakes the fire's hot coals into a small rectangle walled by raised ridges of hot coals; inside the rectangle is sacred ground. He drops pinches of tobacco into the little enclosure and the tobacco flares up, bursts, and throws sparks. A witch approaches. The witch comes from that way, the direction the sparks fly. The shaman cannot as yet see the witch. He was ten years a priest before he was able to see them and even now he often fails. He hears the voices of several witches as they argue and fight in the sky. They will fight over a corpse, and the shaman must stay with the corpse three days and nights, to ward them off with his own voice, his time-proved chants, his remade tobacco.

But the march must continue: there are no days to attend the graves. Bushyhead says we move out tomorrow morning. Think of that, all these corpses, with their souls still inside, are being left for the robbery of the witches.

I saw a lemon once. You ever see one? It was in a white man's sack. My papa killed him for his sack and horse. Of course, he didn't know what was there until we opened it. The scalped man's son said the lemon was to be eaten, and my brother bit into it and was surprised. It must have been bitter. I dreamed last night of that lemon.

Mud and manure, salt meat and slush, coughing your lungs out, wrapped in a blanket lying on the wet ground, sunbaked and snowed on, raindrops in your eyes like tears, tears in your eyes. The Indians and blacks go west.

The soldiers stayed off to themselves. It was not their march. One of them was surprised to find an Indian brave sitting by the trail looking stoically at the horizon, his hair touched by a breeze, a heroic bearing to his head and shoulders, his face shaded by old nobility. Waiting for what message or comfort? What release is coming? Where did his strength weaken, his muscles soften, his body's resiliency and power drain away? He is not yet defeated, but he is cowed, life-thwarted, waiting for a voice to tell him what he ought to do.

A white traveler from Maine:

> . . . detachment of the poor Cherokee Indians . . . about eleven hundred Indians—sixty waggons—six hundred horses, and perhaps forty pairs of oxen. We found them in the forest camped for the night by the road side . . . under a severe fall of rain accompanied by heavy wind. With their canvas for a shield from the inclemency of the weather, and the cold wet

ground for a resting place, after the fatigue of the day, they spent the night
. . . many of the aged Indians were suffering extremely from the fatigue of
the journey, and the ill health consequent upon it. . . . Several were then
quite ill, and an aged man we were informed was then in the last struggles
of death.

We met several detachments in the southern part of Kentucky on the
4th, 5th, and 6th of December. . . . The last detachment which we passed
on the 7th embraced rising two thousand Indians with horses and mules in
proportion. The forward part of the train we found just pitching their tents
for the night, and notwithstanding some thirty or forty waggons were already stationed, we found the road literally filled with the procession for
about three miles in length. The sick and feeble were carried in waggons—
about as comfortable for traveling as a New England ox cart with a covering over it—a great many ride on horseback and multitudes go on foot—
even aged females, apparently nearly ready to drop into the grave, were
traveling with heavy burdens attached to the back—on the sometimes frozen ground, and sometimes muddy streets, with no covering for the feet
except what nature had given them. . . . We learned from the inhabitants
on the road where the Indians passed, that they buried fourteen or fifteen at
every stopping place, and they make a journey of ten miles per day only on
an average.

Pellagra—a disease not yet even named—struck among them.
The shamans claimed to understand it, to be able to cure it.
Into the cold river with the ill. Help her into the water. Look
upstream toward the East. Listen to the chant.

Tuberculosis, pneumonia. Man to family, one family to another. The dead were left alongside the road in shallow graves, to
rot the earth and contaminate the springs. Old campsites were
cemeteries.

A full-blood later recalled his experience on the road:

Long time we travel on way to new land. People feel bad when they leave
Old Nation. Womens cry and made sad wails. Children cry and many men
cry, and all look sad like when friends die, but they say nothing and just put
heads down and keep on go towards West. Many days pass and people die
very much.

The Indians line up at the stream, close to the water's edge,
and stare into the water. Their priest stands behind them,
stretches his hands and arms upward and forward, all the while
staring ahead. "Sge! O Long Man, now you had let the soul slip

from your grasp and it had dwindled away. Now his health has
been restored and he shall live to be old." The chant is to the
river, followed by the chant "O Gĕhyăgúga," the sun. "In the first
upper world, O Gĕhyăgúga, you have the tables. The white food
shall be set upon them. It shall be reached over.

Upstream a congregation of Christians gathers and begins to
sing a Protestant hymn in English.

The shaman: "his health has been restored and he shall live to
be old." The chant continues, seven times repeated to the sun.

The shaman chants to the river, the sun, and the fire; the
black witch doctor chants in a whisper to his hands; the Christians chant to Jesus and the Holy Ghost; the ill move into the cold
wind and water.

Upstream another shaman begins his ceremony of casting
out evil conjurations, sending them on the backs of beavers to
other places, other families, saving this people from the grip of
iron on their guts, the heat in their heads, the weakness in their
legs.

The Christians sing.

The doctor curses, turns to shrug, crouches beside an old
chief who has too little strength to go to any of the priests, even
though there are several holding services nearby. The voices of
the blacks cleanse the morning.

"In the upper world, O Gĕhyăgúga . . ."

What world is that? the doctor wonders.

The doctor moves to a wagon; beneath it a Negro baby newly
born is crying his way into the world, this world just here, with
its chants and songs and perorations. Wash him; there is spring
water enough to wash him. In time explain to him what in God's
name is being done along this trail. How many gods and grunts
and cries, devils and ghosts and spirits are there? Look at those
sick Indians standing naked in the sunshine, bathing in the sun
here in the cold of winter. Dig more graves, cast out more devils,
let even the witches beware this camp as we cleanse our souls.

The shaman tells the mother not to feed the baby for seven
days; instead, let him drink a concoction of herbs.

Oh, go on your way, he is told. She is not Cherokee, she says:
"Christian," the woman tells him.

Feed your baby, black woman, the white doctor tells her. You have milk enough? Black women make milk from corn and fatback. A miracle, a nigger miracle. Let your baby drink. Welcome, baby, into this world of journeys and land speculations, national sovereignties, horse races, willful chiefs, assertive presidents, willing women naked as they receive their men and bear their offspring; welcome to the world of light-horse Indian police calling once more for us to walk our five, six, seven miles for the day in the rain and winter sun. Put the rising sun to your back today, six or seven miles farther it will be—by some miracle as mysterious as fire or the river—at your face. Listen, little babe sucking your mother's breast, the sun is worthy of your following after, but you must understand its character. It changes about.

Where does the evil spirit reside?

Why, in the setting sun.

"Sge! O Ancient White, where you have let the soul slip from your grasp, it has dwindled away. Now his health has been restored and he shall live to be old. *Ku!*"

Was it for the living those Indians went to the water, or for the dead? Or for bad dreams? Or to know if the dead—all the dead along this trail had died of natural causes, or as a result of sorcerers, witches?

Mysteries.

Bad dreams are the result of the hostile conjurations of some secret enemy, and one must perform the ceremony, or else the dream will come true.

What will you name your baby? the doctor asks a black woman.

Ezekiel.

The doctor moves to the wooden bucket of water and waits for the squaw to finish using the gourd dipper. He drinks a little from the gourd and listens to the chants and hymns and bits of sermon and the shouts of the Light Horse as the Indian police try to get the marchers underway. Cherokees sleep late, always have, in winter.

She won't be able to carry her new baby, he says. She ought to be put in a wagon. Yes, even if she is an African.

Ice on the Mississippi, too thick for the ferries to break, too thin to support oxen and wagons. So we have to wait. Story of this trail is wait. That's one story. Have to wait even to die. The other story is moving on.

Dr. Elizur Butler, the American Board medical missionary, had been with the Indians and blacks in the stockades and camps and was serving on this trail, too. He wondered why, God knows, even the storms, the elements conspired to afflict this people. "From the first of June I felt I have been in the midst of death," he wrote. He estimated that one-fifth of the Cherokees had died.

And of the blacks? How many of these dead were black?

Nobody troubled to guess.

March 14, 1839, group number ten arrived in the Cherokee territory, having spent 189 days on the trail.

On March 18 the detachment of John Drew arrived, having passed two others.

On March 24, two detachments—the ones that had left eastern Tennessee on September 20 and October 23 arrived. They were the last ones on the trail, which was called "the Trail Where We Cried,"—"the Trail of Tears."

John Ross was well satisfied by the boat that he and Quatie boarded in eastern Tennessee near his old homeplace, even by the food. They could stand on the decks and watch the sun rise out of the land they were leaving behind, and follow its course as the day passed, the miles being left behind, to the west, where new land lay waiting.

Quatie had a cold, but other than that the family was healthy.

The journey went as planned, down the Tennessee River through all this once-Cherokee land, past white plantations, their slaves seen now and then along the roads driving ox carts, hauling goods, leaning on fences watching the steamer go by. A crowd was gathering: might be an auction, might be a slave sale or a horse race. Ross had been told that Jackson had been a slave trader as well as a land trader, in his day. And Jackson had race horses, indeed, the fastest horse in Tennessee—fastest in America. Not far away he was living, piecing out his daily life.

The voyage went well. There was one passage of land to

cross. As bad luck would have it, the land passage coincided with a winter snow, which made the trail treacherous for the horses and carriages. Night came. Quatie gave her blanket to a sick child. Her own cold got worse, and by morning she was seriously ill. In a vicious stroke of fate, she died. It was all quick. It was unexpected, unkind, gave doubts to believers, aroused questions about God's sense of fairness.

Quatie was buried—there was no coffin even for her—in a shallow grave near the road. All the graves in the West were shallow and near the road. She would have been pleased by the Bible readings, being a Christian.

Lewis Ross took some of the profits and played a hunch. In the West, the backbreaking work of clearing and constructing and planting would create an excellent market for black slaves. He bought a supply of slaves in Georgia and sent them out there. He sent them by water. He sent five hundred.

Lewis Ross, the brother of Principal Chief John Ross, chartered a boat in 1838 and transported slaves from Georgia to the Cherokee Nation. An armed guard met the boat and escorted Ross's property to his plantation for sale to other Cherokees. Some slaveholds went to Arkansas, Tennessee, or New Orleans to purchase slaves.

22

Honey Creek in Indian territory, as this portion of eastern Oklahoma was named, was a tributary of the Neosho, also called the Grand River, which flowed southward about eighty miles into the Arkansas River. John Ridge and his father, the major, set their plantations here, close to the Missouri border. Indeed, one could walk into Missouri in a few minutes, and sometimes Sarah and John did just that, with their children, John Rollin, Herman, Aeneas, Susan, Andrew Jackson, and Flora. Daughter Clarinda, who was slow to learn—in truth "feebleminded"—was usually left nearby with her grandparents, the major and Susanna.

The major and Susanna had brought Clarinda with them to the West, on the water route. The three, their son Walter, and eighteen chosen slaves were the extended family. They had been members of a group of 466, half of whom were children, under the guidance of Dr. John S. Young. It had been a government-run operation, provided with standard government issue: 150 bushels of cornmeal, 78 barrels of flour, and 12,000 pounds of bacon, all stowed aboard the boats tied to the docks at Ross's Landing. A missionary who had been present on March 3, 1837, to see them off, wrote:

> It is mournful to see how reluctantly these people go away, even the stoutest hearts melt into tears when they turn their faces towards the setting sun—& I am sure that this land will be bedewed with a Nation's tears —if not with their blood. . . . Major Ridge is . . . said to be in a declining state, & it is doubted whether he will reach Arkansas.

The major was given no special treatment at the beginning of the journey. His powerful body was bending from the winds of age, it was true. He was sixty-six, an old man for the time, and on the first leg of the journey the doctor thought it wise to move him and Susanna into a cabin.

The passengers had their government money, issued by General Nathaniel Smith in payment for their lost goods, stock, and improvements. Some had more than others; some claimed valuable libraries and blooded stock, more than they actually possessed, and Lumpkin's committee had been forced to pay for most of their claims. Money was plentiful, therefore—and so, as it turned out, was whiskey—so the nights rivaled the stars and moon for glory, to the major's discomfort.

The entire trip was made by water and the open cars of the Tuscumbia, Courtland, and Decatur Railroad, which provided wonderous excursions memorable for the major and the children, awesome really. A train, an outright astonishment, a puffing, boisterous belly-wriggler of a creature, screeching challenges, belching loud noises from its head, throwing off steam and smoke, moving straight as an arrow across the ground.

The train trip took them through Muscle Shoals, the fabled territory that Cherokee chiefs had traded away in return for bribes during the major's younger days. He recalled his anger at the time.

The physician for the journey was Dr. C. Lillybridge. He checked the passengers' health every day, and Susanna's and the major's particularly, careful of the old and the very young, the ones most vulnerable. They proceeded down the Ohio River to the mother of rivers, the Mississippi. Here the "wind makes it difficult for the Indians to cook, as their fires are on top of the Boats," Dr. Lillybridge wrote.

At Montgomery Point, Arkansas, a pilot boarded to navigate the muddy Arkansas River. Progress was slower moving upstream. On the twenty-first they reached Little Rock and boarded keelboats towed by the steamer *Revenue*. The major and Susanna complained to Dr. Lillybridge of severe coughs, which the doctor sought to remedy. On March 27, he wrote in his journal,

Van Buren. Arrived here during the night, patients generally convalescent; left V.B. at 10 o'clock. Good number of Indians drunk. Arrived at Fort Smith at 1 o'clock P.M. Left at 2 P.M. Major Ridge had been advised by a friend, whom he met at Fort Smith, to turn back to Van Buren, as that was the most eligible route to the lands he had selected. About 2 miles above

Fort Smith the Boats landed to set Major Ridge and his friends on shore. Immediately the larger proportion of the Detachment were in motion, and in spite of the advice of the Agents and those who were acquainted with the country, they landed their effects & considered themselves at home.

No deaths on the journey for this group.

The riverbanks were covered with bushes and trees and vines, a healthy looking place. The Indians aboard stared at the horizon line, politely taking in the first sights of their country, assessing its prospects.

The major had decided to settle on Honey Creek, at the northeastern corner of the territory. To travel there he and his family purchased wagons, horses, oxen, supplies of all sorts, and moved northward from the river. An old military highway was available to take them part of the way. They were curious about their world. They were passing through a wilderness, Susanna wrote: there were no bridges; the streams had to be forded. And there were warnings of desperadoes lurking along the way. The Ridges encountered none, but they did meet whites who wanted to sell whiskey.

The major's family and slaves arrived at the blooming time of the redbud trees, the white dogwoods, the wild plum trees. Washington Irving, while working for the federal government, had described Honey Creek:

> the honey-bee swarms in myriads, in the noble groves and forests which skirt and intersect the prairies, and extend along the alluvial bottoms of the rivers. It seems to me as if these beautiful regions answer literally to the description of the land of promise, "a land flowing with milk and honey"; for the rich pasturage of the prairies is calculated to sustain herds of cattle as countless as the sands upon the seashore, while the flowers with which they are enamelled render them a very paradise for the nectar-seeking bee.

The hill forests were predominantly hickory, oak, and ash, with persimmon and some pine and cedar. The bottoms were covered with elm, willow, maple, sycamore, and pecan, all festooned with garlands of wild grape.

The major purchased improvements on Honey Creek itself, where he found rich, fertile land, and he began to plan further clearings. Susanna wrote, "We had to undergo many privations in [the] new Country. But we bore [them] all under the belief that we had found a comfortable home for our children and grandchildren. We expended much money and labor on building houses and clearing land."

The rumor was launched in the East that Major Ridge had died on the way west. When this was proved false, a rumor started that he died a few weeks after his arrival at Honey Creek.

That was proved false, too. He was well and busy, clearing and planting, making another big plantation, starting with the apple and peach trees, and a few cherries and pears.

While still in the East, John Ridge had received $19,741.67 for the improvements and acreage of his plantation in the East. Also, the new owner paid him $1,745 for the crops in the fields and the few hogs. He had a claim for the fees lost while that man Garrett operated his ferry, but the Lumpkin committee had still been adjudicating that at the time of John's and Sally's departure.

They met with Boudinot and his new wife, Delight Sargent, and the two families formed the core of a party that proposed to travel by carriage and horseback to the West. Most of the slaves and horses had been sent along earlier with John's former ferryman, William Childers. Sarah had kept two house slaves with her, to cook and help with the children, and John had kept one man to drive the carriage.

At the ragged, rough town of Nashville, while waiting for their horses to be shod, John went on a little pilgrimage to visit Andrew Jackson, whom he found to be almost deaf, blind in one eye, and generally failing, a companion to the imminence of death, but gracious as John's host.

The party rode north through southwestern Kentucky, crossing the Ohio River at Berry's Ferry. Along the way John and Elias and their wives discussed the challenges ahead: the plantation work; the translation of the New Testament into Cherokee, with which Boudinot was to help Worcester; the founding of a college for the Indians, for which school funds were now available.

They rode across lower Illinois, past marshland and through

swamps, trusting to rickety bridges. They moved across the Ozark plateau on "a good road through a rocky and romantic country." They entered the prairies, saw elk, deer, pheasant, turkey, prairie fowl, hares, bears, possums, foxes. Seven weeks in all were required for the journey—forty-nine days—to Honey Creek. They arrived in cool weather in late November 1837, to find the major and Susanna busily establishing themselves on excellent land. John wrote:

> The country there is best adapted for agriculture & water privileges. It is superior to any country I ever saw in the U.S. Missouri or that part next to the Cherokees is populating very fast and in a few years it will be the garden spot of the United States. The Cherokees have settled here almost altogether in consequence of their being introduced in this quarter by the agents. . . . Honey Creek, near the Senecas, is unsettled, & all the region about there is large enough for the whole Nation. . . . Perfect friendship and contentedness prevail all over this land.

His sister and her husband were already here, and had purchased an improvement on John's behalf from a western Cherokee. At once he and Sally began building a new house. The house had two expensive finished doors and five window frames with shutters. The purchased house had substantial log walls, and the main part had four rooms. The kitchen was in a building of its own. Near the house and kitchen were the apple house, the vegetable cellar, the smokehouse, and farther away the stables, cribs, paddock. It sat among forty acres of pastures and fields.

John and the major built a store on Honey Creek, a big building. Childers agreed to operate the store for them.

John found time to take trips to see the country all around. He wrote:

> I have traveled extensively in that country—once from my residence, near the corner of Missouri and Arkansas, to Fort Smith, through Flint District, where I had the pleasure of beholding fine springs of water, excellent farms and comfortable houses, and mills, and mission schools, belonging to the Cherokees; and every evidence of prosperity and happiness was to be seen among the Cherokees as a people.

He repeatedly asked the Cherokee settlers the same question: would they want to return to the East, if they could have their old rights once more? Most answered no.

He traveled to the "Neutral Ground," a block of territory he had helped to add in the Treaty of New Echota.

> I rode over it, about two days, and I there found Mr. Joseph Rogers, our Cherokee friend, from the Chattahoochee, pleasantly situated in the finest region . . . I ever beheld in any part of the United States. The streams here of all sizes, from the rivers to the brooks, run swiftly over clean stones and pebbles, and water is clear as crystal, in which excellent fish abound. . . . The soil is diversified from the best prairie lands to the best bottom lands, in vast tracts. Never did I see a better location for settlements and better springs in the world. God has thrown His favors here with a broad cast. In this region are numerous mills, and it is of itself capable of supporting a larger population than the whole Cherokee Nation, East.

Meanwhile, Boudinot and his bride settled near the Worcesters, close to the new town of Park Hill, overlooking two prairies. Worcester and Boudinot were as close as brothers, deeply committed to translating, publishing.

John Ridge's intention was to stay out of politics. The governmental structure of the western Cherokees was without a constitution or a comprehensive set of laws, the same condition as the eastern population's some several years earlier; nonetheless, the western elders were honest and skilled. Let them govern. John had his family to care for, his ailing father; each had a plantation; he and his father had the store. Also, he had a new world to explore. John wrote:

> I was pleased to find that religious tracts, in the Indian language, were on the shelves of full-blooded Cherokees, and everyone knew and seemed to love the Messenger, as they called Mr. Worcester. I very often met with new emigrants from the Eastern Nation, either arriving or settling the country, or on their way to Fort Gibson, to draw the balance of their dues for their lands and improvements. These newcomers were formerly of opposite portions in the old nation. There was no disposition to quarrel, but every [one] to cultivate friendship and rejoice together in the possession of this fine country.
>
> I had the pleasure of being introduced to Gen. Arbuckle, commanding at Fort Gibson, and I found him to be an excellent man, of fine personal

appearance, and intelligent. He informed me that the country next to the Osages, on the Verdigris, was . . . yet unsettled. . . . Most all the intelligent men of our nation, our Supreme Judges, and Sheriffs, and Marshals, our Legislators, and our National Treasurers, are . . . already removed, and are engaged in building houses and opening farms. Many of the Cherokees have turned their attention to merchandising, and some have supplied themselves with goods from New Orleans and New York, besides other place more convenient to the nation.

John and Sally hired a teacher, the same Miss Sophia Sawyer. This dedicated, trenchant old-maid teacher came to live with them, as she had for a while in the East. They trusted her implicitly, even left her in charge of the children when in March 1838 they journeyed to New York City, where they marveled at the sights and sounds, attended concerts and plays, and purchased goods for the store from wholesalers. Also he met with religious leaders and discussed the views recently written by John Howard Payne, who remained furious about Georgians and removal. John wrote:

Instead of receiving the late Treaty as a blessing to the Cherokees and as a measure of relief to them, they considered it the source of all afflictions. I attempted to explain John Ross's position in the papers; and many of them are now convinced that the Treaty and its friends are in the right.

John and Sally visited her parents in South Lee, in the Berkshire Hills of Massachusetts; and there John, for the first time in a long while, fell ill. During the summer Sarah traveled home alone, while John followed in September. He had journeyed as far as Kentucky when he heard of a meeting, called by the Cherokees, of ten tribes, to renew alliances and friendships and to remove all stones from the trails, so that members of one tribe living in the West might visit another without bruises. The newspapers speculated about a possible Indian uprising, which was alarming white settlers. John called on the editors of the Louisville *Journal* and talked to them about the pacific intent of the proposed meeting and the responsible character of the Cherokees, and he allayed their concerns.

At about this time the early Ross-planned marches were on

the trails, but John knew little of the plans or routes. He hurried on home to prepare the store for the mass arrivals, hoping to have in place the major stocks of tools, kitchen pans and skillets, clothing and shoes, cloth and buttons, bridles, and dippers. He and his father had decided to sell on credit to Indians who had not received their federal per-capita allowance; they felt that somebody would have to help them get started here. By now John had goods arriving from the Northeast, as well as from New Orleans and other southern cities.

He busied himself building a schoolhouse for Miss Sawyer, to be ready when the masses of Cherokees arrived. A Presbyterian church stood seven miles away down Honey Creek, an hour's ride, and Sally joined that church and attended the services, often taking Miss Sawyer and the children in the carriage. Sarah was the only white communicant; the others were Indians or blacks. The pastor was a Cherokee, an elderly man, John Huss, with whom Miss Sawyer was impressed. She described him in her journal as "one of the best men in the world." She wrote of Sarah, "Our family is nearer what it should be now than it ever has been since I was connected with it. Mrs. Ridge has more influence and moral courage; she also has a brother & sister, with their companions, here, in Mr. Ridge's employ." She praised John's store, but was annoyed and worried about John's growth as a Christian:

> He cannot hear truth without uneasiness. He cannot escape it in the position in which he has placed himself. He has tampered with the cause of temperance, by selling wine, until he has become disgusted with wine drunkards, & says he will sell no more. He has a most interesting family of sons, who, if they follow the instructions he is causing them daily to receive, will shun the path of the destroyer, & loathe the vices of their people. The only daughter who is capable, & of sufficient age to receive instruction, is almost constantly with me—a sprightly, lovely child, full of budding promise, & if we are faithful, this gem of character will open into full-grown flower & finished beauty. . . . The house I occupy & the furniture cost from four to five hundred dollars—probably will exceed five hundred when it is completed. Such presents as Mr. & Mrs. Ridge make in clothing I receive and continue my labours in their family & among their people in the character of benevolence sustained by the patronage of the Board. In

this way they wish me to live & labor, believing it to contribute to my happiness & usefulness.

Early in 1839 John Ridge returned to New York for more supplies for the store. He committed an additional twenty-five thousand dollars, half his, half his father's. The store would be, he believed, the best anywhere about. He visited in Washington "Heads of Departments and other friends" and received "the warmest reception."

In Washington he told Schermerhorn, as the latter later wrote,

> My brother, we have been laboring long together in a good cause—the salvation and happiness of the Cherokees. You for what you have done, have been abused, misrepresented and slandered by your countrymen: and I might yet someday die by the hand of some poor infatuated Indian, deluded by the counsels of Ross and his minions; but we have this to console us, we shall have suffered and died in a good cause. My people are now free and happy in their new homes, and I am resigned to my fate, whatever it might be.

On the journey home, he went by stagecoach to Wheeling, then by steamboat down the Ohio to the Mississippi, then up the Arkansas.

Considering plans for schools, a college, the store, the farms, with rich hopes he returned to find a torn people, bleeding even yet from the trail, an angry multitude in mourning; and they only rarely blamed John Ross and his brother Lewis: their bitterness was directed toward John Ridge and the major, Boudinot and his brother Stand Watie, and their kind.

Rumors were even spread that John's eastern travels had been for the purpose of selling off part of the Cherokees' western lands.

Boudinot's unpopularity with the mass of newly arrived people endangered his work with Worcester on translating portions of the Bible. Even earlier anxiety had often been expressed, but Worcester had staunchly protected him. Now the criticism became a howl.

Politics became turbulent, too. For the past several months, the old settlers and the treaty settlers had got along, but now the Ross settlers, generally called the "late immigrants," were annoyed by attempts at government on the part of the old settlers. Before migrating to the West, Ross and a majority of Cherokee men had met at Red Clay and voted to follow the laws and governmental authority they had established in the East, and they were entering a territory governed by somewhat different laws and other Cherokees.

In May, 1839, Miss Sawyer wrote, "The critical situation of the Nation I cannot communicate. It is such a time of excitement. . . . The atmosphere of the old nation in its most disturbed state, compared to this was like the peaceful lake to the boisterous ocean."

John Ross was one of the last of the new settlers to arrive. The old-settler chiefs called on him to ask about reports of political dissention. Cephas Washburn, a missionary, was present, and reported on the meeting:

> When Ross himself arrived he was visited by some intelligent individuals of the "old settlers," who mentioned this report to him & told him that such a course would occasion great commotion. He denied the truth of the report & said that he & his people were ready to come under the government and laws already existing here. This quieted the people, & the newcomers were everywhere welcomed by the old settlers & aided in finding suitable places for residence. All supposed that the Cherokees were reunited as one people, henceforth to live in harmony.

Ross suggested that a council be called, at which the formal union of old settlers and new immigrants would take place. This was agreed to. The announcements were sent out by the old settlers' chiefs, and on June 3, 1839, at Takatoka (also called Double Springs), Cherokees began gathering. Within a few days six thousand were in attendance. Members of the Treaty Party, the Ridge faction, were invited, but the few who came were solely onlookers. Major Ridge did not arrive with John, Elias, and Stand Watie until June 14. They looked on, visited, and said nothing. Even so, they did arouse resentment, so they left the same day.

Cephas Washburn was present and reported that speeches

were made by old settlers and new immigrants "congratulating each other that they were now reunited as one nation, after having been separated for so long, & expressive of the hope that nothing would ever again occur to divide them."

All went well; however, while John Brown, the first chief, was announcing the close of this highly successful council, John Ross spoke up. He asked on what terms the immigrants would be received. Brown replied that they had been received and had "expressed full satisfaction at their reception." Ross wanted a more formal reception and said that the old settlers should list "the privileges to which they were entitled." Brown did so in yet another speech. As Washburn reported, he said:

> We cordially receive you as brothers. We joyfully welcome you to our country. The whole land is before you. You may freely go wherever you choose & select any places for settlement which may please you, with this restriction, that you do not interfere with the private rights of individuals. You are fully entitled to the elective franchise; are lawful voters in any of the districts in which you reside, & eligible to any of the offices within the gift of the people. Next October, according to law the term of service of the chiefs will expire & any of you are eligible to those seats. Next July will be an election in our districts for members of both houses of our legislature, for judges, sheriffs, etc. At those elections you will be voters & you are eligible to any of those offices. A government was, many years since, organized in this country, & a code of laws was established, suited to our condition & under which our people have lived in peace and prosperity. It is expected that you will all be subject to our government & laws until they shall be constitutionally altered or repealed & that in all this you will demean yourselves as good & peaceable citizens.

The Cherokees responded positively to this statement, Washburn reported, but Ross said he thought it important that his people remain "as an organized body politic, for the purpose of settling their accounts with the United States, and for securing certain claims for spoliations."

As Washburn recalled it, Brown replied,

> For the settlement of all matters growing out of your removal from the old nation & for your subsistence for one year, & for the adjustment of all claims against the United States, you are freely allowed your own Chiefs &

Committee & Council, & Judges & Sheriff, with the name and style of the
Eastern Cherokee Nation.

Ross found this unsatisfactory, Washburn said, and then
made known his objection to the old settlers' codes and government.

Brown replied, "The government is modeled after your own
government & the laws are the same." He said that at the October
council meeting revisions could be begun for revising or enlarg-
ing the code and drawing up a constitution, on which the whole
people could vote. Because the immigrants outnumbered the old
settlers more than two to one, there could not be any hindrance to
their wishes. Ross refused to accept the conditions, and Brown, at
the end of his patience, announced the adjournment of the council.

Ross would not leave. He said he wished a convention to be
called at once to make a new constitution.

Brown, irritated to exasperation, refused to call one, and on
June 19, after two weeks and two days of meetings, he went
home, the other old settlers following.

Ross remained. He asked his people to stay and meet with
him, and for two days longer they had their own conference. At
its conclusion he wrote to Montfort Stokes, a former governor of
North Carolina, now the United States agent to the Cherokees,
that his "reasonable propositions submitted to the consideration
of the representatives of our western brethren have not been received by them in a manner compatible with the wishes of the
whole people," and added that this type of reception would not
"fail to disturb the peace of the community, and to operate injuri-
ously to the best interests of the nation."

Unable to take over the reins of government until after the
October council, the more violent of Ross's followers decided to
execute several policy matters on their own. Even as the Ross
meetings terminated, several dozen of them came together privately, with the intention of invoking the blood laws.

At their private meeting, held at the council grounds—John
Ross himself was not present at the meeting—the specific law
prohibiting unapproved disposal of Cherokee land was read, the

traditional law added to the written code in 1829. The penalty for breaking it was traditional, too, and had been added in fact to that written law by Major Ridge's motion: it was death. The most obvious people to be accused of breaking it were Major Ridge, his son John, and his nephews Elias Boudinot and Stand Watie; also named were John A. Bell, James Starr, and George W. Adair. Actually, the law of 1829 required indictment of the accused and a trial for accusations, and defense, but there was no hint of such formalities.

Three men from the clan of each defendant sat as judges, the accused not informed, not present. Major Ridge was of the Deer clan, and the three judges heard the testimony accusing him of breaking the law and found him guilty. The others were accused and all found guilty.

Among the scores of men at this session was John Ross's son, Allen Ross. Later he prepared a deposition, which said in part,

> A committee was appointed to arrange details and in response to that committee report numbers were placed in a hat for each person present; twelve of these numbers had an X mark after the number which indicated the Executioners. All present were asked to draw. When I came to draw the Chairman stopped me and told me that I could not draw as the Committee had another job for me on that day.

His job was to remain with his father and if possible "to keep him from finding out what was being done."

That very night, before the dawn of June 22, large assassination parties, one for each execution, mounted and rode off. The party assigned to kill John Ridge numbered twenty-five men. They reached Honey Creek at daybreak. They loaded their rifles and, still mounted, surrounded the house. Three of the men left their horses, approached the door, and gently forced it open. In the house were John and Sally and their children, along with her sister and brother-in-law. All were asleep. Quietly one of the three assassins located John, held a pistol to his head, and pulled the trigger. The pistol failed to fire. The three grabbed him as he awoke and dragged him from bed. He fought them vigorously. They hauled him into the yard, the cries of his wife and children and of John himself filling the air, their voices soon drowned by the twenty-five assassins, who set up calls and cries to make appeals impossible. Sally tried to follow her husband into the yard, but men pushed her back through the door, jabbing rifle barrels at her. She could see John as two men grabbed his arms, others his body, and held him up while another raised a knife and stabbed him. The bloody knife stabbed him over and over, while she and her children watched. The men threw his body as high into the air as they could, and let it fall to the ground. As it lay on the red-soaked ground, the twenty-five assassins marched single file over it and stomped it.

Even so, bloody, ripped open, John was not dead. He tried to raise himself onto his elbow. Sally was now allowed to go to him. He opened his mouth to speak and blood flowed from it; he made gurgles, which she could not understand. She ordered servants to carry him indoors. The children watched, dismayed, forever to be haunted. She sat beside the bed; Rollin was nearby. He later wrote:

> Then succeeded a scene of agony . . . which might make one regret that the human race had ever been created. It has darkened my mind with an eternal shadow. In a room prepared for the purpose lay pale in death the man whose voice had been listened to with awe and admiration in the councils of his Nation, and whose fame had passed to the remotest of the United States, the blood oozing through his winding sheet and falling drop by drop on the floor. By his side sat my mother, with hands clasped and in speechless agony —she who had given him her heart in the days of her youth and beauty, left the home of her parents and followed the husband of her choice to a wild and distant land.

The assassins rode south to Beattie's Prairie, the home of Joseph Lynch, a favorite of John Ross. There they slaughtered a steer and ate of it and celebrated the morning's duty. Present were assassins Daniel Colston, John Vann, a man called Hunter, and three Spear brothers, Archibald, James, and Joseph. Joseph Spear had been the wielder of the knife.

Elias Boudinot's children were in New England with their grandparents. He and his bride were living with the Worcesters at Park Hill while building a house on a site near the mission. Thirty riders, assigned to do his murder, waited in a thick woods not far from the house. About nine that morning Boudinot left Delight and the Worcesters and came to the new house to talk to the carpenters, who were at work. From the woods four men approached, and called to Boudinot. Suspecting nothing, he went to meet them. The men needed medicine, they told him, for sick family members. Boudinot was in charge locally of the public medicines, and at once he set out walking toward Worcester's mission station with two of the men. About halfway there, one of the two men fell behind and plunged a knife into Boudinot's back. Boudinot cried out and fell into the grass. The other Cherokee swung his tomahawk, splitting open his head.

The carpenters came running, but they saw at once they were too late to help, or to stop the two fleeing assassins. Delight and Worcester had answered the cry, too. She knelt beside the broken head, the closed eyes. She spoke his name, a name dear to her, and his eyes opened, glazed in death.

Worcester called to a Choctaw Indian working nearby, told him to mount bareback Worcester's own swift horse, Comet, there in the paddock, and ride to the store where Stand Watie worked, to warn him of possible danger to his life.

Major Ridge, on his way to Van Buren to visit a sick slave, left the home of Ambrose Harnage at Cincinnati, Arkansas, that morning. The company of assassins assigned to kill him knew where he was staying and hid in underbrush and trees at a place where the road crossed Little Rock Creek, just a mile outside the Cherokee territory, inside the border of Arkansas, seven miles from Cane Hill. Major Ridge was mounted, as was his attendant, a black youth.

A volley of shots: the youth thought there were ten or twelve shots in all. Major Ridge, five bullets in his head and body, slumped in the saddle. His big horse reared, threw him off.

The black youth, seeing that he was dead, rode swiftly away to spread the word of the fall of the last Cherokee of his breed.

The reports were as strong as great winds in winter that the
major and his two boys, whom he had trained, had been slain in
one morning. The news overflowed the tongue and mind. Nobody talked of it without stammering. There were reports that
Stand Watie was killed, and John Ross. Rumor devoured truth
and other rumors. Dangers haunted the roads and yards and
houses. The truth was three blows, three clangs of the hammer,
three uplifted arms, three shots, with other shots accompanying,
three flashes of the knife, the ax. Three men, who had carried
weights of governing, had been assassinated, young Ridge slaughtered like a hog at an autumn butchering, twenty-five knife
wounds in his body, the stomping feet of twenty-five ushering
him to death. Only once had he been tossed high, no doubt with
expectation that his body would die in flight; but he lingered for
further hatred, his white wife coming to watch from nearby.
What thought she now of life in the wilds? How dare she be
critical of us for what we are!

Who killed John Ridge?

Why, here are the names.

Who killed Major Ridge?

Don't you know? It was Johnston, Money Talker, Car-soo-
taw-dy, Duck-wa, Joseph Beanstalk, Soft-Shelled Turtle. There
were ten or more who fired the volley.

Who killed Stand Watie's brother, Boudinot?

Listen to the men tell all about it. There's no secret, only
pride.

Shot the major from a thicket. Awoke John Ridge from sleep,
did his twenty-five wounds, let him pay in his final minutes for
the arrogance he had shown in life. Now may his white wife
come to know him and us. All men are humble, held up for the
knife. Let his silver tongue be cut out, his right hand be cut off.
His eloquence is mixed with dirt and blood. Let his children remember this particular sunrise and know their place. John Ridge
is humble now, his main soul slowly shriveling in the frontal
division of his head.

Men gathered at John Ross's house, surrounded it. Hundreds
came to protect him from Stand Watie and others of the Treaty

Party, and maybe from the old settlers, too. Ross had not known of the plans for the three assassinations, the men said. Stand Watie was reported seen nearby, he and a group of men were leaving. Ross encouraged his men to ride after them, try to kill them.

Ill, Andrew Jackson at the Hermitage shook his big head at news of the murders, as he did at claims of John Ross's innocence.

Sally Ridge took her children across the border into Arkansas, abandoning the estate she and John had built. Even the merchandise in the store was brought to Arkansas, and John's share was sold at auction for whatever it would bring. Her mother-in-law, Susanna Ridge, had Major Ridge's share returned to Honey Creek, to the store, which she ordered operated as the major had wanted.

Ross held a convention on July 1, which the chiefs of the old settlers and the Treaty Party did not attend in any number. Sequoyah came, however, always attentive to the call for conciliation. One of the first acts of the council was to declare amnesty for all crimes committed by anybody since the arrival of the late immigrants.

Of course, revenge began. What hand killed this Ross man on the road? Or that treaty man in the river? Who killed the treaty man in his field? Who killed the Ross man who had shot the major? Who killed the man who killed the man who shot the major? Who killed that man? Can you count the executions on both hands?

Stand Watie's men ride in the night. Ross's men, too. Old settlers look on dismayed, excluded now from governing their own country.

The public in Arkansas demanded that the murders of the Ridges and Boudinot be brought to trial. The alleged murderers were demanded, but new principal chief of all the Cherokees, John Ross, claimed to have no knowledge of their identities. The federal officials had a list of the accused men and said they were determined to bring them to trial, especially the murderers of Major Ridge, who had killed him on Arkansas soil. Among the accused were James Foreman, Bird Doublehead, two of the

Springstons, and James and Jefferson Hair. United States General
Arbuckle sent dragoons onto Cherokee soil to arrest these men;
the dragoons were accompanied by treaty men serving as guides.
Even so, none of the accused was found, except from time to time
the corpse of one of them, or another, would wash ashore or be
found on a trail.

John Ross, as chief of the western Cherokees, consistently
sought to satisfy his followers, to quell the outbreaks. His government at the meeting in July 1839 passed an act granting forgiveness to treaty men provided they appeared at the council grounds
to confess their sorrow for having signed the treaty of 1835 and
pledge themselves to live peaceably—and to consent to being inel-
igible to hold office for five years. Also, the convention ordered
that a full, free pardon be granted to

> all persons, citizens of the eastern and western Cherokee nation, who may
> be chargeable with the act of murder or homicide, committed on the person
> of any Cherokee previously to the passage of this decree, whether the same
> may have been committed within the limits of the eastern or western Cher-
> okee country or elsewhere.

James Foreman, the man once freed from prison by a "silver
key," who was an organizer of the murders, as he had been of
Walker's previously, was killed; Stand Watie killed him in a hand-
to-hand fight.

To the astonishment and dismay of the old settlers among the
Cherokees, law and order on all counts broke down; even theft
became commonplace, theft of slaves and everything else of value.
These Cherokee men and women from the East became devour-
ers of their own society.

One observer wrote, "Murders in the country have been so
frequent until the people care as little about hearing things as
they would hear of the death of a common dog."

The federal agents informally accused John Ross of complic-
ity in the murders; unable to prove it, they denounced him for
refusing as chief to assist in bringing the guilty to trial. He continued to refuse, and worked to protect them. The agents and

Washington officials called on him to resign as head of the Cherokee government, but he declined.

At the same time he was negotiating payment for costs of the removal. The contract that had been awarded to the Rosses by General Scott in 1838 called for payment of $65.88 each for twelve thousand Cherokees and blacks removed. An additional amount for soap brought the amount to $66.24. On November 3, 1838, Captain Page as disbursing agent had paid $776,393.98 to John Ross, based on the estimate that the time the travel would take was eighty days. The agreement was to provide extra money for extra time, the funds to come from the cash appropriation agreed to in the Treaty of 1835 for the Cherokee nation. Much extra time was consumed, both in starting the march and on the trail, and John Ross filed claims for a whopping additional $486,939.50. John Ross as chief and Lewis as treasurer of the Cherokee government pushed the claim. Even so, the claim was refused by Secretary of War Poinsett and President Van Buren. This left John and Lewis Ross with a desperate crisis, with many creditors. They became busily engaged in appeals, supplying lists of expenses and arguments.

In addition to his financial and personal vulnerability, John Ross was seeking to negotiate a treaty with the federal government guaranteeing permanent Cherokee ownership of its western lands and control of their affairs. He was also planning a school system, trying to buy a new printing press with type in English and Cherokee, negotiating with neighboring tribes, including disgruntled tribes being dispossessed and ancient enemies of the Cherokee, and securing his control of the Cherokee government in the face of old settlers and the Treaty Party opposition; thousands of reparations claims were being assembled and submitted to the federal government and negotiated, among them a claim of his own for an additional $164,250.62, which included $100,000 for false arrest by the Georgians on November 7, 1834. Further, the Cherokee government was negotiating through him the value of portions of its eastern lands, the value of the lost Council Houses and Courthouse, the ferries and turnpike roads, the printing office, the buildings erected for public worship, the eastern schoolhouses, the privately owned improvements of ferries, turnpikes, bridges and roads, claims for spoliation and for lost horses, cattle, hogs, claims for the confiscated rifles, which now the government appeared to be unable to return to the owners as promised.

On all these fronts John Ross fought ferociously on behalf of the Cherokee nation and himself and his brother, the interests of the three sometimes intermingled.

Meanwhile, he was looked to for advice by his nieces and nephews, sons and daughters, several of them in northern schools and colleges. His life was in danger; he was conscious of many warning signs. The troubled national treasurer, his business partner and brother, wrote to him: "You ought to be very much on your guard this winter and keep a good look out and not go out without some of your friends. With you a word is enough." He was lonely, needed affection and a companion, and sought the hand of an attractive social leader, a Quaker living in Baltimore, posting to her a letter he had labored over perhaps too long:

> Having thus set forth, the path of duty blazed out before me in relation to my people; I would beg leave, My Dear E. to tell you in all candour and sincerity, that, it is my deliberate conviction, if I could in any way contribute toward rendering you once more cheerful and happy, that, I should myself, indeed be very, very happy. Therefore, I pray you not to be surprised nor, to consider me presumptuous for thus venturing to communicate to you, feelings, which, in justice to myself, I can no longer repress. To say, that my long cherished friendship for you, has so ardently seized the affections of my heart, as to make my silent thoughts doat upon you as a lover, would be nothing more than an avowal of the solemn truth. May I not then hope to be pardoned through your kind indulgence, for concluding with a petition craving your reply on the subject of my desire for negotiating a treaty with you for the purpose of uniting our hearts in the bonds of Matrimony?

In September 1841, United States President John Tyler, needing to settle the Cherokee matter, consented to pay to John Ross his and Lewis' claim and to negotiate a generous treaty on the remaining matters as well. His death in office tripped up the treaty plans but not the payment. He had John Ross's assurance that any dollars left over after full settlement of Lewis' debt would be paid into the Cherokee treasury.

None was left.

John Ross died in Washington, D.C., the year after the close of the American Civil War. His great home, Ross Hill, had been burned during the war by his enemy, Stand Watie, and his Confederate troops. Ross's slaves were freed, and most of his other wealth was lost. At age seventy-five, on April 3, 1866, he was close to death. When visited by a federal commissioner, Ross was quoted as saying:

> I am an old man, and have served my people and the Govt of the United States a long time, over fifty years. My people have kept me in the harness, not of my seeking, but of their own choice. I have never deceived them, and now I look back, not one act of my public life rises up to upbraid me. I have done the best I could, and today, upon this bed of sickness, my heart approves all I have done. And still I am, John Ross, the same John Ross of former years, unchanged.

No one on that occasion asked specifically about several acts with which his enemies used to upbraid him. Did he, for instance, feel comfortable about having abolished elections at a time that the Cherokees needed national debate? Would he again seek to silence discussion in the Cherokee newspaper? Was it wise to allow the Cherokees to delay, and further delay, making preparations for the move west? Was it wise to assign the removal contract to his brother and business partner? Was it wise to schedule a land route, rather than a water route? Was there more profit in a land route? Was it necessary to disrupt the system of western Cherokee government in order to gain less than a year's advantage? Was being chief for that year of consequence in terms of his and Lewis' bill for almost half a million dollars in additional costs? How much did he personally profit from the contract? Did he have an inkling of the assassinations of Major Ridge, John Ridge, and Elias Boudinot? Did he regret protecting their assassins?

Nobody that day reported asking him anything specific about his tenure, his forty-year hold as the powerful principal chief. Such questions would not have fazed him. He would deny connivance. He was the survivor, living above details, above blame; his followers asked only that he respect them as they were and lead them. Missionaries and government officers and even his enemies acknowledged the remarkable hold he had over his followers. He held them—at least most of them—together as a people. He kept them from responding violently to unfair treatment. He has been called the Moses and the George Washington of the traditionalist Cherokees.

As for Major Ridge, what can be said for him? A youthful hunter, a ball player, a warrior, an obeyer of shamans, a scavenger; later he became a statesman. For vision, for courage, for integrity in personal and public life, he was a human achievement, an honor to any people.

As for Worcester, he continued the work of translating and printing hymns, portions of the Bible, and commentary, first in Cherokee and eventually in Choctaw and Creek. In one year alone, he printed a total of 37,200 copies of books and pamphlets, a total of 1,065,400 pages. He often mentioned Boudinot—a perfect man, he decided—who had made only one mistake in his life, and that was signing the Treaty of New Echota.

If he were to seek a second failure of Boudinot, he might settle on one that would apply as well to John Ridge and the Major; he might have hit upon their underestimating the power of the uneducated Indians, believing their own exaggerated statements about the Cherokees' progress. They trusted a people who did not yet exist. At the time of the Treaty of New Echota, 80 percent of the Cherokees were unable to read or write either Cherokee or English. Most Cherokees were subsisting on small farms, clinging to their ancient doctrines and to the memories of old ways. It was true that signs of change and progress existed; but in the main they were present only among the half-breeds, the slaveowners, not for the general population.

In the battle for the minds and souls of the Cherokees, the missionaries had not won by 1839. The shamans were much too strong. The people as a whole remained wedded to Cherokee lore as passed down orally, garbled in the process. This can be judged most simply in the medicine of the tribe, and of the other four tribes moving west at this same time. Lieutenant Joseph W. Harris reported on his group of Seminoles, sent by boat from Florida, 25 of 407 dying; he said the mortality

> resulted from the perversity of the Indians in adhering to their own peculiar treatment of the sick; which being confined to frequent deluging the patient with cold water, & to a constant kneading of the body, terminated— inasmuch as the diseases consisted of coughs, slight dysentaries, &c—almost invariably in death. And this could not be obviated, although after having exhausted advice, entreaty and expostulation, we resorted to watching, threats and force.

Few died of causes other than disease. The Trail of Tears— or, as Indians more often said, the Trail where they Wept—was a trail of sickness, with Indian sorcerers as doctors. Yes, and African voodoo doctors, too. The blacks' guts, too, were extended and raw, their hearts broken. One must pity them. They and the Cherokees, the Choctaws and Creeks, the government officers and missionaries, all walking into history, which is owned by us all.

EPILOGUE

That portion of the tribe which had stayed in the East remained unaffected by the Western Cherokees. Before the "roundup and removal," about four hundred Cherokee Indians had lived in North Carolina outside the Cherokee boundary, on land of their own, in accordance with the federal treaty of 1819, quite apart from the Cherokee holdings. Living near Quallatown, this Qualla band, as they were called, was not expected by either the national or the state government to go west; they were exempt. There was also a group of fewer than one hundred Cherokees who were given federal permission to remain with them, to join them, as reward for helping troops in the difficult mountain roundup. These were followers of Chief Euchella. In addition there were Cherokees who hid and were not found, and these completed the eastern band in the Great Smoky Mountains, about fourteen hundred in all. These members owned mountain land of their own, and proceeded to buy more. Almost all of them were full-bloods who hunted and farmed small plots. They did not have slaves. In religion they followed Cherokee tradition or were sometimes Methodist—or had selected parts of both. Few spoke English, and few indeed wrote or read it. Their contact with the western Cherokees was spare. They had no official relationship with them and disliked the political leaders, including John Ross, who, they claimed, had become a Jackson man, selling out to the government; they also contended that his hands were recently stained with the blood of his opponents.

As might be expected of a people threatened by extinction, these Qualla Cherokees had an increase in birth rate in the years following the removal. During that period 166 babies were born, while only 53 deaths were recorded, resulting in a total population of 732 people in the Qualla band.

There were at the time Cherokees hiding out also in Tennessee, Alabama, and Georgia. They had no tribal relationship; most were harbored by whites and often were used for farm labor. In an 1851 count, 87 were found in southeastern Tennessee, 50 in Alabama, 321 in Georgia, and 2 Eastern Cherokees were living in Washington, D.C.

The government of North Carolina petitioned the United States to pay its remaining Cherokee Indians the $53.33 earlier appropriated to move each Cherokee west, and after persistent effort this was achieved in 1848, including interest at 6 percent from May 23, 1836. Behind this effort was William H. Thomas, who had been adopted while a boy by Cherokee Chief Yonaguska; he led the effort to acquire the funds, and he used the total amount to purchase mountain land for the Indians' use. In order to protect it, he entered the deed in his own name. Later he transferred title to a corporation set up to hold it in trust, and these maneuvers suffered legal complexities that became severe once Mr. Thomas' senility set in. Apparently he suffered from what years later would be named Alzheimer's disease, or a related ailment. Three times committed to the state hospital for the mentally ill, his personal estate dwindled toward bankruptcy, and the "Cherokee" holdings became involved. After many years the land became the Cherokee Reservation in North Carolina, home of the Eastern Cherokees.

The Arkansas land itself was welcoming, rich and productive. Here were expanses of grass, in places twelve miles wide, the grass three feet high. A ton of grass could be stacked for the cost of only a dollar. Cherokees turned to raising horses and cattle. Between 1840 and 1860, the wealth of the Cherokees burgeoned: the twenty thousand citizens owned 300,000 head of cattle, horses and mules. And they owned four thousand black slaves.

During the first year of the Civil War, 1861, three thousand Cherokee men enlisted in the Confederate Army and fought in the battles of Pea Ridge and Cole's hill. On their return home, these veterans routed out of their homes the Union sympathizers; thousands of them—women, children, old men—fled. An observer reported:

One morning I was at Emporia, Kansas, and saw slopes down the river and the whole slopes were alive with Indians. There were some on ponies and children in blankets, looking like mummies, and there they were, this great multitude of people getting into the timber and getting into the shelter of the timber on the banks of the river. It was an awful sight. We went out to look at them, and they had had two weeks of traveling across that country, 200 miles, and the wolves followed them. Children had died or were frozen to death, some of them frozen almost in their mothers' arms, and as these children died they threw them to the wolves to keep the wolves back.

Thousands fled the raiders. John Ross, who had begrudgingly called for support of the Confederacy, left the territory, traveled to Washington to seek President Lincoln's help—and he stayed there. The raiding parties slaughtered stock, burned barns and houses, looted and destroyed even the capitol, leaving in place only the portrait of Sequoyah behind the speaker's desk. They scattered the volumes of the six-thousand-book library recently assembled.

The blacks left the hovels they had been assigned and fled to the Ozark Mountains, settled off to themselves. Seventy-five miles from the nearest roads and settlements, they found ways to subsist. They remained there until President Lincoln's Emancipation Proclamation. How they knew of it wasn't clear to Indians or whites, but on the day it took effect, they moved out of the Ozarks.

. . . the whole roadways were crowded with black men, women and children, the women with their great bandanas round their necks, all walking. They had sacks over the shoulders containing all their belongings.

The black men volunteered for Union service; two regiments were immediately conscripted.

Once the war ended, all the Cherokees returned, and all the blacks. The devastated country began its life-giving cycles. The blacks this time had their own district of the Cherokee Territory. Hatreds among the Indians one for another continued to be fierce for years, but the fruits of labor were generous, the farms were prosperous.

The American Civil War also involved most of the eastern

Cherokees. Even though they were isolated deep in the mountains and had less interest in slavery or states' rights or tariffs, more than two hundred of their men fought for the Confederacy. The war did impoverish them, along with their white neighbors, reducing the women and children to near starvation.

A traveler through the North Carolina Cherokee country a generation later, in 1893, described the Indians' situation as one of abject poverty, though he found it compared favorably with that of their white neighbors.

Stand Watie chose the Confederacy in the war, as did most Cherokees and as did most members of neighboring Indian tribes. Watie became a general. His men burned John Ross's excellent house, and he lost his own sons—two factors to consider in his lonely old age.

Of course, defeat of the Confederacy ended the plantation system based on slavery and established greater power for the federal government over the states. It also induced the federal government in a fit of temper to abrogate all treaties with the five tribes, confiscating most of their land and forcing them into new treaties. The five tribes were restricted to 20 million acres in eastern Oklahoma.

There are various estimates and several arguments about the social, cultural, and physical damage caused by the 1838 removal. The main portions of all five tribes were uprooted and the people became socially disoriented, their town and clan organizations disrupted. Families dwindled and were divided; many people died. It was sometimes true that those too feeble to travel were left with a kinswoman in the Qualla Cherokee band in North Carolina, but only a few of these handicapped, aged individuals were protected that way. Most elders had been sent along and, weakened by the traveling, assaulted by a different diet of meal and pork, had fallen into illnesses unknown by name to doctors of the time. Traveling five to ten miles daily was not of itself deadly, but the diet, the filth of the camps, the flies feeding at the slit trenches and visiting the food and hands of the people proved to be. Then, too, there was the mosquito, carrying malaria, which struck in summer seasons. And there was smallpox, which struck the Choctaws and became an epidemic among them. There was gonorrhea, a complication for many. And finally, there was the old reaper, who could be relied on to make everyday, standard visits, selecting travelers for that other western journey.

Many of the deaths were of infants whose nursing mothers were ill with intestinal diseases. The sick infants bawled until too weak to cry. One mother carried the corpse of her infant for two days, keeping it company.

How many Cherokees and their slaves died? The answer is a mystery, enhanced, complicated by decades. In the detention camps, from three hundred to two thousand died, depending on the authority accepted; on the trail, from five hundred to two thousand. In other words, the answer is a combined total of between eight hundred and four thousand.

The higher figure was suggested by kindly Doctor Butler of Connecticut, the same medical missionary who had suffered with Reverend Worcester in the Georgia prison. Dr. Butler had recently fallen out with Worcester; almost all the missionaries except Butler and Reverend Butrick favored the western move, and Butler considered this to be traitorous of them. Butler was one who had mailed denunciations of the Treaty of New Echota and of John and Elias and the rest to the antiremoval writers in the East. Recently he had worked as a doctor in the camps, where in spite of his efforts dysentery took many lives; the suffering added to his dismay. Dysentery killed his own little daughter, aged seven months. As for the march, he had accepted Ross's appointment to be the doctor for one of the thirteen groups, and on that march he fought the battles against illness and shamans and African sorcerers, losing forty patients in all. At the end of the journey, instead of multiplying forty by thirteen, to get 520, he stated categorically that two thousand had died, and so he reported publicly. Two thousand plus two thousand in the camps, he said—the judgment. Let the missionaries and the government and the pro-Treaty Cherokees explain why they committed this awful act.

The official figures for the trail, those of government and Cherokee officers including Lewis and John Ross, became available soon thereafter. For the Rosses' thirteen groups of the sixteen:

	Leaving Page's Count	Arrival Stephenson's Count	Ross's Count	Births	Deaths	Desertions
1.	710	654	729	9	54	24
2.	859	744	858	5	34	0
3.	846	898	950	6	38	148
4.	1,079	1,132	1,200	3	33	0
5.	1,205	1,033	1,250	5	71	0
6.	841	921	983	17	57	10
7.	1,031	924	1,035	6	48	0
8.	1,120	970	1,150	0	0	0
9.	745	717	850	3	34	0
10.	1,031	1,039	1,118	0	0	0
11.	897	942	1,029	15	55	0
12.	1,449	1,311	1,766	0	0	0
13.	—	219	231	—	—	—
	11,813	11,204	13,149	66	424	
	+ 213					
	12,026					

SOURCE: *Journal of Cherokee Studies,* III, 3, pp. 187–88.

Dr. Butler's figure of 2,000 contrasts with the government figure of 424.

Dr. Butler's figures became commonly known in New England. They carried great impact, aided the broadside criticism of the removal.

They were given as fact in a few books during the nineteenth century, though historians also used the official figures; however, James Mooney, in 1900, counting deaths in camps, on the march, and after the march of those debilitated by the journey, stated in *Myths of the Cherokees* that "it is asserted, probably with reason, that over 4,000 Cherokee died as the direct result of the removal." Mr. Mooney might very well have got that opinion from William Thomas, the Quallas' benefactor. In 1932 historian Grant Foreman, in his study of the removal of the five southeastern tribes, set down a footnote at the close of his Cherokee chapters: "All told, about 4,000 died during the course of capture and detention in temporary stockades, and the removal itself. See also Emmet Starr, *History of the Cherokee Indians,* 103." The footnote suggests to

some readers that Cherokee historian Emmet Starr provided supporting evidence; but in fact Starr's *History of The Cherokee Indians*
uses only the lower figures. On page 103, the one cited in the
footnote, Starr lists only the official numbers.

Whether one accepts the Butler figures or the government
figures, deaths were numerous, suffering was intense, and of
equal importance the government of the Cherokees, once promising, was destroyed. These losses place in context an extraordinary
message to both houses of Congress by President Van Buren:

> It affords me sincere pleasure to be able to apprise you of the entire removal
> of the Cherokee Nation of Indians to their new homes west of the Missis-
> sippi. The measures authorized by Congress with a view to the long-stand-
> ing controversy with them have had the happiest effect, and they have emi-
> grated without any apparent resistance.

Other aspects of the story have developed variations over the
years. One of them has to do with Tsali, or Charlie. There are
official documents, mentioned earlier relating the murder of two
soldiers and the wounding of a third by the family of this Cherokee. In 1848, Mr. Thomas related an account to a reporter that
gave Tsali justification for the assaults. Some years later still, the
same Mr. Thomas told Smithsonian Institute officer James
Mooney a more elaborate version, one which launched a hero for
the Eastern Cherokees.

> One old man named Tsali, "Charley," was seized with his wife, his brother,
> his three sons and their families. Exasperated at the brutality accorded his
> wife, who, being unable to travel fast, was prodded with bayonets to hasten
> her steps, he urged the other men to join with him in a dash for liberty. As
> he spoke in Cherokee the soldiers, although they heard, understood nothing
> until each warrior suddenly sprang upon the one nearest and endeavored to
> wrench his gun from him. The attack was so sudden and unexpected that
> one soldier was killed and the rest fled, while the Indians escaped to the
> mountains. Hundreds of others, some of them from the various stockades,
> managed also to escape to the mountains from time to time, where those
> who did not die of starvation subsisted on roots and wild berries until the
> hunt was over. Finding it impracticable to secure these fugitives, General
> Scott finally tendered them a proposition, through [Colonel] W. H. Thomas,
> their most trusted friend, that if they would surrender Charley and his
> party for punishment, the rest would be allowed to remain until their case

could be adjusted by the government. On hearing of the proposition, Charley voluntarily came in with his sons, offering himself as a sacrifice for his people. By command of General Scott, Charley, his brother, and the two elder sons were shot near the mouth of Tuckasegee, a detachment of Cherokee prisoners being compelled to do the shooting in order to impress upon the Indians the fact of their utter helplessness.

A romantic concept of Indians evolved in the years following their removal from the Southeast. The Cherokees were generally pictured as living peacefully in their mountain home—though fewer than one in five lived in mountain areas; their possession of black slaves was omitted from such portrayals, their shamans were exonerated; their propensity for warfare was replaced with peaceful coexistence with Creeks, Choctaws, Chickasaws, and the rest. As individuals they were pictured as being free to work out individual relationships with nature. During this period, to be a white man and to have taken part in the Indian wars became reprehensible, and apologies and excuses made by the veterans of Indian wars added to the embellishments. For instance, a letter often quoted as accurately describing the events of Cherokee removal in 1838 and 1839 was written in 1890, fifty years later, by a veteran of the United States Cavalry, John G. Burnett, who on his eightieth birthday sought to assure his grandchildren of his own purity of past actions:

> The removal of the Cherokee Indians from their life long homes in the year 1838 found me a young man in the prime of life and a private soldier in the American Army. Being acquainted with many of the Indians and able to fluently speak their language, I was sent as interpreter into the Smokey Mountain Country in May, 1838, and witnessed the execution of the most brutal order in the History of American Warfare. I saw the helpless Cherokees arrested and dragged from their homes, and driven at the bayonet point into the stockades. And in the chill of a drizzling rain on an October morning I saw them loaded like cattle or sheep into six hundred and forty-five wagons and started toward the west.
>
> One can never forget the sadness and solemnity of that morning. Chief John Ross led in prayer and when the bugle sounded and the wagons started rolling many of the children rose to their feet and waved their little hands good-by to their mountain homes, knowing they were leaving them forever. Many of these helpless people did not have blankets and many of them had been driven from home barefooted . . .

The long painful journey to the west ended March 26th, 1839, with four-thousand silent graves reaching from the foothills of the Smoky Mountains to what is known as Indian territory in the West. And covetousness on the part of the white race was the cause of all that the Cherokees had to suffer. . . .

The doom of the Cherokee was sealed, Washington, D.C. had decreed that they must be driven West, and their lands given to the white man, and in May 1838 an Army of four thousand regulars, and three thousand volunteer soldiers under command of General Winfield Scott, marched into the Indian country and wrote the blackest chapter on the pages of American History . . .

Murder is murder and somebody must answer, somebody must explain the streams of blood that flowed in the Indian country in the summer of 1838. Somebody must explain the four-thousand silent graves that mark the trail of the Cherokees to their exile. I wish I could forget it all, but the picture of six-hundred and forty-five wagons lumbering over the frozen ground with their Cargo of suffering humanity still lingers in my memory.

Let the Historian of a future day tell the sad story with its sighs, its tears and dying groans. Let the great Judge of all the earth weigh our actions and reward us according to our work.

Children—Thus ends my promised birthday story.

This December the 11th 1890.

The exaggerations and factual errors of Burnett and others are regrettable. They are damaging mainly to the reputation of the federal government. That mighty institution is vulnerable in this case, certainly. The government was wrestling in the first half of the nineteenth century with two grave problems, slavery and Indian rights; the first was solved by the bloodiest war ever fought on the continent, and the second by a method of feints and dives and promises and evasions. The government's inconsistencies bother public conscience. Even so, this method was less costly in human terms than an outright war, the alternative Indians would have found more understandable and which would have been consistent with their own history; to them land belonged to the people who possessed it, who won it by force of arms. Jackson's position was extreme, but his successor continued it; and his opposition party, the Whigs, elected four years after he left office, made no changes in it.

One looks back nostalgically to the earlier days when Washington and Jefferson believed a cultural adaptation was possible.

Even then, however, the policy makers did not rest easy. Thomas Jefferson wrote to Governor William H. Harrison in 1803, "Should any tribe be foolhardy enough to take up the hatchet at any time, the seizing the whole country of that tribe, and driving them across the Mississippi, as the only condition of peace, would be an example to others, and a furtherance of our final consolidation."

A practical alternative to Indian removal never came before the government. The alternative of leaving the body of the continent in Indian hands was unacceptable. It was also unacceptable to leave it in French or British hands. One possible solution in the Cherokee case, which received little attention, was made by the federal agent, Return J. Meigs:

> The point had been reached where the Cherokee people should begin to fight their own battles of life, and that any further contributions to their support, either in the shape of provisions or tools, would have only a tendency to render them more dependent upon the Government and less competent to take care of themselves. Those who were already advanced in the arts of civilized life should be the tutors of the more ignorant. They possessed a territory of perhaps 10,000,000 acres of land, principally in the States of Georgia, North Carolina, and Tennessee, for the occupation of which they could enumerate a little more than 10,000 souls or 2,000 families. If they were to become an agricultural and pastoral people, an assignment of 640 acres of land to each family would be all and more than they could occupy with advantage to themselves. Such an allotment would consume but 1,280,000 acres, leaving more than 8,000,000 acres of surplus land which might and ought to be sold for their benefit, and the proceeds applied to their needs in the erection of houses, fences, and the clearing and breaking up of their land for cultivation. The authority and laws of the several States within whose limits they resided should become operative upon them, and they should be vested with the rights, privileges, and immunities of citizens of those States.

A word of praise might be bestowed on Old England, in that they were often protective of Indian rights. Prior to the American Revolution, the English King had placed Indian lands off limits to further settlement. Understandably, predictably, land speculators were furious over this policy. One might go so far as to wonder if "Give me liberty or give me death, but in any case give me Kentucky," was the battle cry in some circles.

Compared with France and Spain, England since Queen Elizabeth had been protective of Indian rights. Consider Spain. When the Spanish conquered Mexico, there were twenty million Indians living there; in the remainder of North America, including Canada, there were two million. Spain's policies of brutal slavery and outright extermination, combined with diseases, reduced the twenty million to fewer than two million population.

Sequoyah, feeble, arthritic, in 1842 found himself buying supplies from Lewis Ross in order to travel to a portion of Mexico, now part of Texas, to look for a remnant of the Cherokee tribe that was known to live there and which he hoped might be persuaded to return to the main body. With him were his son and a few friends, all searchers, all Cherokees. They crossed the Arkansas River below Fort Gibson, passed Edwards' settlement on the Little River, and took the Leavenworth's road to Red River, arriving there fifteen days after starting.

He needed to rest for a few days. He was hungry only for bread and honey, he told his friends, and time to write. His energy was slack. One of the men found ripe, wild plums, and he ate some of them. He mentioned a pain in his chest. What in the world was he doing here? he wondered aloud. Old age gives a man dreams of conquest, but sometimes the reasoning is obscure. For him life was becoming more dream than anything else. Here he was on a journey, unsure of the details of time or place, a seeker of his people. Always the muser, the dreamer, the mender, the teacher.

After the second day of rest, the party moved on. He endured two more weeks of pain and travel. A group of Shawnee, particularly respectful of Sequoyah, the famous chief, gave him camp for a night. He inquired of them directions to Mexico. Six days more he traveled, arriving at a great watercourse. He and his men crossed a mountain, came to a branch, reached a bold spring where Sequoyah bathed. Bees were here in considerable number, and he asked that the group camp long enough to find honey.

Here the horses were stolen by a group of Tewockenees Indians. He and his men discussed returning home, but he decided to go on. They built a raft and crossed the river. Comanches came near. Because they wore caps, the Comanches thought them to be Texans and were about to kill them when they noticed the few feathers in their caps. The Comanches gave them food and listened to their explanation of needing to find the southern remnant of their people, to mend the broken pieces.

Sequoyah was too weary to go farther just now. He asked to be left alone in a cave and instructed the others to find help. They left him in this safe place, or so they believed; but the water from a river rose into the cave and he had to escape. Even though most of his provisions were lost in the water, he started toward the south, dragging his lame foot, now and again marking his trail for his companions, should they try to find him. How near death one comes in life, in old age; he reflected on that.

The others found him days later, alone. He had with him a few pages of his writings. He had honey that he had taken from a bee tree, and a bit of tobacco. He was weak. Indeed, he was close to death. Four or five days of rest did not revive him; he could scarcely move. He sent his companions on to find the Cherokees and give them the message of Sequoyah. Tell them about the great nation of Cherokee emerging to the North, where they would be welcome, where every one was needed.

That night, alone, Sequoyah doused a bite of bread in honey and ate his supper. He read over his few pages of writings: words, words, was there no end to them? He lit his pipe. Death was quietly arriving. He knew that well enough. He noticed the stars are bright tonight.

NOTES

Page

1 Investigations were made: James Adair was one who wrote extensively, seeking to prove the Jewish-Indian relationship. An Irishman, he was in South Carolina by 1735, later serving as an Indian agent under George III. Adair was a trader to the Chickasaws and lived among them and the Cherokees. In 1775 his book, *The History of the American Indians*, was published in London. He left descendants among the Cherokees and Chickasaws.

1 "The Cherokees in their disposition": The characteristics of the Cherokees are described by Adair and also by William Bartram, the English naturalist, who toured the Southeast recording his observations in *Travels Through North & South Carolina, Georgia, East & West Florida, the Cherokee Country*, printed first in Philadelphia by James & Johnson in 1791, p. 483. Bartram elsewhere noted that the Cherokee women laughed at the suspender-secured trousers of the Germans, referring to their condition as "tied-assed."

2 "There are several": Louis-Philippe's visit is described in detail in Sturtevant, "Louis-Philippe."

4 The shaman told: Shamans were the doctors, priests, witch doctors, sorcerers, medicine men. They were paid by the patients' contributions. Extensive information about them and their practices is found in the works of ethnologist James Mooney, who writes as follows:

> One of the most prevalent errors in regard to the Indian is that he knows every plant of the field and forest, and that the medicine man outranks the white physician in his knowledge of the healing art. A moment's reflection must convince any intelligent person that the skill of the Indian doctor, whose knowledge is confined to the narrow limits of a single tribe, and who at best can consult with only half a dozen brother shamans, is not to be compared with that of the educated physician who has devoted years of study under trained specialists, who has the whole world for a pharmacopoeia, together with the mechanical aids invented by modern science, and whose libraries contain the combined experiences of the nations in a thousand years of medical progress. As a matter of fact, the medicine man's knowledge of herbal remedies is about on a level with that of the ordinary farmer's wife, while the best of them are far inferior to her in regard to nursing and the commonsense care of the sick.
>
> (Mooney, "Cherokee Theory," pp. 25–29)

5 he can leave his body: See Witthoft, "Cherokee Beliefs," p. 71.

7 Late autumn, winter: The Creeks were the most powerful enemy and had been known to defeat the mighty Cherokees. On a recent occasion,

in contempt they sent several of their women and small boys against the Cherokee warriors. "They (the Creeks) are so extremely anxious to be distinguished by high war-titles, that sometimes a small party of warriers, on failing of successes in their campaign, have been detected murdering some of their own people, for the sake of their scalps" (Adair, *History*, pp. 275–276). Torture of prisoners was practiced by Indian tribes. Only members of the clans, or families, were considered by Cherokees to be human. Others were enslaved or burned alive or adopted (Gilcrease Institute, John Ross Papers, vol. 1, 120; Perdue, *Slavery*, p. 5). The Cherokees were excellent warriors. Adair predicted that their fondness for war could only result in their complete annihilation (*History*, p. 227).

10   He also had the company: Little people and the Nunnehi are discussed in Fogelson, "Cherokee Little People."

13   Ridge's mother and father: The place Ridge's family settled was the Sequatchie Valley, an excellent hunting ground. To get there, the family poled down the Hiwassee to the Tennessee River, and at a point near present-day Chattanooga, they turned north, perhaps up Sequatchie Creek, poling the heavy canoe to Sequatchie Mountain (Wilkins, *Cherokee Tragedy*, p. 9).

14   This was a place: The Cherokee bow was made of black or honey locust, was slightly longer than three feet, was flat and broad and tapered toward both ends. The string was likely to be bear gut. The arrows were mountain cane, twenty-eight to thirty-four inches in length, with two feathers attached by deer sinew. See King, "Cherokee Bows."

14   "war is their principal": William Fyffe to Brother John, February 1, 1761 (Woodward, *Cherokees*, p. 33).

14   Attacullaculla came by: Attacullaculla was one of the peacemakers of the Cherokees. As a teenager he had been taken to London by an explorer, Christian Priber. A biography of Attacullaculla is provided in Kelly, "Notable Persons." Biographical information on Priber may be found in Farley, "Christian Priber."

16   "Chiefs and Warriors": Sevier's letter is reprinted in King, "Long Island," p. 123.

18   "It is a little surprising": Chief Old Tassel's letter is from a paper by Samuel Cole Williams entitled "William Tatham, Wataugan," pp. 176–178.

19   Of an evening: For a description of Cherokee dances see Evans, "Sketches of Cherokee Characteristics," pp. 16–20.

20   They went on to: Chestowee, at the mouth of Chestua Creek in present Polk County, Tennessee, has been excavated (Wilkins, *Cherokee Tragedy*, p. 13).

20   Often he was left: The material on the training of the hunter is taken from Ethridge, "Tobacco," pp. 80–81, and also Campbell and Campbell, "Wolf Clan," pp. 86–87.

22   At puberty: Theda Perdue says that warriors might attach bear paws to

their feet, or buffalo hooves, and that they walked single file, leaving one set of footprints (Perdue, *Slavery*, p. 31).

23   Even though there were three: Much is written about the ball game, a forerunner of lacrosse; see Mooney, "Cherokee Ball Play."

24   Both sexes took part: Mooney, "Cherokee Ball Play," pp. 14–15.

27   O Long Man: Mooney, "Cherokee Ball Play," pp. 20–21.

27   The ball ground: Mooney, "Cherokee Ball Play," p. 22.

30   An old Indian orchard: The orchard was at Settico on the Little Tennessee River at the mouth of Citico Creek in present Monroe County, Tennessee (Wilkins, *Cherokee Tragedy*, p. 15).

37   At this time: Material for Joseph Brown's story is from Brown, "Captivity Narrative" and King, "Lessons in Cherokee Ethnology."

40   Doublehead took: For more information about Benge and Doublehead see Evans, "Notable Persons."

42   "Proclamation By the President": The original newspapers are in the archives of the Museum of the Cherokee Indian.

42   Washington requested: Coyatee was located in present Ludon County, Tennessee.

45   They confronted Sevier: Etowah, or Hightower, is near present Rome, Georgia (Wilkins, *Cherokee Tragedy*, p. 24).

47   "*Knoxville*, Nov. 29": The newspaper article and Crutcher letter are reprinted in the *Journal of Cherokee Studies* 4.2 (1979): 60–61.

49   James Vann and Charles Hicks: For more information about James Vann and Doublehead, see Wilkins, *Cherokee Tragedy*. pp. 34–49.

52   Ridge, when only twenty-five: Pine Log, between the Oostanaula and the Etowah rivers in northern Georgia, was an old town, associated with a detached southern remnant of the Delawares. It took its name from Pine Log Mountain. "It numbered about twenty houses, scattered for a mile along a creek of the same name" (Wilkins, *Cherokee Tragedy*, p. 16).

55   "knowledge of cultivation": McLoughlin, *Cherokees and Missionaries*, p. 33.

58   The Moravians were makers: The Steiner and de Schweinitz report is found in McLoughlin, *Cherokees and Missionaries*, p. 38 and also in the Moravian Archives, Bethlehem, Pennsylvania. The original report is dated October 28–December 28, 1799.

65   "We now consider": quoted in McLoughlin, *Cherokees and Missionaries*, p. 50.

65   "fain see us gone": quoted in McLoughlin, *Cherokees and Missionaries*, p. 50.

66   "pounded and baked": quoted in McLoughlin, *Cherokees and Missionaries*, p. 50.

69   "We set out": Letter of James Sevier to Lyman Draper, August 19, 1839,

Page

Wisconsin Historical Society, Draper Papers, MS 39S, no. 18 and also in Evans, "Was the Last Battle," p. 32.

70   "Marched first through": Wisconsin Historical Society, Draper Papers, MS 32S.

71   In one of the later campaigns: The Bullard story is in Christian, "Battle of Lookout Mountain."

73   Judge Richard Henderson: Thomas Perkins Abernethy in his book *From Frontier to Plantation in Tennessee* contends that land speculation was the most absorbing enterprise in America. There was no stock market, and there were few publicly held large corporations, few opportunities in most places for starting one's own company. "The insatiable desire for territory manifested by young and land-poor America cannot be fully comprehended unless it is understood that, in those days, the country was run largely by speculators" (p. 19).

79   "This is to inform you": National Archives, Record Group 107; Wilkins, *Cherokee Tragedy*, pp. 41–42.

80   On this trip: Suggestion of Secretary of War Henry Dearborn: Wilkins, *Cherokee Tragedy*, p. 43.

80   "Tell our Great Father": McKenney and Hall, Indian Tribes, vol. 1, p. 383; Wilkins, *Cherokee Tragedy*, p. 43.

81   "My friends, you have heard": McKenney and Hall, Indian Tribes, vol. 1, p. 384; Wilkins, *Cherokee Tragedy*, p. 43.

83   "Father—the underwritten": National Archives, Record Group 75; also Wilkins, *Cherokee Tragedy*, p. 46.

85   "You inform me": Wilkins, *Cherokee Tragedy*. p. 47.

90   "They seemed pleased": Wilkins, *Cherokee Tragedy*, p. 104.

90   "Judge of my surprise": Schwarze, *History*, p. 114; Wilkins, *Cherokee Tragedy*, p. 104.

95   "Some of the females": McLoughlin, *Cherokees and Missionaries*, pp. 92–93.

97   "Don't be afraid": McLoughlin, *Cherokees and Missionaries*, p. 86. McLoughlin points out that reference to the "Great Spirit" in the drummer's declaration was "Gott" in the Moravian transcript.

97   "would return to you": McLoughlin, *Cherokees and Missionaries*, p. 87.

98   "yourselves can see": McLoughlin, *Cherokees and Missionaries*, pp. 87, 88, 89.

98   "If there is someone": McLoughlin, *Cherokees and Missionaries*, p. 90.

99   "My friends": Wilkins, *Cherokee Tragedy*, p. 59.

102 The second sign was: The quake was centered on the present Tennessee–Kentucky border north of Memphis.

112 "This is a phew wordes": Wilkins, *Cherokee Tragedy*, p. 71.

121 "The next day": Wilkins, *Cherokee Tragedy*, p. 83.

121 "These depredations may": Gilcrease Institute, Jackson Papers, roll 10; also Wilkins, *Cherokee Tragedy*, p. 83.

Page

125   The American Board's mission: The site of Brainerd Mission is now a shopping center in a Chattanooga, Tennessee, suburb.

128   "Oh, you don't": Newberry Library, Payne Papers, II. 2–3; Wilkins, *Cherokee Tragedy*, p. 88.

128   "Father, you have": *Religious Intelligencer* (February 1820): 617–618; also Wilkins, *Cherokee Tragedy*, p. 90.

128   "Father: I now have": The conversation with President Madison of February 22, 1816 may be found in Gilcrease Institute, Ross Papers, 16 and also Wilkins, *Cherokee Tragedy*, p. 90.

130   which the new federal Indian supervisor: For biographical material about McKenney, see Horan, *McKenney-Hall;* also Kvasnicka and Viola, eds., *Commissioners.*

131   "a rifle gun": The terms of Jackson's offer are contained in a letter from him to Coffee, July 13, 1817, Jackson, *Correspondence*, vol. 2, p. 307.

132   "forever do away": Resolution of the Cherokee Committee, September 3, 1817: Newberry Library, Payne Papers, VII. 1. 34; also Wilkins, *Cherokee Tragedy*, p. 96.

132   policy of exchanging land: See Royce, *Cherokee Nation*, p. 89.

135   "As we often write": These documents are published in Perdue, "Letters from Brainerd."

136   "Our Society continues": Nancy Reece to Rev. David Green, Newberry Library, Payne Papers.

139   "Stamping with one": Evans, "Sketches," p. 17.

140   "I will now bring": Evans, "Sketches," pp. 19–20.

141   The students complained: Cherokee cooking is discussed in *Cherokee Cooklore*, edited by Mary Ulmer and Samuel E. Beck, published by Mary and Goingback Chiltosky in cooperation with The Stephens Press, Inc., Asheville, N.C. 1951. Featured in it is Aggie Lossiah, granddaughter of Chief John Ross.

143   "I had travelled": Walker, *Torchlights*, p. 66; Wilkins, *Cherokee Tragedy*, pp. 112–113.

144   "with great animation": Wilkins, *Cherokee Tragedy*, p. 113.

144   "I am going to address": Walker, *Torchlights*, p. 67–68; Wilkins, *Cherokee Tragedy*, p. 113. This speech is published in the *Religious Intelligencer* 2 (1818): 713–714, in substantially the same words.

146   "able to read": Walker, *Torchlights*, pp. 153–154.

147   The Seven Brothers: See Wilkins, *Cherokee Tragedy*, p. 117.

148   "Little monitor, by thee": Newberry Library, Payne Papers, VIII. 63, also Wilkins, *Cherokee Tragedy*, p. 123. The poem is dated February 4, 1819.

149   "Like as the damask": Newberry Library, Payne Papers, VIII. 63, Wilkins, *Cherokee Tragedy*, p. 124.

151   "We think with": Ard Hoyt to Samuel Worcester, July 25, 1818, Hough-

Page

ton Library, American Board archives; also McLoughlin, *Cherokees and Missionaries*, p. 115.

152   A silversmith, a mixed-blood: For more on Sequoyah/George Gist see Lowery, "Notable Persons." His English name is commonly rendered "George Guess" in historical sources.

154   "For the information": Letter from Ard Hoyt to Samuel Worcester, American Board of Commissioners for Foreign Missions; also McLoughlin, *Cherokees and Missionaries*, p. 117.

154   "Mr. John Ross": see McLoughlin, *Cherokees and Missionaries*, pp. 117–118.

156   "It will not": McLoughlin, *Cherokees and Missionaries*, p. 119.

156   "You are now": McLoughlin, *Cherokees and Missionaries*, p. 119.

157   The lands to be ceded: These figures are available in Royce, *Cherokee Nation*, p. 286.

157   "I rejoice with": Samuel Worcester to Charles Hicks, March 4, 1819, American Board of Commissioners for Foreign Missions; also McLoughlin, *Cherokees and Missionaries*, p. 122.

158   "You are requested": Royce, *Cherokee Nation*, pp 104–107; McLoughlin, *Cherokees and Missionaries*, p. 121.

158   John Ross was: For a biography of John Ross see Moulton, *John Ross, Cherokee Chief.*

160   "It is not our": Lowery, "Notable Persons," p. 389.

161   most black slaves: Perdue, *Slavery*, p. 106.

162   "the most splendid": J. R. Schmidt to Jacob Van Vleck, September 6, 1821, Moravian Archives; also Wilkins, *Cherokee Tragedy*, p. 131.

162   "his tall and": Boston *Courier*, March 15, 1832; Wilkins, *Cherokee Tragedy*, p. 131.

162   "No memory of": *Georgian*, October 23, 1821; Wilkins, *Cherokee Tragedy*, p. 131.

163   "parties and introduce": Wilkins, *Cherokee Tragedy*, p. 133; Walker, *Torchlights*, pp. 159–163.

164   "Honored Sir": Newberry Library, Payne Papers, 761; Wilkins, *Cherokee Tragedy*, p. 129.

165   "I question": *Missionary Herald* (January 1823): 30; reprinted in Wilkins, *Cherokee Tragedy*, pp. 135–136.

166   "The Osages and Cherokees": *Franklin Gazette*, March 7, 1821; reprinted in *Journal of Cherokee Studies*, 4.2 (1979): 67.

168   "The children of": New York Spectator; reprinted in *Journal of Cherokee Studies*, 4.2 (1979): 68.

168   Atsi nahsa'i: Perdue, *Slavery*, p. 17.

170   "What was it": Tocqueville, *Democracy*, p. 448.

170   President Jefferson had negotiated: Abel, "History of Events," p. 241.

174   "Resolved, That": *Journal of Cherokee Studies*, 6.2 (1981): 72.

Page

174   "The Cherokees may": *Journal of Cherokee Studies*, 6.2 (1981): 72

176   "The buildings at Brainerd": *Journal of Cherokee Studies*, 6.2 (1981): 68–71.

176   "Resolved, That any": Wilkins, *Cherokee Tragedy*, p. 142.

177   "Encouraging prospects": Wilkins, *Cherokee Tragedy*, p. 142.

179   "The fatal hour arrived": *National Intelligencer and Washington Advertiser*, January 29, 1822.

181   "But the Great Spirit": Horan, *McKenney-Hall*, p. 47.

181   "that these people": Horan, *McKenney-Hall*, p. 48.

184   "The appointed time": Boston *Recorder*, February 21, 1824; also Wilkins, *Cherokee Tragedy*, p. 141.

184   "Its whole drift": Wilkins, *Cherokee Tragedy*, pp. 141–142.

184   "Gentle, brilliant": Wilkins, *Cherokee Tragedy*, p. 142.

185   In broken English: Ross, *Papers*, vol. 1, p. 53.

186   "Set him aside": Wilkins: *Cherokee Tragedy*, p. 143.

186   "I now address . . .": Wilkins, *Cherokee Tragedy*, pp. 143–144. Taken from Boston *Recorder*, February 21, 1824.

189   "The affliction": *American Eagle*, March 22, 1824; Gabriel, *Elias Boudinot*, pp. 61–62; Wilkins, *Cherokee Tragedy*, p. 148.

190   "criminal; as offering": Gabriel, *Elias Boudinot*, pp. 76–77; *Niles Weekly National Register*, July 9, 1825.

190   "an enormous painting": Wilkins, *Cherokee Tragedy*, p. 150; see also "Elias Boudinot," p. 212.

190   "I have seen the time": Church "Elias Boudinot," p. 212; Wilkins, *Cherokee Tragedy*, pp. 150.

191   "O, come with me": Gold, *Historical Records*, pp. 31–32; Wilkins, *Cherokee Tragedy*, pp. 146–147.

192   "Why is that": Gold, *Historical Records*, p. 32; Wilkins, *Cherokee Tragedy*, p. 147.

192   "mental powers appear": McLoughlin, *Cherokees and Missionaries*, p. 155. Quoted by Ard Hoyt in his Second Annual Report to the Secretary of War from Brainerd, Records of the Secretary of War, M-221, roll 85, nos. 3323–3324.

192   "Though their skin": McLoughlin, *Cherokees and Missionaries*, p. 155. Found in *Watchman*, March 9, 1822.

194   "Their manner of": Barclay, *History*, vol. 2, p. 128; also cited in McLoughlin, *Cherokees and Missionaries*, p. 165.

201   "They protest against": Savannah *Republican* (August 2, 1825), p. 2; quoted in Wilkins, *Cherokee Tragedy*, p. 166.

201   "In our first": National Archives, Record Group, 75, roll 1, frames 0798–0799; Wilkins, *Cherokee Tragedy*, p. 170.

202   "And these two": Wilkins, *Cherokee Tragedy*, p. 172.

203   "My heart is": *Niles Weekly National Register* 28 (July 1825): 296.

205   "We, the Representatives": Starr, *History*, pp. 55–56. While practicing

Page

medicine, Dr. Starr, a native Cherokee, collected materials for this history.

209   "Resolved by the"; *Laws of the Cherokee Nation,* p. 59, cited in McLoughlin, *Cherokees and Missionaries,* p. 216.

213   "All I ask": Carter, *Cherokee Sunset,* p. 72.

215   "You behold an *Indian*": Boudinot, "Address," pp. 3–4; Wilkins, *Cherokee Tragedy,* p. 188. All subsequent quotations from Boudinot on his lecture tour are taken from this pamphlet.

217   "The ground is": Woodward, *Cherokees,* p. 152–153.

217   "That the policy": Acts of the Georgia General Assembly, 1827, p. 249.

220   "Build a fire": Carter, *Cherokee Sunset,* p. 83.

220   Many blacks: Jahoda, *Trail of Tears,* pp. 89, 106; McLoughlin, *Cherokees and Missionaries,* p. 211. Jahoda gives as her opinion that one-half could read and understand English. McLoughlin states, "most blacks could speak and understand English" and, further, "some Cherokees, when they wished to learn English, turned to their slaves for help." Jahoda also states that in 1835, 12 percent of the Cherokees and 78 percent of Cherokee slaveholders had white ancestry; of those slaveholding families, 39 percent could read English and 13 percent could read Cherokee. Of the nonslaveholding Cherokees, less than 4 percent could read English; 18 percent could read Cherokee.

221   "They get their supplies": Carter, *Cherokee Sunset,* p. 86.

222   In July 1829: For more about gold mining of the period, see Fletcher M. Green, "Georgia's Forgotten Industry: Gold Mining, Post I," *Georgia Historical Quarterly,* 19 (June 1935): 93–111; also Mooney, *Myths,* p. 220.

223   "The dust became": quoted in Mooney, *Myths,* p. 220.

223   "Whereas a Law": *Cherokee Phoenix* (October 28, 1829): 3; Newberry Library, Payne Papers, VI, p. 199.

224   "My sun of existence": *Cherokee Phoenix,* October 28, 1829; Carter, *Cherokee Sunset,* p. 89.

224   "voluntary, for it": Jackson's message to Congress was dated December 8, 1829: Filler and Guttmann, *Removal,* pp. 14–17; Carter, *Cherokee Sunset,* pp. 89–90.

225   "in digging for gold": Georgia's Act of December 19, 1829: Filler and Guttmann, *Removal,* pp. 18–21; Carter, *Cherokee Sunset,* p. 90.

225   "for any person or body"; Carter, *Cherokee Sunset,* p. 90.

226   "I cannot see": Wilkins, *Cherokee Tragedy,* p. 204. Found in January 15, 1830, National Archives, Record Group 75, M-234, roll 75, frame 0054.

226   "the most active": Gilmer, *Sketches,* pp. 263–264; Wilkins, *Cherokee Tragedy,* p. 205.

227   "It has been": *Cherokee Phoenix* (February 10, 1830): 20.

228   "If the agents": Jeremiah Evarts wrote the essays under the pseudonym William Penn. They appeared in the *National Intelligencer* and were reprinted by the *Cherokee Phoenix* beginning September 16, 1829, and in

Page

Cherokee Removal, The "William Penn" Essays and Other Writings, by Jeremiah Evarts, edited by Francis Paul Prucha. Knoxville: University of Tennessee Press, 1981.

229   "overwhelmed by sudden": For a biography of Houston see James, *The Raven.*

232   "long since come": Wilkins, *Cherokee Tragedy,* p. 211. The response to Lowrey is recorded in the 23d Congress, 1st session, Senate Document 512.

235   Thomas McKenney was in trouble: For other details of McKenney's defenses see McKenney and Hall, *Indian Tribes,* pp. 52–53.

237   McKenney was told: The meeting with Jackson is described in McKenney *Memoirs,* vol. 1, pp. 204–206.

239   "Why, sir, everybody knows": McKenney, *Memoirs,* vol. 1, p. 262.

241   On Sunday morning: Colton, *Tow,* vol. 2, pp. 208–210.

241   "We know that": Peters, ed., *Case of the Cherokee Nation,* pp. 157–158.

242   "a domestic, dependent nation": Beveridge, *Life of John Marshall,* pp. 544–545.

242   Jackson was friendly: John Ridge's visit to Jackson is described in his letter to Boudinot of May 17, 1831, published in the *Cherokee Phoenix,* May 21, 1831.

244   "If courts were permitted": Peters, ed., *Case of the Cherokee Nation,* p. 1.

244   "They continued unmolested": *Missionary Herald* 27 (1831): 166.

246   "Sir—It is": *Missionary Herald* 27 (1831): 248–249; see also Bass, *Cherokee Messenger,* pp. 130–131.

246   "The Georgia guard": *Missionary Herald* 27 (1831): 253.

247   "Sir—I have": *Missionary Herald* 27 (1831): 253.

247   "Since Mr. Thompson": *Missionary Herald* 27 (1831): 253. Also Journal of Cherokee Indians, vol. II, p. 367.

247   "I was made": *Missionary Herald* 27 (1831): 300. Also Journal of Cherokee Studies, vol. II, No. 4, p. 368.

248   "Our trial took place": *Missionary Herald* 27 (1831): 363. Also Journal of Cherokee Studies, vol. II, No. 4, p. 370.

248   "We have applied . . ." *Missionary Herald* 27 (1831): 395.

249   "On the 15th": *Missionary Herald* 27 (1831): 395. Journal of Cherokee Studies, vol. II, No. 4, p. 372.

251   "We view within": *Journal of Cherokee Studies,* 4.2 (1979): pp. 85–86. Taken from the New York *Spectator,* Aug. 23, 1831.

252   "The avaricious unprincipled father": quoted in *Journal of Cherokee Studies* 4.2 (1979): p. 94.

252   "Perhaps no event": The item from the Vermont *Telegraph* is reprinted in the *Journal of Cherokee Studies* 4.2 (1979): 2.

253   "that the Attorney General": The full letter was published in the *Jour-*

Page

nal of Cherokee Studies 4.2 (1979): 86–91, as was the reply of Attorney General Lewis Cass.

253 "We are hedged": quoted in Christianson, *"Removal,"* p. 216.

253 "would plant a stake": The chief referred to the Treaty of Doaks Stand negotiated with Jackson while he was chief commissioner: Christianson, "Removal."

254 "Confusion to the": Wilkins, *Cherokee Tragedy,* p. 226. Also, letter of John Ridge to John Ross, January 12–13, 1832, Gilcrease Institute, Ross Papers 32-1; A summary of the letter can be found in Ross, vol. I, pp. 235–236.

254 "His voice is": Wilkins, *Cherokee Tragedy,* p. 227. Reprinted from the New York *Commercial Advertiser* by the *Cherokee Phoenix,* March 3, 1832.

254 "You asked us": *Cherokee Phoenix* (February 18, 1832): 1, Wilkins, *Cherokee Tragedy,* p. 227.

254 "We only wish": Wilkins, *Cherokee Tragedy,* p. 227

255 "Ridge and Boudinot": The decision was published in *Niles Weekly National Register,* March 17, 1832; reprinted in Wilkins, *Cherokee Tragedy,* p. 228.

255 "John Marshal has made": Jackson's remark was reported by Horace Greeley in *American Conflict,* vol. 1, p. 196, and is quoted in Wilkins, *Cherokee Tragedy,* p. 229. Some historians wonder if it was actually made, and others wonder what it meant. The federal courts were, in any event, powerless to act until the laws were challenged by specific cases.

255 "that their only hope": Wilkins, *Cherokee Tragedy,* p. 229. From 29th Congress, 1st session, House Document 185, p. 50.

256 "I believe Ridge": Jackson, *Correspondence,* vol. 4, p. 430; quoted in Wilkins, *Cherokee Tragedy,* p. 229.

257 "the Cherokee Delegation": Wilkins, *Cherokee Tragedy,* p. 231.

257 "It is the wish": Wilkins, *Cherokee Tragedy,* p. 232, 23d Congress, 1st session, Senate document 512, pp. 203–204.

258 "It makes me weep": Wilkins, *Cherokee Tragedy,* p. 232. David Greene to John Ridge, May 3, 1832, Houghton Library, American Board archives, 1.3, I, 1.

259 "one of the most": *Cherokee Phoenix,* July 20, 1833; quoted in Wilkins, *Cherokee Tragedy,* p. 230. McLean's letter to Ross, dated May 23, 1832, is filed in the Gilcrease Institute, Ross Papers 32-4.

259 "Their influence": *Cherokee Phoenix,* August 11, 1832; Wilkins, *Cherokee Tragedy,* p. 236.

260 "I could not": Wilkins, *Cherokee Tragedy,* p. 237

261 "In applying the": Wilkins, *Cherokee Tragedy,* p. 239; 25th Congress, 2d session, Senate Document 121, p. 9.

262 She told him that: Ann Worcester's letter to David Greene that contains the information about the Lumpkin visit is dated October 4, 1832: Houghton Library, American Board archives.

Page
263   "Penitentiary, Milledgeville": Hutchins, p. 373. Letter originally published in the *Missionary Herald* 29: p. 112.

264   "Sir—We are sorry": Hutchins, p. 373. From *Missionary Herald* 29: p. 112. Should Worcester or Butler have brought action against the Georgia arrest and imprisonment, the federal courts would have been required to reach a verdict in light of the recent Supreme Court decision, which would have precipitated a crisis between a state and the federal government. Another state, South Carolina, was at this time threatening to secede unless given its way; two days after Worcester and Butler were released, Jackson "sent to Congress a request for an act empowering him to force the state of South Carolina to give up its absurd notion that it would decide which acts of the federal government it would obey and which it would not" (McLoughlin, *Cherokees and Missionaries*, p. 299).

264   "they thought in the present": Evidence for the American Board's capitulating letter to Ross is in Chief Ross's letter to Elizur Butler of March 1833. In turn, the Ross letter is included in one from Dr. Butler to David Greene, March 18, 1833: Houghton Library, American Board archives: McLoughlin, *Cherokees and Missionaries*, p. 299.

265   "a speedy and favorable": The petition is quoted in Wilkins, *Cherokee Tragedy*, p. 245.

266   "he dismissed the meeting": 23d Congress, 1st session. Senate Document 512, p. 413; Wilkins, *Cherokee Tragedy*, p. 246.

267   "so far as": Letter of John Ridge to John Ross, February 2, 1833, Gilcrease Institute, Ross Papers; Wilkins, *Cherokee Tragedy*, p. 243.

267   "Major Ridge spoke": Gilmer *Sketches*, p. 373.

268   "to love their land": King and Evans, p. 8. Wilkins, *Cherokee Tragedy*, p. 252.

269   "Major Ridge": King and Evans, p. 9. This speech is recorded in a letter from Benjamin Currey to Lewis Cass, dated September 15, 1834, in the National Archives, Record Group 75, M-234, roll 76, frame 140.

269   "It may be that Foreman": King and Evans, p. 9. National Archives, Record Group 75, M-234, roll 76, frames 140–141.

270   "The Council unanimously": King and Evans, p. 10. National Archives, Record Group 75, M-234, roll 76, frame 142.

272   "I have just": King and Evans, p. 13. National Archives, Record Group 75, M-234, roll 76, frame 142; also printed in Jackson, *Correspondence*, vol. 5, p. 288.

272   "By God, sir": King and Evans, "Death of Walker," p. 13.

273   "Sir, it is": Wilkins, *Cherokee Tragedy*, p. 256.

274   "We are prepared": Wilkins, *Cherokee Tragedy*, p. 257. Quoted from Augusta, Georgia, Constitutionalist (July 21, 1835): 2.

274   "And in order": Wilkins, *Cherokee Tragedy*, p. 257. Quoted in the Augusta, Georgia, *Constitutionalist* (July 21, 1835): 2.

275   "Ross has failed": Dale and Litton, *Cherokee Cavaliers*, p. 13.

Page

275 "To the Cherokee": Allegheny *Democrat*, March 16, 1835.

281 "I took occasion": Wilkins, *Cherokee Tragedy*, p. 264. 25th Congress, 2d session, Senate Document 120, p. 390.

283 "They went into": Wilkins, p. 266. 25th Congress, 2d session, Senate Document 120, p. 392.

283 "Ross holds out": Wilkins, *Cherokee Tragedy*, p. 267. 24th Congress, 1st session, House Document 286, p. 60.

284 They heard about an Indian: Several violent incidents are documented in Wilkins, *Cherokee Tragedy*, p. 268.

285 "one Indian stabbed": Hogan to Gibson, June 3, 1835: National Archives Record Group 75.

285 "Is this country": Foreman, Indian Removal, p. 147. Quoted in the *Southern Advocate* (May 17, 1836): 3.

287 Along the way: Foreman, *Indian Removal*, p. 155.

287 "The woods echoed": Wilkins, *Cherokee Tragedy*, pp. 269–270. 25th Congress, 2d session, Senate Document 120, p. 578.

289 "I consider that": Wilkins, *Cherokee Tragedy*, p. 270. *Federal Union*, November 20, 1835.

289 "The question was": Wilkins, *Cherokee Tragedy*, p. 271. 24th Congress, 2d session, Senate Document 120, pp. 533–534.

291 "there was a loud barking": Interesting accounts of the arrest of Chief Ross and Payne are in Wilkins, *Cherokee Tragedy*, beginning on p. 273, and in Carter, *Cherokee Sunset*, p. 184.

291 "You'll know that soon enough": Carter, *Cherokee Sunset*, p. 185.

292 "That address unfolds": Wilkins, *Cherokee Tragedy*, p. 275. 25th Congress, 2d session, Senate document 121, p. 32.

293 "I mixed freely": Wilkins, *Cherokee Tragedy*, p. 276. Cartersville, Georgia, *Courant*, (March 26, 1885): 10.

294 "I am one": quoted in Wilkins, *Cherokee Tragedy*, pp. 276–277.

294 "I know I": quoted in Wilkins, *Cherokee Tragedy*, p. 277.

296 "In this state": Wilkins, *Cherokee Tragedy*, p. 280. 25th Congress, 2d session, Senate Document 121, p. 26.

296 John Ridge viewed the treaty: John Ridge's view of danger is recorded in Anderson's biography of John's cousin, *Life of Stand Watie*, p. 18, and also in Thoburn's *Standard History*, vol. 1, p. 104.

297 "There was a": Wilkins, *Cherokee Tragedy*, p. 282. The Ridges to President Jackson, June 30, 1836, National Archives Record Group 75, M-234, Roll 80, frames 488–489.

297 "But now we come": Also published in Wilkins, *Cherokee Tragedy*, pp. 282–283.

300 "I visited the": "Origin," p. 168.

300 General Wool had been sent: See Corn, "Conscience or Duty."

Page

301 "When I was": Evan Jones to Lucius Bolles, February 6, 1837, Mc-Loughlin, *Cherokees and Missionaries*, p. 322.

302 "New Echota: . . . The duty I": Browder, *Cherokee Indians*. p. 41.

303 "Sir, my communication": Emerson's letter to Van Buren is found in Filler and Guttmann, *Removal*, pp. 94–97, and Carter, *Cherokee Sunset*, pp. 208–209.

304 "My Dear Father": The Boudinot letter is reprinted in the *Journal of Cherokee Studies* 4.2 (1979) pp. 103–107.

305 "Head of Coosa": The letter from John Ross to Sequoyah is published in Lowery, "Notable Persons," pp. 391–392.

307 "a lady of superior": Wilkins, *Cherokee Tragedy*, p. 289. Sophia Sawyer to David Greene, December 24, 1833, Houghton Library, American Board archives 18.3.1, VIII, p. 179.

307 "She was a": Atlanta *Constitution* (October 27, 1889): 5; quoted in Wilkins, *Cherokee Tragedy*, p. 289.

309 "6 November 1836": 25th Congress, 2d session, Senate document 120; Browder, *Cherokee Indians*, p. 43.

309 "30 January 1837": 25th Congress, 2d session, Senate document 120; Browder, *Cherokee Indians*, p. 45.

309 "12 March 1837": 25th Congress, 2d session, Senate document 120; Browder, *Cherokee Indians*, p. 47.

310 "15 March 1837": 25th Congress, 2d session, Senate document 120; Browder, *Cherokee Indians*, p. 47.

310 "30 March 1837": 25th Congress, 2d session, Senate document 120; Browder, *Cherokee Indians*, p. 48.

310 "3 April 1837": 25th Congress, 2d session, Senate document 120; Browder, *Cherokee Indians*, p. 48.

310 "20 April 1837": 25th Congress, 2d session, Senate document 120; Browder, *Cherokee Indians*, p. 48.

311 "12 August 1837": 25th Congress, 2d session, Senate document 120; Browder, *Cherokee Indians*, p. 51–52.

311 "fulfilled in all": The original printed order is in the Georgia Department of Archives and History, General Order no. 74.

312 "greatest scorn": Featherstonhaugh, *Canoe Voyage*, pp. 229–24.

319 "Friends: Our official": Published in the *Journal of Cherokee Studies* 3.3 (1978): 134–135.

321 "Red Clay Cherokee Nation": *Journal of Cherokee Studies* 3.3 (1978): 137.

324 "*Cherokees!* The President": General Scott's address of May 10, 1838 is published in the *Journal of Cherokee Studies* 3.3 (1978): 145.

325 "To ensure to your command": Browder, *Cherokee Indians*, p. 55.

326 "The Cherokees, by": *Journal of Cherokee Studies* 3.3 (1978): 146.

328 "The commanding officer": *Journal of Cherokee Studies* 3.3 (1978): 147.

328 "AFTER Orders": *Journal of Cherokee Studies* 3.3 (1978): 148.

Page

329 "My dear wife": *Journal of Cherokee Studies* 3.3 (1978); 153–154.

329 Scott appealed to: *Journal of Cherokee Studies* 3.3 (1978): 138–139.

333 "28 May 1838": National Archives Record Group, 94; Browder, *Cherokee Indians,* p. 57.

333 "3 June 1838": Univ. of North Carolina, Bynum Papers; Browder, *Cherokee Indians,* p. 58.

333 "4 June 1838": Browder, *Cherokee Indians,* p. 58.

333 "6 June 1838": Browder, *Cherokee Indians,* p. 58.

335 "hereby authorized": Resolution of the general council of the Cherokee nation, Aquohee Camp, July 26, 1838. Printed in *Journal of Cherokee Studies* 3.3 (1978): 150.

336 "My Dear Wife": These two letters from L. B. Webster to his wife were published in the *Journal of Cherokee Studies* 3.3 (1978): 155–156.

337 "The river here": Carter, *Cherokee Sunset,* pp. 240–241. From Deas's Journal, National Archives, Record Group 75, file D-225.

339 "The weather was": Foreman, *Indian Removal,* p. 295; also Carter, *Cherokee Sunset,* p. 242.

339 "Did not move": Carter, *Cherokee Sunset,* p. 242.

340 "Spare their lives": Foreman, *Indian Removal,* p. 297. John Ross manuscripts, owned by W. W. Ross, Park Hill, Oklahoma.

340 "and they well provided": Foreman, *Indian Removal,* p. 297. Smith to Harris, July 3, 1838, National Archives, Record Group 75.

341 "We your prisoners": National Archives, Record Group 94.

342 "18 June 1838": National Archives, Record Group 94; Browder, *Cherokee Indians,* p. 61.

342 "My dear Frances": *Journal of Cherokee Studies* 3.3 (1978): 154–155.

344 "13 July 1838": National Archives, Record Group 94; Browder, *Cherokee Indians,* p. 61.

344 "They obstinately refused": National Archives, Record Group 94; Browder, *Cherokee Indians,* p. 64.

344 "13 June 1838": Univ. of North Carolina, Southern Historical Collection, Bynum Papers; Browder, *Cherokee Indians,* p. 60.

345 Scott told the Rosses: National Archives, Record Group 94; Browder, *Cherokee Indians,* p. 54.

346 "4 November 1831": National Archives, Record Group 94; Browder, *Cherokee Indians,* p. 68.

346 "Sick Report. July 31": National Archives, Record Group 94; Browder, *Cherokee Indians,* p. 65.

348 "*Resolved* by the": Carter, *Cherokee Sunset,* p. 247. The draft of this resolution is preserved in the Gilcrease Institute, Ross Papers.

348 "Ross appointed his brother": The John and Lewis Ross contract may be found in Carter, *Cherokee Sunset,* p. 247.

349 "The contract with": Woodward, *Cherokees,* p. 211.

Page

350   Most of the Cherokees were: Perdue, *Slavery*, p. 42.

350   "To John Howard Payne": Newberry Library, Payne Manuscripts, vol. VI, Ayer Collection.

352   Rebecca Neugin recalled: The 1932 interview with Rebecca Neugin by Grant Foreman is published in *Journal of Cherokee Studies* 3.3 (1978): 176.

356   An Indian man sat staring: Beliefs concerning death are documented in Witthoft, "Cherokee Beliefs."

357   "detachment of the poor": New York *Observer* (January 26, 1839): 4; Foreman, *Indian Removal*, pp. 305–306.

358   "Long time we travel . . ." *Oklahoman* (April 7, 1929): F.6.

358   "Sge! O Long Man": Mooney *Swimmer Manuscript*, ed. Olbrechts, pp. 1–39, is a study of Cherokee culture. James Mooney (1861–1922) did most of his field work in 1887 and 1888 but often returned. This, his last major work on the Cherokees, was completed after his death by Frans Olbrechts. The *Journal of Cherokee Studies* 3.1 (1978) was a "tribute issue" to Mooney.

361   "From the first of June": Wilkins, *Cherokee Tragedy*, p. 351.

362   "Lewis Ross, the brother of": Perdue, *Slavery*, p. 72; See also Oklahoma Department of Archives, Indian Pioneer History, vol. 63.

363   "It is mournful": H. G. Clauder to Theodore Schulz, March 17, 1837, Moravian Archives, Cherokee Mission, p. 290; see also Wilkins, *Cherokee Tragedy*, p. 290.

364   "wind makes it difficult": Dr. Lillybridge is quoted in Foreman ed., "Journey," p. 238; and Wilkins, *Cherokee Tragedy*, p. 292.

364   "Van Buren": Foreman, ed., "Journey," p. 240; Wilkins, *Cherokee Tragedy*, p. 293.

365   "the honey-bee": Irving, *Tour*, pp. 50–51; Wilkins, *Cherokee Tragedy*, p. 294.

366   "We had to undergo": Susanna Ridge to Hon. John C. Spencer, June 7, 1842; Wilkins, *Cherokee Tragedy*, p. 294.

367   "a good road": see Wilkins, *Cherokee Tragedy*, p. 297.

367   "the country there": Wilkins, *Cherokee Tragedy*, pp. 297–298. John Ridge to John Kennedy, January 16, 1838, National Archives, Record Group 75.

367   "I have traveled": Lumpkin, *Removal*, vol. 2, p. 202; Wilkins, *Cherokee Tragedy*, p. 299.

368   "I rode over it": Lumpkin, *Removal*, vol. 2, pp. 202–203; Wilkins, *Cherokee Tragedy*, p. 299.

368   "I was pleased": Lumpkin, *Removal*, vol. 2, pp. 203–204; Wilkins, *Cherokee Tragedy*, p. 300.

369   "Instead of receiving": Lumpkin, *Removal*, vol. 2, p. 204; Wilkins, *Cherokee Tragedy*, p. 300.

370   "one of the best": Extracts from Sophia Sawyer's journal are published in Wilkins, *Cherokee Tragedy*, pp. 302–303.

Page
370 "He cannot hear truth . . ." Wilkins, *Cherokee Tragedy*, pp. 302–303. Sophia Sawyer to David Greene, December 29, 1838, Houghton Library, American Board archives.

371 "Heads of Departments": Wilkins, *Cherokee Tragedy*, p. 303. John Ridge to Eliza A. Northrup, April 30, 1839, transcript courtesy of General Leo B. Washbourne.

371 "My brother, we": Arkansas *Gazette* (October 2, 1839); 2; Wilkins, *Cherokee Tragedy*, p. 303.

372 "The critical situation": Starkey, *Cherokee Nation*, p. 305.

372 "When Ross himself": Wilkins, *Cherokee Tragedy*, p. 318. Washburn to David Greene, August 12, 1839, Houghton Library, American Board archives.

373 "congratulating each other": Wilkins, *Cherokee Tragedy*, p. 319. Greene, August 12, 1839, Houghton Library, American Board archives.

373 "We cordially receive": Wilkins, *Cherokee Tragedy*, p. 319. Houghton Library, American Board archives, 18.3.1, X, p. 55.

373 "For the settlement": Wilkins, *Cherokee Tragedy*, p. 320. Houghton Library, American Board archives, 18.3.1, X, p. 55.

374 "reasonable propositions submitted": Wilkins, *Cherokee Tragedy*, p. 320. National Archives, Record Group 75.

375 "A committee was appointed": Deposition of Allen Ross in Foreman, ed., "Murder," p. 23; Wilkins, *Cherokee Tragedy*, p. 321.

375 "to keep him": Foreman, ed., "Murder," p. 23; Wilkins, *Cherokee Tragedy*, p. 321.

376 "Then succeeded a scene": Wilkins, *Cherokee Tragedy*, pp. 322–323. Documentation for the details of the assassination of John Ridge, his cousin Elias, and his father comes mainly from Wilkins, *Cherokee Tragedy*, pp. 322–324.

380 "granted to all persons": Starr, *History*, p. 119.

380 "Murders in the country":

381 In addition to his: The claims and needs of Chief John Ross were discussed in a letter from him and others to Secretary of War John C. Spencer, June 28, 1842; see Ross, *Papers*, vol. 2, pp. 136–137.

382 "You ought to": Letter of Lewis Ross to John Ross, January 3, 1840; Ross, *Papers*, pp. 4–5.

382 "Having thus set forth": John Ross to Elizabeth Milligan, September 5, 1841, Ross, *Papers*, pp. 101–102.

383 "I am an old man": Moulton, *John Ross*, p. 1.

384 In one year alone: For more information on Worcester, see Bass, *Cherokee Messenger*.

385 "resulted from the": Foreman, *Indian Removal*, p. 332. Joseph W. Harris to General George Gibson, April 25, 1836, National Archives, Record Group 75.

Page
387   "William H. Thomas": For more information about Thomas, see Russell, "William Holland Thomas." For additional information on the eastern Cherokees, see Finger, *Eastern Band*, and Bridgers, "Historical Analysis."

388   "One morning I": Proctor, "Slave Holding Indians," p. 237.

388   "the whole roadways were crowded": Proctor, "Slave Holding Indians," p. 242.

391   "it is asserted": Mooney, *Myths*, p. 133.

391   "All told, about 4,000": Foreman, *Indian Removal*, p. 312.

392   "It affords me": Fleischmann, *Cherokee Removal*, p. 65.

392   "One old man": Mooney, *Myths*, p. 131.

393   "The removal of": *Journal of Cherokee Studies* 3.3 (1978): 180–185.

395   "Should any tribe": Lipscomb, Vol. X, p. 371.

395   "The point had been": Rights, *American Indian*, p. 186.

396   Sequoyah, feeble, arthritic: Sequoyah's final days are documented in Foreman, *Sequoyah*.

BIBLIOGRAPHY

A. DOCUMENTS, RECORDS, AND REPORTS

Archival Materials

Georgia Department of Archives and History, Atlanta
    Acts of the Georgia General Assembly
    General Orders

Gilcrease Institute of American History and Art
    Papers of John Ross
    Papers of Andrew Jackson

Houghton Library, Harvard University
    Archives of the American Board of Commissioners for
    Foreign Missions

Moravian Archives, Winston-Salem, North Carolina
    Cherokee Mission

Museum of the Cherokee Indian, Cherokee, North Carolina
    Early American Newspapers Collection

National Archives
    Record Group 75, Records of the Bureau of Indian Affairs, Department of the Interior
    Record Group 94, Records of the Adjutant General's Office, War Department
    Record Group 107, Records of the Office of the Secretary of War, War Department

Newberry Library, Chicago
    Papers of John Howard Payne, Edward E. Ayer Collection

Oklahoma Department of Archives, Oklahoma City
    Indian Pioneer History

Private Collection
    W. W. Ross, Park Hill, Oklahoma

University of North Carolina, Southern Historical Collection
    Papers of William Preston Bynum
    Papers of John Gray Bynum

Wisconsin Historical Society, Madison
    Papers of Lyman Draper

Government Documents

23d Congress, 1st session, Senate Document 512
24th Congress, 1st session, House Document 286
25th Congress, 2d session, Senate Document 120
25th Congress, 2d session, Senate Document 121
29th Congress, 1st session, House Document 185

B. BOOKS

Abernethy, Thomas Perkins. *From Frontier to Plantation in Tennessee: A Study in Frontier Democracy.* Chapel Hill: University of North Carolina Press, 1932. Reprinted University: University of Alabama Press, 1967.
Adair, James. *The History of the American Indians.* London: E. and C. Dilly, 1775. Reprint of a 1930 edition New York: Promontory Press, 1974.
Anderson, Mabel Washbourne. *The Life of General Stand Watie.* Pryor, Ok.: Mayes County Republican, 1915.
Barclay, Wade Crawford. *History of Methodist Missions.* 3 volumes. New York: Board of Missions and Church Extension of the Methodist Churh, 1949–1957.
Bartram, William. *Travels Through North & South Carolina, Georgia, East & West Florida, the Cherokee Country.* Philadelphia: James & Johnson, 1791.
Bass, Althea. *Cherokee Messenger.* Norman: University of Oklahoma Press, 1936.
Beveridge, Albert J. *The Life of John Marshall.* 4 vols. Boston and New York: Houghton Mifflin, 1916–1919.
Boudinot, Elias. *An Address to the Whites Delivered in the First Presbyterian Church on the 26th of May, 1826.* Philadelphia: 1826.
Browder, Nathaniel C. *The Cherokee Indians and Those Who Came After.* Hayesville, N.C.: Browder, 1973.
Carter, Samuel, III. *Cherokee Sunset: A Nation Betrayed.* Garden City, N.Y.: Doubleday, 1976.
Colton, Calvin. *Tour of the American Lakes, and Among the Indians of the North-west Territory, in 1830.* 2 volumes. London: F. Westley and A. H. Davis, 1833.
Crockett, David. *Davy Crockett's Own Story.* New York: 1955.
Dale, Edward Everett, and Gaston Litton. *Cherokee Cavaliers: Forty Years of Cherokee History as Told in the Correspondence of the Ridge-Watie-Boudinot Family.* Norman: University of Oklahoma Press, 1939.
Featherstonhaugh, George William. *A Canoe Voyage up the Minnay Sotor.* London: R. Bentley, 1847.
Filler, Louis, and Allen, Guttmann, eds. *The Removal of the Cherokee Nation: Manifest Destiny or National Dishonor?* Boston: Heath, 1962. Reprinted Huntington, N.Y.: Robert E. Krieger Publishing, 1977.
Finger, John R. *The Eastern Band of Cherokees, 1819–1900.* Knoxville: University of Tennessee Press, 1984.
Fleischmann, Glen. *The Cherokee Removal, 1838.* New York: Franklin Watts, 1971.
Foreman, Grant. *Indian Removal: The Emigration of the Five Civilized Tribes of Indians.* Norman: University of Oklahoma Press, 1932.
———. *Sequoyah.* Norman: University of Oklahoma Press, 1938.

Gabriel, Ralph Henry. *Elias Boudinot, Cherokee, and His America.* Norman: University of Oklahoma Press, 1941.

Gilmer, George Rockingham. *Sketches of Some of the First Settlers of Upper Georgia, of the Cherokees, and the Author.* Revised edition, Americus, Ga.: American Book Company, 1926.

Gold, Theodore S. *Historical Records of the Town of Cornwall, Litchfield County, Connecticut.* Hartford, Conn.: Lockwood & Brainard, 1877. Second edition 1904.

Greeley, Horace. *The American Conflict.* 2 volumes. Hartford, Conn.: O.D. Case, 1865–1867.

Horan, James David. *The McKenney-Hall Portrait Gallery of American Indians.* New York: Crown Publishers, 1972.

Irving, Washington. *A Tour on the Prairies.* Edited by John Francis McDermott. Norman: University of Oklahoma Press, 1956.

Jackson, Andrew. *Correspondence of Andrew Jackson.* Edited by John Spencer Bassett. 7 volumes. Washington, D.C.: Carnegie Institution, 1926–1935.

Jahoda, Gloria. *The Trial of Tears.* New York: Rinehart and Winston, 1975.

James, Marquis. *The Raven: A Bibliography of Sam Houston.* Indianapolis: Bobbs-Merrill, 1929.

King, Duane H., ed. *The Cherokee Indian Nation: A Troubled History.* Knoxville: University of Tennessee Press, 1979.

Kvasnicka, Robert M., and Herman J. Viola, eds. *The Commissioners of Indian Affairs, 1824–1977.* Lincoln: University of Nebraska Press, 1979.

Laws of the Cherokee Nation: Adopted by the Council at Various Periods. Tahlequah, C.N.: Cherokee Advocate Office, 1852.

Lipscomb, Andrew A. *Writings of Thomas Jefferson,* Memorial Edition. 20 vols. Washington: Thomas Jefferson Memorial Association, 1903.

Lumpkin, Wilson. *The Removal of the Cherokee Indians from Georgia.* 2 vols. New York: Dodd, Mead, 1907.

McKenney, Thomas L. *Memoirs, Official and Personal; with Sketches of Travels Among Northern and Southern Indians.* 2 volumes. New York: Paine and Burgess, 1846.

——— and James Hall. *The Indian Tribes of North America.* 3 volumes. Second edition. Edinburgh: John Grant, 1933–1934.

McLoughlin, William G. *Cherokees and Missionaries, 1789–1839.* New Haven: Yale University Press, 1984.

Mooney, James. *Myths of the Cherokee and Sacred Formulas of the Cherokees.* Reprinted Nashville, Tenn.: Charles and Randy Elder, 1982.

———. *The Swimmer Manuscript, Cherokee Sacred Formulas and Medicinal Prescriptions.* Edited by Frans M. Olbrechts. Smithsonian Institution Bureau of American Ethnology Bulletin 99. Washington, D.C.: U.S. Government Printing Office, 1932.

Moulton, Gary E. *John Ross, Cherokee Chief.* Athens: University of Georgia Press, 1978.

Perdue, Theda. *Slavery and the Evolution of Cherokee Society, 1540–1866.* Knoxville: University of Tennessee Press, 1979.

Peters, Richard, ed. *The Case of the Cherokee Nation Against the State of Georgia.* Philadelphia, John Grigg, 1831.

————. *Reports of Cases Argued and Adjudged in the Supreme Court of the United States* (1828–1842). 16 volumes. Washington, D.C.: 1855.

Rights, Douglas L. *The American Indian in North Carolina*. Second edition. Winston-Salem: John F. Blair, 1957.

Ross, John. *The Papers of Chief John Ross*. Edited by Gary E. Moulton. 2 volumes. Norman: University of Oklahoma Press, 1985.

Royce, Charles C. *The Cherokee Nation of Indians*. Reprinted Chicago: Aldine Publishing, 1975.

Schwarze, Edmund. *History of the Moravian Missions Among Southern Indian Tribes of the United States*. Bethlehem, Penn.: Times Publishing Company, 1923.

Starkey, Marion L. *The Cherokee Nation*. New York: Alfred A. Knopf, 1946.

Starr, Emmet. *History of the Cherokee Indians*. Oklahoma City: Warden, 1921. Reprint edited by Jack Gregory and Rennard Strickland. Fayetteville, Ark.: Indian Heritage Association, 1967.

Thoburn, Joseph B. *A Standard History of Oklahoma*. 5 volumes. Chicago and New York: American Historical Society, 1916.

Tocqueville, Alexis de. *Democracy in America*. Edited by J.P. Mayer and Max Lerner. Translated by George Lawrence. 2 volumes in 1. New York: Harper & Row, 1966. Reprinted Garden City, N.Y.: Doubleday, 1969.

Walker, Robert Sparks. *Torchlights to the Cherokees: The Brainerd Mission*. New York: Macmillan, 1931.

Wilkins, Thurman. *Cherokee Tragedy: The Story of the Ridge Family and the Decimation of a People*. New York: Macmillan, 1970.

Woodward, Grace Steele. *The Cherokees*. Norman: University of Oklahoma Press, 1963.

C. ARTICLES

Abel, Annie Heloise. "The History of Events Resulting in Indian Consolidation West of the Mississippi." *Annual Report of the American Historical Association for the Year 1906* 1 (1908): 233–450.

Bridgers, Ben O. "An Historical Analysis of the Legal Status of the North Carolina Cherokees." *North Carolina Law Review* 58 (1980).

Brown, Joseph. "Captivity Narrative." *Journal of Cherokee Studies* 2.2 (1977): 208–218.

Burnett, John G. "The Cherokee Removal Through the Eyes of a Private Soldier." *Journal of Cherokee Studies* 3.3 (1978): 180–185.

Campbell, Janet, and David G. Campbell. "The Wolf Clan." *Journal of Cherokee Studies* 7.2 (1982): 85-91.

Christian, George. "The Battle of Lookout Mountain: An Eye Witness Account." Edited by E. Raymond Evans. *Journal of Cherokee Studies* 3.1 (1978): 49–53.

Christianson, James R. "Removal: A Foundation for the Formation of Federalized Indian Policy." *Journal of Cherokee Studies* 10.2 (1985): 215–229.

Church, Mary Boudinot. "Elias Boudinot." *Magazine of History* 17 (December 1913): 212.

Corn, James F. "Conscience or Duty: General John E. Wool's Dilemma with Cherokee Removal." *Journal of Cherokee Studies* 3.1 (1978): 35–39.

Ethridge, Robbie F. "Tobacco Among the Cherokees." *Journal of Cherokee Studies* 3.2 (1978): 77–86.

Evans, E. Raymond. "Notable Persons in Cherokee History: Bob Benge." *Journal of Cherokee Studies* 1.2 (1976): 98–106.

———. "Was the Last Battle of the American Revolution Fought on Lookout Mountain?" *Journal of Cherokee Studies* 5.1 (1980): 30–40.

Evans, J. P. "Sketches of Cherokee Characteristics." *Journal of Cherokee Studies* 4.1 (1979): 10–20.

Farley, M. Foster. "Christian Priber—Prime Minister to the Cherokee Indians." *Journal of Cherokee Studies* 8.2 (1983): 97–101.

Fogelson, Raymond D. "Cherokee Little People Reconsidered." *Journal of Cherokee Studies* 7.2 (1982): 92–98.

Foreman, Grant, ed. "Journey of a Party of Cherokee Emigrants." *Mississippi Valley Historical Review* 18.2 (1931): 232–245.

———. "The Murder of Elias Boudinot." *Chronicles of Oklahoma* 12 (March 1934): 19–24.

Hutchins, John, "The Trial of Reverend Samuel A. Worcester." *Journal of Cherokee Studies* 2.4 (1977): 356–376.

Kelly, James C. "Notable Persons in Cherokee History: Attakullakulla." *Journal of Cherokee Studies* 3.1 (1978): 2–34.

King, Duane H. "Cherokee Bows." *Journal of Cherokee Studies* 1.2 (1976): 92–97.

———. "Lessons in Cherokee Ethnology from the Captivity of Joseph Brown 1788–1789." *Journal of Cherokee Studies* 2.2 (1977): 219–229.

———. "Long Island of the Holston: Sacred Cherokee Ground." *Journal of Cherokee Studies* 1.2 (1976): 113–127.

———. "The Origin of the Eastern Cherokees as as Social and Political Entity." In his *The Cherokee Indian Nation: A Troubled History,* pp. 164–180. Knoxville: University of Tennessee Press, 1979.

——— and E. Raymond Evans. "The Death of John Walker, Jr.: Political Assassination or Personal Vengeance?" *Journal of Cherokee Studies* 1.1 (1976): 4–16.

Lowery, Major George. "Notable Persons in Cherokee History: Sequoyah or George Gist." Introduction by John Howard. *Journal of Cherokee Studies* 2.4 (1977): 385–393.

Mooney, James. "The Cherokee Ball Play." *Journal of Cherokee Studies* 7.1 (1982): 10–24.

———. "Cherokee Theory and Practice of Medicine." *Journal of Cherokee Studies* 7.1 (1982): 25–29.

Perdue, Theda. "Letters from Brainerd." *Journal of Cherokee Studies* 4.1 (1979): 6–9.

Proctor, Addison C. "Slave Holding Indians at Time of Civil War."

Sturtevant, William C. "Louis-Philippe on Cherokee Architecture and Clothing in 1797." *Journal of Cherokee Studies* 3.4 (1978): 198–205.

Thornton, Russell. "Cherokee Population Losses During the Trail of Tears: A New Perspective and a New Estimate." *Ethnohistory* 31.4 (1984): 289–300.

Williams, Samuel Cole. "William Tatham Wataugan." *Tennessee Historical Magazine* 7.3 (1921): 154–179.

Witthoft, John. "Cherokee Beliefs Concerning Death." *Journal of Cherokee Studies* 8.2 (1983): 68–72.

D. DISSERTATION

Russell, Mattie. "William Holland Thomas, White Chief of the North Carolina Cherokees." Ph.D. dissertation, Duke University, 1956.

E. NEWSPAPERS AND RELIGIOUS PUBLICATIONS

Allegheny *Democrat*
American *Eagle*
Arkansas *Gazette*
Atlanta *Constitution*
Boston *Courier*
Boston *Recorder*
Cartersville *Current*
Cherokee Phoenix
Federal Union
Franklin *Gazette*
Georgian

Latter Day Luminary
Missionary Herald at Home and Abroad
New York *American*
New York *Observer*
New York *Spectator*
Niles Weekly National Register
Religious Intelligencer
Savannah *Republican*
Watchman
Weekly Commercial Advertiser

F. JOURNALS

Journal of Cherokee Studies, since 1976 published by the Museum of The Cherokee Indian in cooperation with the Cherokee Historical Association, Cherokee, N. C. 28719.

INDEX